Adventures of a Paper Sleuth

To Peter
From Wendy &
Reggie
Oct 15, 2008

FRIENDS HAVE GATHERED TO SAY THANKS
TO MURIEL & HUGH P. MACMILLAN
FOR THEIR PRESERVATION OF GLENGARRY'S
AND CANADA'S HISTORY & CULTURE

LAGGAN, ONTARIO   MARCH 22, 2003

# of a paper sleuth

Hugh P. MacMillan

PENUMBRA PRESS

ARCHIVES
OF
CANADIAN ARTS
CULTURE & HERITAGE

PENUMBRA PRESS
www.penumbrapress.com

Copyright 2004 © Hugh P. MacMillan and Penumbra Press
Published by PENUMBRA PRESS
Printed and bound in Canada
Cover illustration and design by Garth Dittrick

No part of this publication may be reproduced, stored in a retrieval system or transmitted, in any form or by any means, without the prior written consent of the publisher or a licence from The Canadian Copyright Licensing Agency (Access Copyright). For an Access Copyright licence, call toll free to 1-800-893-5777 or visit www.accesscopyright.ca

LIBRARY AND ARCHIVES CANADA CATALOGUING IN PUBLICATION
Library and Archives Canada Cataloguing in Publication
MacMillan, Hugh, 1924-
    Adventures of a paper sleuth / Hugh MacMillan.
ISBN 1-894131-62-2
    1. MacMillan, Hugh, 1924- 2. Archivists--Ontario--Biography.
I. Title.
BX5620.M24A3 2004   020'.92   C2004-906301-4

Penumbra Press gratefully acknowledges the Canada Council for the Arts and the Ontario Arts Council for supporting its publishing programme. The publisher further acknowledges the financial support of the Government of Canada through the Book Publishing Industry Development Program (BPIDP) for our publishing activities. We also acknowledge the Government of Ontario through the Ontario Media Development Corporation's Ontario Book Initiative.

CONTENTS

Foreword
Acknowledgements
Introduction

Chapter	1	The Making of a Paper Sleuth	15
	2	Towboats and Canoes	37
	3	The Remarkable Gravelles	57
	4	Collectors and Their Obsessions	67
	5	The Edgars: a Jacobite Family	82
	6	The Wild Frontier	89
	7	The Canal Builders	101
	8	Glengarry Tales	121
	9	The Ones That Got Away	136
	10	The Last Fatal Duel	148
	11	Taking a Cowan and Other Methods	163
	12	A Gael for All Seasons	183
	13	Adventurers and Explorers	198
	14	Holy Herb	219
	15	Archival Security	233
	16	Loyalists and Other Tales	249
	17	The Semi-Wild West	264
	18	Nigel Drayton: a Real Eccentric	278
	19	Bolsheviks, Buccaneers and Amazons	288
	20	Two Wild Riders	297
	21	Nor'Wester Tales	310

Appendix	1	The MacMillan Method for Saving Canadian History	331
	2	A Note on the Spelling of Names	332
	3	Four Letters	333
	4	List of Acquisitions	336

*Dedicated to my wife and family,
who have listened to these tales
many a time.*

FOREWORD

It is now a quarter of a century since I first encountered Hugh Pearson MacMillan; it was through his son Ian, who thought it might be a good idea if we met. In the Log House at Rockwood, Hugh introduced himself as a Scot. When asked when his people came out to Canada, he replied, without batting an eye, "1793!" To one just off the boat from the Auld Sod, his answer seemed to offer the certainty and comfort of longevity and of the survival of identity. Strangely, that introduction resulted in my becoming more Canadian than I ever intended to be. The meeting marked the beginning of a lengthy adventure with one of the most mischievous MacMillans to adorn the clan since its eponym, almost a thousand years ago, seized a razor to give himself a tonsure, no doubt perched on a rock above Loch Arkaig in the wild country to the west of the Great Glen. It is a great honour to be asked to make a modest contribution to Hugh's book, though the temptation will be resisted to pay him back for innumerable scrapes on two continents, which on occasion brought us sheer frustration and to the verge of arrest, drowning, and heated dialectic. There was, of course, a highly positive side to our acquaintance. There was the incomparable Muriel holding everything together. There were trips to places unimagined, and meetings with characters unimaginable. There were high wines and high gales on tempestuous waters, and good comradeship in abundance. Above all, there was an unrivalled introduction by one of its proudest sons — when he was not masquerading as an archetypal Scot — to the history and culture, to the very essence of Canada, the last great civilized country on the planet.

As he tells us in his book, this son of Glengarry talked his way into an appointment as Liaison Officer for the Provincial Archives of Ontario. This was a job he created for himself when he realized that he was not cut out to be either a farmer or an insurance agent. He had become involved in founding the Glengarry Historical Society and the Dunvegan Museum, and convinced that there were many documents of major historical interest which remained in private hands and should be deposited in an archive to ensure their safekeeping for posterity. He therefore persuaded the Ontario Archives to hire him as a kind of "roving archivist." Neither he nor the institution ever looked back. In subsequent years, he secured the deposit of an invaluable mass of documentation of the greatest significance for the history of the Canadian nation — obviously his primary interest. Led by his ancestry, Hugh also sought out Scottish materials, some of which found their way to the University of Guelph Archives, which houses the finest Scottish collection in the country.

Hugh developed his own methods — apart from piracy and banditry — for tracking down materials. Most notable perhaps was his inventive use of reverse genealogy. He would trace the descendents of people who had made a significant contribution to the development of Canada in the past, and then either phone, visit, or plague them to discover whether they had any papers. This involved a considerable amount of research and sleuthing, and no doubt he still has files, that are incomplete because of infuriating gaps in pedigrees or trails that suddenly ran cold.

Hugh had a nose for documents. He was incredibly lucky, some might say, in encountering people in different places — and not always in Canada — in possession of material with which he persuaded them to part, if not immediately then over a period of years, as he gradually, but persistently, wore down their resistance. On occasion, Hugh operated by hunch. I have been with him on trips across the country when we would suddenly pull off the main road and be charging along a dirt track because he vaguely remembered a possible connection with somebody-or-other who was thought to live on a farm somewhere in the vicinity. Sure enough, he would strike gold. We would end up spending the night and Hugh would further add to the nation's heritage. In this regard, his contribution was truly massive and will never be replicated. Nobody else will have the willingness or the opportunity to spend years painstakingly assembling the evidence necessary to make a strike. In this respect MacMillan was, and is, unique.

All Canadians are in Dr MacMillan's debt for his initiative concerning the reconstruction of the routes of 26- and 36-foot voyageur canoes, which began in 1967. I was fortunate enough to become involved some ten years later. I can honestly say that these represent some of the best times I ever enjoyed in Canada. The numerous good folk who accompanied Hugh on these trips over the years would say exactly the same, and are equally in his debt. The expeditions would last months, weeks, or a few days. The paddlers would stop at various places en route for public displays, tutorials on the canoes and how to build them, and talks on the fur trade. The history of the latter surely represents the most heroic period in Canada's past. Hugh easily convinces us that human achievement, the spirit of adventure and the desire of explorers to push through to the west coast should not be obscured by what is now deemed to be politically correct. Like it or not, the fur trade made Canada. It created a much better than average relationship with the Native peoples (as compared with, say, the US), and eventually led to the opening up of the Asian trade across the Pacific. MacMillan and his voyageurs would tell all of this to anyone who was prepared to listen, and to some who were not! He says himself he was never a great canoeist, but he had the ability to make things happen, to organize, and to involve people. It should be understood that the logistics involved in some of those trips were utterly daunting, not to mention all the potential snags that might occur once the expeditions were actually underway. In a word, he was into recreational heritage long before it became as fashionable as it is now, and in this capacity, he must have had an impact upon thousands of people.

Hugh was a founding member and close associate of the Scottish Studies Foundation, which was set up to finance the establishment of a chair of Scottish Studies at the University of Guelph as a memorial to the contribution made by Scots to the history of Canada. Hugh has always worked tirelessly for this cause, and happily his efforts should come to fruition next year since the organization is now quite close to its target. Hugh has always been a most valuable friend to the University of Guelph, supporting its numerous conferences and generally spreading the word about its programmes. He was a noted speaker himself, forever on the road it seemed, giving lectures and talks for local societies and clubs. His own articles and his good links with the media also ensured that news of Hugh's discoveries reached a wider public.

All of Hugh's friends and innumerable acquaintances will welcome the appearance of this book, which will undoubtedly make him many new friends, as readers yet unknown are invited to share some of his remarkable experiences, his triumphs and his disappointments, but above all his infectious enthusiasm and his appetite for life. Hugh MacMillan is one of a kind. He has made a massive contribution to his country and its heritage. That contribution is by no means transitory or ephemeral; it will be valued and appreciated so long as people continue to investigate the history of this great nation. This is his story.

Ted Cowan

Professor of Scottish Studies
University of Glasgow, Scotland
Candlemas 2003

ACKNOWLEDGEMENTS

A long series of adventures — and misadventures — have accompanied the writing of *Adventures of a Paper Sleuth*. After much searching, I have not found another book that focuses on the art of scouting for historical papers, so I believe it is unique.

The book could never have been written without the help of many people. The inspiration to write it came from reading *Adventures of a Treasure Hunter* by Charles P Everitt, which was brought to my attention by Montreal antiquarian Warren Baker.

Dr Simon Fraser of Cornwall, Ontario, started me out with several important leads in the 1960s. Donald Fraser McOuat, Archivist of Ontario, 1963–1978, and Ian Wilson, now National Archivist, were both supportive of my work. Former Laurentian University president Dr Henry BM Best provided valuable information and assistance on many occasions. Leon Warmski, Ontario Archives, alerted me to numerous potential leads from existing collections.

Before the age of computers, my wife Muriel spent many hours cutting and pasting pertinent information for the book. University of Western Ontario archivist Edward G. Phelps read some of the early drafts and made helpful comments. Journalist Bill Stephenson, formerly with the National Film Board, was an early collaborator on parts of this work.

Rosaleen Dickson (not related to any of the Dicksons in the book) performed an invaluable service as a copy editor. Thanks also to Joan Eddis for her contribution to the editing process. Douglas McKercher of Ottawa contributed immensely throughout the book in formatting, annotating, indexing, and the final edit. He organized the pictures, scanned them, worked Photoshop magic on them where needed, and provided captions. Many thanks to Garth Dittrick of Grimsby, Ontario for his amusing sketches of the bear in the truck, the goat on the bureau and the Cobourg Cadillacs.

Samuel Johnson once said, "A man will turn over half a library to make one book." I have turned over hundreds of collections to make this book. In the process, I was fortunate in making many friends and, I hope, few enemies.

Hugh P. MacMillan

INTRODUCTION

The first two chapters of this book are autobiographical. They are followed by 19 chapters of exciting and sometimes strange tales from my constant search for collections of historically valuable papers.

By age 39, I had been a soldier, farmer, salesman, sailor, and agent for a hypnotist, and had worked with Seal Brothers' Circus from California. The Ontario Civil Service Commission was not impressed by my résumé when Donald McOuat, the Archivist of Ontario, hired me in 1964. I was given the lowly classification of a grade three clerk, but McOuat bestowed the rather grand title of Archives Liaison Officer on me. This didn't really impress anyone, but the title sounded good, and I seized the opportunity to begin travelling around the province of Ontario, honing my investigative skills.

Here are some examples of treasures located and acquired by means of fieldwork all over the country:

- the papers of John Graves Simcoe, first Lieutenant-Governor of Upper Canada (Ontario), found with a farmer from New Zealand
- a station wagon full of the papers of Colonel RR McLennan, CPR contractor, world champion hammer thrower, and Glengarry militia leader
- the bugle from Canada's first warship, *The Rainbow*.
- a piece of presumed human skin in a small tin box, with a note announcing "This is a piece of skin taken from the neck of Cut Nose, Sioux Indian chief hanged at Mankato, Minnesota Territory in 1866."

My career in the field of history and archives began in the late 1950s. I had returned to Glengarry County after several years in British Columbia. I was soon involved in local history, and helped to start the Glengarry Historical Society in 1958. Later, I helped found the Dunvegan Pioneer Museum. In 1967, the Historical Society's Canadian Centennial project was to open the Nor'Wester and Loyalist Museum at Williamstown.

In following the trail of my family history, I visited the islands of Grenada, Trinidad, Antigua and Jamaica in the West Indies. The purpose was to meet descendants of two of my great-great-grandfather's brothers, Archibald and Ranald. They went from Scotland via Glengarry to the West Indies in the first decade of the 19th Century. The Grenadians proved to be a colourful and interesting addition to the Glenpean line of MacMillans. Many of them are described in the pages of my 1994 book, *The Lochaber Immigrants to Glengarry*.

These and many more tales show how much of the written heritage was recovered through the efforts of many people who co-operated with me. I was merely the facilitator. Most of the credit goes to them. Their names and stories fill the following pages.

CHAPTER ONE
THE MAKING OF A PAPER SLEUTH

Much of my life has been driven by a fascination with Glengarry County and its history. That fascination extends back to the 1930s and 1940s, when my father, a Presbyterian preacher, made the pilgrimage back to his roots in Glengarry every summer. Starting in my teens, I took notes from the reminiscences of my grandmother, who died in 1942. Over time, this interest evolved into a unique career in historical research, which continues to this day.

At 16 I left home, lied about my age and tried to join the Royal Canadian Air Force. My father must have intervened, as the Air Force sent me back to school. I did succeed in volunteering for the infantry, but my army career was equally undistinguished. I didn't get overseas, and the pinnacle of my military career must have occurred sometime before I got myself busted from sergeant back to private. Having signed up in the hope of fighting the Japanese in 1945, the only action I saw was chasing Japanese fire balloons in a jeep with a Bren gun during weapons training in the mountains of British Columbia.

When the war ended, I asked for a discharge and went back to school. I signed up for some college courses in English and accounting. After a year's study, I had a passing grade in English and a failure in accounting. I left school for a job in Montreal as office gopher with a Dutch export firm. When I discovered that the manager was shafting the owners, I led an office revolt by the three employees, and the offending manager fired me forthwith.

The summer of 1947 was spent working on my uncle's Glengarry farm, contemplating my next move. To stay and help run the family farm was an appealing option, partly because of my new interest in family history. But I also craved adventure, so I joined a two-month harvest excursion in Saskatchewan, stooking grain and driving a team of horses hauling sheaves to the thresher.

Moving on west, I spent two months on a cattle ranch in Alberta, then out to the Pacific coast. I was by now taking a correspondence course on writing. In Vancouver I thought of going to sea and writing at the same time, in the tradition of Jack London, Joseph Conrad, and Richard Henry Dana.

My timing was bad. There was a seamen's strike in progress, so I had to settle for a coastal towboat, on which I started as a deckhand. So much for writing the next *Moby Dick*.

It was not a glorious or romantic sailing career, but it proved to be the start of a nautical association that would be much longer and richer than I could ever have imagined at the time. I'll come back to my sailing days in Chapter 2.

In one respect, my timing was very good. In Vancouver I met and married Muriel Diver, who had come from Montreal to attend the University of British Columbia. In 1952, we went back to the Glengarry farm.

My true interest lay in family and local history, but that pursuit paid no bills. Not having a university degree, I was in no position to teach. I held a succession of jobs notable more for their variety than their financial yield. Car-top carriers (just as the Korean crisis embargoed supplies of steel to the manufacturer), life insurance (the last refuge of the man who has not utterly given up on the hope of an income) and farming itself (the first step on the road to recovery from expecting to make a living), all were doomed to failure.

Meanwhile, Muriel taught school between raising and caring for our four children. Her contribution to the family finances enabled me to spend time on historical research.

Eventually my interest in family history found a focus in the field of documents and archives. I had begun noting collections of papers in Glengarry that were in private hands, and in many cases in imminent peril of destruction. I was able to take some of these papers to the Public Archives of Canada in nearby Ottawa, keeping copies for myself to use in a column I was writing for *The Glengarry News*.

Then, thanks to the support of Donald Fraser McOuat, I had an opportunity to pioneer in a new job that I helped create, Liaison Officer for the Archives of Ontario. This I found to be remarkable, because I was actually going to be paid to locate and acquire papers!

Moving to Toronto in 1963 was not easy, since our family had long established roots in Glengarry (dating back to 1802), and my lack of success in making a living from the farm of my ancestors was particularly poignant. But in a way, my father's peripatetic career as a minister had helped to ease the separation. After all, only one of his children had been born in Glengarry, and it wasn't me. Besides, I was now in the happy position of being able to convert my hobby to a paying job. I came to terms with the fact that I was not a farmer.

My agenda for this new and untried line of work began without guidelines or direction from the Archives or Civil Service procedures, as there had never been such a position before. I decided, and McOuat agreed, that I would set my own guidelines, following the precepts of any skilled salesman.

I kept in close contact with my Eastern Ontario history buffs and gradually built a network across the Province. I continued to gather family history information in the form of documents, both originals and copies, and combined it with the recording of oral history. Along my career path I unearthed many stories that relate to my Glengarry relatives.

Over the years I have received help from a host of friends. Information for this book too has come from across the continent and abroad.

While every family's history is unique, every family *has* a history. Each is worth knowing, for the knowledge gives depth to the lives of every member of the family and their understanding of why they are where they are in this life.

I have been in the privileged position for much of my life, of seeing how my family history intersects with the history of Ontario, the history of northern and western Canada and even the West Indies! I have related disjointed bits on occasions through the years, no doubt boring some while delighting others. The rest of this chapter places these anecdotes together for the first time, hopefully putting me into my own historical context. Like many Scottish families, mine has spelled its name with joyous inconsistency as MacMillan or McMillan as whim and fashion took it.

An anonymous statement I have kept for years sums up how important this type of history can be for my family and yours:

> "We stand to gain a new understanding about ourselves as we learn more about our ancestors and the lives they lived. In today's mobile, often unstable, society, it is important for people to have knowledge of their larger family connections, both here and abroad."

My father, who died in 1976 at age 91, had his share of faults as well as virtues. He was rigid, unbending, and intolerant of human frailties, but he persevered in his beliefs. He left a prosperous Glengarry farm to become a minister. At 85, he was still preaching the gospel without the aid of notes. For him, the Presbyterian work ethic was real and he could not understand why I was being paid to chase around the country after other peoples' old papers. After my sessions of trying to mine his highly retentive, but selective, memory for nuggets of family history, his regular comment was, "But Hugh, when are you going to get a real job?" I explained that I was sort of a preacher, travelling around the country persuading people to preserve our history. He never accepted that idea; it was still not a real job in his mind.

The only historical relic that has been saved in our family is the Brown Bess flintlock musket that was carried by my ancestor John Roy McMillan when he served as a yeoman in the Royal Canadian Volunteer Regiment (1797–1802) and later with the Glengarry Militia in the War of 1812–1814. He was in the regimental company of his own brother, Capt Alexander McMillan. It is pure luck that the flintlock musket has survived the housecleaning efforts of my cousins.

There were several John McMillans in the RCV Regiment. Differentiating my relative from the others was made easier by a mix-up in the paperwork that was part of the process of granting crown land.

Capt. Alexander McMillan returned from Scotland to Canada in 1793 with a number of young kinsmen including his brother, John Roy (my great-great-grandfather), and recruited them into the Regiment soon after he arrived. When it was disbanded in 1802, our John Roy would have been in line to receive a grant of 200 acres of land from the Crown. Instead, his grant specified 600 acres in the north end of Lancaster Township, later Lochiel, in Glengarry County. Normally there would only be 2 or 3 items in the file for a lot, but this file has a dozen or more letters and papers attesting to the identity of the three John McMillans. As the land board had mistakenly granted him 600 acres instead of 200, not knowing there were actually three John McMillans being granted land, the other two John McMillans must have been outraged until the error was corrected.

The fortunate result for me as a researcher was that Captain Alexander had to supply an affidavit attesting to the antecedents of the three John McMillans, which provided valuable material for people searching their McMillan family histories. Occasionally bureaucratic mix-ups can yield some advantage.

Thanks to Mary Beaton of Ottawa, the following item was extracted from an article in the *Glengarry News* of September 7, 1894 celebrating the 100th anniversary of the Glenelg settlers:

> Died 1870 at Torbolton at 101 years, late of lot 24, 5th con. Lochiel Glengarry, Mary (Grant) McMillan relict of late John McMillan elder of St Columba, emigrated to Canada in 1791 at 22 years of age. 15 children,

8 survive, eldest is now 80 years of age. Leaves 138 grandchildren and 185 great grandchildren.

The obituary helped to prove the authenticity of information I had previously recorded and to correct a mistake. I had assumed that Mary Grant McMillan was part of the United Empire Loyalist migration from the Mohawk Valley of New York, but the information in this obituary reduced my loyalist ancestors from 4 to 3.

My research had already revealed Mary Grant McMillan's link to Cuthbert Grant, Warden of the Plains, and I also discovered a connection with former Nor'Wester Alexander Grant, of Duldreggan Hall at L'Orignal on the Ottawa River.

My father was told by his father that, after her husband John Roy died in 1841, Mary Grant McMillan walked over 100 miles north along the Ottawa River to the Fitzroy Harbour area, to join her oldest daughter Mary, who was married to Captain Alexander McMillan, not the same as mentioned above but possibly her cousin, son of Lt-Col Alexander.

They could have made their trip easier by a trek to L'Orignal and thence upriver by boat. Mary Grant McMillan's late husband's cousin, another Mary McMillan, daughter of Archibald of Murlaggan, was married to Thomas Kains, captain of the Ottawa River steamer *Shannon*, which might have taken the family at least as far as Bytown.

Thomas Kains was a half-pay officer in the Royal Navy. He had been in the party that set fire to the White House in Washington during the War of 1812. Kains was called back to active service as a purser on the *Victory*. I have located portraits of Kains and his wife Mary, as well as his naval uniform, now in the hands of various descendents. They were as far afield as New Jersey and as near as Waterloo, Ontario.

Archibald Kains (1865–1944), a grandson of Mary McMillan and Thomas Kains, retired from banking to spend the last years of his life collecting papers and information about the Kains and McMillan families. In 1942, he journeyed from his home at 9 Rideau Gate, Ottawa, to return to President Franklin Delano Roosevelt in Washington, DC, some sterling silver that his grandfather had looted from the White House in 1813. I am still searching for items Thomas removed from Admiral Horatio Nelson's flagship, *HMS Victory*, when it was a hospital ship during the Crimean War.

The portrait of Thomas's grandson Archibald, who began his banking career at Brantford, shows a handsome figure in a kilt. I located Archibald's letters to Pauline Johnson, the famous Indian poet from Brantford, and the letters are now with the National Archives of Canada.

Captain Thomas Kains (1790–1855) was a member of the party that set fire to the US Presidential residence during the War of 1812. After being whitewashed to cover the smoke damage from this fire, it became known as the White House. During the Crimean War, Kains was purser aboard HMS Victory. Victory had been Nelson's flagship at Trafalgar, but by Kains's time, it was a hospital ship. (Author's collection)

According to notes from my father, lot 24 on the 14th concession, today the 5th of Lochiel, was the home of John Roy McMillan, and a meeting place for the 1802 emigrants. John Roy probably built a log house around 1802 when he took up his land grant, and built the stone house that still stands today between 1815 and 1820. This fine old stone house is set away from the road on the slope of a hill well back from a small private cemetery by the roadside.

In 1802 John Roy McMillan was just out of the army when his brother Allan and cousin Archibald arrived in Montreal with over 400 kinfolk. John Roy, along with the other two John McMillans, may have been in the forefront of those trying to lure the new arrivals to their area.

I could never find John Roy's headstone in the cemetery that was on his land. Someone had taken some of the stones away. My grandfather's brother John sold the farm early in the 20th century to Henry Vogan who had to rebuild the chimney on the stone house. Having difficulty finding flat stones, he thought of the abandoned cemetery at the road. Sometime I'd like to try to convince the present owners to take the top portion of their chimney down and return the stones to the cemetery.

Father told me during one of my note-taking sessions that a cousin, Lily McMillan, had a wooden leg and went out west in the 1890s, but he offered no word of explanation about how she lost her leg. At a later note-taking session I asked if she had any nickname. Well, yes. "She was called Klondike Lily!" That answer got my full attention! But the only further information I gleaned was that "she sinned!" My comment was that most of us have sinned, and I asked my father, "So what was her sin?" The question was met with silence.

A dram of single malt in a later session with an elderly cousin succeeded in drawing out an answer. I was told "She was one of those, you know ... madams with the Gold Rush." Elated at this success, I kept up the questioning but no more information came forth. I told this story to an aunt noted for her lack of humour and delusions of grandeur. She was most indignant when I told her I intended to record the story in our family history as an unproved legend. I've spent a lot of time and some money researching Klondike Lily, though so far with no success. There are moments when I think "Klondike Lily" may have been a figment of my imagination — or my father's.

Pierre Berton and a few other Klondike experts claim to have heard of her, but lack details. Dear Aunt Grace did not appreciate my view that it's not every family that turns up a madam in the family record.

Another family anecdote worth recording here is about finding the portrait of Allan McMillan of Glenpean, probably painted in 1802, around the time he came to Canada.

In 1970, I made my first official trip to the west coast for the Archives of Ontario. One of my assignments was to acquire the papers of Archibald McMillan of Murlaggan from his great grandson, Dr John MacMillan in West Vancouver. Dr MacMillan's sister Marjorie, wife of Judge Oscar Orr, had photographs and paintings, while John had the papers and had arranged in his will for the original collections to go to the Public Archives in Ottawa. Marjorie had sent the portrait of Allan McMillan of Glenpean to the Argenteuil County Historical Society's museum, a fine old stone building twenty miles downriver on the Ottawa from Archibald McMillan of Murlaggan's old home. There was no portrait of Archibald, but a fine one of his wife Isabella Gray was with a descendent, Jack Barker of Cowansville, Quebec.

On this same visit in 1970, Judge Oscar Orr saw me eyeing a jagged piece of metal 4 inches long mounted on a pedestal. On inquiring what it was, I was regaled with this explanation:

> That is a piece of shrapnel that hit me above my right eye in World War I and lodged in my mouth. Luckily I survived this ordeal, but was left with a tiny open wound above my eye.

This resulted in a strange phenomenon that lasted many years before the wound finally healed. When I used my pipe, smoke issued from my forehead. I dined out for years on the following incident that resulted from this oddity.

The judge continued:

> Marjorie and I were riding on a train in England soon after I had sustained this injury. A very stern looking bishop, arrayed in all his regalia, got into our compartment. Being a very proper Englishman he made no chitchat with a colonial soldier. Indeed, he buried his head behind the paper he was reading while I lit up my pipe.
>
> At one point he happened to lower his paper just as a large puff of smoke escaped from my forehead. The paper quickly went back up but he kept taking a peek. Still not a word from the good bishop, but he was seen to be crossing himself as he got off at the next station. No doubt it confirmed his worst suspicions about colonial troops.

Marjorie sent me on my way after dinner with a photograph of Allan's portrait and extensive notes about our family connection. I deposited the photo of the painting in the Archives of Ontario and the notes were added to my growing pile of material intended for this book. Marjorie died soon after this and my notes did not survive a 1972 fire in our home.

In 1990, I went to the Argenteuil museum to compare my photograph of Allan with the original portrait which, much to their embarrassment they were unable to find. Did Marjorie send it to some other museum? Was it stolen? It never did turn up.

In the fall of 1991, I went to the North American Fur Trade Conference at Michilimackinac, Michigan, hoping to garner more information on James McMillan. I stopped at Eureka, Montana, to pick up Doc Smiley, a fur trade history friend. Smiley was the last veterinary surgeon in General George Custer's ill-fated 7th Cavalry, the last US regiment to have horses. When Hitler's Panzer divisions cut through Poland in 1939, the regiment wisely switched to tanks and Doc was out of a job.

I was to meet Doc Smiley at the Elkhorn Bar, where there is a clever replica of an alligator chained to the waterpipe of the men's urinal. It is just dark enough that you don't notice this creature in the swirling water of the trough as you unzip. When you do spot his head with open jaws amidst the foaming water you get a sudden urge to zip up and leave fast. After a second look at this mean-looking critter you realize you've been had. Many a tourist has arrived at the urinal well into his cups but departed sober.

The bartender couldn't stand my lack of reaction when I came back from the loo and finally asked if I noticed anything unusual, "Not really," I said, "but aren't you afraid that little alligator in your urinal will drown?"

Travelling across the vast open grasslands and mountains of Montana, we stopped at Three Forks in the "Big Sky" country of Madison County with the towering Gallatin Mountains to the east of us. Here we got a great welcome from cousin Catherine McMillan Shirley, whom I had last seen 42 years earlier, in 1949, at a party her father Peter Miles McMillan had organized for expatriate Glengarrians.

Peter Miles McMillan had been a compulsive gambler. I recalled that when his party ended, he drove me 200 miles west to Butte in his big Frazer car (now a collector's item). Here we met my colleague Harry Dixon, who had a contract to sell advance tickets for Seal Brothers circus. At that time, Montana did not welcome paper money, so Peter went to his bank and got out a bag of silver dollars with about fifty for me. We must have stopped at every bar en route to Butte. By the end of the day I had just about doubled my stake by playing the slot machines and Peter had accumulated several bags of coins.

Peter's brother Archie had been given the farm by their father. Peter had received a $100 gold piece as his patrimony, with which he had headed west to make his fortune. This he did — several times — but lost it just as often through his compulsive gambling.

Gathering even these few stories about family history takes time, patience and luck. The year before she died, my cousin Catherine McMillan Shirley told me a tale which none of the rest of her family had heard.

> In 1917 father and mother left Goldfield, 200 miles west, and headed for this area. The trek took all summer, but they were not alone. The slow progress was on account of them driving about 3000 head of sheep. They could make only 15 to 20 miles a day, as the sheep had to graze and find water. Dad must have done well in the short time he had been in the West. He and mother had the two oldest of our family but I was not yet born. Dad had a Model T Ford for Mother and the kids to ride in while he and his French-Canadian sheepherders rode horses, driving the sheep with the help of a dozen or more sheep dogs. There is not even one picture to show this strange cavalcade on the move. Dad also had about $25,000 in silver dollars, which was some fortune in those days.

Within a short time he was near to being broke through his gambling. Luckily for him, Mother had had enough sense to get some money from him beforehand, and she bought an old house, which she named the McMillan Hotel. Mother grubstaked him many times when his incessant gambling would make him broke again.

My grandmother Annie McIntosh McMillan (1860–1942) was a handsome woman, judging by her photograph. She was raised on a prosperous farm in Charlottenburgh Township, Glengarry. All her McIntosh relatives moved to the West Coast just before the First World War. Many of her interesting letters have survived. She told me her great-great-grandfather had been killed at Culloden and the English were still anathema to her. One time she warned me never to marry a Sassenach. Years later, when I learned what the word meant, I did go and marry one. I don't suppose Granny is pleased. I am wondering what my pious grandmother's reaction was to the following portion of a letter she received September 12, 1882 from her cousin Isabella Grant at Cashion's Glen, South Branch, Glengarry:

> Dear friend Annie — I am sorry to tell you that I was up to Crawfords last night and the girl has decided not to go from home at present. I think she is expecting a few husking bees and she dont want to loose the fun the next time John goes for a girl he must do as we were telling him he must sleep with her and she will be sure to stay.

Well! And some of us had the idea our elders rarely thought of sex, except of course for the pleasure of creating us. Annie would have been 22 at that time and she married my grandfather two years later. Who was "the girl" and who was "John," and was Isabella or Annie sleeping with John? We will likely never know, but it does throw a new light on Granny and cousin Isabella. Aunt Grace would not have approved of such a letter being made public, notwithstanding the worthy cause of advancing social history.

Great-uncle John Archie Roy McMillan (1851–1917) is one of my grandfather's five interesting brothers. He remained a bachelor, but judging by his correspondence, had several admiring women available. He must have been an indifferent farmer, a part-time drover, and a gambling land speculator. This is documented in some of his papers I managed to salvage from my housecleaning cousins' bonfire. His business records show him to be the owner of almost a block of land and buildings on Green Avenue between St Catherine and Sherbrooke streets in Montreal. This must have been too slow a way to get rich, because he sold out before World War I to buy prairie land near Saskatoon. He overextended himself, and a cash flow problem lost the lot, along with his grandfather John Roy's stone house and farm.

John Archie Roy spent his last years with Sandy, another bachelor brother, who owned the farm where Muriel and I lived from 1952 to 1963. He was a skilled cabinetmaker and, according to my father, went to the shanty every winter from around 1870 to 1900, taking a crew of men, horses and supplies by train to Saginaw, Michigan.

The Lochaber emigrants were already familiar with the handling of big timber when they came to Canada in 1802. Their part of the Highlands was heavily timbered and had streams along which logs could be rafted. We preserved the cast iron stove that Sandy took to the shanty and it now rests in the Dunvegan Pioneer Museum. The door casting reads "Copps Bros, Hamilton 1879," a family relic with a story.

John and Sandy Archie Roy McMillan, were look-alike brothers, with lean craggy features, faces clean-shaven except for handlebar mustaches and slicked-back hair parted in the middle. I can remember great-uncle Sandy's frugality, which extended to cutting hard peppermint candies in half. The following excerpts from two unsigned letters to John indicate that two ladies he knew had very dissimilar problems for him to solve:

> Dear Friend — I have heard you were talking about coming down the time of the fair be sure and call I will be on 171 St Urbain St, Montreal. The fair is commencing on the 11 ending on the 19 you come down some of those days if you don't feel to high. I haven't been sick since you came down you know what I mean I didn't tell them at home as they would take a fit. I wish I had some of the stuff you were telling me off. I dont think you deceived me in doing anything wrong. J. A. you will burn this letter as soon as you read it. I think of the last night we were together. I was dreaming about it last night.
>
> xxxxxx yours ____

There are indications in John's cash books that in the following years he was paying to support an unnamed orphan in Montreal.

Little Jack McDonald, a famous Glengarry fiddler, knew JA, as John Archie Roy McDonald was known, from stopping over at the Dalhousie Hotel on his way to and from Montreal. This would be an overnight stop if he was taking his horse and rig, and he'd get a room for a tune or two on the fiddle. Little Jack, the Glengarry fiddler, said, "that uncle of yours could stepdance, play the fiddle, and sing Gaelic songs all night long. He was a caution with the ladies, and not feared to spend his money, or pay for his mistakes, as when he got Betsy in a fix."

The second letter, undated and also unsigned, is circa 1895. It outlines a completely different sort of problem:

> John, Why dont you be smart for yourself and others you have a bill against Mrs. M Cameron ... she has that house insured at $1,000.00 and that is more than she will ever get for it and if you would watch your chance when there is a storm and set that big shed next to the house in a flame. Set it inside and up near the roof and then we will all get our money and she will not loose everything and of course watch the wind is not hie so not to hurt anyone ... or after a rain or towards morning no one in gods world would ever no. Be sure and burn this paper....

For the sake of social history, we can be thankful that my uncle JA did not put his own papers to the torch. There is no indication that he followed her detailed instructions.

Lt-Col Alexander McMillan was the first of our Glenpean line known to have crossed the Atlantic. His presence in America as early as 1773, when he came to New York City on the Pearl, was noted in JLH Neilson's *Quebec Almanac* of 1796, which records the following charming description of Alexander by Col Landemann of the Royal Engineers:

> McMillan was a jolly fat Scotchman, with a very plump, round face, sandy hair and a rosy complexion. In the course of the evening, after dinner at McLean's, he treated us to a tune on two Jews harps, performing on both at once, and as he asserted, playing first and second. His Jews harps were great pets, and he kept them in a neat case made for the purpose, well supplied with cotton to protect them from injury.

All my efforts to find these Jew's harps have come to naught.

In 1967, I located Donald MacMillan, a great-grandson of Alexander, who owned a trucking firm in East Brunswick, New Jersey. He had carefully preserved his great-grandfather's handmade French-Canadian style armchair. Family legend had it that the chair was made by the St Regis Indians near Cornwall, Ontario, as a token of their regard for his leadership in the successful raid on French Mills, New York, on November 23, 1812. At that time, he was Lieutenant-Colonel of the 2nd Regiment of Glengarry Militia.

Artifacts like this are more likely to survive if they are left with an institution or collector rather than in someone's attic, so I asked Donald to donate the chair to the Nor'Wester & Loyalist Museum in Williamstown, Ontario. When he came up from New Jersey in September 1967 to present the chair at the opening of the museum, the brigade of three fur trade canoes that I had organized arrived from Grand Portage, the old North West Company rendezvous at the head of Lake Superior. Our piper led us ashore. Several with Nor'Wester or Loyalist connections took turns being photographed in the chair.

Lt-Col Alexander McMillan's military career is documented in the Public Archives of Canada, RG 8, C-series, vol. 17, 793. He was appointed to DeLancey's Brigade in 1777, served in the Revolution, was present at the reduction of Savannah and elsewhere. Appointed to the Royal Canadian Volunteer Regiment in 1796, he remained until it was disbanded in 1802. He later served as Lt-Col of the 2nd Regiment, Glengarry Militia. From January 1809, he commanded the flank companies of the 1st and 2nd Glengarry and was appointed to the Militia Pension Board of Upper Canada. He had a son who was a Captain in the Glengarry Fencibles during the War of 1812. This son was probably the Captain Alexander McMillan who married Elizabeth Crites, United Empire Loyalist, and the ancestor of Donald MacMillan in New Jersey.

Captain Alexander McMillan was at the military settlement in Perth, Lanark County, soon after its creation in 1816. He was a half-pay officer from the Glengarry Fencibles with an outstanding record in the War of 1812. He built a stone house there about 1842 and was the first Warden of the district, but he was better known for a duel with a Dr Thom at Perth. Apparently Thom had neglected to invite the less socially favoured wife of McMillan to a year-end levee. This insult led McMillan to challenge Thom. Pistol shots were exchanged but no casualties ensued. Presumably honour was satisfied.

Alexander McMillan received large land grants in Glengarry after the Revolutionary War. He was a founding member of the Highland Society of Canada in 1818. In 1823, the year he died, his nephew James, a former Nor'Wester but by then with the Hudson's Bay Company, came to the village of Williamstown by canoe very much as I was to do 144 years later in a recreated canoe brigade in 1967.

With James McMillan on that 4,000-mile canoe trip were two of his Métis children, Margaret, 8, and Allan, 7, whom he had brought from the Columbia River on the west coast, to be baptized at St Andrew's Church of Scotland in Williamstown.

The next record I have found suggests that the little boy, Allan, may have stayed in the east with his grandfather Allan, because he is listed in 1836 as a Nor'Wester apprentice clerk hired to go from Lachine to Red River.

It's interesting how this information came to light. My fur trade history friends often exchange leads. Prof. Jennifer Brown, a fur trade academic at the University of Winnipeg, showed me an unpublished manuscript by a Hudson's Bay Company trader, Henry Conolly, son of William Conolly who was a North West Company partner. Henry died on a steamship en route to Labrador in 1910 with the unedited manuscript of his father's memoirs. Jennifer had this copy on loan from Jim Morrison, another of my researcher friends. It was an exciting moment when I came upon the reference to my McMillan antecedents.

On contacting Jim, I discovered the original copy of the manuscript was part of the Robert Bell papers in the Public Archives. Robert Bell of the Geological Survey of Canada was a renaissance man who carried on a correspondence with everyone from Charles Darwin to a Hudson's Bay Company clerk in the Arctic. It is not surprising that he would have such an item among his papers. Robert Bell's daughter tried to get the memoirs published in New York when she lived there in the 1920s, and Jim Morrison also has plans to edit and publish this important material.

In 1966, I acquired a transcript of the 1801 journal of a canoe voyage from Fort George on the Niagara River to Fort Malden on the Detroit River. The writer was Lt Miles McDonell of the Royal Canadian Volunteer Regiment. He was stationed at Fort George while Alexander McMillan was at Malden. I assume my ancestor John Roy McMillan was also at Malden because he was in his brother's company. Miles McDonell, who was a Glengarry man, was later to become agent to Lord Selkirk at Red River and the first Governor of the Red River Colony. In his diary, he wrote, "We gathered for dinner with my old friends Captains McMillan and McLean. We drank toasts and Alex entertained us." Probably he played his Jew's harps.

In the *Dictionary of Canadian Biography*, an entry on Col James DeLancey (1746–1804) gives a vivid account of the guerrilla-type tactics of Delancey's Brigade, in which Capt Alexander served for seven years. Delancey's Brigade was a picked force of horsemen drawn from Westchester County to procure supplies for the British Army from the neutral ground between the British and American positions. Gen William Tryon of New York commented, "this troop is truly the elite of the country ... I have much confidence in them for their spirited behaviour."

Picture of Bartle Bros. photographic studio on wheels in summer, on a sleigh in winter, served Glengarry County late 19th and early 20th century.

Malcolm and Hugh MacMillan presenting Brown Bess Musket carried by great, great, great grandfather of the Royal Canadian Volunteer Regiment and the Glengarry militia to Joan P. MacDonald, Director of the NorWester Loyalist Museum, Williamstown, November 2002.

Because they supplied the British Army and the inhabitants of New York with cattle, they were called the Cowboys and over the next five years they became one of the best known and most feared of the Loyalist units. Also known as the Outlaws of the Bronx, they harassed the enemy throughout the war. Washington was well aware of this activity and sought the capture of Alexander McMillan. I have been unable to learn more about him despite many years of searching.

In 1962, I had the pleasure of meeting Charles McMillan's widow, Grace, at the Cowansville, Quebec, home of her grandson, Jack Barker. Then in her 90s, she had many stories to tell of her late husband, a grandson of Archibald Murlaggan McMillan.

My tapes of several hours of tales about the family were lost in our 1972 housefire, but one of them stays in my memory. About 1890, Charles and Grace McMillan left the Grenville, Quebec, area for the Oregon territory. They established a business there and operated it for about ten years. In 1901, Charles's father Duncan McMillan died. On inheriting the property, Charles sold the business, stashed the proceeds of about $20,000 in his money belt and headed east with Grace by train through the western states to Chicago, then on to Montreal.

Somewhere in Montana, the train came to a halt in a narrow rock cut. Word spread through the cars that it was being held up by train robbers. It was a certainty they would be searched and all valuables taken. While other passengers were hiding valuables in their shoes and skirts, all places the bandits would be sure to look, Charles took his money belt from under his shirt, handed the large denomination bank notes to Grace, then pitched the belt out the window. Charles kept some money in his pocket along with his watch, and Grace kept a few dollars in her purse. Like most ladies at that time, Grace had her waist-long hair coiled in a large bun on top of her head. Her nimble fingers soon had the banknotes in tight little rolls, which she shoved into the mass of hair atop her head. The bandits took her wedding ring, his watch, and all their available money, at which point Grace burst into tears exclaiming, "But we have no money to get us back to Montreal!" One of the bandits felt sorry for her and tossed her a $5 gold piece. She was still chuckling sixty years later when she told me the story of how she had fooled those Montana bandits.

Many stories came from my father's memory. Others were handed down through four generations of collective memory, despite the loss of the Gaelic, which would no doubt have improved them.

Alex Willie MacMillan from Lochiel was a well known undertaker in Alexandria whose ancestor came out in the 1802 emigration. He had a black sense of humour, exemplified by the tales he liked to tell. He once said to me, "The first decision that a Glengarry lad gets to make is choosing his father's coffin." There was some truth to that. Many Highland heads of households fancied themselves as the monarch of their own glen. *My* father certainly had such leanings.

Alex Willie once stopped my father on the street for a little chitchat. Father asked about Alex Willie's health and his business. Alex Willie's succinct reply was, "Well, Rev JA, it would be tolerably better if you could fix me some funerals real quick."

In the 1930s, Alex Willie and a friend were driving back to Alexandria on a cold winter's day, transporting a corpse seated upright in the back seat of his old touring car. They had to get out and shovel, as the road wasn't ploughed. Another car caught up to them and two men got out to help push them through the worst drifts. It was getting dark, and one of the men noticed the person in the back seat, so he called out to Alex Willie, "What's the matter with your friend in the back seat? Why isn't he out here pushing?" Alex Willie's quick answer was, "Seems he had too much of the grog and fell asleep, but reach in and give him a shake." The stranger's reaction was not recorded.

In 1914, my grandfather Hughie Archie Roy MacMillan died at age 61 from pneumonia, possibly brought on by a lengthy sojourn in a snow bank on a cold winter's night, following a visit to the Quigley Hotel a short distance from the farm.

The ledger kept by the Wildcat Chisholms for their store and hotel has frequent entries for Wee Hughie taking home a jug of high wines, a lethal mix of overproof alcohol and a variety of other ingredients. These entries commence in the 1860s, when he would have been a lad of ten or so. My father explained about all these purchases from the Quigley Hotel. Hughie's mother, Margaret Grant came to this farm in the 1830s as the bride of Archie Roy MacMillan. The farm was located where the stage from L'Orignal on the Ottawa River stopped to change horses before proceeding to Lancaster on the St Lawrence. My great-grandmother served food and drink and would need these spirits for the travellers. Father said she smoked a clay pipe, which she kept on the mantel. One day a traveller picked it up to smoke it. Before she used it next, she broke a piece off the stem. When she died in 1893, she was said to have left $20,000 in her will, all of it made from the sale of food and drink.

Margaret Grant MacMillan was of Loyalist stock from the South Branch of the Raisin River near Williamstown. From her portrait (lost in our 1972 housefire), she appeared to be a handsome woman. Despite her false teeth, which fit badly in those days, she had fine features with a sharply chiseled nose and piercing eyes; not someone you would want to cross.

There are mysterious chapters in our family saga that I have yet to pry open.

Father once told me of when his grandfather Archie Roy "dressed up for me in his top hat and tails to show me how he looked when he went to see lawyer McLennan in Cornwall about his uncle Ranald's estate in the Indies." When I pressed for more details, Father changed the subject. This is a fragment of an elusive story of ships, money, and poison, first intimated to me by my grandmother when I was 15.

In 1995, while I was visiting my relatives in Grenada, Lynessa Leid mentioned the same story about Ranald saying that he had been poisoned in the West Indies. My grandmother had also told me the same story. I have had records checked , but to no avail. Many such stories have some sort of basis in fact, but with no records they are usually impossible to verify.

In my last note-taking session with father, he told me that in 1906, when he was 21, his father had given him money to go to Illinois and buy a Percheron stud horse, which he brought back by train. With that horse, my father raised enough money to study at McGill University to become a preacher.

Some of these stories as recounted and recorded may not seem terribly significant to a family history, but tell much about the social history of the times. They are worth committing to paper to keep them safe so people yet unborn can better understand why people in the past acted as they did.

A bill dated 1893 shows that it cost $252.03 to roof my grandfather's barn with slate. The priest in the Catholic church next to our farm, one Father McMillan was proud of the slate roof on his own house. He thought it the only slate roof around until he was told that Hughie Archie Roy McMillan had put a slate roof on his barn years before. It was around this time that the Orange Lodge people needed a white horse for their July 12th parade, as the one they had used in past years had died. A lodge member suggested, "Why not ask Father McMillan if we can borrow his white horse for the day?" This seemed an unlikely prospect, but ask him they did. He told them he would like to help them, but his parishioners would not be pleased at him aiding this Protestant group. However, he said, he would be away that day and the horse would be in the barn. They got the message, and before daylight on the Glorious 12th, they were leading the horse down the road. At first light they were shocked to discover that someone had painted the horse green. This was the only recorded instance of an Orange Walk that starred King Billy riding a green horse.

The business records to do with the slate roof were in a wooden chest of documents I found at my uncle's house in 1972, the year he was killed in a car accident. It was while looking after his estate that I was pleasantly surprised to find that my cousins had not destroyed this chest of historically valuable records, a fine collection of 19th-century letters and business papers that has since been deposited with the Glengarry Historical Society. Among the papers is the 1907 Glengarry telephone book consisting of only one page and listing 19 subscribers, my grandfather being one of them. The rules in the phone book are interesting.

You are instructed to:
- Read these rules before and after eating.
- Always hang the receiver on hook with ear down to keep out dust.
- Outsiders will not be permitted to run in and use the telephone a minute.
- 3 minutes is a goodly time to talk business and should also satisfy those socially inclined.

Donald John MacGillivray was a first cousin of my father's and a veteran of the Boer War. Donald's ancestor came from Scotland in 1794 with the Glenelg settlers to Glengarry. Donald John told me about his father courting Isabella, my grandfather's sister. He drove down to Lochiel with his horse and buggy to see her father, Archie Roy, and ask permission to marry her. Archie Roy considered this request and answered, "No, you can't marry Isabella, because she is keeping house for her two brothers, Sandy and John, but you can marry my older daughter Henrietta." Donald claims his father left in a fine rage and headed back for Kirkhill. When he cooled off, he decided, "Well, they are sisters and they look alike — so why not?" He married Henrietta.

Donald John made many fine cedar chests, which he gave to certain select women in Glengarry. The criterion was that they must allow their husbands to have a dram in the house, so my wife Muriel was given a cedar chest many years ago.

Before I joined the Ontario Archives, my own interest in history had been on a personal, family, level but I was intrigued by Alfred Silver, author of *Red River Story*, and *Where the Ghost Horse Runs*. In his notes, Silver explained how he mined historical sources to create novels, which were based on a mix of historical fact and conjecture. Concerning our western Canadian Métis connections and the early fur trade, Silver's notes also help to explain the connection between the Grants and the McMillans: He wrote:

> I wouldn't have been able even to start on this book ... if it hadn't been for an amateur historian named Margaret Arnett MacLeod. Among her many other endeavours, including editing the letters of Letitia Hargrave and contributing to *Women of Red River*, Mrs. MacLeod developed a passionate obsession for researching Cuthbert Grant. When someone asked me for an explanation for Mrs. MacLeod's obsession, since she wasn't a descendent of Grant, nor did she appear to have any other vested interest, the only theory I could come up with was the gap left in her life by the death of her only son.
>
> Lieutenant Alan MacLeod was a World War I flyer and was unusual among recipients of the Victoria Cross in that it wasn't awarded posthumously. He came home to Winnipeg with all his arms and legs intact and died in the influenza epidemic of 1919. Mrs. MacLeod's husband also died before his time. The result of her loneliness was a book entitled *Cuthbert Grant of Granttown*, written in collaboration with a budding young professional historian, because by that time Margaret was unable to read her notes, her vision was too weak.
>
> The book has an interesting mission in it, because Margaret had a romantic concept of Grant, and her collaborator appears to have been rather, well, jealous. Unfortunately there were further editions after Margaret MacLeod's death, allowing her collaborator (we used to shoot collaborators) to insert an introduction asserting that the dotty old half-blind lady's vision of Grant was flawed, because Grant was not, in fact, 'heroic' (whatever that means). One reason given is that Grant, on one occasion at least, drank more than his position of responsibility allowed. Another is that Grant was used by the North West Co and the Hudson's Bay Co for their own ends, while 'heroes, even when young, are not used; they pursue their own objects.' I suppose we will have to eliminate that brandy-sodden Churchill from the list of fit subjects for biography, not to mention that eager young Corsican who was so effectively used by Robespierre and was Josephine de Beauharnais's sugar daddy.

William MacMillan, a Métis buffalo hunter in the Edmonton area, died in 1903 claiming to be 103 years old. He is seen here with his wife. William's father was James MacMillan of the North West Company, first cousin of my great-grandfather, Hugh Roy MacMillan. (Ontario Archives photo no S 7198, reproduced with permission)

My own sentiments about the collaborator mirror those of Silver. Let us keep Cuthbert Grant as a hero, warts and all. Cuthbert Grant (1793–1854), known as the Warden of the Plains, was the leader of the Métis in 1816 when they killed Governor Semple of the Hudson's Bay Company and twenty of his men in the battle of Seven Oaks near present-day Winnipeg.

Isaac Cowie, a writer on the subject of the Red River, said of Grant:

> Under Grant, the Métis of the buffalo hunting brigades were organized as a disciplined force, which repelled every hostile Indian attack so successfully as to win renown as the most skillful and bravest warriors of the Prairies. They protected themselves from overwhelming numbers of Sioux, guarding the agricultural settlers of the Red River Colony from molestation by the bloodthirsty Tigers of the Plains and other warlike tribes.

Over 20 years ago, while tracking down the papers of Cuthbert Grant in Manitoba and North Dakota for the Ontario Archives, I also had a personal interest. My Métis McMillan relations around Red River would have known Cuthbert Grant and may have been on many of his well organized buffalo hunts.

I have referred from time to time in this chapter to articles I lost in a housefire. In 1972, a firebug torched our home in Toronto in the middle of the night. When the 15-year-old arsonist was caught a year after setting his 42nd fire, he told the police it was random chance. He did not know us and could as easily have burned down the house across the street. What attracted him to ours, he claimed, was a huge canoe sitting on a trailer in front of the house.

He poured gasoline over our two cars, then tossed a match on them, but didn't touch the canoe as he claimed it was magical. A passing taxi driver saw the flames outside the darkened house and with great presence of mind, kicked in the front door, shouting "Get out! Your house is on fire!"

We had planned to leave that morning to take the fur trade canoe through the Minesing Swamp, part of the North West Company's alternate route during the War of 1812–14, and be the first to re-enact this trip. The crew, four teenage friends of my sons, were asleep upstairs, ready for the big adventure.

When the fire broke out, they all escaped, but our eldest son Malcolm went back into the house looking for his sister, not knowing that she had picked that night to sleep at a friend's place. My wife rushed back to get Malcolm out, just seconds before the station wagon blew up, spreading the flames into the house. We didn't paddle our canoe on the Minesing that day.

We salvaged much of the contents of the house, storing things with relatives and friends, whence odds and ends continued to resurface in the years that followed. Looking for information recently among some of these papers that my sister-in-law returned to me, I came upon five pages of smoke-blackened notes from interviews with my father in 1970. He recalled that in 1907, when he was 22 years old, his father told him that my great-great-grandmother, Mary Grant, was related to a fur trader, Cuthbert Grant, who was out west and was said to have visited her when he came back from Scotland.

I immediately thought of Alfred Silver's novels that portrayed Cuthbert Grant as a heroic figure, with shortcomings. I was also reminded of the value of keeping track of old or new papers, which has been my lifetime habit.

(Information in this chapter has been adapted from material I wrote for Lochaber Emigrants to Glengarry, *published in 1994 by Natural Heritage, Natural History Inc, and from an article I wrote for the 1998 issue of* Glengarry Life, *the annual publication of the Glengarry Historical Society.)*

CHAPTER TWO
TOWBOATS AND CANOES

On a fine spring day in 1965, Ken Macpherson and I were sipping wine at The Mermaid, our favourite seafood bistro on Bay Street in Toronto, contemplating Canada's upcoming 100th birthday bash. Ken enquired, "And what will your centennial project be for 1967?"

My reply was ready. "The Glengarry Historical Society and I plan to start a museum about the North West Company, many of whose partners came from Glengarry. To publicize this project, I'm thinking of organizing a canoe trip from some distant point to arrive at Glengarry for the opening of the museum."

The whole concept was vague at that time and needed much more thought and planning. Most people I talked to, including Ken Macpherson, thought it would never work — far too many problems. But I was determined to make both the museum and the canoe trip a reality. My inexperience was monumental and it was as well I couldn't see the many problems ahead or I might never have embarked on the venture.

The proposed project did start me on 20 years of canoeing in large 26 and 36-foot canoes. Over the years from 1965 to 1985, our colourful crews helped spark a renewed interest in Canada's fur trade history.

First, though, I must relate my earlier seafaring adventures, how I got into them, how I survived them, and how I escaped.

In the fall of 1947, I was standing with my cousin Claude Fraser in the dust of the main street of Carstairs, Alberta. We were about to make a fateful decision on the flip of a coin. Would we head north to the recent oil strike at Leduc, or west to Vancouver on the Pacific Coast? Our jeans weighted down with cash after several months of cow-punching on the Hays ranch, we were ready for a new challenge.

The coin came down for Vancouver. Within a month, I was a greenhorn deckhand on the steamboat *Prosperative* headed up the British Columbia coast for a tow of logs.

Thus began my four-year career as a West Coast towboater. My cousin joined the crew and that became his life's work. I was thinking of getting on a deep-sea vessel as source material for writing exciting sea stories!

Reality struck when I reached Vancouver and went to stay with my father's cousin, Alpine McIntosh, superintendent at Burrard Dry Dock. Tall, lean and taciturn, Alpine had come to Vancouver with his parents from Glengarry in 1904. He assured me I would not get on a deep-sea ship, as I had no experience. He was right. Ten days walking the Vancouver docks proved the union wanted no greenhorns.

Alpine had a solution. Coastal towboat companies were always short of deckhands for the ships that towed log rafts and barges up and down the coast. Within days, Alpine had me a berth as a deckhand on the *Prosperative*, owned by Cliff Towing Co. She was a 100-foot wooden-hulled former sealing schooner, converted during World War II to a steam-powered towboat. I signed on and a few hours later, we had loaded our supplies and were headed out Burrard Inlet and under the Lions Gate Bridge in the dark.

There commenced a series of errors that, although comic, had great potential for tragedy. I had never been in a vessel bigger than my grandfather's canoe. Ballantyne, the dock superintendent for Cliff Towing, desperate to get the *Prosperative* on its way, had told Captain Bert Balkwell that I was experienced. This, I found out later, was based on my having told him that I could paddle the canoe.

The captain, lulled thereby into a false sense of security, put me on the mate's watch and retired with a ferocious hangover to his cabin.

The mate, Bob Evans, a swarthy Siwash Indian, had just come off a month-long bender. His hands shook so much he could hardly hold his mug of coffee. He showed me my bunk below the bow deck, then took me up to the wheelhouse, where he commenced explaining about keeping on course by the compass, and making entries in the ship's log. Assuming that an experienced sailor like myself would have no problem, he then lay down on the wheelhouse settee and went to sleep.

It was panic time for me as I tried to hold to the course he had given me, a near impossible task. The ship would fall many points off course in one direction, I would over-compensate and she would fall off in the other, meanwhile frantically dodging huge inbound and outbound freighters. By sheer luck and some improvised wheel-handling, I made it out of Vancouver Harbour. We stood six-hour watches, so I was to be on till midnight, but I shook Bob awake and confessed my inexperience, which put him in a great rage. "You mean you can't read a compass or

I was first posted as mate on the steam tug "Queen," owned by the Cliff Towing Co. (Author's collection)

We lost this entire tow — over $1,000,000 worth of logs in 1949 dollars! — during a storm in the Gulf of Georgia. (Author's collection)

hold a course? You are useless to me!" he snarled. "You would be fired, except I'm stuck with you until we're back in port in a month!" He took over the wheel, assuring me he would make my life hell for the rest of the trip, which he did.

Worse was to follow when Captain Balkwell came on watch at midnight. He was in a foul mood made worse by the discovery that the dockmaster Ballantyne had stuck him with not one but two greenhorns. It turned out that Dave, the deckhand on *his* watch, was a prairie farm boy who had never been on a ship either.

Verbal attacks by the skipper and the mate kept up for the rest of the voyage, but under their iron tutelage we learned the details of navigation, and the use of steel cables and boom chains in making up tows of log booms.

Each section of logs was about 64 by 72 feet. The huge logs floated free inside a boom secured end to end by 90-pound boom chains, with logs chained across the top every ten feet to hold the floating logs down. It was our job to go to a logging camp's booming ground and chain together 30 sections of logs, made up in booms of six to eight sections. We would then let out our ⅞ tow cable from the winch and proceed on the long tow back to the mills around Vancouver and up the Fraser River at a slow 2 knots.

By the end of the trip, we had learned the basics and won the grudging respect of both the skipper and the mate, who decided to keep us on. As the skipper put it, "You two are getting a free education at our expense."

On the second voyage up the coast to Desolation Sound, our tormentors had been sober for over two months, so it was prank time at the expense of the greenhorns. All these years later I still cringe as I recall the riotous response of sailors up and down the coast to an oft-told anecdote about the Great Oyster Chase. How could we have been so gullible?

It all began when Captain Balkwell casually enquired what we knew about oysters. Neither Dave the prairie boy nor I had ever seen a real oyster. The skipper assured us they were a great delicacy but hard to catch despite having no legs.

Headed for one of the best oyster beds on the coast, the crew flattered us shamelessly, talking of our youth and fleetness of foot. We were to go ashore on the late low tide, equipped with flashlights and whistles, and run along the beach shouting, waving our lights and blowing our whistles. This was supposed to frighten the oysters into the shallow water where the rest of the crew would be waiting to catch them in nets. Late at night we neared the oyster beds and rowed ashore with our gear in one of the tug's lifeboats.

The chase was on, and we were hyped up to do our part. The skipper assured us that our reward would be the best of the catch, deep-fried by our Chinese cook. We were told not to worry if we saw no oysters, as they blended in with the rocks. Just keep shouting and waving those lights, he said. This we did, while the rest of the crew stayed out of sight in the shallow water, encouraging us to keep up the good work, telling us they were filling bags of oysters. After an hour of this, our voices were about gone and the skipper called the chase off.

Back on the tug, we were shown the results of our efforts: piles of oysters in their shells. Dave and I were walking a mile high. We had a big feed of oysters at midnight with plenty left over for days to come. It was some days later that the truth sank in. Skilled pranksters had sucked us in, and the story of our Great Oyster Chase was spreading up and down the coast by radio telephone.

During all this learning process, I continued my writing course by correspondence. I became the butt of many a joke for having gone to sea armed with a typewriter, but it stood me in good stead when I got caught up in the strike. I had passed the exams for my coastal mate's license and had an inflated opinion of my abilities as a seaman, but it was my writing that made me most proud when I sold a story based on an exciting incident aboard the tug.

The *Prosperative*, towing an oil barge, was hove to alongside a deep-sea freighter anchored and on strike in Vancouver harbour. As I stood on the deck of the barge, ready to heave a line up to the ship, I noticed a small boat approaching at high speed. Having been warned about the low esteem in which union goons held strikebreakers, I dashed to the bridge and turned on the searchlight just in time to see the crew lash onto our barge bearing baseball bats. With no time to alert the skipper, I seized the high-pressure firehose, called out to the deckhand to turn on the pressure, and scythed a jet of water across the legs of the bat-wielding thugs. They were washed into Vancouver harbour and retreated soggily to shore. The skipper issued a generous dram of rum to celebrate our presence of mind.

Some time later, I was working on a 100-ton tug, the *MV French*. One rainy day, we were approaching the Skookumchuck, a fierce set of rapids up the coast from Vancouver. Log tows could only come through this narrow passage when the tide was changing, which meant slack or quiet water. Our skipper was heading into the dreaded rapids on a short towline. He misjudged slack water by mere minutes, but it was enough for us to suddenly find ourselves in a swirling mass of whirlpools. The tug spun around end for end like a top. The towline came under the keel and we were in imminent danger of capsizing.

I grabbed an axe and chopped the tow cable where it ran taut over the rail, which was already under water. The cable parted with a twang and the tug slowly righted itself. Though the skipper praised my quick action, he also pointed out it was a foolhardy act. I could easily have been cut in half by the backlash of the severed cable.

We came shooting out of the rapids, and with great difficulty eventually retrieved our tow, which had headed for the open sea.

What might seem to be a routine job was never without excitement, danger, and a new adventure on every sortie. Once the skipper got his orders, we would head north up the coast to whatever remote logging camp had a tow of 20 to 30 sections of logs to haul back to a sawmill. There were hundreds of mills and hundreds of camps. This was the exciting part, steaming up long inlets with spectacular scenery all around us. Running without a tow, we could make a brisk 10 knots.

Weather was the all-important factor. The flat booms would break up in rough water. The captain kept close to the radio telephone for weather reports. A prudent skipper always kept in mind the location of the nearest sheltered bay he could duck into if the weather turned bad. His dilemma was that too much caution (and not enough speed) meant the towing company would lose money, while excessive risk could result in lost logs and insurance claims.

Making up a tow could take upwards of a day, particularly in a booming ground with hundreds of numbered booms tied to the shoreline of a sheltered bay. The captain had a list of numbered booms we had to find. This necessitated steaming back and forth to locate our booms. We walked out on the logs wearing spiked boots, carrying a four-foot peavey with an iron hook at one end for burling logs and a spike at the other.

Both mates and deckhands worked on the booms, doing a balancing act on the huge logs, bobbing up and down with every passing swell. Falling in between these grinding timbers could be fatal. Another potentially career-ending move was to carry a 90-pound boom chain around your neck instead of over your shoulder. Soon after I became a mate in 1949, I hired a young deckhand who had that bad habit. He ceased the practice the day he sank like a rock and we managed to rescue him only moments before he would have drowned.

When we spotted one of our booms, we would undo its boom chains. The skipper would force the tug through the narrow opening between the booms, drop a line on the boom and back out, hauling it into open water. We would repeat the process until we had all the booms we came for out in the open water, then commenced the job of chaining those 20 to 30 booms into a huge square with a towing bridle at the front end. Hot and sweaty from hours of heavy labour, we were ready for a rest as the tug moved slowly out of the bay for the open sea.

To keep the tow well away from the propeller wash, we would let out several hundred feet of 1 inch steel towing cable. We never made more than 40 to 50 miles every 24 hours, so it was a long haul back to Vancouver. Moving at this pace, there would be no way to reach a sheltered bay faster than two hours, so keeping in touch with weather forecasts was a priority.

One stormy night, we pulled into the lee side of Savary Island, some 200 miles north of Vancouver Island. We anchored the tug, then winched in the log tow to our stern. We stood 6-hour watches. Shortly after I came on at midnight, the easterly gale suddenly swung around to the west. We beat a hasty retreat to the east side of the island, but the wind kept changing all night and we had to up anchor with each wind change. At daylight, we discovered we had lost over half our tow.

A few months after the Savary Island mishap, we were one of five towboats assigned to take a gigantic tow of over one hundred booms across the Gulf of Georgia and up the Fraser River. Fitting a tow of this size with many boom chains and towing bridles took several days. Then we waited for a favourable weather forecast to start the 30-mile tow across open water. Perfect weather, with a report of good weather to follow, came two days later, so we were away, the five boats straining on taut towlines.

All went well past the point of no return, when suddenly we found ourselves heading into choppy seas and an increasing easterly wind. At the mercy of the waves, our situation worsened. We had to keep going, though we were losing logs at an alarming rate. The beachcombers would be out in force with their landing craft, making a fortune picking up stray logs. Several hours later, we were at the mouth of the Fraser River with little left of our tow but the boom sticks, having lost over a million dollars worth of logs. So much for weather reports!

In the fall of 1949, I passed my navigation tests and became mate of the *MV French*. She was my first experience with an oil-fired diesel, noisier and dirtier than a steamboat.

My new skipper was a deep-sea man. His own ship was strikebound, so he signed on with us as a relief officer. He had difficulty with our bell-whistle system of controlling engine speed, being accustomed to the more modern telegraph system. He had to adjust to the reality that this was a small boat, in contrast to his former command.

We spent hours practicing in open water: half ahead, full ahead, full astern. The Fairbanks-Morse diesels were started up by air pressure. Each time he rang for astern from ahead, the engineers stopped the engine by giving the up cylinders a shot of air to force the boat into reverse. They were appalled at his waste of air pressure. When we ran low, we had to circle till the air pressure in the tanks built back up. If we ran out of pressure, the engineer on duty would light the punks (black-powder cartridges fitted to the up cylinders) and minor explosions would drive the up cylinders down to restart the engine. The engineers cursed us if they were to use the punks even once, never mind several times.

I couldn't teach the captain fast enough, and the inevitable happened. One sunny afternoon on Bowen Sound, headed for the Bowen Island boom yard, 15 miles from Vancouver, we ran out of air pressure *and* punks. The profanity from the engine room was awesome!

An embarrassed skipper had to radio Vancouver head office and order our seaplane to bring out a large box of punks. Head office was not amused and partly blamed me for not teaching the captain the new routines fast enough.

Hours later, we were under way, headed for the boom master's dock to pick up our orders. Our fearless captain stayed at full speed ahead; even as we neared the dock, he was not slowing down. When I cautioned him, he replied, "Relax, Mac! It's only a little towboat." The boom master, sitting on the dock in his deck chair sipping his gin and tonic, was getting visibly nervous at our fast approach.

The skipper suddenly realized he had misjudged and said, "Here, Mac. You take her." I rang for full speed astern and swung the wheel hard to starboard, but it was too late. We hit the dock almost head-on, cutting through at least 10 feet of it, and sending the boom master into the water. The skipper, to his credit, took full blame for his misjudgment. The boom master was in a foul mood, but he did help us get our tow back together. The crestfallen skipper had made his one and only towboat trip. He was grateful to get back to his deep-sea berth.

For the next three years, I made many trips up and down the coast towing log booms. I kept up my writing and continued to gather family history from relatives in Vancouver. During long stretches ashore, I took other temporary jobs, including advance agent for a circus and then for The Great Orlando, an Australian hypnotist, all the while dreaming about moving back to Glengarry to live on the family farm.

It was of course in Vancouver that I met and married Muriel. Our migration back east to the farm in 1952 began the series of career and house moves that resulted in our arrival in Toronto and my work for the Ontario Archives. It would be some years before I returned to sailing and watercraft of a different kind, namely canoes.

By 1965, Centennial fever was in the air. Plans for every conceivable type of project were being discussed and argued about all across Canada. There were big and small projects, practical and impractical projects. Funding was a three-way split among the federal government, provincial governments and municipalities.

Glengarry was gearing up through the recently created historical society to launch a project. There were many proposals, often sports-oriented. Ian McMartin and I, both past presidents of the Glengarry Historical Society, had our own proposal. Ian was a World War II RCAF veteran of Loyalist descent, a teacher and an active local historian with some good ideas.

We wanted to establish a North West Company and Loyalist Museum in Williamstown, the oldest village in Glengarry County, 15 miles east of Cornwall. Williamstown had several historic structures dating back to 1784 and the arrival of the first Loyalists. Our rationale for this project was simple. Many of the clerks and partners in the North West Company came from Glengarry and were sons of Loyalists. What better place to have such a museum?

Ian and I researched the idea and found that no other community in Canada had made this exciting suggestion for a centennial project, so we were free to start.

Even Archie McDonell, the Reeve of Charlottenburg Township, where Williamstown is located, was a Nor'Wester descendent. The vision quickly caught the imagination of the public and we had the citizen support we needed. Other ideas were brought forward, but after a referendum our idea won out. We were empowered to spend up to $25,000 to buy a suitable building for the proposed museum.

We were really hoping for a location in Williamstown. The town was named after a great friend of the Iroquois, Sir William Johnson, who died in 1773. Sir Alexander MacKenzie, another famous Nor'Wester, donated the bell for the 1812 church in the village. The names of fur traders and other Loyalist settlers are commemorated in street names throughout Williamstown.

Our first choice was the Sir John Johnson Manor House (now a community library), which was built in 1784 for the Loyalist leader (and son of Sir William), but never lived in by him. It was owned at this time by an order of nuns, who turned down our offer to purchase.

A similar offer was made to the owners of a Williamstown house built in 1784 for Rev John Bethune, the first Presbyterian minister in Upper Canada. On his death in 1815, it was bought and lived in for over 20 years by David Thompson, the famous surveyor and trader of the North West Co. This offer also was turned down.

Finally, we made a deal in 1966 to take over the Georgian-style 1860 grammar school, which the local school board had recently closed. The board deeded it to us for a dollar. Using the available three-way financing, we were fortunate to engage the services of Peter J Stokes, a restoration architect from Niagara-on-the-Lake, Ontario.

In 1965 I was introduced to 26 foot and 36 foot fur-trade canoes by Canada's canoe authority, Bill Mason, who had been taken on as an advisor to the Centennial Commission. His mandate was to help organize a cross-Canada canoe race with 26 foot North canoes. A crew from each province would race from Rocky Mountain House, Alberta to Montreal, Quebec. This plan, combined with my increased interest in the fur trade, helped formulate my idea of our own canoe trip, a journey, not a race, to publicize the opening of our unique museum in September 1967.

As a novice to this aspect of our involvement in North West Company and fur trade history, I had much to learn. Under Bill Mason's expert tutelage, my knowledge of fur trade canoes increased dramatically. I was hooked, and determined that the Glengarry Historical Society should own a 26 foot Chestnut replica of a North canoe for its own use. Ian McMartin and I also wanted to have a real birchbark canoe to go on the proposed trip and later be an exhibit in the museum. For these ambitious plans we had to raise several thousand dollars.

All the available government funding went to remodelling the grammar school into a museum. We each contributed money and many hours of time. Ian was able to raise $2000 to acquire the canoes, the birchbark one to be built by César Newashish, a Cree canoe-builder in northern Quebec.

By the summer of 1966, we had our Chestnut canoe and were on the water getting badly needed practice in handling a big canoe. By this time, my volunteer crew was fairly confident. Our first mishap occurred that summer, when we took a CBC interviewer for a turn around Toronto Harbour.

We warned the CBC man with all his taping equipment to keep still. He didn't get the message. Standing up in the canoe, he managed to upset us into the débris-strewn water. A CBC television crew in a nearby boat recorded this embarrassing mishap for posterity. It was not our finest canoeing hour.

Weeks later, we were out with the brand new Chestnut North canoe on the Crow River east of Peterborough, Ontario. This was to be our first test of running rapids. The crew was presented with a wild scene, white water cresting at six to eight feet. Following the advice of Eric Morse, the expert on fur trade canoe routes, we first walked the shoreline of these awesome rapids. The idea was to pick a logical course through the towering white caps. With much trepidation, we started our run into the raging white water. To our amazement, we made it through without capsizing, but the boat was almost awash to the gunwales with water. Our crew, eager for more, ran these same rapids again successfully several times and continued to train in 1966, racing, running rapids and portaging, readying us for the big trip the following year.

My knowledge of the fur trade grew as I continued to read and find out more about the activities of James McMillan, the only McMillan in the North West Company, therefore easy to trace among the many Grants, McDonnells, Camerons, and McGillivrays.

By the summer of 1967, I had recruited several other descendents of North West Company Partners to help paddle two canoes from Grand Portage, Minnesota, the old mid-continent headquarters of the North West Company, to Williamstown.

As it became increasingly obvious to us that Glengarry had been a prime ground for North West Company recruits among their own Highland kinsmen, we were persuaded that we had the right museum in the right place!

Publicity about the museum, including the historical columns I wrote for the *Glengarry News*, helped promote our canoe voyage, which was set to commence in August 1967. We planned to arrive in time for the official opening of our museum by the Hon J Keiller McKay, Lieutenant-Governor of Ontario.

The Chicago blacksmith and canoe-builder Ralph Frese was to meet us at Michilimackinac with his 36 foot silk-screened fiberglas Montreal canoe. This legendary, super-skilled craftsman called his canoe design "Chicagoland birch bark." He also was hooked on fur trade history, so we had a great common interest. Ralph often said that one of his aims in life was to show the people of Illinois that their State had a proud history even before Abraham Lincoln, as the French and British were there long before the Americans.

On this Canadian Centennial venture, the American crew in the 36 foot Montreal canoe was experienced and dressed in authentic voyageur costumes. Recruited because they had a connection to someone in the original North West Company, our own crews of six to a canoe were mostly inexperienced. One was Richard Hubert, about 60, of Greenwich, Connecticut, a descendent of Hugh McGillis from Glengarry, who had been a North West Company Partner. Richard had been a CPR agent in Tokyo at the start of World War II, and helped introduce ice hockey to the Japanese. Another of our crew was Donald MacDonell, 20, a direct descendent of John "le Prêtre" McDonell, a North West Company Partner and brother to Miles McDonell, one of Lord Selkirk's agents. Grant Campbell, great-great-grandson of John Duncan Campbell, a North West Company Partner, was also one of our crew.

When short-handed, we resorted to taking on hitchhikers who would agree to paddle the distance. The best recruit snared enroute was Charles Laberge, superintendent of Champlain Park on the Mattawa River. With years of paddling experience, this Métis descendent of a voyageur had a great interest in the fur trade. One other recruit who stayed with us was a well muscled young Maritimer with no paddling experience, but lots of enthusiasm and a willingness to try anything.

My brother Roy was also a useful addition to the crew. He had little paddling experience, but plenty of interest in our project. He was a career External Affairs officer, and diplomacy was his strong suit. We needed diplomatic skills for some of the personality clashes that arose among men working close to each other in a canoe over extended periods.

As I reflect many years later on that very first major canoe voyage that I planned as a rank amateur, I realize how fortunate I was that so little went wrong.

Surrounding myself with some experienced canoeists helped. Allan Bell was the canoe captain. He was a chiropractor, and we did use his expertise. John Gadsby was the epitome of a voyageur, short, stocky, with the legendary appearance and attributes. I recruited him from the Ontario Archives to be the bow man in the Chestnut North canoe.

Our first day on Lake Superior provided a wild ride to test our collective skill. Deep waves and a following sea drove us up the coast toward Fort William, our first stop, at the mouth of the Kamanistiqua River.

With our big square sails set, we went upriver to be met by the Fort William pipe band, a dramatic moment. Our ragamuffin voyageur crews could have stepped from the pages of a Grace Lee Nute voyageur tale. Since we had limited time and finances, we had to travel some of the route by land to reach Williamstown by September 2.

We were to meet Ralph Frese at Michilimackinac, at the juncture of Lakes Superior, Huron and Michigan. This had been the mid-continent headquarters of John Jacob Astor's American Fur Company, major competitors of the North West Company and later of the Hudson's Bay Company. Ralph Frese, looking very much the 19th-century fur trader, had 12 men in his crew including a dentist, a self-styled anarchist, and professional photographer Robert Lightfoot. The Americans gave us a fine welcome at Michilamackinac and blended very well with my crews, who were looking scruffier every day.

Our route led upstream on the French River through magnificent Precambrian Shield country. Under sail, we did Lake Nipissing in a day. The Mattawa River was a real challenge, with many rapids to shoot under the supervision of our newfound expert, Charles Laberge.

By the time we reached Arnprior on the mighty Ottawa, we caught up with some of the friendly, hard working, cross-Canada canoe racers who had been on the go for two months. In Ottawa a short time later, we were invited to a reception on Parliament Hill arranged by Glengarry MP, Viateur Éthier. Our American companions were most impressed, assuring us this could never happen in the US Capitol.

Reaching Montreal and paddling through the narrow canals at Expo 67 gave us plenty of public exposure. We carried our own piper, who kept the crowds entertained. The last leg of our voyage was up the Raisin River from Lancaster to Williamstown. The banks were lined with people cheering us on and listening to the pipes. A huge roast of buffalo was part of the reception at the Nor'Wester and Loyalist Museum, which was now open to the public.

Friends, neighbours, visitors and families were on hand to see our spectacular landing. It was a grand opening, with Lieutenant-Governor the Honourable John Keiller MacKay officiating. Just as thrilling for me was to see my wife Muriel with our four children, Malcolm, Ian, Neale and Jocelyne all on hand to see us land. Thanks to the help of so many people, my dream of a fur trade museum had become a reality.

A wildly elated crew carried the bark canoe up the steep stairs to the second floor of our museum. The main floor is devoted to the Loyalists, many of whose sons were also prominent Nor'Westers, and the bark canoe is still the centrepiece of exhibits upstairs.

Complementing the canoe in the second-floor exhibit were many priceless relics. I was getting to know many Nor'Wester descendents and their belongings, aside from the papers I could find for the Archives. Many had relics that I encouraged them to donate to the museum.

A prime relic was Simon Fraser's snuff mull, which I acquired in Calgary from Mrs Eileen Street, a McDonell lady whose ancestor John Roy came from Glengarry. Ordered by Sir John Johnson to conduct a group of women and children to Upper Canada in 1783, John Roy

McDonell took Simon Fraser's mother and her young family through the wilderness from the Mohawk Valley into the future Glengarry. Years later, Fraser, discoverer of the Fraser River, gave the snuff mull to the McDonell family in memory of John Roy's service to the Fraser family. It was a ram's horn with the great explorer's initials engraved on its sterling silver lid.

In 1968 and '69, I organized voyageur canoe trips to retrace the route to James Bay, starting at Lake Nipissing near North Bay, Ontario. While on Lake Nipissing, we had a huge 40 foot bark Montreal canoe that Charles Laberge and Andy Green had built. We were using it along with the 26 foot North canoe for film footage being shot by Christopher Chapman, the cinematographer who had won an Oscar in 1967 for *A Place to Stand*. Commissioned to do a film for the 300th anniversary of the Hudson's Bay Company in 1970, Chapman contracted me to provide men, costumes and canoes. During that film, we all had some great canoeing and a lot of fun.

On the first night camping out at Nipissing, my canoe captain, Allan "Basher" Bell, cooking up the T-bone steaks, complained that his cooking oil was giving off bubbles. I discovered to my horror that he had mistaken dish detergent for olive oil. The fish got a good feed of steak that night and we settled for canned corned beef.

Our crew of seven voyageurs, with the famous cameraman and canoeist Bill Mason, then started down the Missinabi River, a rough leg with very shallow water in the rapids. We were overloaded and broke 22 of the 60 ribs in the canoe before we hit the Moose River crossing, where we had to take the canoe out of the water and abort the trip.

After all these canoeing initiatives, I was lucky enough to have a corps of fur trade canoe enthusiasts who could make themselves available on short notice as voyageurs in costume with the big canoes for a movie shoot.

The Nor'Wester group also entered races in the big canoes. We ran a race in 1969 between Lancaster and Williamstown on the Raisin River. It was a hot humid day and we were racing under a blazing sun. We had stripped to our shorts on the last portage, when I managed to step into a wasp's nest concealed in the long grass. Pursued by enraged wasps, I never moved so fast! That night, a local doctor pulled a dozen stings from my throbbing back.

Our next big trip was in 1970 from Grand Portage, Minnesota, to Winnipeg over the old voyageur canoe route that ran along the international border. The first portage tested our stamina. It was eight miles long, at a 45-degree slope over rough terrain. We slept well that night. It had taken months of planning to organize that brigade of five 26 foot North canoes. Crewing were Mark Stiles from Frontier College, Dave Chester, a journalist from the *Toronto Telegram*, John Gadsby of the Ontario Archives, Muriel's nephew Michael Diver and cousin Brian Liboiron, a skilled artist, and our two elder sons, Malcolm, 16, and Ian, 14.

Glen Fallis and Greg Cowan of the Voyageur Canoe Co from Millbrook, Ontario, provided another canoe and crew. They were also our cameramen for the half-hour documentary they filmed, titled *Again the Voyageur*.

Kirk Wipper, from Camp Kandalore and Canoe Museum, provided two North canoes and crews. The fifth canoe to make up the brigade was Maurice Parkin's, with his crew from Chicago.

We packed enough food for a month in waterproof containers, all packs colour-coded to save confusion, particularly at portages. It was a difficult trip over 800 miles through the beautiful canoeing country of Quetico Park. There were many portages and as many opportunities to take the wrong route. Everyone on these outings had to admire those first French traders and canoe men who made their way west with no maps and very little idea where they were headed.

Most of our crews were tough and hardened, ranging in age from Greg Badger and our son Ian at 14, to Leo Krusak, 70. There were always a few voyageurs who were not prepared for such a tough grind despite my pre-trip newsletters warning everyone to get into shape both mentally and physically. Some were great, a few were slackers, and each had his own idiosyncrasies.

The camera crew shot several thousand feet of film and were particularly attentive to Wobay Kitpou, a colourful Indian with all the trappings and regalia of a real shaman. He had been adopted in Sherbooke, Quebec, by Col Munster, who named him James Munster, so he had two personæ. The trip was enlivened by his flamboyant presence. He insisted on bringing along his teepee, but its poles never made it past the first portage up from Grand Portage, being too much of a drag.

We were a weary, unkempt crew of voyageurs by the time we reached Lower Fort Garry at Selkirk on the Red River, some 20 miles north of Winnipeg. This was not only the 300th anniversary of the Hudson's Bay Company, but also the 100th anniversary of the Province of Manitoba. The five canoes made a dramatic water display, with races across the Red River and a tug-of-war between two canoes tied end to end.

Spectators at these events were getting the message that canoeing was great fun and great exercise, in addition to the considerable excite-

A pair of modern-day voyageurs near the shore of the French River for the filming of a BBC documentary, "The British Empire Around the World." (Author's collection)

ment of paddling the big canoes over historic routes. I was also imparting the message to anyone who cared to listen that it was birchbark fur trade canoes that were Canada's first means of inland transport. The crews of French-Canadian voyageurs with their mostly French or Scots leaders were the first to explore Western Canada and much of what is now the United States.

I pushed this point constantly in private conversation and with a slide lecture on *Fur Trade Canoe Routes in Canada*. I tried to build on what Eric Morse had done so well in retracing many of these old routes and writing or talking about his experiences.

Hundreds of other canoe and fur trade history buffs across Canada were staging races and historical pageants using the big canoes. This activity continues today, though with little publicity.

In the late 1970s, the National Capital Commission was the main sponsor of the Canada Canoe Festival, a week-long celebration centred on the voyageurs and the exploration of western Canada by the fur traders and the voyageurs. There were races, demonstrations and heritage events, with the finale on July 1st, Canada Day. Thousands of visitors thronged to Victoria Island in downtown Ottawa to see these exciting activities firsthand. The event was developing into a unifying force for the country.

The BBC in London asked me to organize three canoes to create scenes of canoe exploration for their series on the British Empire around the world. We ran rapids, portaged, and even arranged to have the top BBC producer chased up a tree by an irate black bear. That adventure gave him plenty of cocktail chatter back in London.

For the American bicentennial in 1976, I gathered several canoes and crews to transport the Sieur de Cadillac and his French troops to Fort Detroit. Our men in colourful voyageur gear and our piper impressed the American spectators, while General Motors got some great publicity.

Through these contacts with other history-conscious people, I was always alert for tips about papers for the Ontario Archives, which thus benefited from some of our publicity stunts. Once people heard about my unusual line of work, the tips would flow. I am constantly grateful that so many perceptive people chose to point me to many caches of priceless papers. Often it was idle chitchat that produced the best leads. My antennæ were always up.

In the late 1970s, we started Simcoe Brigade trips to publicize John Graves Simcoe, the first Lieutenant-Governor of Upper Canada, now Ontario. The man who played Simcoe with great *élan* and verve was Charles Humber, a history teacher at Oakdale Collegiate in Toronto. A heavy-set man with an infectious grin and a wicked sense of humour, he knew Simcoe's background well and fit the role perfectly.

I met Charles Humber when the Simcoe Foundation hired our canoe and crew to transport him and his party on a voyage that Simcoe had taken in 1793 from the Holland River near Lake Simcoe through to Georgian Bay. It was an exploratory trip, and we followed Simcoe's route in detail, landing Humber and his party of three at prearranged points to be met by crowds of people anxious to know more about Simcoe's career.

We met descendents of the Selkirk settlers who had been lured east to the area around Lake Simcoe from Red River (now Winnipeg) by the wily Duncan Cameron of the North West Company. This was in the early part of the 19th century, when the North West Company was trying to rid the west of the Kildonan settlers brought via Hudson Bay by the Scottish philanthropist Lord Selkirk. In our crew were descendents of some of the Nor'Westers who had forced these settlers out of Red River many years before.

Charles Humber, aka Simcoe, was well liked by our crew in part because he taught them some history. When they landed him in his resplendent uniform, they always referred to him as "Your Excellency."

Several voyages later, our crew presented him a special paddle with a twisted haft that made it almost useless. The paddle had been signed by all the crew and inscribed "to His Royal Impotence." Charles still has this symbol of our affection hanging on his wall.

One of our historical re-enactments took us on an all-day trek from Kingston, Ontario, across the lower end of Lake Ontario to Oswego, New York, on the American side. Oswego was a British port in the Revolutionary War. From here we went down the American shore to Sackett's Harbour, an important naval base during the War of 1812–14. The American crowds were impressed by our precision paddling, executed to the shrill drone of the piper. On this voyage we went from Brockville to Fort Wellington, another British fort near Prescott, Ontario, now restored for the tourist trade. Our voyageurs fought a mock battle with two British schooners. The Governor General and party were treated to a rare spectacle. Gavin Watt and his King's Royal Regiment of Re-enactors performed this intricate drill with our very informal voyageurs. Some of our crew were women attired as male voyageurs. They did an excellent job, and were a great asset to the expeditions. Our crews were a mix of all ages, and they all learned much more about Canadian history through reliving it.

On another voyage, we crossed Lake Ontario from Toronto to Fort George, at the mouth of the Niagara River. Here Charles Humber, aka Simcoe, put on a stellar show which we took across the river to Fort Niagara, originally a French, later a British, and eventually an American fort. We like to think we gave our American cousins a more balanced view of history.

The last major voyage was from Ottawa to Montreal in 1985 to attend the Fifth International Fur Trade Conference. I had attended all these affairs for academics and fur trade history buffs since 1965 at St Paul, Minnesota, Winnipeg, Manitoba, Grand Portage, Minnesota, and Fort William, Ontario.

Victoria Stewart of the Macdonald Stewart Foundation organized the 1985 conference at Lachine, near Montreal, where Canada's fur trade started. For this occasion, I assembled my last Nor'Wester canoe brigade to show some living history.

My longtime paddling partners, Phillip Shackleton and Ken Roberts, whose classic book, *The Canoe*, had recently been published, were valuable supporters. This 1985 crew of voyageurs included a variety of occupational backgrounds: a sheep farmer with the appropriate name of Woody Lambe, who was also a teacher, wildlife biologist and artisan Mike Buss, a blacksmith, an airline pilot, a filmmaker, and an actor.

We also had one canoe-load of whom only two, the bow man and the stern man, were sighted. Their racing rivals were a crew of Mohawk Indians from Kahnawake, and my son Malcolm's crew of voyageurs from Acton (Ontario). I first lent the local high school our 26 foot North canoe, but when the teachers gained more insight into the history of the voyageurs, the school bought its own canoes, with students raising much of the money.

On the 1985 journey to attend the Fifth International Fur Trade Conference, our flotilla set off on a Sunday afternoon from Victoria Island in the Ottawa River behind Parliament Hill and enjoyed a leisurely three-day paddle to Montreal. As usual, we had an assortment of Nor'Wester descendents, several with a connection to Glengarry County and the Nor'Wester and Loyalist Museum, which we were helping to publicize. With us were two new enthusiasts, former federal Cabinet Minister the Hon Alastair Gillespie, a descendent of North West Company Partner George Gillespie, and Juan Cameron from Washington DC, a descendent of North West Company Partner Duncan Cameron. These new paddlers had been valued sources of important archival material, and were most anxious to join a modern-day Nor'Wester canoe brigade. This was their only chance and they performed admirably.

Our second major stop en route to Montreal was at L'Orignal, where the 1804 Georgian-style home of North West Company Partner Alexander Grant stood. Named Duldreggan Hall after Grant's birthplace in Scotland, it was a magnificent old mansion, owned at the time by Dr Drummond Smith and his wife Betty. Duldreggan Hall had been a traditional stop for Nor'Wester canoe brigades from 1804 to 1821, and the Drummonds put on a great party for our voyageurs, as they had in 1967, on our first Nor'Wester canoe brigade trip.

When the brigade reached Lachine, we encamped at the old Nor'Wester warehouse now owned by Parks Canada. Here the blind canoeists, Acton voyageurs, Mohawks and others in our party, put on three days of demonstrations for the benefit of busloads of schoolchildren and visiting tourists as a highlight of the Fur Trade Conference.

One hilarious happening on this voyage was the night of the big banquet at the Queen Elizabeth Hotel. Juan Cameron decided to host a cocktail party at the nearby Ritz-Carleton Hotel. Our small group included Woody Lambe, Mike Buss, Ken Roberts and Phillip Shackleton, all in voyageur gear, myself and Wilfred Johnson in kilts, Wilfred's wife Joan and my wife Muriel both dressed in elegant gowns, and our son Ian in casual attire. For some unfathomable reason, we were mistaken for a wedding party. The waiter seated us all and instantly brought us an assortment of snack food and a magnum of champagne. Our hungry crew quickly demolished this unexplained windfall. However, when the waiters realized we were not part of the wedding party, they took a second look and decided that Voyageur dress gear did not conform to the Ritz dress code. They brought jackets for the men to wear over their outfits. Our host was incensed and explained that we were on our way to a fancy-dress banquet at the near-by Queen Elizabeth Hotel. To no avail, we left since it was obvious that service was being denied. Other patrons complained to the management saying that they were being ridiculously officious.

Many times since 1985, I have been asked when I will organize another of these spectacular canoe brigade trips. My stock reply is 'Never.' I want to go on a fur trade canoe voyage when I just have to take my paddle and gear, with someone else organizing. It has yet to happen.

I was never a great canoeist. Many were better, but I was able to draw together a wide range of canoe history buffs. It was a great 20 years and I am game for another trip, but not as the instigator.

CHAPTER THREE
THE REMARKABLE GRAVELLES

Considering my natural affinity for all things Scottish, it was no coincidence that one of my first major cases as roving representative of the Ontario Archives should be centred upon Renfrew, that pleasant Ottawa Valley community near the confluence of the Ottawa and Bonnechère Rivers. The town and the county were named after a town and shire in Scotland, one of the ancestral seats of the Royal Stuarts. The family of interest, however, were French-Canadians, a group often found in close proximity to the Scots.

My curiosity had been tickled by tales I'd heard of the remarkable Gravelle family, residents of Renfrew for well over a century. If only a fraction of the stories told about them were true, perhaps I could get a handle on some Gravelle pictures, manuscripts or artifacts that might be displayed for public enlightenment and benefit. One pertinent item already in my possession was a pamphlet called The *Story of Renfrew*, in which the *Renfrew Advance* listed profiles of area pioneers. One of these was Father Joseph Gravelle's admiring portrait of his dad, Arthur, born in Renfrew in 1857. The opening lines, penned in 1965, were startling:

> As long as my father, Arthur Gravelle, continued to live, he was in danger of death at the hands of those ruthless persons who put the unjust acquiring of wealth as foremost in life's ambitions. At any moment, he could have been kidnapped or forced at the point of a gun to join a band of robbers who had planned to rob a bank.

When I got that far, I wasn't sure whether it was Father Gravelle's dad who was being discussed, or the plot for an Italian opera. As I read further, I became even more intrigued, for the next words were "and all because he had fallen on the great secret of secrets...."

What was he talking about? Of course! Joseph Gravelle was a priest! The great secret of secrets he was writing about was no doubt some mystical religious experience. But in the next line, I learned the truly astonishing nature of Arthur Gravelle's secret of secrets: "knowing how to open the door of a safe without having to know the combination." Well, that was more like it! If safe-cracking had been Gravelle senior's sole talent, he would have rated merely a notation in my casebook, but it was only one of many. Educated at the University of Ottawa, the senior Gravelle had started his own newspaper, *The Renfrew Union*, when he was only 19. A mathematician and chess whiz, he played international chess masters by mail. A fine magician, he entertained friends with his sleight of hand. Well before Alexander Graham Bell, Gravelle had a communications system connecting people in a number of Renfrew buildings.

Arthur Gravelle's abiding passion, however, was genealogy. Early in life, he began compiling information on thousands of families on both sides of the Ottawa River, a gigantic task. Eventually becoming publisher of Renfrew's then largest newspaper, *The Mercury*, Arthur Gravelle was the town's mayor in 1909 and 1910, and served on many different boards. How he discovered the power to cause intricate safety systems to fly open at his touch was never revealed to his children, Joseph, Roy, Arthur Jr, Millie or Claire, nor to anyone else, as far as I know. Quite early on, however, Arthur Gravelle became famous for this unique skill, not only in the Ottawa Valley and Ontario, but all over Canada, the USA and even in Europe. He was said never to have used his talent for personal gain. Only rarely did his son Joseph have the chance to see him in action:

> One evening I fortunately accompanied my father to the post office to get the mail. As we passed in front of Alex Fraser's clothing store, we saw this merchant standing in his doorway, appearing rather worried. He told my father that his safe would not open, and he was sure he hadn't forgotten the combination. He asked my father if he'd try to open it, as there were papers he needed inside. My father sent me to the post office and went into the store with Fraser.
>
> I hurried to be there to watch him at work. But I didn't hurry enough. Mr. Fraser had gone to get a lamp, as it was too dark to see clearly in his office, and he was just returning when I arrived on the run. What was our disappointment when we found the safe had already been opened and my father was ready to leave!
>
> He had done it all in the dark, the way most good robbers like to work.

No lock seemed too tough for him. Once he put on a demonstration of his skill with sensitive timelocks at the Merchant's Bank in

Ottawa. He repeated the performance a short time later at the Taylor Safe Company, with an American lock claimed to be of such radical new design that it was guaranteed to defy unauthorized entry. Onlookers familiar with his style were surprised this one took Arthur almost ten minutes to crack. They had been ready to bet that with such a stuffy, skeptical audience he might have tried his grandstand caper, using his special shortcut method, which usually caused safe doors to spring open dramatically in less than three minutes.

> I would say it was not a gift, exactly, but the result of long years of study. His mathematical sense was undoubtedly one factor, but he had a mind that could follow the hidden workings of the wheels, the intricate knowledge of safes themselves.

One of Arthur Gravelle's most publicized performances was in the 1890s, when he appeared as a witness for a Napanee, Ontario, bank teller, accused of stealing large sums of money from his own bank's vault. It was an open-and-shut case in the crown attorney's opinion, hardly worth the bother and expense of a trial.

"He's the only member of the staff who knows the combination of the vault, so who else could possibly be doing the stealing?" asked the crown attorney, gazing smugly around, daring anyone to contradict him.

When called to the stand, Arthur stated, "I don't know the combination. But I can open the safe." He proceeded to do so, with the whole courtroom looking on. The case was dismissed.

Father Joseph Gravelle's theory that safe-cracking skills were learned rather than inherited was contradicted by the experience of his brother Roy. During most of the First World War, Roy was on active service with the Canadian forces in France. It was common knowledge among his comrades and the high command that he had a way with locks, even though Roy had never yet gone beyond parlour tricks. Several times he had earned the gratitude of his comrades by opening doors to French wine cellars. On one occasion, he had used his talent to defuse a German landmine that was menacing the whole area. "It requires the same kind of tinkering," he said as he confidently levered the lethal detonator out of its socket and tossed it to his pals cowering behind sandbags 30 feet away.

Roy's safe-opening talents, passed on to him by his father, remain a mystery. It has been rumoured that after the war, he was kidnapped by French safecrackers and forced to tour Europe opening safes for them, but there is no proof of this.

The more likely story comes from Renfrew people who knew him and recall that Roy Gravelle remained nearly ten years in Europe after the war. When he returned, he had money, dressed well, drove a Model T Ford, had several female friends, held no regular job, and worked at being mysterious. He visited friends and relatives in Sudbury, Blind River, Toronto and Vancouver, and stayed with a daughter of Renfrew timber baron JJ McFadyen. Roy Gravelle was said to be a professional visitor who always paid his way, and might stay a week or much longer. Cecilia McCrea, a witty retired teacher living in Toronto, knew him well. "Roy was always fun to be with and full of pranks," recalled Cecilia. "I taught in Renfrew from 1925 to 1935, and had many a ride in his Model T."

Roy Gravelle stayed for a while in the old family hotel after it closed. Hydro cut off the lights, so the ingenious Roy ran a wire to a nearby store. He seldom spoke of his time in Europe, except to say it was very profitable opening safes damaged in World War I. He confided that he gave some of his money to convents, but came back with enough cash so he would never have to work again.

As a teenager in the 1930s, Alfred Kallies, who had worked in the Gravelle hotel, then known as the Ottawa House, tells us more about the mysterious Roy:

> I never heard of Roy till one night a rap came on the side door of the hotel, which I nervously opened. A well dressed, bearded stranger carrying a satchel presented himself as Roy Gravelle. He always dressed in a dark suit and wouldn't do anything to damage his hands. He was often called away, sometimes to Europe, to open safes. Roy lived like a gentleman, and would always send you out of the room when he worked on a safe.

This is as much as we know about Roy and the mystery of how he made use of this unique talent passed on by his father.

As a busy parish priest in a succession of rural Ontario and Quebec communities, Joseph Gravelle had little free time at first for any of his family's traditional interests. As he became more experienced and at ease with his various flocks, he began to immerse himself in the Gravelles' favourite hobby, the one which had so fascinated him as a youngster that it undoubtedly helped direct him into a life of service to others. This preoccupation was the compiling of histories and interconnections of people on both sides of the Ontario-Quebec border, and then tracing the families back to their roots in Europe.

I caught up with him not too long after I started my job at the Ontario Archives. Well into his eighties, he was serving the St Charles

Borroméo parish at Otter Lake, Quebec, and I liked him the moment we met.

He came up to all my expectations from what I'd heard about him: a parish priest with authority but an innate sense of modesty, a *raconteur* once you got him talking, and a dedicated genealogist in the broadest sense of the term.

I spent two days examining the names he had so painstakingly compiled over two generations and found myself overwhelmed. He had cross-indexed the families to enable trained genealogists or even amateurs to uncover unsuspected connections or missing heirs. His collection totaled nearly twice as many souls as his father's already formidable tally of 350,000. On the wall was a huge map of the area covered by the collection, from high up on Lake Temiskaming to the suburbs of Montreal. The low-cost filing system consisted entirely of 8 inch x 3 inch strips of paper gleaned from the scrap bins of the printshop in nearby Shawville where the county's weekly newspaper, *The Equity*, also published regular articles on genealogy by this versatile priest. Upon each of these varicoloured strips of newsprint, bond, Bristol or whatever was available on a given day, Father Gravelle would pen the information about one family unit. The cards were fitted snugly into cornflakes boxes from which he had neatly sliced away the front panel and carefully resealed the top end through which the corn flakes had been poured. These flimsy but compact trays were then tucked away safely in hundreds of incubator trays, which he had rescued from somewhere, probably a defunct egg-grading station in Shawville.

When I excitedly informed Don McOuat at the Archives about this fantastic cornucopia of genealogical data, he was less than enthusiastic. He professed not to like genealogy, and as the collection transcended provincial boundaries, he decided it was obviously far more suited to the Public Archives Collection in Ottawa than to the provincial archives in Toronto. At Father Gravelle's death in 1973, the collection contained more than two million names, with ancestors going for many generations back in France. The Public Archives of Canada bestirred itself to accept and reorganize this remarkable labour of love to their own specifications.

Even this show of interest by the national body came about only after I lobbied the Ontario Genealogical Society to hound them into action. Today, the Gravelle Collection is considered one of the most important genealogy collections in the possession of the National Archives of Canada.

Undaunted by the poor reception of my genealogical find, I was elated on my second visit to Father Gravelle, by then retired in Renfrew, to learn that the priest was, in his own way, a film magnate as well. Not just any old run-of-the-reel Hollywood, British, Japanese or other foreign flicks. In his possession were almost 2,500 reels of film, each in its own metal canister, the majority not only of priceless historical interest, but bearing the all-important, (to me and McOuat, at any rate) inscription: "MADE IN ONTARIO." How a back-of-beyond prelate had come into possession of this cinematic treasure trove was one of those all-too-typical Canadian tales of official apathy, buck-passing and Scrooge-style penny-pinching. It should make all loyal Ontarians weep.

The sorry sequence of events leading up to my discovery of the collection goes back to the early days of motion pictures in Ontario. Concerns about wartime agricultural production led to the establishment of the Ontario Motion Picture Bureau in May 1917. A series of vegetable planting films led to more ambitious subjects that documented industry, agriculture and natural resources in Ontario. Most of the films were contracted to two competing Toronto firms, Pathescope and Filmcraft. But by 1922, charges of graft and corruption had become such an embarrassment for the government, that it decided to start its own studio. Anxious to move the problem out of sight, Ontario Treasurer Col. WH Price, agreed to purchase an abandoned film studio in Trenton Ontario.

The studios had been built in 1918 by Canadian National Features and after a series of owners and productions, had been idle for several years. Cameramen and other technicians were hired to work at the newly revitalized facility. About the same time as this was happening, the government bought the Pathescope distribution library and greatly expanding the provincial film library rental operations.

The aim of this service was to distribute educational movies for a small fee to church groups, service clubs, women's organizations and other private agencies. The film-lending service was expected to be particularly welcomed in rural areas of the sprawling province where regular movie theatres were scarce and radio was still sorting out its own faint, squeaky beginnings.

The Film Rental Library proved a huge success, bringing glimpses of the outside world to many who had only read about the miraculous new communication medium. Miners and lumberjacks, railwaymen and construction gangs, toiling in the bush with only dog-eared magazines or the inevitable card games to lighten their few leisure hours, were among the major beneficiaries of the service. So too, were patients in hinterland hospitals, children at summer camps, and old people living in villages far off the beaten track. Customers could select what they wanted to see from a descriptive catalogue of titles, under a variety of general headings: Travel, Customs, Sports, Industry, Ontario Agriculture, Engineering, Health and Sanitation, Topical and Historical Events, and so on. All the films were silent, of course, sound not making its far-reaching debut until nearly the close of the 1920s.

An odd feature of the films was their size. The half-million feet of black and white projection prints were originally shot and edited on 35mm stock. They were then transferred to what was called non-standard 28mm format, which was introduced by Pathescope to Canada in 1914. The 28mm format was on non-flammable diacetate stock, and thus could be shown in schools, churches and halls around Ontario. Special projectors were required to show these films. Among the most popular were scenes of Canadian troops in France during World War I, the Prince of Wales's Canadian Tour of 1919, and the funeral of former Prime Minister Sir Wilfrid Laurier in Ottawa that same year. Low down on the list, though keenly watched because it was "like you were just looking out the window at them," according to a farm wife at the Haliburton Fall Fair, were dignitaries cutting ribbons, laying cornerstones, turning sods, pinning medals on athletes or horses, and judging pie contests. Early treasures were the 1908 opening of the Haileybury Mining School, where so many prospectors would learn where to look for minerals and what to do if they found them, Toronto's Central Tech, a noted art school, and a round-up of the Canadian auto industry in 1922.

Among the educational offerings and scenes of Canada and Canadians at work and play, were also such pure entertainment as cartoons, Charlie Chaplin comedies, a 20-reel 1907 production of Victor Hugo's *Les misérables*, "rendered in Paris by the most talented French actors"; several episodes of the *Exploits of Elaine*, the famous cliff-hanger starring serial queen Pearl White; a creditable production of *Macbeth*; and even a four-reeler entitled *Il Trovatore: Tense Moments from Opera*, minus music, singing and sound effects, of course.

By 1934, however, major changes had taken place in the Canadian way of life. Most homes had radio and newspapers to keep them informed. Watching Hollywood movies on Saturday, at as little as a dime apiece if you got to the theatre before six, was a regular family ritual, except in the most isolated regions. The biggest change, however, was in the economy. Ontario, like the whole of Canada and the rest of the world, was deep in a depression. In October 1934, populist Liberal premier Mitchell F Hepburn abruptly closed the Ontario Motion Picture Bureau, firing the entire staff from director and lab supervisor to cameramen and clerks, with only a month's severance pay. Totally disregarding the massive library's value as historic provincial documents, he also ordered the immediate destruction of all 35mm negatives. The prints themselves, in their cans, were offered up to anyone who would take them off the Province's hands, at 25 cents per film.

Deep in his small rural parish, Father Gravelle somehow heard of the sale. Many of his flock lived so far from civilization that any sort of film fare would be a treat, so he scraped together $750, drove to Toronto and relieved the Ontario Government of its redundant motion picture library. Perhaps because of his collar, they also gave him, at no cost, several 28mm projectors and spare parts.

Gravelle made good use of his booty, brightening the lives of thousands of the old and the young, the poor, the ill, and the isolated. Well into the 1950s, by which time he had also become an integral link in the National Film Board's rural circuit, Father Gravelle and his 28mm films were familiar sights over the whole region. They survived radio, Hollywood and many other popular modern amenities. Finally, with the advent of television, even the National Film Board offerings lost their appeal, since they were all made available on TV, and the gatherings to watch a community screening became a thing of the past.

In confident expectation that the films, or at least that portion of them portraying historic Canadian subjects, would again be valuable in a few years, Father Gravelle arranged for them to be stored in a parishioner's barn near North Bay, Ontario, then went about his manifold other duties. By the time I heard about the films in 1964, just after I had viewed his genealogical files, Father Joseph Gravelle was ready to sell the collection in the barn for the nominal sum of $1 per can.

I drove to North Bay to examine the inventory, a mission that proved to be a painful one. The barn where they were being kept was also a haven for wasps, and I was badly stung. Environmental threats would turn out to be merely one of the dangers of my new profession. Nevertheless, I persisted and selected a representative sample of these valuable films to take back to Toronto for screening. Father Gravelle had stipulated that he would only sell the films in one lot, and since it was quite evident that only a part of them had any bearing on Ontario, this made it easy for Ontario Archives to refuse the collection. This refusal closed the door on my official interest in the collection, but my personal interest in seeing that the library found a good home continued unabated.

I began contacting all the possible agencies whose mandate might permit them to handle the huge collection. The Public Archives of Canada just said, "Not interested; we have no set-up whatsoever for films." The Canadian Film Institute was intrigued but lacked the funds for the purpose. The National Film Board also wanted them, but its charter did not cover the gathering or holding of any vintage films but its own.

I then began canvassing private filmmakers in the Toronto and Montreal areas. They expressed interest, but none was prepared to chance buying the collection. This was understandable as the 28mm format had long been obsolete and no labs in Canada had any equipment that could copy, or even view the films. The only equipment to do this was in Hollywood.

In 1966, just when I was at my lowest ebb, two Toronto film producers, Michael Jacot and Greg Hoy, co-owners of Graphic Consultants Limited, agreed to purchase Father Gravelle's stash of cinematic history. Then their troubles began. With visions of the triumph they might have at Expo 67 with this historic Canadian collection, they moved the films to Greg Hoy's garage and his whole family joined in organizing and cataloguing them, sending samples off to Hollywood for transferring. The cataloguing took them well past the summer of '67 and it was not long before Greg found himself paying startling sums in shipping charges, insurance, and even duty to get the Hollywood-doctored films back into Canada again. The last irony was that no government agency would help salvage the collection, but when a patriotic private company put up money to do so, the Canadian government made life difficult for them at the border.

Problems began to beset the Hollywood transfers. Finally, Hoy had to import a Scottish technician, Alan Bullock, who designed and built a special optical printer that could copy the delicate material.

Looming large in the centennial year was an event that forever changed the history of film preservation in Canada. In July 1967, a fire started in a hot semi-abandoned wooden building near Beaconsfield P.Q. Inside were the best 35mm copies of all the earliest NFB films, original army films from the first and second world wars, the films of the Canadian Government Motion Picture Bureau, thousands of newsreels and the nitrate collections of the new Canadian Film Institute archives. The entire cache, some 80,000 cans or more, went up in flames as a result of spontaneous combustion. But lack of interest was the real cause.

A similar lack of substantive interest and funding plagued the Graphic Consultants 28mm project team. They received ample publicity and praise for their efforts, but, despite a documentary on the unique collection by well known Canada-booster Pierre Berton, and laudatory feature stories in several magazines, official Canada maintained a stony silence. Graphic got no response to its letters from Secretary of State Judy LaMarsh, Ontario Premier Leslie Frost or several other VIPs, while all they received when they presented Prime Minister Lester Pearson with a complimentary film print of Sir Wilfrid Laurier's funeral was a polite thank-you.

By the start of 1969, Graphic Consultants were so close to bankruptcy that they were seriously contemplating sale of the collection to the only agency that had expressed an interest, a New York-based commercial film archive. Had this deal gone through, the collection would have been lost to Canada forever. In the nick of time, the Public Archives of Canada came to the rescue. "Canada to have National Film Collection" trumpeted a press release from the office of the Secretary of State on July 18, 1969. "This program will ensure the collection and conservation of all motion pictures of enduring value to Canada."

Former hockey player Bill Galloway had risen through the ranks of the National Film Board to become head of its film library and director of film research, He persuaded National Archives of Canada chief Dr Wilfred Smith to include motion pictures among the historical items it would collect and store. Galloway had traveled extensively in North America and Europe procuring material for NFB productions. He had been engaged by the major US television networks to gather film footage for such well known documentary series as *Victory at Sea*, produced in 1949, *D-Day Plus 20* in 1964, and the 1965 series, *Canada at War*. The head of the new Public Archives of Canada film department would be none other than William Galloway, age 40.

As soon as possible, Galloway got some money to Greg Hoy. Michael Jacot had long since gone his own way, and the firm Graphic Consultants Limited had gone down the drain.

Hoy generously said he didn't blame anyone. They thought they could make money out of being good citizens, but it didn't work out that way. After this sad episode, Greg Hoy gave up filmmaking altogether and became a lawyer.

I was relieved to hear the films had found a home, for it was on my conscience over the years that I had been an instrument of Graphic Consultants' downfall. The collection that no one wanted is now known to be the largest cache of 28mm film ever found in North America.

CHAPTER FOUR
COLLECTORS AND THEIR OBSESSIONS

People save old paper for various reasons, often because they just let it accumulate, sometimes over generations. Without these caring people (and packrats), there would have been few useful historical documents left for me to collect for the Ontario Archives.

My own obsession was with collecting for an institution, to make the material available for researchers, rather than building a private collection for myself. My success in ferreting out collections was due partly to naïve luck and a nose for it, but mostly to the rapport I learned to establish with the collectors, from the very serious to the most casual.

Arnold Bennett, an American collector, saw it thus: "Collecting is a world habit. Collectors practice it consciously and with a definite recognized aim. The rest of us practice it more or less unconsciously."

Few archives make an effort to co-operate with serious collectors, seeing them only as competitors. My approach has been the opposite. I fed the collectors tips about their own particular obsessions, as long as they didn't conflict with my employer's collecting mandate. Most were so pleasantly surprised by this novel approach that they, in turn, fed me leads that were outside their own collecting agenda.

My theory about maintaining contact with an expanding circle of friendly collectors operated on the same premise as that of any successful salesman. Some archivists thought it improper to go out soliciting material as I did, but Don McOuat and other government people changed their views very quickly when they witnessed the results of such liaisons.

Why do people collect? What impels, compels, drives, seduces otherwise normal men and women to forsake useful, rewarding vocations and spend their lives grubbing through attics or outbuildings for elusive bits of paper or other objects?

"To the public mind, collectors are one vast, grasping consciousness, greed personified. Avarice is a sin we are taught to avoid — and avarice is collecting's organizing principle," writes art gallery curator Joan Murray in an article about the late Charles de Volpi.

As Ms Murray goes on with her article about The Great Collector, Charles de Volpi, it is evident that this scholarly Quebec paper company executive, who signed even important documents with a simple, friendly "Chas," was a charming individual as well as a consummate, incredibly broad-ranging acquirer of early Canadiana.

Starting with stamps when he was 12 and broadening out to encompass an enormous range of Canadian decorative art, Charles de Volpi, who also rejoiced in his role as Honorary Colonel of Montreal's Royal Irish Hussars, was the envy of other Canadian collectors. A millionaire with as much leisure as he chose, he became perhaps the leading acquisitor of Canadian prints and illustrations, Staffordshire china imprinted with views of Canada, furniture, toys and sugar moulds, to name but a few of his passions.

De Volpi not only collected, he confounded colleagues by using his treasures in ordinary life. Virtually every piece of furniture and ornament in his home carried its own fascinating history. Among the first to appreciate Eskimo carvings and other primitive works, he could discuss each carver's peculiarities amusingly and at length, as his seemingly disembodied fingers took apart a complex wooden maple sugar mould and put it back together.

He never failed to show visitors his weathervanes, especially an exquisitely balanced cock created c1865 for the church of Ste Scholastique, Quebec. De Volpi recognized these works as an art distinctive of his beloved province. On a level with the finest folk art produced anywhere in the world, they reflect an art trend that does not appear in American models, but is associated with European examples.

Margaret de Volpi told Ms Murray that she'd always resented her husband's collection, which overflowed their house in the small skiing village of St Sauveur des Monts, north of Montreal. "After his death, she must have watched it go to Montreal's McCord Museum with relief," wrote Joan Murray. "Especially the ... highly breakable Staffordshire china."

Though fearful each time she dusted his treasures, Mme de Volpi was never as close to breakdown as the wife of David Brown, a well known Ontario book collector. Having filled all available space, he stacked so many of his recent purchases under and even upon the nuptial bed, that a good night's sleep became impossible. Finally, she'd had enough. "Make up your mind," she told him. "Either the books go, or I do."

David Brown died in 1997, leaving over 100,000 books in a very small house along with many other relics and collectibles. These items were left to his two closest friends, both former teachers. One friend was given all the books; the other friend was given the house plus the other collectibles. The books were a mixed blessing, because many had not been looked after, were not inventoried, and created problems in their disposal.

David Brown will be remembered for having what is considered one of the largest and most eclectic collections imaginable, from volumes about the Cossacks, through over 100 books on the Crusades, to hardcore pornography.

A major question for me was: who are the chief collectors? They are mainly males, but with a fast-growing crop of keen, enterprising women. Most collectors are patriotic; Canadians tending to specialize in Canadian or even their own province's papers, Americans in Americana, Europeans in their own country's collectibles. This is not because collectors are more nationalistic than other people, but because an intimate knowledge of a nation's history is absolutely vital to success; and few have an encyclopædic acquaintance with more than one country's antecedents.

Nevertheless, a collector's nationalism is not confining. If a search for Canadiana should lead across boundaries or oceans, no major collector will hesitate to follow, or have an agent act for him. Serious collectors must have enough funds not only to travel but to pay for the desired manuscripts or artifacts they find available. Time must also be taken into account. Few people can drop everything at a moment's notice and go haring off on what might be a wild paper chase.

Most collectors — with the exception of the independently wealthy or the offspring of established collectors who may gain their own knowledge and experience acting as dogsbodies for daddy — usually have some other job to put bread on the table. Initially, weekends and holidays are devoted to prowling around museums, antique shops, flea markets and libraries, and nights are spent studying dealers' catalogues and reading all the books available on the chosen subject. As they gradually gain an overview of the subject, addicted collectors usually select a particular focus suited to their tastes, temperament and available time.

I spent my first 39 years unknowingly readying myself for a career as the Archives' collector. I was also preparing for the day when I'd retire and become a private dealer and collector, specializing in items with the scent of the fur trade and the Highlands about them. In a 1983 issue of Air Canada's *En Route* magazine, Frank Rasky wrote, "MacMillan looks and talks like a history book character ... often given to wearing kilts or buckskin. One sometimes has the impression that he is related to every Scot in North America ... an impression he shrewdly fosters when seeking private papers from Scottish families."

Being from Glengarry and Scots-oriented hurt me not all when I made my first major coup for the Archives: the entire private library of parish priest Ewan J MacDonald, one of Canada's largest single collections of manuscripts relating to Glengarry County, dating back to the 1780s.

My easy choice of Scottish and fur trade memorabilia, however, leads to another question: how do others know what to collect?

In his 1952 book, *The Adventures of a Treasure Hunter*, famed American collector Charles P Everitt noted that the word "Americana" was once thrown around very carelessly. It could mean "the *Mayflower Compact* or a hoop skirt or a whiskey label or just nothing in particular."

Only when he was preparing for retirement, after 50 years in the business, did he feel qualified to define what Americana meant to him. "It means," he wrote, "anything showing how and why people came here, and how they lived after they got here. In booksellers' catalogues, it generally covers printed material alone, but I see no reason for any such limitation."

Substituting other nations' terms for Everitt's "Americana," this definition of their craft could well become every collector's *raison d'être*, the pot of gold gleaming at rainbow's end. Like the mountain that draws climbers to its peak simply because it's there, collecting is its own valid reason for existence.

Another Canadian collector with a military background is Leo Heaps, son of Winnipeg socialist firebrand Member of Parliament Abe Heaps. Handsome, rugged Leo left Queen's University at 19 to parachute into Europe. Taken prisoner at Arnhem, he escaped, joined the Dutch underground and arranged escapes for others, earning thereby the Military Cross and a Mention in Dispatches. After the war, he opened an art gallery in Ottawa, but left in 1948 to fight for Israel and again in 1956 to help Hungarian refugees. By 1963, he was riding high on a Montreal real estate boom, when the bottom fell out. "I lost my house and all my possessions," Heaps recalls. "With only $200 total assets, I decided to head for England, which had always been good to me."

England had not only been kind to its colonial soldier of misfortune, but in his special field, landscapes, portraits, Eskimo carvings, and explorers' diaries, it held promise of being the mother lode, because English travellers, military personnel and civil servants had played a large role in Canada's early development.

Leo Heaps' first coup was of a size and value to make veteran collectors gasp with envy. It was 1967, Canada's 100th birthday, when he set out to find the fabled Kamchatka Venture Collection, some 250 ancient Eskimo carvings amassed by fur trader Vernon Elphick during a hazardous 1921 sled trip across the Alaska-Siberia wasteland. Archaeologists and museum curators who had seen them marveled at their beauty and dreamed of the bonanza to be reaped by some lucky institution. When Elphick died, there was no sign of the carvings among his belongings and no indication of whom Elphick may have sold or given them to.

Heaps spent two years on this quest, grubstaked by two angels he has refused to identify, and the trail finally led to a village just outside London, England. Here, a brace of retired Hudson's Bay Company factors, who had seen their chance and grabbed it, were sharing the fabulous collection.

Shortly afterward, Leo Heaps was intrigued by a footnote to a story about British Admiral Sir George Back's Arctic explorations, which recalled that this early 19th century seadog was a keen amateur watercolour artist. That was enough to lead Heaps to a filthy, stinking Dorsetshire cowshed, where, under a fetid pile of manure and crumbling old harness parts, he unearthed a battered suitcase belonging to Sir George's great-granddaughter. It contained several paintings of Eskimos and polar bears, along with the admiral's diaries, journals, medals and other memorabilia. "It paid for all the time I'd spent, with a bit over for me," said Heaps.

Leo Heaps accumulated other notable acquisitions: some fine pictures by John Webber, an artist accredited to Captain James Cook's third expedition, 1779–80, including an oil painting of Friendly Island natives and a number of watercolors of West Coast Canadian Indians; the journal of *HMS Centurion*'s globe-girdling voyage of 1740–44, which proved to be very valuable; 51 previously unknown works by self-taught Canadian Impressionist Henry Sandham, a charter member of the Royal Academy, who died broke in 1910. Sandham's early paintings were in traditional style, but Heaps' new finds were fresher, far more colourful, and more valuable, especially to Sandham admirers in Winnipeg and Montreal.

"The attics of England are still full of treasures, even though the public is unaware of their value," Heaps declares. "I only hope a few more come my way."

Historical documents have been preserved for posterity by civilizations dating as far back as ancient Greece, but public archives, as cultural forces in communities, are still not as well known as museums, libraries and art galleries. The first Historical Archivist of the Dominion of Canada was Douglas Brymner, a former journalist from Greenock, Scotland, appointed in 1872. He did a creditable job, despite the benign neglect and penny-pinching of the federal civil service.

Brymner's successor, named to the post of Dominion Archivist and Keeper of the Public Records in 1906, Sir Arthur Doughty, continually jolted civil servants out of their well padded seats. He once journeyed to the Maritimes just to buy Benjamin West's dramatic painting of General James Wolfe dying on the Plains of Abraham. In Halifax, he was chagrined to learn that the director of the newly created National Gallery had just bought it.

"It's in our baggage room at this very moment, ready to be shipped to Ottawa," the Halifax stationmaster informed him. Casually ambling toward the crated treasure, Sir Arthur waited until the stationmaster was busy elsewhere, then whipped out his pen and changed the name and address on the crate to his own. In the uproar that ensued, Sir Arthur remained icily calm. "Who knows how long the National Gallery itself will last," was his invariable retort to most criticism, "if they can't even address a parcel properly?" It wasn't until the 1950s, when Kaye Lamb headed Public Archives, that the National Gallery regained that painting.

Doughty hit his stride in World War I, first with captured enemy cannon and then with a full range of British and French weapons. He amassed a huge collection of military equipment and sent exhibitions across Canada and the then neutral United States. These were acclaimed by a public eager to know and share the experience of their military forces a wide ocean away.

One large exhibit of Sir Arthur Doughty's weapons touring in the USA for a 1918 war bond drive attracted more than eight million visitors over nine months. Even after the war was over, no Canadian fair or exhibition was complete without a sizeable array of these armaments, including field artillery and a captured enemy aircraft, the bullet holes and dried blood still visible on its flimsy fuselage.

In September 1919, a German grenade launcher on loan to a fair in Parry Sound, Ontario, carried its own array of ordnance. The explosive charges had, of course, been removed but, unfortunately, the propellant had been left intact: when a spectator inserted a bomb into the machine, it was launched into the crowd, killing a bystander. The government paid $1,500 compensation to the victim's family. But later that same month, when a Canadian veteran was hurt demonstrating a grenade in the T Eaton Company's Winnipeg store, he was refused compensation on the grounds that the exhibit was for display, not demonstration.

For years, Sir Arthur pressed vainly for the establishment of a proper military museum. At the outset of World War II in 1939, his splendid collection of war trophies was finally put to use — as scrap metal — but he had never lost sight of the goal itself.

"Of all our national assets, archives are the most precious," he constantly reiterated. "They are the gift of one generation to another and the extent of our care of them marks the extent of our civilization." Sir Arthur Doughty's philosophy is contained in a letter he wrote May 16, 1917, qualified as non-official, to WC Milner, his agent in the Maritimes.

> When I was in England, I heard someone who had come from Nova Scotia say that there was a fight for the papers and that you were threatened with all sorts of proceedings. I stated that I did not care anything about the proceedings so long as he gets the papers. To be prosecuted in the course of getting hold of papers so long as you get them is a matter for rejoicing and if you did advertise your triumph I am not going to blame you. You must remember the mysterious manner in which you have gathered papers has aroused a great deal of animosity, not because your opponents have any particular love or regard for the papers but simply because you have been able to do what they could not do. The only time I have been inclined to find fault with you was for not sending the things to Ottawa quicker. Because if you once get them out of the reach of your opponents, they would never get them back again without armed force.

No one can accuse me of being quite this militant. However, after receiving an honorary D Litt degree in 1984 from Laurentian University, I was granted an honorary CPO by my old pal Edward "Fast Eddie" Phelps, head of the regional collection at the University of Western Ontario in London. Ed was one of my fiercest competitors, and the initials stood for Chief Pirate of Ontario.

Alice Munro, one of Canada's best short story writers, managed to work my job description into one of the stories in her book, *Moons of*

A "Priest" assault gun mounted on a Ram tank chassis — part of Bill and Carol Gregg's complete collection of World War II Canadian military vehicles — out for a spin, 1986. (The Ram was a Canadian variant of the American M3, built at the Montreal Locomotive Works.) Bill is second from left, I am on the far right in the tam-o'-shanter.

Jupiter. Here a woman is trying to explain to her friend Julie what her pal Douglas Reider does for a living: "He is in charge of collecting, buying for the provincial archives, all sorts of old diaries, letters ... that would otherwise perish, or be sold to collectors outside the province or the country. He pursues various clues, hunches.... He often has to

View of the living room of David Brown, a dedicated book collector. When the number of books in the house reached 30,000, his wife gave him an ultimatum: either the books went or she did. The collection is seen here at approximately 100,000 volumes.

The rare 1940 Ford 60 H in Charlie Lassiter's junkyard in Tillsonburg, Ontario. Charlie had buried it in a pile of scrap lumber so he wouldn't be tempted to sell it to Bill Gregg, but a flash of sunlight on metal gave it away, and after two years of negotiation, it was added to the Greggs' collection. Bill is on the left, Charlie at right. (Author's collection)

persuade reticent or suspicious or greedy owners, and to outwit private dealers. He's sort of a pirate, really."

It sure sounds like my *modus operandi*, but the physical description is wrong. Though Munro describes the character as very tall and lean, at 5 foot 8 inches I am decidedly on the short, stocky side. However, let's face it, Sir Arthur would have approved, in fact he would probably have hired me on the spot.

Sir Arthur Doughty's *alter ego* might well have been not one person but two: veterinarian Dr Bill Gregg and his wife Carol. This Rockwood, Ontario, couple's obsession was to obtain at least one specimen of every World War II vehicle built in Canada. Unique among collectors in at least two ways, they achieved their goal in only nine years and, unlike most collectors, who never stop searching for better, rarer, more historic specimens of their particular *objets d'art*, the Greggs quit when they had acquired a representative sample of each.

One of their merry chases involved *The Case of the Truck in the Woodpile*, the pile in question being located in Charlie Lassiter's vast junkyard in Tillsonburg, Ontario. Dr Bill had mooched around the yard many times, but had never paid any attention to the woodpile. One sunny afternoon in the early 1980s, he thought he caught a flash of light on metal, or perhaps glass, from inside the pile. As thrilled as Schliemann discovering Troy or Harry Oakes breaking into his subterranean Kirkland Lake river of gold, Bill began flinging the boards and beams aside and saw, to his delight, a 1940-vintage Ford truck buried in the débris.

He was fondling the windshield wipers while clearing a path to the driver's door, uttering little yelps of joy, when Charlie came racing up, crimson and bellowing with rage. "I've had that truck hidden there since 1954, just so's I wouldn't be tempted to sell it to the likes of you," he screeched. "You won't find another 1940 Ford 60 H in the whole dang country!"

It had taken a keen, searching eye to spot the hidden treasure and it now took two exhausting years of persuasion to get Charlie to part with it, but patience paid off in the end and the happy couple finally drove off in their mint condition 1940 Ford, to wind up their collecting careers.

The Gregg collection, amassed from all over Canada, the United States and Europe, is now on display at Camp Shilo, Manitoba.

Peter Trower, my West Coast poet friend, saw the collection one dark and foggy night. He composed the following poem, which really captures the essence of the Gregg collection.

"Night Manœuvres"
from *The Slidingback Hills**

In a silent barn of war
in a rainy Ontario meadow,
the death wagons sleep
strange stock for a farm to harbour
tank and howitzer gun carriage
armoured car and a mobile command post
once used by Gen Crerar.

The collector has summoned them here
with a wave of the money wand
he tends their fractures oils their rusty works
a curious exercise
to husband a herd of life size Dinky Toys
it is like a childhood hobby gone berserk.

At night when the field is still
and the shepherd of ordinance
gone to his marching dreams
something stirs in the barn like mice in a sack,
the battered command post glows
and there they are —
dapper Montgomery
moustached mournful Crerar
and unsinkable Churchill sipping his cognac.
The old expenders of blood
the crafty chess-kings of carnage
juggling lives, they foddered the cannons well
when the years ran red,
now they are met again like ominous echoes
to mount a phantom campaign
to sift the unquiet ashes of battle
and summon the dead.

The orders are given and heard
the locked barn doors swing wide
the rag-tag force rolls forth — an army reborn
to scout the war-spared land
at the dimly remembered whim of an old command
and hunt for ghostly panzer divisions till dawn.

---
* Oberon Press, 1986

This tribute to the Greggs is rare. Seldom is such moving poetry composed to tell the story of a collector. It must have been a painful reminder to Peter Trower, whose father was killed shortly before World War II commenced, while testing a Supermarine Spitfire.

Trucks, grenade launchers and tanks may seem unwieldy items to collect, but they are dwarfed by the private railway cars which Toronto businessman Andrew Merilees set about acquiring, none of them less than 79 feet long. The Merilees collection of papers and photographs are at the National Archives in Ottawa. The railway cars are in private collections of railway equipment in Toronto.

Protecting his treasures from the weather, animals, thieves and other assorted perils is an important part of every collector's life, but few have gone to the lengths Sam Weir has. In January, 1981, this prolific Queenston, Ontario, amasser of Canadian paintings, historic documents, sculptures, antiques, and memorabilia relating to his own legal profession, included in his will the proviso that his house and all its wonders should become a public museum and he should be buried by its front steps to make damn sure it remained inviolate. And it came to pass exactly as he specified.

"Very few requests for home burials are granted," explained John Francis, of the Ontario Ministry of Consumer and Commercial Relations, after Sam was properly planted. "However, we granted a special order because Mr Weir had stipulated all his art treasures be turned over to the public."

On what might be called the borderline, or shadowy area of the collecting mania, are men like William Ready, of Irish descent but born and raised in Wales, who made his fame in Hamilton, Ontario as a librarian.

Hitherto renowned chiefly for its smoking steel mills, the Tiger Cats football team, and its location on the most westerly and most thoroughly polluted bay of Lake Ontario, this city is now a mecca for scholars from all over the world, and is likely to be so for ages to come.

This is why prominent citizens, both in and outside of Hamilton, believe a statue or other suitable monument should be erected to honour William Ready. Bill did what many considered impossible: he brought the complete papers of British peer, mathematician, philosopher and radical reformer Bertrand Russell to Hamilton's McMaster University. Ready had to bid against 29 other universities, museums, foundations, booksellers and private collectors, including a couple of oil-rich Sheiks, to obtain this invaluable find.

The collection of letters, books, tapes, photographs and manuscripts include a 30-page letter to Russell from Russian premier Nikita Khrushchev, demanding to know why the Americans were "massacring their Indians." There is also a tender 1904 letter from Earl Russell to his fiancée, thanking her for sending her photo "with thy Gainsborough hat ... and thy dear middle-class hands." All together, the bonanza numbers more than 200,000 separate items and was obtained for McMaster for a mere $520,000.

The deal for the Russell papers was initiated during Canada's centennial year, 1967, when the total amount in Ready's hands for bidding purposes was only $5,000. It was consummated in March 1968, two years before Russell's death. Ready topped this triumph by acquiring for McMaster the papers of Irish playwright Samuel Beckett at a bargain rate, scant days before Beckett copped the Nobel Prize for Literature, which sent his reputation and value skyrocketing.

Though he made great deals, William Ready could not be classified as a dealer or a collector in the same way as private collectors, most of whom find themselves with extra copies or inferior specimens of a desired item to trade or sell for needed cash or better goods. Ready approached me at one stage with a proposition to work for McMaster University collecting literary papers, but after much thought I decided it would be too narrow a field. I chose rather to put out my own catalogues and buy and sell as an ordinary dealer.

John Davis Barnett (1845–1926) was a brilliant engineer who came from England at age 17 and spent most of his life in Stratford, Ontario, as mechanical superintendent of the Grand Trunk Railway. A highly cultured man, interested in everything, he left a collection of 40,000 books to the University of Western Ontario, dwarfing its existing library.

In addition to the books, Barnett left hundreds of 'Barnett bundles,' large manila envelopes into which he stuffed "that which others were not keeping." These included thousands of trade catalogues, posters, advertising flyers, and clippings from long gone sources, along with all sorts of engineering and architectural drawings. All together, they represented a superb record of technological advancement, a background against which Canada's industrial growth can easily be charted.

The University of Western Ontario didn't quite know what to do with Barnett's bundles, and they gathered dust on shelves for almost 50 years. Only in 1977, with the help of Canadian Heritage and Public

Archives, were they re-catalogued. The credit for this fine piece of work goes to Edward Phelps of Western and Dr Norman Ball, currently teaching about the impact of technological change at the University of Waterloo. These two teamed up to process the massive Barnett collection. Much of the technical material was donated to the Public Archives, where Dr Ball had been teaching.

The grand opening of the Barnett Collection in 1983 was an epochal event in the University of Western Ontario's history. I heard later that a local builder discovered he'd recently paid $10,000 for detailed information that was freely available in Barnett's bundles. He was almost in tears.

Another collector for whom I had a wary admiration was Borden Clarke, owner of Old Authors' Farm, almost straddling the Canada-US border at Morrisburg, Ontario. Old Authors' Farm was actually a bookshop with "30 years of honest business in Canada" according to its literature, specializing in Old and Rare Books, Stamps, Maps and Documents, as well as First Editions, Americana, Canadiana and Law Books." H (for Harold) Borden Clarke, a native of Annapolis, Nova Scotia, was certainly one of the world's great collectors, having had in his possession first editions of *Moby Dick*, *Elegy in a Country Churchyard*, *Evangeline*, *Leaves of Grass* and other equally famous works by authors like Thoreau, Emerson, Longfellow and Whittier.

Clarke obtained these treasures from public libraries across New England, his favourite and nearest stamping ground. He would see priceless volumes on the open shelves where trusting librarians had placed them.

One day in 1930, he asked chief librarian in Salem, Massachusetts, why they didn't put cheap reprints on the open shelves and keep their first editions under close lock and key.

Clarke was told that the main Boston Library is the depot for all New England libraries and recipient for discoveries in rare books. He was told they have the finest reference works and their staff gives valuations on books to all comers, but that the Boston Library reports such low sums for first editions that it would hardly pay to sell them and buy reprints. This was not quite true, though Salem's chief librarian undoubtedly believed it to be so.

"Staff members (in Boston) bought this stuff the year round, from unsuspecting small libraries and passed them on down to New York at ten times what they paid," Clarke later testified. "The poor little village library was caught between thieves who paid nothing and those who paid almost nothing."

Seeing a whole nation's literary and historical treasures being so wantonly plundered, he wrote to ten of the largest libraries, including Harvard, warning them of their peril and telling them how to foil the thieves. Most ignored his letter, but Harvard thanked him and acted on his advice.

David C Mearns was a well known American collector I met several times in Washington, where we compared notes. Here are David's views on why fieldwork is necessary for any collector: "To be successful, an acquisitions program, particularly in the field of manuscripts, must be imaginative, constant, aggressive, patient, prepared for protracted negotiations, definable, flattering and fun. It must also be based upon personal relationships established by those shameless beggars, the acquisitors, and their often coy, or confused, or reluctant, or hesitant, or (dare I say it?) stupid prospects. It is these considerations which impose that necessity of fieldwork."

No doubt Sir Arthur Doughty would have endorsed this line of thinking. I would love to have teamed up with Doughty and Mearns. We would have made a great team of collectors.

CHAPTER FIVE
THE EDGARS: A JACOBITE FAMILY

A column by MacKenzie Porter in the old Toronto Telegram during the 1960s sparked my hunt for the Edgars, and like many of my cases, this one will probably remain unfinished forever. Porter's column described the unusual nature of the work I was doing for the Archives. After it appeared, I received a number of phone calls, suggestions, criticisms, and one good tip, which at first seemed improbable.

I was told that a gold snuffbox and duelling pistols that had belonged to Bonnie Prince Charlie were in Scarborough, Ontario. Unlikely as that might have been, I did listen carefully to the tale told me by Elizabeth Hay Trott and promised to go and see the treasures she was holding for her former companion, whose name she said was James Edgar.

Some months passed before I was able to meet Elizabeth Trott. She was a charming middle-aged school teacher and part-time writer, living in an old farmhouse at the intersection of Kingston Road and Lawrence Avenue. Her house had been expropriated and was due to be demolished the following year, so she would need to vacate the premises. Elizabeth, it appeared, doted on the colour purple. She met me at the door dressed in an all-purple pantsuit, and the entire interior of her house was coloured purple, the only exception being a bedroom papered from floor to ceiling with maps.

I took a tour of this unusual house, hoping to find some Edgar papers, but I was unsuccessful. Somehow, I missed a major cache of papers. Good luck rather than good management would bring the valuable cache my way the following year, but on this first visit with Elizabeth, I only saw a large collection of Jacobite paintings, which she was storing in her home for her friend James Edgar. Most of these were of the Royal Stuart family.

One of the portraits might have been of Bonnie Prince Charlie, the Young Pretender (1720–88) as a youth. Another seemed to be his father, King James, the Old Pretender (not the king who actually ruled as James VII of Scotland and II of England from 1685 until he was deposed by King Billie in 1689, but his son James, styled VIII and III, b 1688 and d 1766 in France). A haughty, middle-aged beauty was probably James's wife, Clementina Sobieska, daughter of the King of Poland; a younger woman wearing a diamond necklace could have been Martha Walkinshaw, one of Prince Charles's several mistresses.

The paintings were all in bad condition, but I took them for safekeeping to the Ontario Archives and set about finding their owners, James Edgar and his two sons. This search involved me in a complicated chase. Through 48th Highlander connections and pension files, I eventually found former Captain James Edgar, an employee of the federal Department of Health, living in a rooming house on Charles Street in Toronto. He gave me a miniature of Prince Charles, handed down from his grandfather, Sir James. I left it in the charge of the Canadiana branch of the Royal Ontario Museum. Eventually James Edgar's son, David, of Victoria, BC, who already had the gold snuffbox and duelling pistols, took the miniature over from the ROM as well. These items that David retrieved, along with a lock of Prince Charles's hair, the ribbon of the Order of the Garter that Charles wore at Culloden, the miniature of Mary Queen of Scots, and other relics, were of no interest to the Ontario Archives.

When I asked James Edgar if there were any Canadian family letters or manuscripts around, he was vague. He seemed to remember some, but had no idea where they might be.

However, he showed me two 18th-Century oil portraits of Captain Thomas Pearson and his wife. Thomas had skippered a ship for the House of Edgar, the family mercantile business based in Scotland. When I mentioned to James that my mother's maiden name was Pearson, he insisted on giving me the two portraits, which were in dismal condition. I had them restored and reframed, and eventually sold them to a collector of Jacobite items in L'Orignal.

It took me longer to find the other son, John Jr, but he finally turned out to be living in Toronto too, and he inherited the royal portraits.

While tracking down the Edgars, I had various misadventures, and found out more about this remarkable Jacobite family. Emigrating to Canada in 1840, an earlier James Edgar of Keithock had bought land near Lennoxville, Lower Canada, where his son, the future Sir James David, was born the following year. When he was 17, James David moved to the Toronto-area hamlet of Woodbridge, where he apprenticed as a lawyer. Called to the Bar in 1864, he had a natural gift for writing that led him to accept the position of Legal Editor of the Toronto *Globe*, then headed by its founder, the fierce Liberal crusader George Brown.

Knighted for services to Canada by Queen Victoria in 1898, Sir James David Edgar died the following year at his Toronto home, aged 58. He had a life-long love affair with his wife, the former Matilda Ridout, daughter of a prominent Toronto family. She adored the tender, often funny, *billets doux* he dashed off to her in tense moments snatched from debates in Parliament. His letters to her covered such topics as Louis Riel, international arbitration procedures, women's suffrage and copyright legislation to protect Canadian writers. Matilda applauded when he became the first Ontario Protestant to openly berate the powerful Protestant Protective Association, whose virulent attacks on Catholics were threatening to break up the country.

Matilda Ridout Edgar also made a name for herself as a patriot, writer and mother. Born in Toronto in 1844, and married to James Edgar at 21, she was best known for her historical tome, *Ten Years of Upper Canada in War and Peace, 1805–1815*. This book tells the story of her family's adventures during the War of 1812. She also wrote a volume on Sir Isaac Brock in the *Makers of Canada* series. At the time of her death in 1910, she was president of the National Council of Women of Canada.

James and Matilda Edgar had nine children. Among them were James Frederick Edgar, KC, and Pelham Edgar, a Professor of English at Victoria College, University of Toronto. Pelham was a widely admired author, critic and champion of Canadian writers. Usually seen at the wheel of an ancient Rolls Royce, with the Edgar coat-of-arms on the door, this university don published a scholarly biography of Henry James in 1927 and *The Art of the Novel* in 1938. He was an intimate of Bliss Carmen, EJ Pratt, Sir Charles GD Roberts, Valency Crawford and many others.

Pelham Edgar was a prime mover in the establishment of the Canadian Writers' Foundation, whose mission was to ensure that fine Canadian writers need never again spend their last years in poverty. He died in 1948 and was buried with his parents and other Edgars in the family plot at St James Cemetery. The family, once known by the Scottish baronial title Edgar of Keithock, have become, in the history books of Canada, the Edgars of Toronto.

Elizabeth Trott was a mine of information about the Edgars during the Scottish rebellions of 1715 and 1745 (known as *The '15* and *The '45*), most of the information having come from James Keithock Edgar. I was certain that I had found the correct descendents of the James Edgar who had been private secretary to King James, the exiled Old Pretender, for the better part of half a century.

Though Protestants, John and James Edgar had been hunted down after the failure of the '15. John was captured and imprisoned in Stirling Castle, where he died. James escaped and made his way to Rome, where he entered into lifelong service as private secretary to King James, the man he looked upon as his legitimate sovereign. The exiled court lived frugally, supported by a few faithful Jacobite followers, selling family heirlooms when in dire need. Apparently James, the Old Pretender, shared any windfalls with those who, like James Edgar, had chosen to be with him in exile.

The depth of the private secretary's loyalty was apparent when British prime minister Sir Robert Walpole, believing that another attempt to restore the Stuarts to the throne was planned, decided on the strength of spies' reports that this younger son of a poor Scottish laird must at all costs be won over to the Hanoverian side.

When an offer of a handsome sum of money was made to Edgar in exchange for information about the whereabouts and intentions of James, Edgar is said to have thrown the letter in the fire without bothering to reply. Several further offers, each larger than the one before, were made. He spurned them, too. Walpole, believing they had not yet come close to the secretary's own idea of adequate payment, then wrote a personal letter to Edgar, advising him that £10,000 had been deposited to his credit in the Bank of isVenice.

This got results. Edgar, after consultation with his employer and withdrawing the money, dispatched his own personal note to Sir Robert, thanking him for his most generous gift, and adding a stinger that must have made the English politician's blood boil.

"I have laid it at the feet of my royal master," he wrote, "who has the best title to gold that comes, as this has done, from his own dominions."

King James was, of course, deeply moved by his faithful adherent's munificent gesture. Along with other expressions of gratitude, he presented Edgar with his own richly engraved gold snuffbox.

Secretary Edgar cherished this box above all other royal gifts until his death in 1764. It was part of the dozen-odd Jacobite treasures that his collateral descendent James Edgar gave to some member of the family. The collection included the brace of duelling pistols Prince Charles had used in the Rebellion of 1745–46, which was bequeathed to Secretary Edgar's nephew.

Recently, when I was in Victoria, BC, I discovered that the list of books in the personal library of James Edgar, the secretary to the Old Pretender, still exists. It is a slim volume with title and author recorded in neat copperplate script. James would have had those books in Rome during his 18th-Century exile. Along with the list are a few of the books and some letters, many written under the alias "G Guthrie" that he used while he was plotting to put King James on the throne. What a find!

It was another year before my luck with the elusive Edgar papers turned. A Mrs Hobbs phoned to tell me an odd story. Her mother had been Elizabeth Trott's housekeeper for many years, and it was in her old farmhouse that a large tin trunk holding 450 or more Edgar family letters had lain from World War II until 1966. Mrs Hobbs had thrown them into the garbage at one point, she confessed, and the rain had got at them. But next morning, she rescued them because she thought the tin box would make a good toy box for her children. Noting the papers inside, she dried them in the oven and even ironed the messiest ones.

Mrs Hobbs had seen the story about me in the *Toronto Telegram* but had been deterred from calling me because her husband was afraid she could be charged with theft of the papers. She was calling me now because she realized this was nonsense, since Mrs Trott had left the old tin box holding the Edgar papers in the house when she turned it over to Mrs Hobbs and her family.

I went to see Mrs Hobbs and found, after a cursory examination of the trunk's contents that they were indeed the papers I'd been looking for and had missed on my first visit with Ms Trott.

They included valuable personal and political letters of Sir James David Edgar and his wife Matilda Ridout. These documents were added to the collection of Edgar papers which had already been deposited in the Archives by the Edgar family, and I persuaded the Ontario Archives to pay Mrs Hobbs $600 for all the trouble she'd gone to in preserving these papers.

The tin box was about a yard square. Inside were miscellaneous records of the Edgars back to 1680 in Scotland, poems by various family members, a partial draft of Lady Matilda Edgar's book on The Old Pretender, genealogy charts on the Edgars compiled by the Grampian Society in 1873, loose clippings from the marvelously named Miss Edgar's and Miss Cramp's School for Girls in Montreal which had been started with the financial aid of Sir William Van Horne, builder and first president of the Canadian Pacific Railway, a letter from William Gladstone, Prime Minister of England, praising Lady Edgar's history of the war of 1812, and a handwritten Shawnee-English dictionary compiled by Thomas Ridout while he was a prisoner of the Indians in 1788. By strange coincidence, several years later, I located the other copy of Ridout's dictionary, with a Radenhurst descendent in Paris, France (about whom more later).

Also in this exciting collection were 197 written records of *séances* staged by Lady Edgar shortly after Sir James died, attempting to make contact with him in the spirit world. "There is no great gulf fixed between the two worlds, as we had always thought," she reported her late husband as assuring his dearly beloved, sorrowing widow. "There is only the great difficulty of communication." On another occasion, he was reported to have said "I am learning many different powers that are unknown to you now, but which are all to be learnt sometime by everyone." Another admonition by Sir James from the spirit world was, "Service from love is the highest privilege of man in all worlds. It is begun on earth, it is continued with more and more opportunity here..."

In September 1969, I was leading a voyageur canoe trip with the famous canoeist/filmmaker/author Bill Mason to obtain film footage for a Hudson's Bay Company documentary film by Chris Chapman. At Moose River Crossing awaiting the train back south, our voyageurs chatted up the recently arrived school teacher, an attractive, petite, cigar-smoking woman named Betsy, who tended to stand out in a tiny native community.

Not entirely to my surprise, but as a consequence of my insatiable curiosity, I learned that Betsy's mother, Margaret Wood back in Huntsville, Ontario, was born an Edgar, a cousin of the 48th Highlanders' James! In my profession, it is a given that you should always ask that one more question, so of course I did. It turned out that she knew a couple of people who might have other papers relating to the Edgars in Canada. One of these possible holders of Edgar papers was an Edgar family lawyer in Toronto, who, with the blessings of both Mrs Wood and her daughter, turned over a bundle of documents and letters to me a few months later. The gods were smiling on me when I found that Betsy's mother had a great cache of blueblood Edgar papers that I had been seeking and was later able to acquire. Finding this lead to such a valuable trove was another of those co-incidences that continue to come my way. I am convinced that it is more than random luck.

A second surprising new source was another cousin of James named Maud McLean. She had been a pupil at Miss Edgar's (her aunt) and Miss Cramp's School for Girls in Montreal, but confided to my query that all the Edgar papers her own family had held had already been deposited with the Ontario Archives by her father. Maud was an exceedingly knowledgeable family member. She and co-author Robert Stamp have written a well researched family history, *My Dearest Wife: the Private and Public Lives of James David Edgar and Matilda Ridout Edgar* (1998).

The importance of family records in an Archives can usually be roughly gauged by the space their written documents occupy. I gazed with satisfaction on the more than five feet of wall space devoted to the Edgars. This Scots family suffered greatly for their steadfast loyalty to the Jacobite cause they espoused, and then poured the same energy and love into the country they chose for their new home, Canada.

I deeply appreciated my good fortune in discovering this material, finally, in spite of my earlier bumbling failure to spot the tin trunk containing hundreds of items the first time I searched Ms Trott's house. People talk about the luck of the Irish, but it's nothing to the serendipity I have experienced as a paper sleuth!

CHAPTER SIX
THE WILD FRONTIER

Tom Barnett and his son Sidney were Canadian showmen of the stature of their contemporary, Phineas T. Barnum, though in typically modest Canadian fashion, they lacked the Yankee promoter's absolute abhorrence of giving customers an even break. Nowhere in the Barnetts' magnificent museum was there any cruel put-down like Barnum's infamous "This Way to the Egress!" sign that vaguely hinted at a rare avian display as it lured the unwary and unsophisticated outside instead, forcing them to pay again to get back in. Nowhere in the Barnetts' marketing philosophy was there room for sham or misrepresentation.

Thomas Barnett arrived from Birmingham, England, at the age of 25 to found the Niagara Falls Museum. Established on the Niagara River front in 1827, it was one of North America's oldest museums. Barnett started modestly with mainly historical relics and border memorabilia. The museum became so popular that in ten years it had to be enlarged, even though its first premises, a former brewery with high ceilings, had seemed ample space for exhibits. The 1837 museum, a two-storey affair, was built on land adjoining the first one, and a connecting passage was turned into a zoological garden.

A Toronto newspaper declared the expanded museum was "unsurpassed as the collection of one individual in the world ... galleries of large dimensions, each well filled with curiosities, animals from the smallest to the most gigantic size, birds of every known kind, being especially rich in this department, reptiles and fishes of every description. Canada should feel proud of having such a magnificent collection fit to grace any capital of Europe."

The paper went on to marvel at Barnett's well-nigh incredible generosity. "Mr Barnett has done much for the progress of knowledge by throwing open his museum to all public schools of Canada and the United States free," it stated, "and his public spirit and enterprise have added important features to that beautiful place, Niagara Falls."

By the late 1850s, though pleased with the prosperity of his New World enterprise, Barnett was unhappy with the way the whole area surrounding the museum was developing. "Far too commercial" he might have phrased it, "Too many factories, not nearly enough cultural institutions." Not an environment to attract the thousands of tourists from both sides of the border who were his meat, potatoes and good living. A man of action as well as ideas, he set about finding a spot away from the smoke, noise and rough industrial atmosphere, where he could build a museum from scratch to satisfy his own dreams and leave as an inheritance to his son Sidney.

From his tenderest years, the boy had been a great help, representing his dad in many distant parts of the world. On trips to Egypt and Cuba, he had acquired specimens and curiosity items that were highly popular with a broad spectrum of the paying public. He was truly a chip off the old block.

The new museum opened to much fanfare and acclaim early in September, 1860, just in time to greet Queen Victoria's eldest son, Edward, Prince of Wales, on his first solo journey abroad. The Victoria and Albert Museum in London, named in honour of the handsome 18-year-old prince's parents, had opened only three years before. Edward was able to admire its colonial counterpart, especially since the new premises boasted the uniquely enterprising addition of a hotel, a kind of accommodation the playboy prince would prize for the next 40 years. Other notables who would view the wonders of the new Niagara Falls Museum were Abraham Lincoln, Ulysses S Grant, and the Barnetts' competitor, PT Barnum.

Another unique service the Museum offered to the public from its site at Table Rock, near the Horseshoe Falls, was a guided tour of the falls themselves, under the Sheet of Water thrown off as spray. Though it appears that the Barnetts had not built the spiral stairway giving access to this tourist attraction, they held an exclusive government lease on it. This was contested by their archrival, a sinister figure named Saul Davis, owner of Table Rock House, who coveted the staircase for himself and made life a continual jurisdictional struggle for the Barnetts.

In 1860, the year his new museum opened, Sidney Barnett and archaeological expert Dr James Douglas traveled to Egypt, then just coming into its own as a favourite search area for relics from the days of the Pharaohs and the Pyramids. They returned in triumph, bearing several mummies which admiring scholars unreservedly acknowledged as the finest examples of Egyptian antiquities existent in the whole of North America.

The following year, though still as deeply involved with the affairs of the Museum as his father, Sidney reacted to the start of the Civil War across the border by joining the Canadian militia as an ensign. The bloody fraternal fracas, in which more Americans were slaughtered than in any war before or after, made no unusual inroads on Ensign Barnett's way of life.

But the Fenian uprisings of 1866 posed a different, and potentially far more dangerous, problem. Backed, if only nominally, by a victorious northern army seeking new territories to conquer, even these stage Irishmen might mount a successful invasion of Canada. To help head off such a coup, Ensign Sidney Barnett was elevated to the rank of Colonel and made Commanding Officer of the Welland Battalion. Friction with his commanding officer, whose incessant demands to "fix militia matters right in your own battalion" were as hard to take as all the Fenian forays directed at the Eastern Townships and New Brunswick. When local skirmishes in the nearby Fort Erie area died down, Col Barnett resigned his commission in disgust.

In the meantime, Tom Barnett's civilian enterprise was beset with many problems, mostly involving legal squabbles with rival impresario Saul Davis, roving gangs of hoodlums from across the border and financial difficulties resulting from the unsavoury reputation the whole Table Rock neighbourhood was now earning for itself. The Barnetts began looking beyond their beloved museum for other moneymaking opportunities.

They hit upon the idea of re-enacting an Indian burial. It must have been a successful show, because it inspired the Barnetts to hold a far more elaborate and expensive re-enactment of a prairie ritual often described in the press of the day, and more luridly by writers and artists with wilder imaginations in the illustrated weeklies, a buffalo hunt.

Though the Barnetts couldn't foresee it, this dream of recouping the family's fortunes by staging a true to life buffalo hunt on the Niagara Falls littoral would prove to be their ruin.

A fascinating figure for most North Americans in the years following the Civil War was William "Buffalo Bill" Cody, chief Indian scout for the United States Army in Nebraska. (Cody's father was from Oxford County, Ontario.) A Pony Express rider while in his teens, decorated Indian fighter, supplier of buffalo meat to the Kansas-Pacific Railway, said to have killed 69 of the huge beasts in a single day, dashing young Cody personified romance, excitement, the unruly element that lies dormant in men, and craves to be set free. No one was more mesmerized by the idea of Bill Cody than Sidney Barnett, not quite

Thomas Barnett, proprietor of the Niagara Falls Museum, which has laid claim to being the oldest museum in North America. "Buffalo Bill" Cody, the partner of Barnett's son Sydney in the original Wild West Show, drove the museum into ruin and bankruptcy, then stole the idea. (Canadian Illustrated News, 8 June 1872)

TO VISITORS TO THE FALLS.

On your arrival at the Falls of Niagara, your first desire is to obtain

THE BEST & MOST COMPREHENSIVE VIEW OF THE CATARACT,

That you may take in at a glance the Sublimity of the whole, and be enabled to mark out the points you wish to visit in detail. *Such a View you will obtain by going at once to*

THE MUSEUM!

From the Observatory of which one of the most magnificent

PANORAMIC VIEWS

On the face of the earth is spread before the observer. If you wish to descend the Stairway below the Table Rock, and see the mighty rush of waters and the overhanging rocks,

Go to the Museum, and you can descend Free

You cannot spend your time to a better advantage than by a Visit to the Niagara Falls Museum, where you will see the Finest Collection on the Continent of America, consisting of *Twenty Thousand Specimens*, such as

BIRDS, ANIMALS, MINERALS,

Insects, Egyptian Antiquities, &c., &c.

Attached to this is the Beautiful Pleasure Garden, with its

FISH POND, Indian Wigwams, SUMMER HOUSES,

(always cool and pleasant). Living Animals, comprising

Buffalo, Wolves, Deer, Cranes, &c.&c.

The thousands of Visitors every year testify to its richness, variety, and beauty and to the fact that this is THE place of all others for spending a while delightfully, with pleasant memories ; and all for the low price of .25 cents.

THOS. BARNETT, *Proprietor.*

Niagara Falls, (C. W.) 1862.

---

30 when the Civil War ended, but already thoroughly domesticated, with a wife, a brood of daughters, a raft of debt and aging parents who depended on him in their declining years.

Recently retired as a Colonel in the militia, Barnett knew he could never be a Cody. He saw no reason, though, why he couldn't become an intimate friend of this colourful figure. If things worked out, he would be the enterprising Canadian promoter who would introduce this American hero in all his flamboyant but modest glory to the whole world.

Barnett opened his campaign in early 1869 with a letter to Cody, asking his advice and possible assistance in capturing some buffalo for a Grand Buffalo Hunt that he was planning to stage in Niagara Falls, Canada. He was deliriously happy to receive a short but extremely encouraging letter from Buffalo Bill in late March. The 23-year-old scout agreed to obtain the required animals. "It is a big job but it can be done," he wrote, "... money will do anything."

Barnett lost no time in informing the public that the famed frontiersman would soon be appearing in their midst, in a magnificent show devised and staged by Cody and Barnett, or perhaps, to retain alphabetical order, Barnett and Cody. Any day now he would be hearing from the picturesque American West that the animals were rounded up and awaiting his order to entrain for the East. Though he hadn't had the chance to discuss the whole extravaganza with his partner, as he liked to call Cody, he believed they should wait until the animals, Indians and cowboys were actually present in Canada's honeymoon capital before they finalized the details of the show. Meanwhile, he'd have to be patient.

It was only two years after Cody's phenomenal one-day slaughter of 69 animals had earned him the moniker "Buffalo Bill," so even if he'd kept up that pace, there must still be thousands of buffalo left. Of course, capturing them alive was different from shooting them dead, but if Bill was even half as expert as claimed, he must have some system for accomplishing this. Especially when he had a partner who was waiting to reward him handsomely for each and every one of the big, shaggy beasts, C.O.D. Niagara Falls, Ontario.

All that summer, Col Barnett waited.

Having resigned his original commission, he'd since become Colonel of the St. Catharine's 44th Regiment. He had enough problems with the museum, the rowdies and the various government agencies that would alternately buoy his hopes for financial assistance and firmer new leases, then, exasperatingly, sit on their hands for months. Cody's excuses for the non-delivery of the beasts from the big sky country was stretching his patience.

All the next summer, 1870, Barnett continued to wait in vain. By now, he had prudently stopped talking about the upcoming Big Show. There was a brief flurry of messages back and forth in 1871. Buffalo Bill, it seemed, hadn't realized there was haste involved. He and his sidekick, Texas Jack Omohundro, had tried a couple of times to lasso the beasts for which he expected $1,000 apiece, but without success. He was sorry if he'd wrecked the Colonel's plans, but as soon as Texas Jack passed Bill's way again, they'd surely get him as many buffs as he wanted.

By now, the Colonel had had enough of Bill's promises. The scout couldn't get it through his head that you didn't just ship a bunch of the beasts one day and put them on show the next. You had to advertise, or nobody would be there to see it. What Colonel Barnett needed was someone as famous, as great a drawing card, as colourful as Cody but with some sense of responsibility and showmanship. Someone like James Butler "Wild Bill" Hickock, perhaps. At 34, Hickock was earning enormous respect as an Indian fighter, frontier marshal and proven "Dead-Eye Dick" with his pearl-handled six-shooters and a rifle. Hickock had already responded to Barnett's requests, agreeing to be his Master of Ceremonies. Furthermore, he would supervise the roundup, engage some Indians and cowboys, see to the transportation and be at the Colonel's disposal for advice on the authenticity Barnett was stressing.

Col Barnett was eager to have an early summer show. Tourists were open to suggestion then, and more important, free with their money, after the long, dreary winter and the fickle, interminable spring. The grandstand facing the 80 acres near Falls View would hold almost 50,000 people. Barnett would need that many customers just to cover costs. He hoped that souvenirs, endorsements, sideshows and other sales items and commercial concessions would help recoup his own badly needed profit on the event.

To make sure nothing interfered again with his announced plans, Barnett headed west himself. He found that negotiations of the simplest kind on the home turf of the buffalo, with the men who shot or captured them for a living, were not as readily concluded as he felt they would have been back East. He wrote to his wife from Fort McPherson, Nebraska, on 1 June 1872:

> It takes time to accomplish anything in this country. I had expected to be all through my business here and be back home by at most or latest, the 3rd of June. But here I am, and likely to be for some little time yet … I have no doubt of the perfect success of the undertaking, but I must say at times my patience almost gives out and my courage sometimes weakens as I think of the magnitude of the enterprise. My anxious thoughts are respecting my dear family and my dear mother and father. Should I fail in this, the consequences would be fearful.

The next line is a surprise. Seemingly abandoning his vow not to rely any longer on Texas Jack or his pal, Bill Cody, he wrote a laconic, astonishing final morsel of news before he wished them all his kindest love:

> Omohundro came in yesterday morning and we at once proceeded to business. I expect we will be able to ship the buffalo in the course of five days and then it will take about ten days for the whole to arrive at Niagara Falls ... I go out with the men on the hunt and will not be back for several days.

A wildly erratic account of this hunt appeared in the Lincoln, Nebraska, *Daily State Journal* on 2 July 1872, under correspondent WD Wildman's byline.

> Buffalo, the wild cattle of Nebraska, are here in countless numbers. A gentleman from Saratoga, New York, came to Fort McPherson and hired three ... scouts to capture eight full-grown buffalo, to astonish Saratoga on the 4th of July at a grand celebration. Three gentleman known ... for their daring were chosen, *viz*, Dashing Charlie, Texas Jack and a man named Barrett (His initials my informant did not know ...) They started from Red Willow early ... on the 9th of June and ... before noon, the eight bulls were prisoners and loaded on wagons. The mode of capture was as follows: one would throw a lasso over the neck and follow with a slack rope until another could lasso the foot. Then they'd proceed to down the 'baste.' Texas Jack lassoed one ugly old bull ... but he turned short, caught the horse and pitched both of them into the gully. I was told the next morning seven of the eight died.

Barnett must have been promised that some new buffaloes would be rounded up and shipped to him as soon as possible, because he entrained for Niagara Falls shortly afterward. New snags were arising on all sides. The 100 or so Pawnee tribesmen Hickock expected to bring with him to add real-life dash and colour to the show, wouldn't be coming after all. The US Government flatly refused to permit this large a number of "hostiles" — well, actually any number for that matter — to leave the reserve to which they had been assigned. Once more, the Colonel could only gnash his teeth in rage as he had to announce another postponement of his extravaganza. Once more, Barnett headed west to now wearily familiar territory. What did it matter what kind of Indians could come, he demanded? And who cared if the *vaqueros* weren't authentic Mexicans, as long as Hickock was satisfied they could ride, shoot and rope? But the buffalo, the wild Texas steers, and everything else had better be authentic.

The world's first Wild West Show, after three unbelievably frustrating years in planning and rehearsals, was finally staged on 28 and 30 August 1872. Accounts of this unique spectacle differ widely. Most agreed the 50 Sac and Fox Indians, in war paint and bonnets, uttering bloodcurdling screams, were horrifyingly real. So were the Texas steers, lassoed by the dark-skinned cowboys, and the attacks of the mustang-mounted Indians on the huge buffaloes (using only blunted arrows, to comply with local by-laws). The tribal and war dances performed by the Indians were interesting; as was the demonstration of their ancient sport of *baggattaway*, meaning 'ball' in Ojibwa. A precursor of lacrosse, baggattaway is the oldest organized sport in North America, believed to have originated with the Algonquian tribes of the St Lawrence River Valley. This wild game was conducted under stern admonitions from Master of Ceremonies Hickock not to kill or maim opposing players.

The non-native portions of the program were the music provided throughout by the band of the 44th Regiment and, to give the combatants, animals and dust time to settle, several breathtaking exhibitions of tightrope-walking by a young Lundy's Lane daredevil who died shortly afterward trying to walk across Niagara Falls.

Wild Bill Hickock was everything Barnett and the spectators could have asked for. In command throughout, the epitome of a picturesquely garbed, flowing-maned frontier lawman, he loved his work and was proud to demonstrate it for *effete* Easterners who would never experience it themselves. That these effete Easterners could be quite as savage as any Indian soon became evident, however. The Toronto *Globe*'s front-page headline read:

THE BUFFALO HUNT, THE WHOLE THING A FARCE

The Toronto *Mail*'s story imitated its rival's approach with:

> About 1,500 people were present on the grounds.... But they were doomed to be disappointed ... a few Indians amused themselves playing lacrosse ... then seven Mexicans, headed by "Wild Bill" ... commenced chasing a poor steer who was quietly browsing and having succeeded in getting it to trot, it was lassoed and quickly thrown to the ground....

Only Sidney Barnett knew the real story. Because it was the end of August, tourists were more concerned with their kids getting back to school, so the potential audience was only a small local one. Costs had skyrocketed and concession receipts plummeted. The Barnetts lost $20,000 on the venture and faced bankruptcy. Five years later, unable to meet even basic taxes and expenses, they lost their beloved museum to Saul Davis. Davis did the unpardonable; moving it across the river to the US side. It was repatriated in 1958 by Jacob Sherman and operated by his grandson, also Jacob Sherman. Now bankrupt, Col Sydney Barnett was reduced to peddling Bibles in South America, where the time and place of his death went unrecorded. His daughter Julie, who went with him to the Amazon, died in the old Barnett mansion at Niagara Falls in the 1960s.

It was shortly after her death that Gauthier *dit* Landreville, a shirt-tail relative, came on the scene looking for Barnett books and papers. Long before this, the chief author of Barnett's misfortunes, Buffalo Bill Cody, was rolling in wealth from the more famous Wild West Show he staged worldwide for 20 years. With the proceeds he would buy land in the western States and create the town of Cody, Wyoming. There is little doubt that he got the idea for a hoked-up Wild West entertainment from Sidney Barnett's effort to put on an authentic show — which could have succeeded if the faithless scout had kept even part of his promise.

I was alerted to the colourful, tragic epic of the Barnett Family by a short squib in the September 1970 *Canadian Magazine*, a Saturday supplement of the *Toronto Star*. The story, by Toronto writer Peter Moon, was entitled "Buffalo Bill Blew It," and sub-headed "And Wild Bill Hickock didn't do much better." As illustrations, the article had a studio photograph of three men, Wild Bill, Texas Jack and Buffalo Bill, along with a huge poster advertising the Grand Buffalo Hunt at Niagara Falls, cutlined "the buffaloes captured for this purpose near the foot of the Rocky Mountains."

Sensing the wealth of documents I might obtain from this absorbing human drama, which would eventually cover a whopping 7½ feet of Archives wall space, I contacted writer Moon. From him, I extracted the names of a preliminary cast of fascinating characters I hoped might in turn lead to the Barnetts. The central figure in the case was a short, swarthy Métis named Gauthier *dit* Landreville, proprietor of the Author's Shop in Winnipeg.

Though hardcover books were the backbone of his business, Landreville traveled widely, with an eye always open for posters, letters, broadsides and other published material to sell to collectors. While he was away, a succession of lady friends minded the bookshop.

The poster advertising the hunt led Landreville to a pile of old letters in the Barnett mansion at Niagara Falls, from which he deduced that Sidney Barnett had deliberately and callously been taken for a ride by Cody and Texas Jack Omohundro. All the delays, postponements and frustrations, Landreville believed, could have been avoided. It was only when Hickock entered the picture and realized what was going on, that Barnett's authentically intended Grand Buffalo Hunt, fiasco though it turned out to be, was staged at all. Hickock got his fee out of it, and left his saddle, which is still in the museum, but it was Cody who saw what a gold mine a Wild West Show could be, resulting in his riches and today's Rodeos, Round-ups and Stampedes.

An interview with Ernie Rentz, a London, Ontario, dealer in rare books and other printed matter, yielded a few more scraps of information. "*Dit* loves books. He positively glows when he shows you prize items, but he has no fixed prices for them," Rentz told me. "If rent time is near, he'll let items go for a fraction of their value. He sold me a $100 book about the Battle of Jutland, for only $4."

Convinced now, for many reasons, that Landreville was a man I could warm to, I looked forward to meeting him. Scheduled to be in Winnipeg to attend the three-day Canadian Fur Trade Conference on 30 September 1970, however, I learned to my horror and dismay that Landreville had just committed suicide, by hanging himself!

"Got on the phone to Mr de Landreville's sister at noon today and set up an appointment with her for this evening," reads my notebook entry from my first day in Winnipeg. "I also spoke to the Winnipeg Police Department and arranged to see the officer in charge of the case...." On 3 October, I spent part of the afternoon at the police station going over their file on Landreville. It had been rumoured that Landreville had hanged himself because his partner and companion, Marilyn Bartalette, had sold his Riel Diary, which he valued at $25,000, for a mere $1,000, but the police record revealed that she was in the clear as far as having taken any of his manuscripts. The police also discovered she had power of attorney to sell books and manuscripts on his behalf.

I spent considerable time locating Marilyn Bartalette, and after a day spent at her house discussing the sad fate of de Landreville, I took her out to dinner. She said she had sold most of her Barnett items, including five posters for the Wild West Show, pictures of Buffalo Bill and Wild Bill Hickock, letters about the Fenian Raids, and others of Col Barnett's letters. Ms Bartalette said she would get in touch with the buyers of these items to see if they would sell them back to us or provide copies. But she never followed through on her promise.

Marilyn was evasive about the location of the Barnett papers, but did inadvertently let slip that they might be with a bank on Portage Avenue. Armed with this bit of information, I visited all the banks on Portage. I finally found the papers at the Banque Canadienne Nationale, where they were being held as security for a loan. We negotiated their acquisition for the Ontario Archives. The cost was $400, about half what de Landreville owed the bank.

Further conversation with the manager revealed that de Landreville had more papers with the BCN on Bay Street in Toronto. Marilyn told me that her partner had obtained a small collection of papers taken from Louis Riel after his capture in 1885. Back in Toronto, I visited the bank on Bay Street and persuaded the manager to add the papers in de Landreville's safety deposit box to those I had obtained in Winnipeg. Marilyn's earlier comments proved correct: there were indeed Louis Riel papers — a small but valuable collection.

Back in Winnipeg five years later, I got a line on more Barnett papers with a Métis relative of de Landreville, so the search was still on. Though the main events of the lives of two people, Sidney Barnett and Gauthier *dit* Landreville, were fairly clear, I had a feeling of incompleteness, dissatisfaction, of something lacking. I strongly sensed that more papers, casting new lights on some aspects of the lives of these two deceased Canadians, would undoubtedly turn up in the future.

I never totally wind up any search; my memory can usually recreate the salient factors in any case, what made it worth the Ontario Archives' time, the human foibles or heroics it illustrated, and where the descendents of the people in question are now living. I grieve for Sidney Barnett. Striving for perfection, he was betrayed by individuals for whom he'd had only the highest regard. His letters reveal discouragement and defeat, telling all too graphically how he ended his days, peddling Spanish and Portuguese Bibles to South American peasants.

As for Landreville, it is tragic to contemplate the horrible death of this complex, fascinating personality who loved books so passionately that he glowed when he talked of them. If I'd met him in Toronto, would things have ended differently?

Another unsolved puzzle!

CHAPTER SEVEN
CANAL BUILDERS

In the 1880s, my grandfather, William J Pearson, had several men with teams of heavy horses and scrapers moving earth as a small sub-contractor on the building of the Trent Canal from Lake Ontario to Georgian Bay. Jim Angus, in his book *The Incredible Ditch,* tells of this longest running public works project in Canadian history, begun in the 1830s and still being worked on in the 1920s. Stories my grandfather told me of those days sparked my first interest in canals, which have played a much larger part in the development of Canada than our landlubbing population would ever imagine.

From modest little Canal Flats in British Columbia, dug in the last century to connect Columbia Lake with the Kootenay River, to Nova Scotia's St Peter's Canal, which joins the beautiful Bras d'Or Lakes and the broad Atlantic, Canada is furrowed by man-made waterways of all sizes and purposes. Most were built by public bodies to correct problems Mother Nature created when she was laying out the general contours of the country. Examples of this are Ontario's Welland Canal, constructed to bypass the mighty Niagara Falls, and St Andrew's Lock at Selkirk, Manitoba, meant to tame the rapids of the Red River.

Ontario's Rideau Canal was built by British army engineers as a backdoor supply line between Montreal and Kingston, detouring around the main St Lawrence River route, which is adjacent to an occasionally belligerent United States for most of the way. The Trent Canal, almost 100 years in the completion, simply connected a number of isolated pioneer settlements with each other and the outside world. A considerable number of the country's canals were made redundant by the arrival of railways and passable roads. Others, like the St. Lawrence Seaway, provided an alternative — complementary and often much cheaper — mode of transporting cargoes to and from the heart of the continent.

Certain canals have been advocated to expedite commerce. Millions, perhaps billions of dollars are just waiting to be spent by private industry digging a ditch across the Isthmus of Chignecto, connecting Nova Scotia to New Brunswick, if and when governments decide the time is politically ripe. An ironclad assurance that Fundy's mammoth high tides won't inundate Prince Edward Island in the process would be needed.

Among the many and varied reasons for wanting a canal to be built, none has been quite as imaginative and breath-taking in its scope as that of Narcisse Maxime Cantin (1870–1940), a direct descendent of the 17th-century French shipbuilder, Nicholas Cantin, whose family name is sometimes spelled 'Quentin.'

I came to hear about this French-Canadian visionary, entrepreneur and organizing genius in 1966, in a roundabout way. It all started while I was on a field trip to the USA. I spent two days in Boston renewing contact with an old friend, Professor Charles Dunn, head of the graduate school of Celtic Studies at Harvard University. I was bringing him up to date on my manuscript recovery operation when he gave me several good leads. One resulted in his putting me in touch with Jim Scott, writer, political organizer and former head of public relations for a large Ontario brewery. Scott was one of Dunn's Canadian friends who had gone to Harvard with him years before.

Several months later, I made contact with Jim Scott in Seaforth, Huron County, Ontario. He gave me some more leads. The most promising was about the French-Canadian entrepreneur Narcisse Cantin, born 1870 in the tiny hamlet of French Settlement, Parish of St-Pierre-aux-Bouleaux on the broad, open shore of Lake Huron south of Goderich, Ontario. His family had been driven out of Joliette, Quebec, in 1846, by bad harvests, poor land and a dearth of good jobs. Many other Quebecois were leaving for New England, but the Cantins chose Lake Huron's shore because of glowing reports from ex-voyageurs of fertile soil, a pleasant climate and a great big lake that was "lousy with fish."

The family bought land from the Canada Company at about $3 an acre. Though they planted wheat and what vegetable seeds they could obtain, it was years before they climbed out of their near-starvation existence. Often the only food they had was berries, nuts, roots, groundhogs and whatever fish they could catch. If they had anything to sell for cash, it meant a walk of many miles to Goderich, Seaforth or even London. The scarcity of food meant they had to work in all weather, even in dangerously high winds that could snap off the ice floes on which the fishermen plied their nets. In one incident, three men and their dog spent four days and nights on a floe, suffering exposure and frozen feet. Finally, the wind drove their free-floating shelf of ice ashore near Grand Bend, where an Indian family took them in and looked after them.

By the late 1880s, when Narcisse Cantin was out of elementary school (his only formal education) and growing into muscular manhood, living was becoming easier. He did his share of the farm work, but knew this lifestyle was not for him. At 17, he began buying cattle from the neighbours and shipping them via Hensall, the nearest railway point, to Buffalo, New York, the largest and most prosperous city in the border region. To accommodate local markets, he also opened an abattoir.

At 19, Cantin married Josephine Dénommée, the daughter of a neighbouring farmer. He moved his bride and his centre of operations across the border to Buffalo, the bustling terminus of the Erie Canal, which connected the Great Lakes with the Hudson River and thence to the Atlantic Ocean. Here he spent the next seven years, and came into his entrepreneurial own. He vastly expanded his cattle business, became an agent for all sorts of American products in Canada, and turned his keen mind to marketable inventions. Among these were a type of glue he sold as Instant Crockery Mender and a liquid furniture polish, a remarkable achievement for someone with only basic education and an incomplete command of English.

"He made friends easily, however" Scott told me. "And because of his size and muscularity, he became a sparring partner of the great bare-knuckles fighter, world heavyweight champion John L Sullivan, whenever the Boston Strong Boy was in Buffalo. As you can imagine, this didn't hurt his popularity among the city's best people."

It was in Buffalo that Narcisse Cantin first envisioned a deep-water canal system to accommodate the world's largest ships, running from the head of the Great Lakes to the Atlantic Ocean. The vision exploded in his brain with a thunderclap. It overwhelmed and dominated his life from then to his death. He would pay for his canal by selling the incredible amounts of electric power to be extracted from the 580-foot drop of the world's largest volume of fresh water, between Lake Superior and the St Lawrence. It would make Eastern Canada and the northern USA the greatest industrial area on earth, and revolutionize the lives of the region's inhabitants.

With Cantin's drive and salesmanship, and the financial resources of two rich nations, the dream might have become a reality back then. It would have brought a big chunk of prosperity for his own people, the displaced, semi-literate Quebec *habitants* who had given up 200 years of close kinship among people like themselves to start a new life in an alien Anglo environment. They needed a big new boost if they were ever to succeed. To this end, Narcisse Cantin proposed that a full-sized canal should be built from a spot near Port Stanley on Lake Erie to Lake Huron, not far from his birthplace. This plan would cut 150 miles off the journey, though it would probably be unpopular in Windsor, Detroit, Sarnia, Toledo, Sandusky and Port Huron.

At the Lake Huron end, he would create a city to be called St Joseph, in honour of his patron saint. He would construct a harbour for his new metropolis out of concrete and steel. As the western terminus of the mammoth transportation and electrical power grid, St Joseph would attract its own industries, provide well-paying work for Cantin's compatriots, and would rival Toronto and Buffalo as centres of commerce and culture.

"Nobody on God's green earth could ever accuse Narcisse Cantin of thinking small!" said Jim Scott with a grin, continuing his account of the life and work of his energetic fellow Huron County native.

Cantin began promoting his idea of a deep-water canal system among influential Buffalo businessmen, even knowing that a powerful US bloc led by the railroads, the coal mines and private power companies, bitterly opposed any such project. Nothing daunted, Cantin kept pitching the tremendous power output currently going to waste which, once tamed, would go on forever, making fabulous profits for men smart enough to see the possibilities. As for the waterway, another gold mine, his plan envisaged the need for only 14 locks, from the head of the Great Lakes to the Atlantic.

"Amazingly, the St. Lawrence Seaway as we know it today, has 16 locks to cover this same distance," Scott marveled. "This largely self-educated French-Canadian youth figured the whole thing out more than 60 years earlier, and did his damndest to bring it to fruition."

Cantin, more of a nationalist than he might seem, had argued for an all-Canadian power grid and seaway, fearing that if it were shared with the USA, the far more aggressive and ruthless Yankee approach to business would eventually lead to them taking over. US investors, yes, and glad to have them, glad to pay them all the dividends accruing to them, but US partners, no, except perhaps for the interests moving the great American Mesabi iron and Canada's grain harvests to market.

Though still nowhere within sight of the financial backing required, or Canadian permission to start construction, Narcisse Cantin put phase one of his plan into motion in 1896. He bought the plans for a village called Lakeview, which had been registered in Goderich away back in 1857. Lakeview had been surveyed, divided into residential lots, commercial properties and common recreational grounds. This 26-year-old dreamer then bought up all the real estate in Lakeview and all the land for a considerable distance around. He changed the name to St Joseph, which the village is still called today.

As part of his plan, he said, he would be repatriating French-Canadians from his home area who had found life too difficult in Canada and were now making more money but living miserably and without soul in Chicago. To accommodate them, he immediately began promoting new industries in St Joseph: a sawmill using logs which had to be floated to St Joe's from far up Lake Huron, a small brick and tile yard, followed immediately by a second, much bigger one, a pipe-organ factory, and a winery. Not everyone was pleased with his progress. Many who wished they had bought up land, or neighboring communities that expected to be cut out of profits, were caustic in their criticisms.

The London *Free Press* published an editorial on Cantin in September 1897: "A few are trying to injure this gentleman in his large undertaking. Indeed, the smaller merchants in the villages adjacent are leaving no stone unturned to injure a man who is alive — so far at least as business ability is concerned — while they are sleeping."

Development of a real estate empire was not Cantin's main aim, though. It was only a means to fulfilling his dream. "It is rather a drum to beat upon," he explained, "so that I might draw attention to my Great Lakes and the Ocean Waterway project." In 1898 Cantin made his first application to Ottawa for a charter for his Huron and Erie Canal Company to run from St Joseph, "that hive of industrial activity," to a point on Lake Erie between Port Talbot and Port Stanley. He had explained the project to federal engineers and they had agreed it was both possible and feasible, but he was turned down. Again in 1902 and 1903 he pressed Ottawa for the needed charter. Each time the bill to incorporate his company received first and second readings in both Commons and Senate, but was withdrawn prior to the final reading and never got to the vote.

Still optimistic, loath to burn bridges to possible future backers, he only spoke darkly of "the opposition of large capitalists to any scheme, however profit-producing on a vast scale, which rested in the hands of others." There was no slackening in his promotion of St Joseph as a western metropolis and his canal as "the hub of North America" despite Ottawa's discouraging response. During the years 1897–1907, Cantin constructed a three-storey hotel covering an entire city block of downtown St Joseph. He became a good friend of Brother André (Alfred Bessette), of the world famous Mount Royal Oratory in Montreal. Brother André marked a place in the St Joseph Memorial Park, for a statue honouring St Joseph. It was erected there in 1972, along with a Provincial plaque honouring Narcisse Cantin.

Though he couldn't persuade Parliament to grant his charter, Cantin managed by strenuous lobbying over a six-year period, to get them to make a tiny start on a harbour for St Joseph by allocating $15,000 for a government wharf. The first wooden structure was washed away by autumn storms, but by 1907 a stone replacement was actually in operation, despite a local weekly paper's ill-natured comment that "St Joseph needs a harbour as badly as a goose needs side pockets." Narcisse could wine and dine potential financial partners in either the still unopened New Balmoral Hotel or at his own spacious home. Now if they desired, he could take them deep-lake fishing and be certain of a safe place to land them with their catch. They could even have their pictures taken there, with the hotel, houses and business establishments of St Joseph in the background, proof positive that there actually was a new town taking shape on Huron's shore.

In 1904, Cantin made yet another request for a charter. When this one died too, he appealed personally to Prime Minister Wilfrid Laurier and was advised that nothing could be done on such a vast scheme until "another government proposal" had been ratified.

This other proposal, Cantin learned to his baffled dismay, was the completion of the Inter-Colonial Railway. Like most Canadians, he believed the ICR had been declared complete in 1891, when the Cape Breton Railway's last spike bit into a creosoted tie. Cantin wasn't asking the government for money, only a piece of paper giving him the right to start digging.

He finally did get his charter on May 30, 1914, for plans for all the required canals, stipulating standard depths of 35 feet and widths of 400 feet. Today's Seaway is 27 feet deep, and, in recent years, increasing it to 35 feet has often been suggested. During the summer of 1914, Cantin was tooling up to amass the required $500 million. But in August, war broke out and men and money rushed to the colours. Though he kept on trying, he and his company were unable to make any headway over the next four years.

The opening of the Panama Canal in 1917 gave him opportunity for a short flurry of publicity, when he declared his ditch would be much easier to construct. "They had very difficult grades to overcome," he said. "We don't." In the 1920s, Cantin saw that a whole new ballgame was in progress. Interest in the waterway aspect of his own development plans was on the back burner. Up front was a growing realization that the water power potential of the part of the proposed seaway closest to Montreal was the prize to be won.

The organization to grab the lion's share of this wealth would not necessarily be the one with the best, cheapest, environmentally safest or publicly beneficial method of extracting the power. All these skills could be bought, rented or counterfeited. The outfit exiting with the mazuma when the dust settled would be the daring, lucky, opportunistic, financially street-smart folks who knew how to stickhandle through the seamy, multilayered morass of Canadian politics. Cantin had been a *naïf* to think that just having logic on your side was enough. As a lower-class French Catholic promoting a thinly populated part of Protestant Ontario with Yankee money, he was seen as an embarrassment, a joke, a liability to any party, not the popular public figure he'd pictured himself.

Cantin tried his best to join the big-money bettors in what he could legitimately characterize as "the only game in town." His bid to have his new Great Lakes and Atlantic Canal and Power Company win the existing rights and properties would necessitate construction of a mammoth generating plant at Beauharnois, on the site where Quebec Hydro's 2.2 million horsepower plant now stands. Unfortunately, it involved him, even if only peripherally, in the sordid and now infamous Beauharnois Scandal of 1931–32. One of the biggest political embarrassments in Canadian history, it included under-the-table deals and huge payments to Ontario premiers and Canadian prime ministers, among others. Narcisse Cantin's major error in judgment was in employing a respected Quebecker named Robert Oliver Sweezey, as his chief engineer and instructing him to do what was necessary to "get the Beauharnois ball rolling." When success was in sight, the two men clashed. In late 1926, Sweezey tendered his resignation. Cantin refused to accept it, but Sweezey located new backers and obtained the permits and finances for completing the Beauharnois job, with himself as the company president. Cantin sued, claiming Sweezey had done all his research and financial calculations as a Cantin employee, so the permits for the huge generating station should belong to him. Narcisse Cantin won some preliminary bouts but, probably because the hidebound federal bureaucracy had always considered him a joke, he lost the main battle.

Some four years later, when the Beauharnois Scandal broke, Cantin and his Toronto lawyer, Frank Regan, supplied opposition politicians with all the ammunition they needed to crucify the principals in the case, among them — sweet revenge — Bob Sweezey.

In the 1970s, I tracked down many of Robert Sweezey's papers. The tip came from one of my entrepreneurial friends, Hugh Fitzpatrick, who was trying to buy Sweezey's old mansion near Kingston, Ontario. The papers were with a daughter in Montreal. It is another example of getting on a roll for a certain type of papers and more of the same falling my way.

Unfortunately, because both major political parties desperately desired to keep the public mind off the nasty ways politicians raise money, perjure themselves at the drop of a silk topper and skewer innocent protesters at will, Cantin received neither credit nor gratitude for helping them to "clean house at Beauharnois."

Cantin's planned community, St Joseph, decades ahead of its time in concept and development, had been demolished in the early 1920s, and when he died in 1940 his company was broke. Known at the end as the Transportation and Power Corporation, it was sold in bankruptcy court for a mere $15,000 to the Beauharnois Light, Heat and Power Company. As with other personalities of interest to Ontario Archives, once famous or infamous but now no longer in the public eye, Narcisse Cantin aroused my compassion and feeling of shame at the shabby way he'd been treated by a WASP-dominated society.

Cantin's major problem was that he was a passionate man who believed in what he was doing, whether it was selling beef or charting the future of a continent. Sadly for him and the continent, we would have to wait a lifetime to obtain the benefits he was proposing in the 1890s. He was dealing with bloodless, two-dimensional civil servants and businessmen whose idea of triumph was acceptance for membership into an exclusive club or causing a stock market issue to rise.

I was looking forward to meeting members of Cantin's family, sons and daughters who would be in their 70s by then, or perhaps a grandson. Jim Scott hadn't known which member of the family was currently in possession of the family papers. Checking through other Ontario Government files, I learned that papers in the possession of Napoleon E Cantin, of Royal Oak, Michigan, had been the source of a long essay on the history of French Canadian settlement in Huron County. The bound essay, titled *A Drum to Beat Upon: the story of St Joseph, Ontario, the city that never was on the shores of Lake Huron and Narcisse Cantin, the Wizard of St Joseph* was published in 1958 by Joseph L Wooden, of Exeter, Ontario. The same material was consulted in the preparation of a 1964 Master's thesis on the life and activities of Narcisse Cantin by Derek Blackburn, of the University of Western Ontario. Bibliographies appended to these two works revealed that the papers consisted mainly of:

- drafts for promotional articles and propaganda
- drafts of reports to various boards of directors with whom Cantin worked
- published reports and other informational or promotional material relating to water power and navigation schemes in North America

- maps, blueprints, proposals, plans, atlases
- commercial records relating to St Joseph, the Huron-Erie Canal, Beauharnois
- a large volume of newspaper clippings.

A memo appended to the list of papers notes that "Much of the material is written or published in French, since Cantin was French-Canadian and worked for much of his life in Montreal. The major portion of the collection was undoubtedly accumulated by Cantin as evidence for his court battles against Sweezey, Beauharnois Light, Heat and Power Co Ltd., and Beauharnois Power Corp."

Knowing where most of the Cantin papers were and who was in charge of them, I was optimistic about acquiring them for Ontario Archives, assuming it would be a relatively simple, speedy business transaction. Here is the actual timetable:

September 13, 1966 I arrived at Royal Oak and spent some time talking with Napoleon Cantin, grandson of Narcisse. Massive like his grandfather, Napoleon was in the construction business with several brothers. The collection of his grandfather's papers would run to 44 linear feet, somewhat larger than most other exhibits in the Ontario Archives. Much of it would be controversial, as it involved the Beauharnois Scandal.

Napoleon Cantin said he would consider giving us the collection if he could have copies of certain parts to keep for his family. He would also like our department to place a plaque to his grandfather at St Joseph.

February 23, 1967 I contacted Napoleon Cantin again about the papers. He was undecided whether to send the material to me in Toronto or send it first to his cottage in St Joseph. Apparently some group there wanted to memorialize his grandfather in some way. He finally agreed to have me pick up the collection on my next trip to Windsor and bring it back to the Archives to be organized and have an inventory compiled.

May 3, 1967 I drove to Windsor and phoned Cantin about picking up the papers but, since talking to him the previous day, he had a change of plans and had to go to a meeting that night, so was unable to sort the papers and put them in the station wagon.

September 22, 1967 I went back to see Mr. Cantin and arranged to pick up the papers in November but that, too, was postponed.

January 12, 1968 I spoke to Mr. Cantin about the papers again. He said he had been sorting out all the duplicate items and suggested I wait till March, when he would be finished.

Studio portrait of Narcisse Maxime Cantin (1870–1940). Cantin was a sparring partner of the bare-knuckled world heavyweight champion boxer John L Sullivan. He was also the inventor of crockery glue and liquid furniture polish, visionary, and almost builder of the St Lawrence Seaway.

Oil portrait of Nicol Hugh Baird (1796–1849), scion of a well known Scottish family of engineers and canal-builders. As Clerk of the Works on the Rideau Canal, Baird was responsible for completing the canal under arduous conditions. He was involved in a number of other transportation projects in North America. He died in Brattleboro, Vermont, while working on a railway. (Portrait now in the National Portrait Gallery)

May 31, 1968 I contacted the Cantin home in Michigan. Napoleon had to go to Canada and his son said to call before I went to Windsor next time and he would have the papers ready.

December 20, 1968 I drove to see Napoleon Cantin. He had nearly completed sorting this large collection. He said he expected to be done some time in February.

February 28, 1969 I called Cantin and found that since talking to him he had lent part of his collection to someone doing research in New York State. The material was to have been returned in February as he knew I'd be in touch with him in March, but it had still not been returned. He suggested I wait until he called me after he had the material back, and I could then go and pick up the entire collection.

August 8, 1969 I met Cantin and he agreed to turn over the collection to us in October.

November 5, 1969 I called Cantin in Detroit, prepared to go and pick up the papers but his wife informed me that he had just got out of the hospital after a bout of hepatitis and I would have to wait until later that year or early January to bring back the collection.

March 16, 1971 I drove to Detroit, called Cantin, who said he would see me the following day about his grandfather's papers. It appeared that after four years of delays he was actually going to turn over the papers.

March 17, 1971 I went to Cantin's home in the morning. We spent the day sorting and packing papers. I loaded all I could in my car and finally made arrangements for a truck to come later and pick up the balance, which filled 14 cartons. I took the Cantins to dinner, then drove through to London. I had some problems with Canadian Customs regarding the manuscripts but after a two-hour discussion we settled on dealing with the manuscripts as antiques.

By 1972 the following historic plaque was erected at St Joseph, Huron County by the Archaeological and Historic Sites Board, Department of Public Records and Archives of Ontario:

NARCISSE CANTIN
1870–1940

Descended from a long line of French-Canadian shipbuilders, Cantin was born on a nearby farm, which his grandfather acquired about 1850. An energetic entrepreneur, inventor and cattle trader, Cantin began work here in 1897 on a city named St Joseph from which he hoped to construct a canal linking Lake Huron and Erie. Undaunted by his inability to raise sufficient funds for this project, he initiated and, between 1900 and 1930, tirelessly promoted the concept of a Great Lakes seaway system which would take passengers and freight from all ocean ports on the globe direct to all the principal ports of the Great Lakes.

Contrary to the inscription on the official plaque, it was not an inability to raise money that killed Cantin's canal project but his inability to persuade Parliament. to grant him a charter.

March 1, 1974 I drove to St Joseph and contacted an aunt of Napoleon Cantin about some more Cantin papers to add to the large collection I had picked up in Detroit. Mrs. Cantin wanted her sister to look over the collection before she turned it over to us.

August 9, 1974 I drove back to St Joseph and went through the 14 cases of Cantin papers which had been separated from the main collection of manuscripts and the entire Cantin collection came finally into the safety of Ontario Archives. Persistence does pay off!

Though he didn't achieve his dream and never built a canal, Narcisse Cantin was indeed the Father of the St Lawrence Seaway.

Nicol Hugh Baird (1796–1849), a noted civil engineer in Canada from 1828 until his death, had been more successful though much less heralded. On Baird's shoulders fell the massive challenge of completing the building of the Rideau Canal. He took up tasks originally carried out by the first Clerk of Works, John MacTaggart.

Baird came to my attention in January 1968, four years after I began looking for historical papers. Hearing me talk in a television interview about preserving historical papers, a perceptive viewer put me in touch with Mrs Jennie Foley, wife of a grandson of Baird. This was a stroke of good fortune. Mrs Foley, her son Michael, cousin Cynthia Bunnell and other relatives had most of Baird's business and personal papers, which I examined in great detail. After protracted negotiations, I secured the Baird papers for the Archives.

Some time later, I was contacted by Arthur Dunn, an Ottawa engineer who was searching for papers about Baird for Donald Braid, a friend in England and great admirer of Baird's engineering ability. Braid wanted to do a monograph on Baird, so I worked with him and Arthur Dunn on a detailed account of this man's amazing achievements.

Baird worked on the canal for four years and saw its completion under Lieutenant-Colonel John By, who had been responsible for it from its start in the early summer of 1826. The story of John By and his vital part in the building of the Rideau Canal is well documented, but Baird has received little mention in recent times.

Nicol Hugh Baird's important part in the Rideau project was recognized in January 1831 when he was admitted as "corresponding member Nicol Hugh Baird, Civil Engineer at Rideau Canal, Bytown, Upper Canada," by the Council of the Institution of Civil Engineers. His original application form is still preserved at the Council's headquarters in Great George Street, Westminster, London. His sponsor was the first president of the Institution, Thomas Telford, himself renowned in Britain for his work on the Highland Roads, the Caledonian Canal, the Holyhead Road, the remarkable cast iron aqueduct that carries the canal across the Vale of Llangollen (127 feet high at Pont Cysyllte), and other fine works.

Telford had sponsored the younger Baird for the job of Clerk of Works on the Rideau Canal in 1828. He had long been familiar with Baird and his famous Scottish engineering family. The Bairds were also associated with the Forth-Clyde Canal. The connecting link between the Forth-Clyde and the city of Edinburgh was surveyed by Thomas Telford and built between 1813 and 1821. Baird's father acted as engineer for the enterprise.

Nicol Hugh Baird was born into this family in Glasgow on August 26, 1796, the eldest son of Hugh Baird and Margaret Burnthwaite. He was given a good sound education, similar to his famous uncles. One of these, Charles Baird, went to Russia, becoming an engineer in St Petersburg. It is understood that Nicol also worked for a time in Russia, that being a usual family experience. It is also known that Nicol worked with his father, Hugh, on the Glasgow Union Canal, having entered the family profession of civil engineer in 1816 at the age of 20.

In 1827 and early 1828, John MacTaggart had health problems in Bytown, Upper Canada (now Ottawa, Ontario). He is known to have suffered from malaria and was suspected of drunkenness. Whatever the true cause, he was a very sick man, and was unable to carry out his duties. The engineers and surveyors on Baird's team spoke well of MacTaggart, as can be seen clearly from their reports in the Baird papers I was able to secure for the Ontario Archives. MacTaggart had been recommended by another engineer and fellow Scot, John Rennie, for whom he had once worked.

On this occasion, it was Thomas Telford who was asked for his recommendation and Nicol Hugh Baird arrived in Bytown.

Just how harsh and dangerous life was in Upper Canada can only be imagined. The whole area was still almost primæval forest except for small, scattered settlements where land grants were still being slowly cleared by discharged veterans and British immigrants who were encouraged to make their homes there after the 1814 peace. The military authorities were responsible for laying out new townships close to proposed military roads. Clearings did not penetrate far into forests where travel was difficult. The settlers depended mainly on rivers for transport. Unless roads were of strategic military importance, they were virtually nonexistent. Occasionally wagon tracks were upgraded to local roads for site development in a few places where capital and manpower were not in short supply.

Mosquitoes were a curse. These voracious flying insects attacked everyone journeying in the region. Female mosquitoes need 1–4 millilitres of blood to mature their eggs. The common Anopheles mosquitoes were normally merely irritating creatures found in all similar environments from Canada to Siberia. But when humans with malaria arrived in a district, the bites suddenly became dangerous. The mosquitoes spread malaria from person to person.

In Upper Canada, occasional settlers carrying malarial infection may have moved up from seriously affected areas of Virginia, but more likely sources were troops transferred from the West Indies or India. Many workers and settlers along the canal site sickened or died from malaria, which they knew as 'ague' or swamp fever. MacTaggart's book, *Three Years in Canada*, gives a firsthand account of malaria along the Rideau.

Baird arrived in August 1828 and by May 21, 1830, John MacTaggart obtained a doctor's certificate that his malaria attacks were of such severity that a "change of air" was indicated. (*Malaria*, Italian for 'bad air,' was believed to be caused by noxious emanations of swamp gas.) Amongst the Baird papers are notes and correspondence about the indications for and dose of laudanum drops, a tincture of opium, used to relieve the paroxysms of ague. As MacTaggart became more disabled by malaria, he returned to Scotland, where he died a few years later.

Even without malaria, mosquitoes and flies were a torment to those living in the rough, often chilled by rain-soaked clothes, eating hardtack washed down with lakewater fouled by nearby latrines, and avid for the all too available but fleeting comfort of whisky.

The magnitude of the work on the Rideau is obvious to all who have seen the canal, even if only in pictures. It is difficult to appreciate that it was built by manual effort. Power equipment did not exist, and the most sophisticated labour-saving devices were derricks made of wood, operated by hand winches. Gunpowder was used for blasting, stuffed into holes bored into the rocks with hand-operated bits. Without roads to reach their sites, the workmen depended on boats to shift their tools and supplies to the nearest landing, then hacked a trail through scrub and undergrowth for rough horse-drawn sledges.

As Clerk of Works for the last four years of the undertaking, Nicol Hugh Baird had the difficult task of balancing the demands of contractors and directing workers, and settling how much each should be paid. He had to sign off on the amount of work completed, certify that it met the agreed standard, and instruct the office at Bytown for their payment. There were often disagreements over what had been originally accepted as a contract and what constituted extras that became necessary in the course of the work owing to unforeseen circumstances. Local landowners with dams to work their grist mills or with riverbank property were always quick to complain that their livelihood had suffered and to demand compensation for loss of water or, more frequently, for flooding.

Canada is exceptionally fortunate that Baird kept considerable amounts of his paperwork and, even more so, that later members of the family preserved them. This important archival material was donated to the Ontario Archives in 1968. It is remarkable that it had survived from the time of his death in 1849, nearly 120 years.

I was also able to acquire copies of many of Baird's drawings of the canal, which show the immense amount of detail and measurements that he had to handle. This is clearly illustrated in the diaries and field notebooks, many prepared on his site inspections between August 1828 and August 1832. Numerous small personal accounts record how people lived in those days, what things cost, and the daily lives of these Canadian pioneers.

Although the Rideau was built as a military canal, paid for by the British government, and under the charge of Lt-Col John By of the Royal Corps of Engineers, it was ultimately dependent on Canadian labour, under the leadership of contractors. Contractor for the first flight of locks was Thomas McKay, a partner in McKay, Redpath, Phillips and White. Andrew White and Thomas Phillips of Montreal were partners contracting for the first sector from Kingston to the Ottawa River and for the work at Black Rapids and Long Island.

As the Rideau Canal was nearing completion, political discontent arose in Britain over the cost of this tremendous waterway running across 123 miles of godforsaken Upper Canadian wilderness. A look back year by year at the rising complexity and cost of the project more or less explains the discontent of English voters.

Much had changed since the initial simple project of improving the transport of men and materials from the Lachine Rapids near Montreal to Kingston. This task, so vital to the defence of Canada, had required the use of bateaux and overland transport at a number of points along the St Lawrence River, particularly at two 9-mile-long rapids. Stores were portaged over these stretches by oxcart, so the lightened boats could be poled through the rough water. It took 11 to 14 days to deliver stores to Kingston. Every week from Lachine, two hundred bateaux, 40 feet long by 6 feet wide with 20 inch draught, were brought upriver. Ten thousand men, including 3,500 bateauxmen, had to be recruited, and the Ordnance Office tripled its expenditure in three years. The demand had reached the limit of local sources of labour, so further expansion was virtually impossible.

In September, 1824, Samuel Clowes was appointed to report to the legislature of Upper Canada on the feasibility and cost of building a number of canals in the region. His obviously cursory and only preliminary estimate of costs created difficulties because his figures for the Rideau were later treated as firm and reliable, proving to be both stupid and disastrous assumptions. Cost overruns based on his estimates resulted from difficult construction problems and the expenses of excavating in hard rock. Anything from 200% to 300% overruns became common.

In 1825, the Duke of Wellington, then the United Kingdom's Master General of Ordnance, dispatched a Commission of Royal Engineers to report on the defence of Canada and vital communications and fortifications. The Rideau scheme was deemed at that time to be critically important to the defence of Canada and was to be the first phase of construction.

The heavy work of charting the wilderness started with MacTaggart's November 1826 survey, with further surveys in May, July and August 1827, but it was not until late 1827 and early 1828 that the first construction projects began.

This period co-incided with significant progress in the development of steamboats. Their advantages over the small flat-bottomed bateaux would be clear once there were adequate locks for the 20 x 80 foot gunboats. Progress was exceedingly difficult because the decisions were being made in England. For Lt-Col By, correspondence was frustrating, the time lag in communications between London and the Rideau being two months, made worse by delays in the decision-making.

On June 25, 1828, Lieutenant General Sir James Kempt, Lieutenant Governor of Nova Scotia, arrived in Kingston to begin a methodical examination as president of a second engineering committee sent out by London. They were surprised by the size of the project but highly pleased with the way that it was organized and the amount of work already accomplished. There had been considerable discussion and differences of opinion in London over the final size of the locks proposed by By to accommodate larger steamboats and this committee was to make the final determination on site.

The decision, not completely in accord with John By's ideas but acceptable to him, provided for locks sufficiently large to take the smallest of the steam towboats operating on the open waters of the Ottawa River. These were 108 feet long, 30 feet wide across the sidewheeler paddleboxes, and 4 feet in draught, capable of towing the new and larger Durham boats fully laden, two at a time at a speed of 4 to 5 knots. The Kempt Committee handed over its instructions, and work on the locks to these new dimensions began on August 1, 1828. Nicol Hugh Baird arrived on the site at a crucial stage in building the Rideau Canal.

In 1828, before Baird arrived, there were sudden floods in February and April that caused damage to the dam at Hog's Back near Bytown, and the last of the seven bridges, still under construction, collapsed. Bedrock in several excavations for locks proved unsound and masonry floors had to be laid in some locks. Meanwhile, malaria was rampant at several of the sites. It was supposed that better circulation of air would help, so forest was cleared from these areas. The mosquitoes did not react to the removal of trees but the clearance probably removed many of the stagnant pools that were their breeding grounds.

Little or no work was undertaken after October, when the labour force dispersed until spring. The rivers were scoured each spring by floods that could range as high as 15 feet above the mean level of the river, and could arrive as early as February or as late as April. Partly finished works had to be made safe from such dangers. It was soon recognized that these huge volumes of water also needed special handling during the danger periods on the finished canal. By 1830, several of the dams had been damaged by spring run-off. The engineers then realized that these low dams were incapable of handling the heaviest floodwater, so they laid out and constructed waste weirs at a heavy additional cost.

Baird faced many problems that had not been visualized, and serious new outbreaks of malaria at the Cataraqui lock sites brought work to a complete standstill in August and September. Some contractors died of malaria and many were reluctant to work on the sites, demanding higher rates and decamping when their heavier costs were not compensated. Some of the unforeseen work then had to be carried out during the difficult winter season to meet special deadlines. All this added substantially to Baird's responsibilities and his workload. The fact that he satisfied his superiors despite these obstructions, is obvious from various comments made in letters and documents that he received.

Nicol Hugh Baird was also asked by Lt-Col By to undertake special work beyond the Rideau. He reported on the work required to provide steam navigation at the Back River and Rivière des Prairies, north of the Island of Montreal. He also examined and reported on improving conditions for rafts and boats on the Chaudière Rapids between Bytown and Lac des Chats, and did a survey of the Ottawa River and the country between it and Lake Huron.

The Rideau Canal was completed in remarkable time, despite daunting conditions of climate and environment, and has earned the admiration of professional engineers ever since. At the time of its completion, the canal was an unequalled feat of engineering, and cost the Treasury more than any other project at the time in the British Empire. Great political difficulties arose from misunderstandings, lack of appreciation of the problems, and failure to recognize its strategic and economic importance.

In November 1830, Wellington's government was replaced by a Reform government, which saw fit to blame John By for every cost overrun. They summoned him to England in June, 1832, and involved him in bitter infighting between the Treasury and the Ordnance Department over expenditures on the canal, but charges of improper conduct and extravagant expenditures could not be sustained, thanks to the detail in Nicol Hugh Baird's careful estimates and itemized accounts for the work at each site. And thanks to Baird's descendents, we still have these records.

Nicol Hugh Baird had several occasions to be concerned about his health and had a real anxiety about what would happen when he was no longer required on the Rideau Canal. This is clearly shown in a letter from John By dated August 16, 1830:

> I can most fully enter into your feelings and anxiety, to be placed in some settled form of life, as your present situation will cease early next year on completion of the works of the Rideau Canal. Be assured should either of the Provinces require a Civil Engineer to superintend the construction of Public Works, I shall be most happy to give my

Certificate of your zeal and ability. You may rely on my mentioning to his Excellency, Mr James Kempt when I have the honour of meeting his Excellency that I am of the opinion that Canada would be much benefited by Employing you in Constructing Bridges, opening Roads and improving the Water Communications in the around parts as the necessary funds from time to time would be provided....

On September 21, 1831, during his difficult period of work on the Rideau, Baird married Mary Teller White, the daughter of Rideau Canal contractor Aandrew White, in Montreal. They had eight children, Mary, Andrew, Hugh, Charles, Margaret, Hamilton, and twins Charlotte and Jane. Mary White Baird died on August 20, 1847, a week after the birth of the twin daughters in Montreal. Nicol Hugh Baird died two years later in Brattleboro, Vermont.

Before the completion of the Rideau Canal, Baird visited Trenton, Upper Canada and noted a need for a bridge over the River Trent. His first design, in January 1831, was presented to Sir John Colborne, Lieutenant-Governor of Upper Canada, and he was invited the following year to recommend the best location for the bridge. It was finally built between July 1833 and the spring of 1834, with six spans covering 750 feet.

Navigation on the Trent River was attracting attention, both for the transport of supplies and people, and for the movement of timber, an important resource in the economic development of Upper Canada. In 1833, Baird was asked by Colborne to make a survey and submit a report and estimates to make the waters between Rice Lake and the mouth of the Trent River navigable. In 1835 this work was extended to cover a route between Rice Lake and Lake Simcoe.

The whole of this program was to suffer from underfunding, but Baird was appointed as Engineer in Charge of the works. Work was started in 1836, suspended in 1839 when the money was exhausted, and did not start again until September 1841. It again ran into difficulties when work on the Trent Canal came under control of the new Board of Works formed after the union of Upper and Lower Canada in 1841. Baird finally worked on the 53-mile waterway from Peterborough to Healy Falls. His records for the site end in 1843.

Nicol Hugh Baird's close association with steam propulsion on the Great Lakes is illustrated by the considerable amount of information I was able to acquire for the archives on his design of a Sweeping Paddle Wheel. He obtained a Canadian patent in January 1842 but it was 1846 before it attracted the interest of the Admiralty. It was agreed to convert one of the Lake gunboats, the *Mohawk*, in January 1846. The first trial in November of that year was a great success. Like many brilliant ideas, however, this came too late. The age of paddle wheels was drawing to a close.

Railways were making small local starts in the late 1830s, but even in the 1840s, many were only short links between trading terminals or to open up farming land and timber resources. Connections to the American coast were envisioned as enabling transport of people and goods to open seaports when the St Lawrence was icebound for months in the winter. The Lake Champlain and Connecticut River Railroad issued a prospectus in August 1845 for a line intended to run from Burlington to Rutland and Bellows Falls in Vermont and then on to Boston. After meeting in February and March 1849, it appears very likely that Baird and WB Gilbert of the Rutland Line came to an agreement for discussions between their principals. Their meetings and combined surveys yielded an agreement that a cedar post should mark a point for the junction of their lines near the Canadian border on the route to Burlington. Among the Baird documents are a few draft pages on the subject.

Nicol Baird was obviously deeply involved with the project but after more than five months passed, the only information in the archives is that he died in Brattleboro, Vermont, south of Bellows Falls through which the railway was to pass on its way to Boston. None of his reports, field notebooks and other material about the project beyond Brattleboro are to be found.

Baird's children all seem to have done well. A close bond of affection between the brothers shows through in the archives of Andrew Hugh Baird, the eldest son, who was less than fifteen and a half when his father died.

There is always the possibility that Baird was keeping his usual careful records in Brattleboro when he died. Perhaps someday someone may find personal papers from the records used by the Railroad Engineering Department to complete the work that had engaged Baird for those nine months. Nicol Hugh Baird was a man of purpose and careful attention to detail, and he justified the reputation that so many Scots earned when they transferred their technology to other countries.

CHAPTER EIGHT
GLENGARRY TALES

Charles William Gordon, who wrote about his birthplace under the pen name Ralph Connor, helped perpetuate an idyllic image of Glengarry County with his homey, sentimental turn-of-the-20th-century novels, *Glengarry School Days* and *The Man From Glengarry*. (Writing seems to run in the Gordon family's blood. Alison Gordon, Charles's granddaughter, was a sports columnist for the *Toronto Star*, and is the author of five baseball mystery novels. Her brother, also Charles, is a well known newspaper columnist, humorist and, at last count, also the author of five books.)

For well over two centuries, this stretch of farm and forest along the St Lawrence at the eastern extremity of Ontario held an almost mystical attraction for a host of fur traders, military men, wanderers, ex-voyageurs and woodsmen, as a working base when young and as a welcome haven of peace and security in their declining years.

Canadian explorers Simon Fraser and David Thompson were among them. So were many leaders of the North West Company, the upstart fur-trading group, most of them Scots, who challenged the mighty Hudson's Bay Company's monopoly.

Captain Walter Sutherland, a fierce loyalist who played the dangerous game of spying for Britain during the American Revolutionary War, also chose Glengarry for his retirement years, which he called "borrowed time." I first heard about Walter Sutherland's espionage in 1939, when I was 15 and already keenly interested in family history, quizzing my grandmother, Annie McIntosh McMillan and writing notes that, amazingly, I have managed to keep to this day.

Grandmother Annie's story about my great-great-grandfather Walter Sutherland takes place in the Revolutionary War. He was being hunted down by the enemy, when an old woman named Humiah sheltered him and his brother Joseph, giving them food in the bush. All she asked for her trouble was that if he ever had a daughter he would name her Humiah. I found this interesting, because I had a first cousin whose name was Humiah Fraser. I kept looking for other Sutherland descendents, especially after becoming a paper sleuth. Persistence was rewarded in 1970 when I discovered that Jean Sutherland Boggs, former head of the National Gallery, was also a descendent, and her mother's name was Humiah.

The next year, in the course of settling an uncle's estate, I came on a clue to the whereabouts of Walter Sutherland's papers. A letter written on February 9th, 1909 from New York City by Wm G Schram stated that an old photograph of Walter Sutherland's wife, Nancy Campbell, was from a lost painting by Wm Sawyer, of Kingston. I already knew that Nancy was the daughter of Moses Campbell, a sergeant with the Black Watch, who settled near Crown Point on the east side of Lake Champlain, New York in the late 1760s, after the Seven Years' War with the French. I set aside other cases I was working on at the time in order to find out about Schram. Also a descendent of Sutherland, he was likely of my grandmother's vintage, and probably dead. I was in Glengarry at the time and knew Russell Harper, an authority on Canadian artists. I set off to see Harper at once. He got out his file on William Sawyer.

Photograph of an oil portrait of Nancy Campbell (1764–1848), by Wm Sawyer, ca. 1870. Born in New York City, to Moses Campbell (b 1733), an immigrant from Killin, Perthshire, Scotland, and a descendent of the Earl of Breadalbane. She married Walter Sutherland of the King's Royal Regiment of New York. Her father was an officer in the Black Watch, the 42nd Highland Regiment, and fought at Ticonderoga. Her daughter married Duncan McIntosh, and her granddaughter Annie married John Roy MacMillan, grandfather of Hugh P MacMillan.

To my surprise, the information on Sawyer had been provided by Wm G Schram, then of Winter Park, Florida. There was no phone listed for him in Florida, but the file gave locations for two daughters, one in Wisconsin, the other near New York City. Unlisted phones slowed things down but I finally located the daughter in Wisconsin. Her father, aged 93, was still very much alive, and wanted to see me. Within a short time, my wife and I, along with Humiah Boggs, were in White Plains, New York, having dinner with Mr Schram.

This chase was a winner. Bill Schram had a filing case full of documents and papers that I was able to acquire for the Ontario Archives. Schram had a fat genealogical file he had been building for 80 years, having started his family history quest as a teenager, as I had. Humiah Boggs continued her own research and recorded a backhanded compliment from a Sutherland descendent about my persistent methods of chasing papers: "Hugh is a con man with a heart."

The name Humiah, sometimes spelled Humia, appears often among Walter and Nancy Sutherland's many offspring, supporting the story told by my grandmother Annie in 1942.

Among the papers I had acquired was a letter from Maj James Gray dated April 2, 1782, written from Montreal to Col Claus summarizing the many risks encountered by Walter Sutherland in his career as a spy.

> As Mr. Sutherland has had a great deal of fatigue upon many scouts, I wish you would use your interest to get him in Capt Crawford's place.... Sutherland deserves some encouragement [sic] for his Risques and Services and I know Col Campbell's sentiments as to him which is very favourable.

Recording the Sutherland story, the late Humiah Sutherland Boggs had the following bit of family lore about Captain Walter Sutherland. After he settled in Glengarry, but was still a militia officer on active service, he was ordered back to duty, and posted to Fort George at Newark on the Niagara frontier. Nancy and their 10 children followed him to Newark, where they had the use of a small frame house. The American General M^{C}Clure and his ragtag army of militia torched most of the town the night of December 10, 1813 and Nancy found herself out in the snow with her brood huddled on mattresses before finding other shelter.

By another of those strange coincidences that seem to crop up in my eternal chases, I found another descendent with the same story. I called to see an old friend, Lorraine Hovey, who lived near Barrie.

Lorraine figured in another case where I had scooped some of the papers of John Ross Robertson, founder of the Toronto Telegram. After her husband's death, Lorraine Hovey had married his former roommate from Queen's University at Kingston. I was to meet them for dinner and wouldn't you know it, the new husband turned out to be Walter Sutherland, an engineer from North Carolina, descended from my great-great-grandfather Capt Walter Sutherland, the spy.

Lorraine's husband had a few more papers from his 98-year-old father, also Walter Sutherland, who was still living in North Hatley, Quebec. I met the father and he repeated the same story about Nancy being put out in the snow, and the origins of the name Humia or Humiah! We agreed that Captain Walter Sutherland had more than earned the 2000 acres of land he was awarded in Glengarry to spend his 'borrowed time' on.

One of the longest and most pleasant associations of my lifetime was with Monsignor Ewan John MacDonald, MC, born in Glengarry in 1883. I met him in 1954, when we were attempting to found the Glengarry Historical Society.

Msgr MacDonald had amassed, and agreed to turn over to me, the largest single collection of letters, memos, telegrams, pamphlets, newspaper clippings, receipts, broadsides and other documents dealing with the subject closest to both our hearts, Glengarry County.

By the time I began working with the Ontario Archives, MacDonald and I were bosom buddies. Our common goal was to make sure the priceless collection of Glengarry memorabilia would become the first, and a truly magnificent, acquisition of my fledgling career as a manuscript sleuth.

To prove my worth at the Archives I wanted Ewan's collection passionately and he wanted his collection to have a secure home, where it would be properly preserved, respected and available to future scholars. Thus continued and expanded the unusual business and social relationship between Ewan MacDonald, Roman Catholic priest, monsignor of the church, Vicar-General of Alexandria, chaplain of the Alexandria monastery, Glengarry County, and me, child of the manse, son of a Presbyterian minister.

Father MacDonald had not led as quiet and peaceful a life as might be expected from his easygoing small-town manner. Shipped overseas as chaplain of the 154th Battalion in 1916, he was awarded the Military Cross for his work with the wounded at the bloody battle of Amiens.

Home again, he maintained military ties as militia chaplain for the Stormont, Dundas and Glengarry Highlanders. He was also an outstanding lacrosse player, an athlete in many different sports and the prime mover in setting up a local game preserve.

In the mid-1920s, Father MacDonald established a small experimental farm, wrote and directed a pageant about Bonnie Prince Charlie with descendents of many who died for the Stuarts at Culloden as cast, and began laboriously compiling genealogical charts of many local descendents of Highland Scots.

In later years he would have audiences rolling in the aisles as he related true stories of Glengarry's past, his eyes twinkling as he mimicked habits of speech, manners or physical traits for which their present day descendents were noted. In 1942, Father MacDonald went overseas again as senior Roman Catholic chaplain of the 4th Canadian Division, returning the following year to resume his parish duties.

When he and I got down to serious business in 1964, Father MacDonald was in the process of moving from the monastery to his sister's home in Greenfield, a few miles from Alexandria. Local nuns, trying to be helpful, dumped his meticulously indexed and cross-indexed files of manuscripts into shopping bags for easier carrying. When we learned what had happened we were aghast, though no word of reproach was ever directed at the good sisters.

In one way it was a disaster of the first magnitude, requiring years of painstaking labour to return the manuscripts to their proper order, but in another way, it was a godsend, a pleasant little error, since it gave me an excuse to visit the Monsignor any time I happened to be anywhere near Glengarry, to sort out a few more bags. In the process each time, there was a certain amount of whisky consumed, Scottish songs sung, fiddles and pipes played.

Among the manuscripts Father MacDonald had collected were some which outlined details of the trials and tribulations of the Roman Catholic Church over more than 200 years of Glengarry's past. The Monsignor was willing to hand over all of these papers to the Archives, free of charge, except for a few that St Francis Xavier University in Antigonish, Nova Scotia had asked for, though there were certain letters dealing with private church matters, politics and other sensitive issues, which he would have preferred to have removed from the collection.

"I have about persuaded him, however, to include all this material," I wrote in my diary of December 10, 1964. "If he feels it is necessary, he can place restrictions on same. He raised this latter point himself, inquiring if it could be done."

MacDonald also provided me with the names of people from nearby Ottawa or Montreal to as far away as New York and New Orleans, who had borrowed some of his papers, and had not yet returned them. He said he would write to them or telephone, but that I might have to go and get them in person.

On August 12, 1966, I spent the day going over manuscripts with the Monsignor. There were still at least 20 shopping bags full of papers to be sorted. Father MacDonald was inclined to destroy any material that was controversial with respect to the church. I spent some time retrieving items from his discard pile.

"When we finish the sorting," I wrote in my diary, "I will have to search the house, as I'm sure he has forgotten where he stored much of his material. He has taken a diary of Father John's to Cornwall and is going to read it through before he turns it over to us.… He is ready to spend some time speaking into the tape recorder."

By August 9, 1967, Msgr MacDonald helped negotiate a deal that had been hanging fire for three years over some 300 letters dating from 1776 to the 1860s. The compromise reached was that we would get copies and the originals would go to St Francis Xavier in Antigonish.

On December 20, 1968, while in New Orleans, I contacted Donald Coleman of the *Picayune Times* and found he still had possession of letters and other material from Father MacDonald's collection. I called to see Msgr MacDonald in Cornwall on November 14, 1969 when he was 88. He was still sending people to us about his large manuscript collection.

While rummaging through one pile of papers, I came across several envelopes containing more than $700. Examining the envelopes, the Monsignor explained that the money was obviously intended for masses, which had gone unsaid during the months he had spent in the MacDonell Memorial Hospital in Cornwall. Now, to honour their trust, he would have to say all those masses. "MacMillan," said the Monsignor, holding up the money and fixing me with an accusing eye, "you've certainly made a lot of work for me!"

I have wonderful memories of this celebrated raconteur, war hero, genealogist and humanitarian. On my last visit, two months before he passed away, the nuns had cut off their venerable patient's daily dram of scotch, but I ignored these restrictions in the sincere belief that this Highland elixir, in moderation, could not possibly do any harm. "Hugh," I remember him saying to me with a deep chuckle, "I wonder what the Sister Superior would think about the son of a Presbyterian cleric smuggling whisky in to the Vicar-General of the diocese."

Monsignor Ewan MacDonald died early in 1972, having spent most of his last four years in the Cornwall hospital.

One of the more courageous and foolhardy politicians of the last century was the Honourable Richard Cartwright, a graduate of Trinity College, Dublin, who started political life in Canada as a Conservative, crossed the floor after the Pacific Scandal, and became Canada's Minister of Finance in the new Liberal cabinet.

Cartwright's scandalous behaviour was reported in a pamphlet, published in 1877, which I acquired from Clarence Ostrom of Alexandria. Clarence's specialties were repairing watches and collecting gossip and ephemera — transitory items not intended to have lasting value, but which can become valuable collectibles. The item read:

> While this gentleman and the others of the Ministry were travelling through the country, he made a very insulting reference to Sir John Macdonald and to Senator MacPherson in a speech he delivered in Aylmer, Ont. He averred that those two gentlemen are dishonest, and that they have a right to be so because they are Highlanders; and because, from time immemorial, the Highlanders have been plunderers and thieves.

Scots all over the country erupted in rage when word of this calumny reached them, and the Highlanders of Glengarry were so incensed that they sent a delegation to Senator David Lewis MacPherson in Ottawa, to thank him for bringing it to their attention, and for rebuking Cartwright to his face for daring to cast such unwarranted aspersions on a noble race.

> In the blindness of his partisan rage [stated a Major Fraser, who read out the Glengarry delegation's address to the senator], Mr. Cartwright stigmatized us as having inherited dishonesty from our forefathers and in possessing 'predatory instincts' … that these instincts with us were stronger than reason and that we are compelled to be thieves, robbers and outcasts.

> This monstrous assertion was made before thousands of people … and it is now being disseminated throughout the country.

Fraser went on to deplore "a whole race slandered to promote the ends of unscrupulous partisanship," and added that if it had not been for Highlanders it was doubtful "whether this Dominion would ever have belonged to the British Empire, or would have been preserved to it in 1812 and 1837–38."

In his reply, Senator MacPherson thanked them for coming "from a great distance … to vindicate the memories of our sires and the good names of their children." He brought them to their feet with his words, "A further duty remains to be performed — the punishment of our traducers! … In discharging that duty, not with the claymore, as of old, all of us must bear a part. It is most fitting that Glengarry, the Highland heart of Canada, should be the first to move and that her manly sons should send forth the fiery cross to … show that neither man nor government shall insult them with impunity."

A much longer peroration was delivered in the Gaelic tongue, followed by a reception for the men from Glengarry. At the reception, Senator MacPherson pointed out, facetiously, that if Cartwright had wanted to insult Highlanders he could have done so without incurring their lifelong enmity. "If he had any imagination, he could have quoted the satirist and called us 'a motley crew of bare-legged beggars, McLeods, MacDonalds and Macgregors.' If he'd wanted to get really insulting, he could have put it into broad Scots:

> There's naught in the Highlands but syboes [onions] and leeks,
> And lang-leggit callants [fellows] gaun wanting the breeks
> — Traditional, quoted by Sir Walter Scott, *Waverley*

At the next election, in 1878, Richard Cartwright was defeated in his riding of Lennox and Addington and had to go looking for a new constituency with a scarcity of Scots among its voters.

Angus MacDonnell was the postmaster at Apple Hill. He had one of the biggest paper collections in Glengarry County, filling his post office, home and several barns to overflowing with papers, antiques and *bric-à-brac*. Angus had his mailmen and their rural route customers well trained. Farmers knew Angus would pay modest amounts for any old thing they had lying around that they didn't want. They would leave items at the road to be picked up by the mailmen, and the cash would be in their mailbox the next day.

This system went on for many years. After Angus died, an auctioneer took several days to sell off his collection. Unfortunately for me and the Ontario Archives, Queen's University in Kingston got most of these paper treasures, probably through Angus's auction sale competitor,

Melvin Ferguson from the nearby hamlet of Avonmore. They were a tough pair of bidders at an auction sale. Melvin frequently prefaced all chitchat at sales, except for the bidding, by stating, "I would like you to know that I am a graduate of Queen's University."

From MacDonnell's voluminous collection comes the following poignant slice of life, described in one of the few items I gleaned. A document dated April 19, 1803, sets out the indenture of Michael Gray, son of the late Philip Gray, of Glengarry, in the eastern district of the province of Upper Canada. The handwritten deed states that Michael had been

> put and placed as an apprentice to Alexander Urquhart, farmer, to learn the art or occupation of a farmer, and to serve from this date unto the full end and term of fifteen years ... during all which term the said apprentice his said Master shall well and faithfully serve, his secrets keep.
>
> The goods of his master he shall not embezzle, waste nor lend, without his consent, to any; at cards, dice or any unlawful games he shall not play, taverns or ale houses he shall not frequent, fornication he shall not commit, matrimony he shall not contract, from service he shall not at any time depart or absent himself. And the said master, in consideration that the said Apprentice doth in all things well demean himself, will teach and instruct the said apprentice in the art or occupation of a farmer, as well as he can, with one suit of wearing apparel and one suit of holiday apparel, with one year's schooling if a school should be kept in the neighborhood, convenient for the said apprentice to attend, and shall also find and allow unto the said Apprentice, meat, drink, clothing, washing and lodging and all other necessities fit and convenient for such an apprentice during the term aforesaid. In witness thereof the said parties have here unto ... set their hands.

Had Michael's father's death left a widow with too many mouths to feed, forcing the oldest boy, Michael, to sell himself into virtual slavery for his entire youth? Was Michael an orphan glad of a place to be lodged, clothed and fed? One can only hope that Glengarrian Sandy Urquhart proved to be a kindly man.

The North West Company of fur traders was founded in Montreal in the winter of 1783–84, made up of partners, many of them Loyalists or sons of Loyalists from Glengarry. When these Nor'Westers established their string of trading posts from Montreal to the Pacific Ocean and began competing aggressively and violently with their well established but often lacklustre rival, the Hudson's Bay Company, many of their clerks were recruited from Glengarry.

For more than 40 years, all-out rivalry between the Hudson's Bay Company and the North West Company persisted, but in the end the more solid financial position of the HBC won out over the enthusiasm and enterprise of the Nor'Westers. In 1821, the two companies became one, under the name of the Hudson's Bay Company but in the hearts and memories of its retired members, many of them in Glengarry or surrounding counties, the old North West Company survived.

After 1821, at least 70% of the chief HBC factors and traders were former Nor'Wester partners. To resurrect the stirring saga of that pioneering Canadian firm, Ian McMartin and I spearheaded the establishment of the North West Company Museum in Williamstown, Glengarry County, as a 1967 Canadian Centennial project, re-enacting a voyageur canoe trip as a dramatic opening act.

Genuine documents, papers, letters and other memorabilia dealing with the North West Company's active days, have been very hard to come by. I discovered that most, but not all, documents relating to the North West Company had been destroyed.

But in 1968 I was able to obtain the snuff 'mull' (box) belonging to the illustrious Nor'Wester Partner Simon Fraser. It came to me, as these things so often do, in a roundabout fashion. One of the voyageurs on our canoe trip re-enactment, a descendent of Angus Roy "The Mast" McDonell, put me in touch with Elaine (McDonell) Street, another descendent, in Calgary. In addition to the snuff mull, Elaine Street had a fine collection of 19th-century business records of Angus Roy McDonell's, which I also acquired. Angus Roy was nicknamed "The Mast" because he was in the timber trade and provided masts for the ships of the British Royal Navy.

While in Calgary, I was recruited by Canadian author WO Mitchell to speak to a history conference in Banff, about my experiences on the trail of the Nor'Westers. In a foolhardy moment I pulled the snuff mull from my pocket to show the audience of westerners, and exclaimed, "This is an example of the sort of relic you can find out west and take back east." It's a wonder I wasn't run out on a rail!

Simon Fraser was born in what is now Vermont, came to Canada with his family, and in 1792 at age 16, was apprenticed to the North West Company.

After an adventurous career, including discovering the hazardous British Columbia river which bears his name and following to its

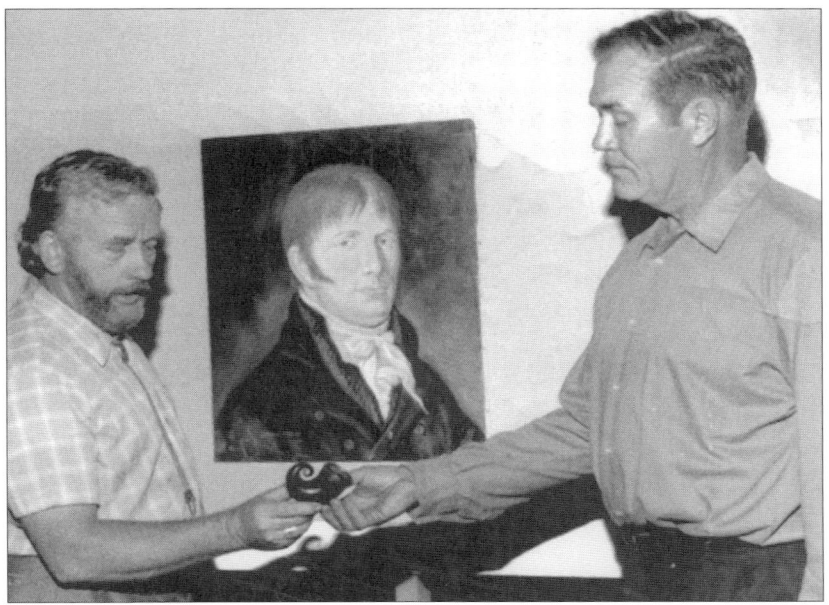

Hugh MacMillan presents Simon Fraser's snuff mull to Iain McMartin of the Nor'Wester and Loyalist Museum at Williamstown, Ontario, 1968. Portrait of Henry McKenzie in background.

mouth on the Pacific Ocean, he retired to St Andrews West, near Cornwall. The snuff mull, which he probably carried all his life, is as its name suggests, meant to hold snuff.

Crafted in Scotland, the mull has a horn lid, with an embossed silver Scottish thistle design. The date 1790 and Simon's initials are also etched in the silver. It is thought the mull had been owned by his father and grandfather. It is now on display in the Nor'Wester Museum.

How the mull came into the possession of Elaine Street's family is a drama in itself. Mrs Street's great-great-grandfather, John Roy McDonell, sailed from Scotland to upper New York Province in 1773. He soon became personal secretary to Sir John Johnson, son of Sir William, the leader of the Iroquois confederacy. When war with England erupted, loyalist John Roy McDonnell was assigned the task of leading a group of women and children through the trackless wilderness to Montreal. MacDonnell carried out this assignment faithfully. From Montreal, they eventually made their way to what is now Glengarry. Among this group of Loyalists was a very young Simon Fraser, his mother and her other children. His father had died a prisoner of war during the early stages of the American Revolution. Some time after his retirement to St Andrews, Simon Fraser presented his snuff mull to the McDonnell family, in appreciation for John Roy McDonnell bringing his mother and the family safely to British territory.

I acquired a great collection of medical records concerning Glengarry from a dealer in Toronto. While loading the papers in my stationwagon a fierce gust of wind blew many of them up and down the road. Luckily for me the road was damp from a recent rain and stuck to the pavement. Frantically running and dodging traffic, I managed to gather them. A near disaster. They covered three generations of a family of medical practitioners who had served the early Glengarry communities. Ebenezer Hunt, his son Henry Hunt, and a grandson, also called Henry Hunt, spanned the better part of the 19th century applying their healing skills to the settlers in Glengarry's Indian Lands.

Dr Ebenezer Hunt, whose English grandfather Jeremiah was known as a "celebrated old dissenting minister" ('dissenting' not in reference to a cantankerous personality, but as contrasted with the all-powerful 'established' [official national] Church of England, which we now call the Anglican Church) lived from 1688 to 1744. As strong-willed as his feisty ancestor, Ebenezer studied medicine and practised in Liverpool and London for several years before emigrating to the United States in 1804. Though not bothering to register as an MD in any American city, he did quite well there for some years, as far as can be ascertained.

In 1810, however, Dr Hunt, his wife Leah (*née* Alcock), their son Henry, 13, and 8-year-old daughter Hannah, 8, headed north to Upper Canada. Dr Hunt was a multidimensional individual. His interests included the penning of poetry, philosophy and medical books, chief among the latter being *Praxis Medica; A Comprehensive View of the Cause, Nature and Cure of Most Disorders Incident to the Human Body, and Illustrated with Cases*, by Ebenezer Hunt, MD. The title page features a lengthy quotation in classical Greek from the writings of Hippocrates, the Father of Medicine, whose Hippocratic Oath is still taken by all who aspire to be medical doctors.

Also quoted at some length in Latin is the German physician Ettmüller. *Praxis Medica* is dated 1788, which suggests that Dr Hunt must have been indeed precocious to have summed up so weighty a medical text with notes on actual cases, so shortly after receiving his degree. A second medical book, entitled *Fever*, may also have come from his own pen. Among cases listed is the following on Pleuritis:

A healthy young man of 27 years named Reuben Alcock of florid complexion ... from being exposed to all sorts of weather ... in the end of May, 1796, after being much heated, imprudently took a large draught of cold spring water. The next morning he complained of a pain in his stomach, which he supposed to arise from wind.... He continued to struggle with it for about ten days, drinking spirits and taking black pepper, but this only ... increased the symptoms. When consulting me, his pulse was hard and wedgelike ... with the usual concomitant of fever.

June 11: I took about eight ounces of blood from his arm and followed it with a purgative of Sal Glauber [Glauber Salts — sodium sulphate]. In the course of the day he was much easier but at night the paroxysm returned with great violence and continued till morning when ...
June 12: I repeated the bleeding and purgative with like effect ...
June 13: I again repeated the phlebotomy ... with the happiest effect, applied a blister to his side and in a few days he recovered.

Another large section of *Praxis Medica* was headed "Venereal Disorders: the principal of which are Gonorrhea and Syphilis," with indecipherable notations underneath, mentioning "Gonorrhea, Clap and Syphilis, Chap 3." One case of Gonorrhea with Phimosis involved a young tailor named Thomas Mason, who had "improper relations with a bad woman" eight days earlier. Dr Hunt put him on the "antiphlogistic regimen" and in order to bring down the inflammation, gave him calomel and Glauber Salts. A week later, Mason "informed me that he had taken the medicines as directed. The phimosis is entirely gone, his mouth is sore, the running thinner and paler and though the scalding ... reported while making water, is still bad, the medicines operated well. He came no more to me."

Dr Ebenezer Hunt's son, Henry, wished to follow in his father's footsteps, but the nearest medical school was too far away so his dad undertook to instruct him in the healing arts and he became an "irregular practitioner" until an increasingly rigid and bureaucratic Medical Society forced him to stop. It was said that irregular practitioner Henry Hunt had been so well and thoroughly trained by his father that the only give-away was that his language and handwriting on prescriptions were "quite different from his father's."

It was fortunate that the research into the Hunt family carried out in 1941–42 by Toronto physician Norman B Gwyn, was included with the Hunt papers. From Dr Gwyn's papers, I discovered that Ebenezer's grandson, unlike his father, had the benefit of the finest formal medical education. He practised in Williamstown for 12 years before moving to Toronto, where he continued to serve for another 38 years. When he died in May 1926, he was buried at Woodlands, an old family retreat on the St Lawrence.

The second Dr Henry Hunt's journal, which he kept during his entire medical career, was also a part of my acquisition for the Archives. An archivist, inspecting and evaluating this medical coup, wrote: "Certain social and political events are duly noted. A description of diseases and treatments and the general state of medicine and nursery in the country, is provided … as well as conversations, life style, pastimes, social activities and outings. One interesting episode recounts Dr Hunt's visit to Oliver Mowat in 1889. His journal notes 1884–1907 give an account of diphtheria, which prevailed about Williamstown in the early days of his practice."

The evaluator concluded, "The Collection [of Hunt family papers] is interesting and informative as it documents the practice of medicine in Ontario in the late 18th and early 19th centuries. The earlier writings *Praxis Medica* and *Fever* reflect early medical education in England and on the continent and the relationship between medicine and classicism. These writings are useful in that they demonstrate the type of authority referred to by 19th century Ontario physicians."

Years later I acquired an 8 foot by 3 foot chart dated 1809, the only known map of the Indian Lands in Glengarry, showing the names of all the settlers at that time who leased this land from the Mohawk Band at St Regis. It was originally their 3-mile wide right of way stretching from the St Lawrence to the Ottawa River. On lots 7 and 8 of the 13th concession appears the name of our pioneering medic, Ebenezer Hunt.

Captain Alexander Stickler was a Scot from the Orkney Islands north of mainland Scotland. Unknown in Glengarry today, Captain Stickler at one time operated steamboats to Montreal and beyond. They were called the *St Francis*, *Fashion*, *Star* and *Manitoba*. He later built a huge barge, which he named the *Glengarry*.

I used to drive by his fine old brick home in South Lancaster and speculate what cache of papers were in the huge safe to be seen through the dirty fly-specked window on the river side of the unoccupied building. Its owner, Mrs. McCallum, lived in Winnipeg and it took years of visits before a deal was made with her niece who inherited the place.

The safe was stuffed with all of Stickler's old business papers, maps and pictures. Alexander Stickler, the great Orkneyman entrepreneur of Glengarry has left a major cache of papers that I was able to acquire for the Ontario Archives, where they are now waiting for an author who can write the story in the detail it deserves.

CHAPTER NINE
THE ONES THAT GOT AWAY

The Jarvis-Powell case started as a routine one, but took on new life in dramatic fashion when I finally made contact with Denise Wile.

A complete stranger named John McMillan, no relation to me, appeared at our door one day looking for his family's roots. We were living in the Rockwood, Ontario area, near Guelph, and the local postmistress had sent him to see me, hoping I could help. Such chance encounters sometimes start a new case, or, as in this instance, reopen an old one.

John McMillan was an engineer from North Carolina. He told me that his wife's niece, Denise Wile, had a collection of papers, art and relics, inherited from her father, who had died several years before in Boca Raton, Florida. He gave me her phone number, but she was never at home when I called. Finally I contacted her ex-husband in Markham, near Toronto, who gave us her address in Scarborough. Not long after, I was sipping tea in her living room.

To my amazement, Denise turned out to be a daughter of William Dummer Powell Jarvis, from whom I had purchased a station-wagon load of Jarvis papers back in 1967 for the princely sum of $2,000. Being new to the game then, I never thought to ask him about other things he might have, a mistake I seldom repeated, but here I was by sheer chance talking to his daughter. She had a jumbled-up mixture of papers, medals, ephemera, and a lock of hair from General Sir Isaac Brock, who died in 1812 at the Battle of Queenston Heights, turning back the sneak attack that opened the American attempt to invade Canada during the War of 1812.

In the 1970s, thieves broke into the old Jarvis house north of Toronto and stole many items, leaving other valuables scattered in the fields behind the house.

Denise moved these things many times over the years, so we will never know for sure how much was lost or stolen. We do know, however, that Interpol has some of the stolen art on its wanted list. The pistols that

Samuel Peter Jarvis used to shoot John Ridout in July 1817 were also taken. Thieves missed the powder horn and the spectacles worn by Mrs Anne Powell when she had her portrait painted.

The thieves also missed the mourning brooch, miniature, and letter identifying her daughter Anne's body when it was washed ashore onto the Irish coast in 1822. I was fortunate to acquire these unusual relics, thanks to Denise having the good sense to save as much as she could. Unfortunately, a collection of Brock's letters had been lost, but I trekked to Boca Raton to recover what was left there in a neighbour's garage. My wife and I were going on a holiday to Florida anyway, so we decided to make a detour to Boca Raton to recover what had been left there many years earlier by Denise's father. The neighbours were delighted to have the boxes removed at long last.

When I spread the papers from several boxes onto the carpet at the motel for some preliminary sorting, an army of silverfish scurried every which way. But cleaning up that mess was well worth the effort. We had opened up an untold drama.

Anne Powell, daughter of William Dummer Powell, was infatuated with John Beverly Robinson, Attorney General of Upper Canada. In the winter of 1822, Robinson and his wife went by stage coach from York (now Toronto) to New York City to catch a ship to England. Anne, in her 30s, had been confined to her room by her mother, one of the leading lights of York society, but sneaked out and pawned her gems to pay a driver, who set off in pursuit of the Robinsons. She caught up with them, but Robinson had told the ship's captain not to allow her aboard.

Undeterred, Anne Powell caught the next brig to sail, the *Albion*. It foundered in a gale off the Irish coast and Anne was drowned. The mate of the ship wrote the letter that identified her body by the brooch she was wearing, which contained a swatch of hair, presumed to be Robinson's. The letter has two holes burnt through it from the acidic action of the copper in the brooch. These articles are permanently preserved in a frame with the story mounted on the back, and I eventually sold them to a Montreal collector.

General Brock's lock of hair, which was also saved for posterity, had been collected by Samuel Peters Jarvis, who was at the battle of Queenston Heights. He married Mary, a sister of the tragic Anne Powell. Impressive proof of provenance was saved in the form of a letter from Sam to his future wife documenting how he obtained the hair. This case illustrates a collection missed, that by the fickle finger of fortune was recaptured. It remains open, as I am still following tips about other Jarvis items around Parry Sound, Ontario, and further leads in New Jersey.

For every collection of manuscripts and memorabilia that I brought home to the Ontario Archives, I knew there might be another dozen equally valuable ones I had missed. Some of these were probably — maddeningly — just around the corner from my home or in buildings I passed on my way to work. Missing a collection caused me as much pain as the successful conclusion of other cases afforded me pleasure.

When I retired in 1989 after 25 years as a liaison officer, acquisitor, paper sleuth and house-scourer, I was able to look back on more than 2000 paper chases, using every mode of transport from Ski-doo to canoe, helicopter to swamp buggy, Rolls-Royce to horseback, and even an icebreaker.

Of my 2000-odd cases, I have scored successes in some 70%. Naïveté, weariness and sheer bad luck accounted for a fair number of the misses. The others could be ascribed to a variety of causes. Among these would be:

1. hearing about it too late; someone else copped it first
2. having trouble persuading the owner to make a deal for the public good, tax credits or even money
3. hearing of it through a friend of a friend of a friend, who may not have checked it thoroughly or reported it accurately
4. discovering, after much legwork, that it was of broader interest to the whole of Canada, and therefore should be in the hands of the National Archives of Canada (NAC), rather than the Ontario Archives or some other institution.

The latter was the case of the detailed, fascinating annals of several generations of Scots by the name of Mickle, who lived just north of Guelph, Ontario in 1832. It was felt that the University of Guelph should have the papers, with the Ontario Archives receiving copies of any manuscripts they particularly desired.

One poignant miss that still haunts me concerns the papers of Dr Robert Bell and his grandfather, the Reverend William Bell. The Bells were that rare breed who combined genuine piety with an insatiable curiosity about everything around them. Robert (1841–1917) joined the Geological Survey of Canada at 15 and later became a director, after obtaining degrees in medicine and applied science at McGill University and teaching chemistry at Queen's University, Kingston.

Dr Robert Bell (1841–1917) of the Geological Survey of Canada named more than 3000 Canadian topographical features, a record. He corresponded with Alexander Graham Bell and Charles Darwin. His wife would follow him into the bush, toting their daughter papoose-style in an Indian moss bag.

Known to his Indian friends as *Wasagisik*, meaning 'clear sky' because they had always found him as dependable as a cloudless sky, Dr Robert Bell was happiest when in the northern bush, wading through swamps, shouldering a 100-pound pack and ignoring bloodthirsty black flies as he bent to smell a flower or probe a rocky outcropping with his geologist's hammer. He charted much of northwestern Ontario, followed its rivers to their outlets, recorded the northern limits of the conifers and did the reconnaissance mapping for laying the tracks of the Canadian National Railway. He was famous for the names he gave to at least 3000 topographical features, more than any other Canadian mapmaker. Many of the names credited the Indians before him, whose choices of names were sheer poetry. Wabigoon Lake was named after its lovely water lilies, which were likened to white feathers, and Manitouwadge was the cave of the Great Spirit. Atikokan was buried caribou bones, Keewatin was home of the north wind and Nakina was a warning cry, "Hold on tight! Don't let go!" they presumably exclaimed as their yellow birchbark canoes hurtled through the rapids.

In the early days, the only way Dr Robert Bell's Glasgow-born wife Agnes could spend a few days with her footloose husband was to accompany him into the bush, toting baby daughter Margaret on her back, papoose-style, in an Indian moss bag. I'd heard about these fabulous people all my life, and in Perth, Ontario, I met and interviewed the incredible Peggy Cavanaugh, of Baton Rouge, Louisiana, the great-granddaughter of Rev William Bell. She was also the great-granddaughter of John Haggart, a contractor on both the Welland and Rideau canals, in whose old downtown Perth mansion on Haggart Island in the Tay River, Peggy was living.

Peggy Cavanaugh was an unforgettable figure, with her billowing gown and mane of red hair, flitting from Perth to New Orleans to Ireland, all the while managing her nephew's jazz group. She sent me to Laval-sur-le-lac, Quebec, to meet her cousin Robert Douglas, a descendent on the maternal side from Rev William Bell, the first Presbyterian minister of Perth, and on his father's side from James Douglas, who founded the first mental hospital in the province of Quebec.

In the mid-1960s, I had heard that this Robert Douglas had sold a considerable portion of his grandfather Robert Bell's papers to the Public Archives of Canada (PAC). Checking with Douglas, I learned that PAC had sent back a large proportion of these papers. I assumed, since PAC had sent the papers back to their owner, that they must be of little or no value, because PAC was usually pretty shrewd about such matters. Because of that, I made no effort either to acquire the papers or even to examine them for any portion that might possibly be of interest to us in Ontario. What a mistake that was!

About 1979, I heard that Douglas was thinking of selling the stuff PAC had returned to him 15 or 16 years before, but because of my *idée fixe* that it must be worthless, I paid no attention.

The PAC had made a monumental blunder in this case, and possibly because I was a neophyte at the outset of the case, I followed them with a similarly monumental blunder of my own, to my everlasting regret. It turned out that these papers included thousands of valuable letters to and from such famous personalities as Charles Darwin, Alexander Graham Bell, and Sir Sandford Fleming.

After that, anything Peggy Cavanaugh had left, I decided we must buy. Robert Douglas's papers included many letters from Andrew Bell to his father in Perth. There was also a diary of Bell's, now owned by Queen's University. More papers are with Norman Bell in Douglas, Arizona. I tracked these papers from Arizona to Toronto to Ottawa, where Airdrie Bell Guppy, daughter of Norman, had them. This, in part, made up for missing Bob Douglas's mother lode.

Among these papers was a rare pamphlet from a disgruntled parishioner of the Rev Wm Bell at Perth. It is undated and signed simply "A Presbyterian." It is a vitriolic diatribe, full of ringing phrases like:

> You have once again come under the influence of your besetting sin, ie. your anxiety to become an author.... Are you not aware that Presbyterians of Bathurst and Drummond are dissatisfied with your unpleasant temper and tyrannical conduct....

> [It concludes] I shall take my leave of you for the moment, but not in your own uncharitable spirit, by hoping you will fall in the pit dug for your enemies, but by advising you to forgive them who spitefully use you.

This opinion of Bell is at odds with the generally high regard in which he was held by the community. It just points up the fact that even the most highly regarded may still have their detractors! On May 22, 1979, I drove to Laval-sur-le-lac, met Robert Douglas, and acquired a collection of Toronto newspapers and a condensed version of his great-grandfather's journals.

Another failure that still rankles, probably because of the great lengths to which I was willing to go in pursuit, is listed in my files simply as "The French Count." The story starts at Fort William (now part of Thunder Bay), a fur trading post for three centuries, where North West Company wintering partners met Montreal-based partners each spring to exchange a continent's harvest of furs for trade goods. The occasion was always marked by colourful, native-pleasing ceremonies where round the clock dancing, socializing and merrymaking were the order of the day. My fascination with Fort William stemmed partly from my great interest in the short-lived North West Company. Equally important to me was the on-going provincially funded building project aimed at restoring Fort William to its former picturesque glory.

On December 11, 1977, I drove out to see the restoration site, where several buildings were almost finished. I tried to contact Roy Beebee, who had been working as a photographer there the previous summer. In 1968, Beebee had met a French count on a train between Switzerland and northern France, whose ancestor had been with the North West Company at Fort William. The Count said he had all that ancestor's papers. Unfortunately, Beebee lost the Count's card and couldn't remember his full name. But I was determined to follow up this lead myself. After many phone calls, I finally contacted Beebee on December 20 and got more details about that 1968 train encounter. I decided I would need to contact the French embassy.

A week later, I met Pierre Jolin at Henry Best's Christmas party and told him my story. As a member of the French Royalist Association, Jolin had many contacts that I hoped would be useful. He did what he could for me when he got back to Europe, and in due course, I received a letter from Ontario's Belgian agent, Ennio Vita-Finza in Brussels:

> It was a pleasure meeting you in Toronto, and your story was most interesting.... I dropped into the Association of Nobles of France and told them your problem. The result was the names of three nobles now living in Canada, who may be useful to you.... You might also consult two books: Dictionnaire de la noblesse française, and Bottin mondain, and write to France's national archives, c/o Archiviste Baron Durye, 60, rue des Francs-Bourgeois, Paris 75004.

I contacted the three nobles, one a count and one a viscount, all in Quebec, but to no avail. I received another letter written in French and addressed to me as "Canadian Archivist Researching French Count." After reviewing the request, the writer, identified only as "J de B," wrote:

> Unfortunately, the information provided is very imprecise. It could possibly refer to a member of French nobility, a resident in 1969 of northern France or Switzerland, whose name might just possibly have been St Predue. M MacMillan has asked us to insert an appeal for assistance in our bulletin. This is somewhat like throwing a bottle into the ocean, but after all, why not?

While touring southern France in March of 1980, I did more work on the French Count case and was given the name of a Mr Gilles or perhaps Jean Compan, who I understood was with the Tourism and Commerce Bureau in Nîmes, so should be relatively easy to trace. I was told he had been with Roy Beebee when they met the Count so I looked for his address, hoping for a break in this case, which had been dragging on for years. Somehow or other, however, even the name and address of the elusive French aristocrat proved as ineffective as all other clues, and the following year, on May 22, 1981, I wrote to M Compan at his home:

I made every effort, while in Nîmes … to find you at the address the travel agency provided. Unfortunately, you weren't there, though we tried for a week or more. We would deeply appreciate it if you could help us find the French Count (perhaps named St Predue) whom you and M Beebee met in 1968.

I have never come any closer to learning either the correct name of the mysterious nobleman or his alleged collection of early fur-trading lore, but I never close the books on a case. One fine day I will get a phone call out of the blue, probably in French, and the caller will provide *la clé* that unlocks the whole enigma.

I have always wondered why there are few or no Greek, Chinese, Ukrainian, German, Italian, Latvian, native Indian or various other ethnic Canadian collections among the Ontario Archive treasures, missed or captured, considering they are all well represented in the population of Ontario. If a Greek or Ukrainian citizen had ever approached me with news of a trunkful of letters or other family papers connected to Ontario's past, I would have deluged him or her with tears of gratitude, but nobody ever has. Our own Native People, who were here before the rest of us, were never known for written records, outside of the rare map drawn up before the white man came.

I see this lack as collections missed, diminishing the variety and richness of the Archives' files. I was hoping my successors as Archives Liaison Officers would have more luck with other sectors of our society. Unfortunately, there will not be any follow-up, because my former position has been eliminated.

My work was a free-wheeling operation that would not survive under compartmentalized modern archival portfolios. The present policy is for portfolio managers to operate within narrow parameters such as medicine, fur trade, politics, education, or business. They are responsible only for collections in their particular categories as they go about actively collecting new material. But in actual practice, there is very little activity. Like many organizations, the archives have been subjected to severe financial restraints. Funds have had to be allocated for computers, microfilm readers and other equipment to keep pace with modern technology, leaving very little money available for the purchase of actual documents.

Another major problem is lack of space. Archives have had to become highly selective in what they collect, and in many cases have had to turn certain material over to regional archives or historical societies. The original mandate of archives to locate, acquire and store papers has been diminished in the process.

One donor I wouldn't wish on my worst enemy was the woman with complete files of two early Ontario newspapers, which she had obtained when the papers stopped publishing. She kept these in her home, most of them in the basement, and was not interested in giving them to the Archives. She had reservations about even allowing us to microfilm them until she finished copying local news from each volume. In March 1970, I asked her if we could purchase the newspapers and she suggested I keep in touch. A month later when I stopped in to see her again, she hadn't yet finished copying what she wanted out of the papers. A year later, March 1971, she let me take two volumes of the papers for purchase. The other volumes, approximately 26 in number, would be available soon, she said. On 31 August 1971, I drove out to see her again. She had had a radical change of heart since I was last there, and she now wanted to sell. Her basement had been completely flooded, and the papers were in a very bad state. I took the papers back to Toronto to have them dried out and microfilmed. They took months to separate and dry out, and it took an extra two months to remove the odour of the dozens of cats that had enjoyed those papers in the woman's basement.

One time-consuming long-distance paper chase that was neither a total disaster nor a raging triumph either, came to be labeled The LaMothe Case. It started in 1965 when I dropped into H Borden Clarke's antiquarian book shop in Morrisburg, Ontario, to get some leads for new collections.

Borden Clarke related that in 1939, while he was running a bookstore in Montreal, a man walked in and produced a small collection of manuscripts, which he said were for sale. Examining them, Borden noted they were reports and letters about the western fur trade circa 1780–1815. He grew more and more excited as he saw they included a lengthy report by Jules Maurice Quesnel after whom BC's Quesnel River, Quesnel Lake and the community at the junction of the Quesnel and Fraser Rivers were named. The documents related to the trip Quesnel took in 1808 with Simon Fraser down the waterway later named the Fraser River.

The man with the Quesnel collection explained that he was selling these family papers for $25, because he needed that much to buy liquor supplies for a party being held at his club that weekend. He was surprised when Borden gave him the $25 immediately, but added that if he'd come back on Monday he'd give him another $75, which the bookseller didn't happen to have in his cash register just then. At this point, the stranger invited Borden to come to his home with him on Monday and he would sell him several trunks jammed with more of the same material. His said his name was LaMothe. On the Monday, Borden made sure he opened early so as to be ready for his welcome client's return. He waited anxiously all morning and, not daring to leave the premises for lunch, all day as well, but there was no sign of the man to whom he was eager to pay the $75, along with much, much more if things turned out as he hoped. Borden contacted every person by the name of LaMothe in the Montreal telephone book, ran ads in both English and French newspapers and finally hired a smart private detective who had served him well on several other occasions, all to no avail. He never saw the man calling himself LaMothe again.

For once I had the edge on Borden Clarke. Hearing this strange story almost 30 years after it happened, I was in the catbird seat position of having a Montreal sister-in-law called LaMothe, from this same old seignorial family. Two days and countless interviews later, I knew the stranger's full name was Lucien LaMothe and that he had died in the old Taft Hotel in downtown Montreal back in 1959. During his last days, Lucien had very little contact with his family, I was told. So it was only by reading the coroner's report and interviewing his pals that I discovered Guaranty Trust in Ottawa had handled his estate, which was larger than any of his relatives realized. A trip to Ottawa and lunch and dinner with a charming lady named Velma Reid, the trust officer assigned to the case, resulted in my taking over most of the retired file on Lucien LaMothe. This elicited some two dozen names of Lucien's friends, to whom I wrote, inquiring if they knew what had happened to the LaMothe papers. Heading the list was Fernande Linstead, of Los Angeles, who inherited LaMothe's estate.

Several months went by before I heard from any of these people. The first letter to come back was from Guy Fisher in Ojai, California. It turned out he'd met Lucien in 1953, on a tramp steamer from Capetown to Montreal. They became friends during the voyage and LaMothe discovered that Fisher was a collector of stampless covers (letters from the days when they bore no stamps but were paid for on delivery by the person to whom they were addressed). As a token of his esteem, LaMothe had sent Fisher a collection of fur trade letters written from Fort Michilimackinac in the 1780s. Also included in the generous gift was a North West Company fur trade journal for the winter of 1818–19, kept by a clerk named Nelson, at Tête au Brochet ('pike's nose') on the Saskatchewan River system. I later discovered that the complete set of Nelson's North West Company diaries, except for those of the winter of 1818–19, were donated by some unknown person in Calgary to the Metro Library in Toronto.

We were fortunate in being able to buy this unexpected windfall from Guy Fisher. I had noted that a copy of Fisher's letter had gone to Mrs Linstead, so I phoned Fisher, who promised to contact her about the trunkful of papers her husband had inherited. This was the good news. The bad news followed almost immediately. Some two months earlier, Mrs Linstead had moved into a new home. In the inevitable bustle, disorder, last-minute emergencies and hurly-burly attendant upon even the best planned of such operations, she had thrown out the entire priceless collection of fur trade papers. All she had retained, apparently, was the death mask of Sir Wilfrid Laurier. LaMothe's father had once been his secretary. As the only one in existence, it would be quite valuable, and I hoped to buy it from her, but this hope came to naught.

In 1991, I finally met Fernande Linstead and her husband Bob in Desert Springs, California. I had flown to Los Angeles, rented a car and driven to meet them for dinner with the firm expectation of being able to purchase the mask which the Laurier Museum was naturally most anxious to acquire, but Bob, unbeknownst to Fernande, had donated it to a church bazaar. More than likely some Californian has it hanging on his wall as a curiosity, without any idea of Sir Wilfrid's place in Canadian history.

There was a sequel to the sad ending of this chase. I located another of LaMothe's pals in Old Montreal, a Mr Methuen who also had a few fur trade letters and, a while later, a relative of Lucien LaMothe offered me several more. Then in 1977, Mrs. Linstead's daughter got in touch with me on behalf of her mother, who had just recalled that other letters may have been given away as gifts or curiosities to friends of her mother's in California. While on a trip through that part of California the same year, I asked them to keep an eye open for more of the precious papers. I'm still waiting for further results in this frustrating case, which has dragged on now for many years.

Had I only talked to Borden Clarke a few months earlier and so heard about Linstead that much faster, the whole affair might have had a much more satisfying ending. One puzzling aspect still remained to be explained, and I had hoped to be able to satisfy Borden Clarke's still burning curiosity about it before he died; why hadn't Lucien LaMothe come back for his money that Monday? Some of his friends said he was like that, not careless exactly but given to concentrating on one thing at a time, to the utter disregard of others equally if not more important to his own welfare. If he'd had a good time at the party for which he needed the $25, for instance, he might have met someone he found interesting and gone off with him on a ship bound for the Orient or South America, forgetting his rendezvous with Borden.

That's what makes manuscript sleuthing so fascinating. As unpredictable as the stock markets or the weather, are the probabilities of what human beings will do under any set of circumstances when it comes to saving or not saving paper ephemera.

CHAPTER TEN
THE LAST FATAL DUEL

The most famous fatal duel in Canada was the last one, fought in Perth, Upper Canada (now Ontario), on June 13, 1833. The true story behind the senseless tragedy was obscure until the 1960s, when I located two sets of papers that brought the facts to light.

It was not the traditional "pistols for two, breakfast for one." Differing from affairs of honour in other nations, this lethal engagement took place in the evening, instead of dawn. Two pistols were fired simultaneously in a drizzling rain, with the astonished, grieving victor violently retching as he saw his shattered friend lying face down in the mud.

Principals in the famous duel were Robert Lyon, 19, handsome, personable, a fine athlete in all sports from foot racing to pistol shooting, related to the town's leading Radenhurst family, studying to be a barrister in their law office, and John Wilson, an impecunious farmer's son, about 20, studying law in James Boulton's law office, paying his way by tutoring the lawyer's son and other children.

Friends despite their vastly different social and financial backgrounds, both had flirtations with Elizabeth Hughes, a recent newcomer from England, where relations between the sexes were less rigid than in Canada. Elizabeth taught at a select ladies school run by Mr and Mrs Gideon Acland, and was an object of widespread sympathy because her father had died of cholera. She was thus in the perilous position of being without a natural protector in a male-dominated society.

The only villain in the case was another law student, Henry Lelièvre, son of a French sea captain who had prudently switched sides after Trafalgar and attained respectability in the British Navy. Lelièvre lusted after Miss Hughes and hated John Wilson, who he believed had the inside track with her. Actually, Wilson was in love with Joanna Lees, the miller's daughter next door.

Like Lelièvre, Robert Lyon also believed his friend Wilson had a crush on the newly arrived young teacher, and resolved to tease him about her.

Their respective chiefs frequently sent Lyon and Wilson on legal business to Bytown (Ottawa), some 50 miles away. Meeting Wilson in

Bytown for a few drinks, Lyon casually mentioned the newest bit of gossip from home, that Miss Hughes was allowing men to indulge in unbecoming freedoms with her. Even worse, he went on, she was seeing Lelièvre, who had sat alongside her with his arms about her in a position which no woman of spirit would permit.

Wilson, angered at his friend's remarks, wrote a letter to Gideon Acland, the employer and self-appointed guardian of Miss Hughes, quoting what his friend had told him about the English girl's behaviour.

Within hours, everyone was talking about how young Bob Lyon had made a dishonourable remark about an unprotected female. By the time they returned to Perth after their brief business sojourn in Bytown, Robert Lyon discovered that he was considered a pariah, a cad and a bounder. To make matters worse, he was invited to no more tea parties, virtually the only occasions where one could meet pretty girls in summer. Tracing his troubles to their source with the accommodating, highly-solicitous help of Henry Lelièvre, the young Lyon was astounded to learn that the cause of all the cold shouldering was a remark attributed to him in a letter by none other than his supposed friend, John Wilson.

Furious, Lyon went prowling in pursuit of the author of these calumnies. An article I wrote for *Maclean's Magazine*, edited by Robert Marshall, describes what happened next:

> The two came face to face on the afternoon of June 12 in front of the town's court house. Had Wilson written that letter? Wilson admitted he had, and Lyon immediately knocked him to the ground. Wilson, bruised and bleeding, made some effort to explain. But Lyon, too angry to listen, turned on his heel with a parting insult. "You're a damn lying scoundrel, sir," he shouted, "and I'll treat you as such every time I meet you!"

Wilson was in several quandaries, most devastating of which was that his heart's delight, the lovely dark-eyed miller's daughter Joanna Lees, now spurned him, using his unread letters and passionate poems as confetti to strew around other chums' wedding paths. As for the trouble with Bob, John Wilson was sure he could smooth it over, once the hothead cooled down enough to talk, friend to friend.

There still remained the other, more difficult dilemma. Having been publicly thrashed, Wilson feared he could never again hold up his head and be regarded as a man of honour unless he sought satisfaction by challenging his friend to a duel, much as he abhorred the very thought of such things. He took this problem to his patron, James Boulton, who was later to explain it in court thus: "If John's standing in society had been higher, he might with less danger to his reputation have treated the matter with contempt." Believing he had no choice in the matter, but trusting that good sense would somehow prevail, Wilson issued the challenge, which was immediately accepted. As his second, Wilson chose a student friend of Lyon's named Simon Robertson, who he hoped would talk some sense into Robert.

"Indeed, the details of an agreement, with Lyon offering an apology and Wilson clarifying the intent of his letter, were worked out," wrote the Toronto *Sunday Star*'s Frank Jones some 30 years ago in his "Murder Most Foul" series, "but then Lyon, perhaps egged on by his second, Henry Lelièvre, backed out of the agreement at the last moment."

The impressionable Lyon's selection of Henry Lelièvre as his second was the worst choice possible, if cool-headedness was the desired end. Many times that evening and the following day, Lyon wavered on the verge of sending a conciliatory message to his friend. At one point he tried to cook up a scenario that would allow both of them to retire from the field with all the honour the bristling protocol-mad town demanded even of civilians, especially where the purity and reputations of defenseless maidens were concerned. Each time Robert Lyon wavered, his young second Henry Lelièvre talked him out of his resolve, convincing him that he was the injured party who must at all costs, even against his own wishes, defend his noble name.

The site chosen for the duel by both seconds was a ploughed field beside the Tay River, about a mile from town, just beyond the Perth sheriff's area of jurisdiction, to spare that popular officer any possible embarrassment. As the appointed hour of 6:00 pm approached, black clouds were gathering and thunder rumbled ominously in the distance. A light rain began to fall. The furrows in the field were ploughed in ruler-straight lines, as if deliberately to make it easier for duellists to line up their sights. The two parties aligned themselves accordingly along the furrows while the preparations were being observed.

There were instructions from Dr William Hamilton, the surgeon in attendance, about procedures to follow if one or the other received a mortal wound in the initial volley. In Canada at that time, the victor and his second in this duel would both be charged with murder if a death should occur, not, as in the United States where guns were carried openly and even fatal shoot-outs by two men facing each other resulted in minor penalties, if any.

Both principals and seconds having nodded their grim acceptance of these draconian conditions, they also agreed that the dropping of an umbrella should be the signal for them to fire. Then the two white-lipped friends, back to back, holding identical, clumsy, foot-long pistols, began the fateful paces, turning to face each other at a distance of some 30 feet and trying to wipe each other off the face of their lovely green earth.

James Boulton was running toward the scene of conflict when he saw the twin puffs of smoke and then heard the crash of the weapons. He had known the duel was on, but might have been late because he had been trying to locate Wilson's father, or perhaps Bob Lyon's half-pay officer brother George, to urge the boys back to sweet reason.

Nobody died or was even scratched on the first volley, both of them firing wide, either out of courtesy or the unmanageable heft of the weapons. "Boulton, peering through the rain, saw both men still standing and breathed a sigh of relief," the *Star* story continued. "In these affairs, apologies were usually exchanged after one shot had satisfied honour."

With this in mind, the surgeon in attendance hurried forward and asked the seconds to stop the affair for a few minutes with a view to reconciliation. "That's impossible," Lelièvre told him. "Then let me speak to Lyon," said the doctor. Lelièvre said that wasn't possible either, until both guns were reloaded. "However," Dr Hamilton was to testify, "I went to Lyon and said, 'For God's sake, Lyon, is there no way to put a stop to this unfortunate business?' 'Doctor, it's impossible,' said Lyon."

Dr Hamilton then hurried over to where Wilson and Robertson, his second, were standing and found them, as he'd expected, ready to exchange apologies and forget the whole thing. But as he turned back to the others, he saw that Lyon was taking up his position with the gun in his hand. The doctor then turned away, defeated.

The story in the *Star* concludes:

> Advised by a frustrated Robertson that he must also resume his position, Wilson did so with obvious reluctance. As he was setting his feet firmly in place, he was horrified to see that Lelièvre had directed Lyon to move over to the same furrow as his own. From the young Frenchman's gesticulations and the cool, decisive way he was showing Lyon how to aim, it was plain he meant his man to use the arrow-straight furrow as a helpful gunsight.
>
> Once more the signal was given. Once more, two heavy, smoothbore duelling pistols exploded together, but this time only one man was left standing when the smoke cleared. John Wilson, looking amazed, stunned, incredulous, dropped his weapon to examine himself all over, half-expecting to see blood gushing from a mortal wound. Only when his sec-

ond assured him that the pistol ball had missed him entirely could he gaze around to see his friend, face down in the muddy field and at Lelièvre, horrified as he looked down upon his handiwork. Lelièvre swiveled about and walked rapidly, almost running, toward the distant town.

What happened then is mired in controversy. Dr Hamilton rushed over to the stricken Lyon, but there was nothing he could do. The ball had pierced the right side of his chest and shattered his lungs. He died within a few minutes, according to Hamilton. Others say he was carried on a door to a nearby house, *Inge-va*, where Thomas Radenhurst, his employer and brother-in-law, lived, and that he died while a servant was being sent next door to borrow more rags to staunch the bleeding. The Rev William Bell had a third version. He reported seeing the body in a farmhouse close to the duelling spot, while two magistrates and a jury conducted an inquest. Radenhurst was sitting beside the body drunk, crying and swearing by turns and abusing Mr Boulton and his connections.

Henry Lelièvre, his murderous machinations revealed for everyone to see, was making tracks, metamorphosing from the idle, well dressed nobody the community despised, into an equally scorned backwoods vagabond who was later reputed to have died in Australia. His other victims, Wilson and Robertson, languished in the Perth jail until their trial for first-degree murder, Wilson as the principal, Robertson as his accessory, which came up before a judge at the August assizes in nearby Brockville.

The case created a sensation with its promise of scandal in high places. "The courtroom was crowded to excess," reported the *Brockville Recorder*. "Among those present were a number of respectable females."

One of my major sources for this file was the memoirs of a Perth woman, Winnifred Inderwick. She records that Robertson and Wilson took their own defence; both had legal training, of course. Four people first told what they had seen. The surprise witness was Adam C Muir, a close friend of Robert Lyon's, so close, indeed, that he swore Lyon had come to him at 6:00 AM while he was still in bed and asked him to be his second. It was only after Muir declined the honour that Lelièvre offered his services and was accepted. James Boulton's testimony made himself appear idiotic: "I learned about five o'clock on the 13th that a meeting was expected … and shortly after that they were going out. I thought it impossible at that time, as it was raining."

The other two were William C Reade, a lad of 13 or 14, who was working in his dad's potashery (potash plant) when he heard the first shot fired, and Deputy Sheriff Alexander Powell, who testified he stopped about a quarter mile from the parties, asked George Lyon if he should interfere, was told not to (it was outside Powell's bailiwick) and then heard the shot fired.

Wilson himself then addressed the jury, telling them that it had all been a terrible mistake:

> I was led from step to step, still in hopes nothing serious would occur until the fatal moment when the pistol was put in my hand for the second time. Then indeed I felt the awful reality of the situation. I expected to be killed. But death was less terrifying than the frowns and reproaches of my friends and a scornful world.

Robertson's speech was just as flowery and grandiloquent: "If the jury thinks the lives of two unhappy youths are necessary to vindicate the majesty of the offended laws, for the purpose of putting down a practice [duelling] which, if permitted, I should long deplore, I would without a murmur resign my life to the sacrifice."

Both young men, obviously coached by older, wiser heads, stressed that toward poor Robert Lyon they felt only good will, not malice, the essential ingredient to constitute murder. The jury of their peers took the point and in a short time returned verdicts of not guilty. Rev Mr Bell wrote, "The jury ... were Irish, who consider fighting commendable rather than a crime."

Both *Maclean's* magazine and the *Toronto Star* did a fine job of winding up the loose ends, using insights provided by my ever-increasing piles of relevant material.

> Wilson, his lesson learned, renewed his attentions with Joanna Lees, writing her long letters, pleading for a second chance in the months following his acquittal, [said the Star]. But her parents were outraged and firmly opposed the connection. Repulsed, Wilson turned again to the maligned Miss Hughes. Short of funds and with her reputation in tatters following the duel, she gratefully accepted his hand, and in the spring of 1835 they were married. The couple moved first to Niagara and then to London, where Wilson, perhaps fearing creatures he could not put a name to, built a fortress-like stone house, Elmhurst, with walls 2 feet thick and deeply recessed windows.

As mysterious and dramatic as the event itself are the Radenhurst, Sanford and Inderwick adventures which we came upon while tracking down the story of Canada's last fatal duel.

I came by the new material as a result of an energetic gameplan to make the Ontario Archives a household name in the world of manuscript collection. Delivering speeches to any group who would listen, often dressed in buckskin or kilt, writing news and feature stories about the work at hand and the philosophy behind it, I was also collaborating with any organization even remotely connected with my field. One of these was the Royal Ontario Museum (ROM), which then as now was far more famous than the Ontario Archives. The ROM had fine collections of fossils, totem poles, Chinese relics and other interesting items that visitors could actually touch, and had been giving lessons about them to generations of Canadian school children, in Ontario and beyond.

The Museum even sponsored its own archaeological expeditions to such exotic places as Persia, Iraq, and fabled Samarkand. The Canadiana branch of the ROM maintained particularly harmonious relations with the Archives because, being perennially strapped for space, they shared any spare niches and crannies.

When I joined the Ontario Archives I was greatly assisted by Verschoyle ('Vers') Benson Blake, dean of Ontario historians, and grandson of the second Premier of Ontario. Blake was shy and retiring, but had an awesome knowledge of Ontario history. As I was the new boy with the Archives, he took me under his wing and freely shared his knowledge. This included *entrée* to many an old Ontario home stuffed with papers. Vers Blake styled himself as the last of the Edwardian gentlemen. He played this role with great gusto and made his contacts available once he discovered that I was prepared to ask people for their papers, which he couldn't bring himself to do. He delighted in field trips, and it was on just such a trip that he introduced me to the woman who owned the papers that included the story of the duel.

Mrs Winnifred Inderwick was a Perth socialite with family and business ties to important people all over Ontario. Her frank reminiscences and shrewd insights into her own and her forebears' ways of thought and action provided a piquant counterpoint to the more somber aspects of the case. Her lovely old stone house (to which the mortally wounded duellist Lyon may have been carried), was called *Inge-va*, meaning "Come here" in the Tamil language of Ceylon (now Sri Lanka) where her husband's parents had lived. A plaque commemorating *The Last Duel in Canada* sits at the entrance gate, but her own family history is just as fascinating. Her husband Cyril Inderwick, a founder of the Architectural Conservancy of Ontario, donated the house to the Ontario Heritage Foundation.

The unhappy house to which Robert Lyon, fatally wounded in the Last Fatal Duel was carried on a door. Inge-va (which means, "Come here!" in Tamil) was bought by the father of Charles Inderwick to house the remittance man's family. (Photo courtesy of the Ontario Heritage Foundation)

The pair of flintlock duelling pistols used in the last fatal duel in Canada, in 1833. Appropriately, the fight was over a woman's honour. The silhouette is of Robert Lyon, who died. But everybody involved (including the lady) ended up losing. (Pistols in possession of the Perth Museum)

Soon after the Canadian Pacific Railway was built across the prairies in the 1880s, Mary Ella Lees, a daring and independent young lady from Perth, was on a train headed west to survey some family land near Calgary. Her father forbade her to go, but the fiery redhead borrowed money from her brother, and off she went.

Out west, she met Charlie Inderwick, a charming remittance man with some bad habits. He owned a ranch into which his English father had poured a fortune. Charlie's father tired of the ranching game and sent the young couple, with funds, first back to Perth then on to Ceylon to run his tea plantation. Charlie continued to drink and gamble, and soon chalked up another failure, so his father came up with another drastic financial solution. He brought Mary Ella back to Perth with her

A hand-tinted studio portrait of Charles Inderwick in Alberta, ca 1900. An English 'remittance man,' sent by his father with an allowance to a ranch in Alberta, Charlie married a spunky girl from Perth, Ontario. His father, tiring of the drain on his finances from the ranch, set Charlie's wife and three children up with a house in Perth, and Charlie was sent to a tea plantation in Ceylon (Sri Lanka), where he remained for the remaining 30 years of his life. The Perth house, Inge-Va, played a part in Canada's last fatal duel. (Private collection)

three young boys, and set them up with the house named *Inge-va*, and a lifetime income.

Winnifred Inderwick was the widow of Cyril, one of those three boys. Her father-in-law, Goodtime Charlie, remained in Ceylon and never saw his family again, though he wrote love letters to Mary Ella for over 30 years, and these have survived. As he degenerated through drink and gambling, the letters became more pathetic; a sad ending to a romantic tale.

The opening lines of Winnie Inderwick's memoirs give a hint of the gossip and delicious tidbits to come:

> In the south-west corner of Scotland ... lived a family by the name of Lauderdale. Yes, they were the Lauderdales of Fort Lauderdale, Florida. To get to my Lauderdales, Margaret Lauderdale, a daughter, married a steward on her father's estate, a man named Shaw, and was ostracized. She came with him to Canada about the 1820s ... and settled near Almonte, Ontario. They had 10 children, many of whom died of TB.... I knew only two, my grandfather, William Shaw and his brother Alexander, both of whom became lawyers, Alex in Walkerton, and William remaining in Perth. Before they practised their profession, they were both articled to Dowdy McMartin, one of the earliest lawyers here. He was called Haughty Mac [because] he never allowed a client to sit in his presence....

I was quite familiar with the McMartin name, as some time before I had bought a major collection of papers belonging to Haughty Mac's brother, Alexander McMartin (1788–1853), postmaster, Member of Parliament, and sheriff for Glengarry County. These papers had been stored in the basement of the old McMartin Mill in Martintown and were overlooked until I got on the trail. Unfortunately, I was too late for Haughty Mac's papers.

Mrs. Inderwick's gossipy memoirs are a bit confused over the events leading up to the Wilson trial, perhaps because of her strong personal emotions. She writes that Radenhurst and Boulton had just about come to dueling before Wilson and Lyon tangled, though it was Dowdy McMartin — Haughty Mac — who had challenged Boulton to a duel. Then again, she avers, surely wrongly, that "according to the law of the time, you were not allowed counsel."

Eventually Wilson did have counsel, to the extent of advising him what to say to the jury. At another point she says Rev Mr William Bell went to see John Wilson "and severely admonished him" for his behaviour, reporting back that Wilson was very non-communicative.

As a youngster, Winnie Inderwick's grandfather had boarded with the Wilsons while taking his schooling, and Robert Lyon had lived in *Inge-va*, her home, so her memoirs are indignant on this point: "The doctor, lawyer Boulton, the Radenhursts should have stopped those crazy kids. What was the matter with them to let it go on and that young man to die for nothing, next to nothing?"

Adding to the accounts that had been so well preserved by Mrs Inderwick, I later was able to acquire for the Archives another great resource about Canada's famous last fatal duel. One day, the ROM's Helen Ignatieff, daughter of Col Alexander Fraser, the founder of the Ontario Archives, and wife of Nicholas Ignatieff, warden of Hart House, University of Toronto, told me she had Nora Radenhurst in her office. Nora, an elderly lady from France who had not been in Canada since the 1920s, returned to sell family collections of furniture, art and papers which had been stored in a friend's barn near Barrie for nearly 40 years.

After her parents died in the 1920s, Nora Radenhurst left Canada, with a young artist named Sanford, to live in France. When she became pregnant, Mr Sanford walked out and she never saw him again. Betrayed and abandoned, Nora stayed on in Europe right through World War II, now returning to Canada only because the family house and barn were being sold.

Nora Radenhurst's mother was Emma G Sanford, daughter of SM Sanford of Barrie. If what Nora told me about the name of her child's father was correct, there may have been a family connection. Another possible connection may have been another Mr Sanford, who was reputed to have absconded to South America with funds raised to build the Barrie Opera House, returning the "borrowed" money at a later date. We may some day sort out these Sanfords, or it will be a conundrum for future paper hunters.

When Nora Radenhurst decided to come back to Canada and sell her belongings, her daughter, Daphne, thought it was a poor idea because she had never been to Canada and assumed that Canadians would not appreciate such antiques. Nevertheless, Nora made up her mind to come, so she went to the Canadian Embassy in Paris for information, and was told to contact the National Museum for the artifacts, the National Gallery for the art and the Public Archives in Ottawa for the manuscripts.

Her plane, however, landed not in Ottawa but in Toronto, so she sensibly decided to check out similar institutions in Toronto, and ended up at the ROM Canadiana Gallery, which also housed the Ontario Archives. When Helen Ignatieff introduced me to Nora, I persuaded her to let me handle the Radenhurst papers.

From the documents I purchased from Nora Radenhurst for the Archives, I learned that the Radenhursts were Swiss immigrants who came first to Quebec and then, in 1824, to Perth, in Upper Canada, where Nora's grandfather, Thomas M Radenhurst, opened a law office and prospered. His son, Nora's father, George Radenhurst (1850–1921), was a well known Barrie lawyer. After his death, Nora stored the family treasures, including the papers, in the barn of a neighbour, Marjorie Laidman, next door to her old family home. Soon afterwards she and her companion Sanford left for Europe. The papers remained in the barn for 44 years, until I ferreted them out!

In the Radenhurst case, as in many others, I regarded the hundreds of letters and documents I bought from Nora Radenhurst as a prime source for leads to other collections. Historians could have access to the papers, after I had mined them for tips to other papers that might allow synchronicity to take effect. Often this was a time to use reverse genealogy, which entailed tracking down descendents of other players in the drama of the last fatal duel. Within weeks of obtaining the first batch, after Nora insisted on sorting through the material she hadn't seen for 40 years, I was chasing numerous leads to other possible sources suggested by the papers.

In September 1990, my wife Muriel and I were in Brussels. We had just finished a two-week Scottish tour. The group we were leading had gone back to Canada and we planned to spend 10 days touring parts of Belgium, Germany and Holland. At dinner, we were discussing the Radenhurst case, when Muriel suddenly remembered that Nora Radenhurst's daughter Daphne had lived in Brussels. So I was away to find a telephone and check directory assistance to see if there were any Radenhursts or Sanfords listed. Nora had told me, 30 years before, that her daughter worked for NATO in Brussels and Paris. I had never been able to locate the daughter before or after Nora died, so I was following a very old and cold trail.

There were no Radenhursts listed in the Brussels phone book, but there was one Sanford. When a female voice answered I stated who I was and gave a few tidbits about this strange tale. It seemed to work; people are intrigued by any tale that hints of mystery. No con man would have concocted the elaborate tale I spun for Terry Sanford and she didn't hang up. We took her to dinner the next night. When Terry met us at our hotel she was accompanied by her teenaged daughter, as she said, "in case you turned out to be a weirdo."

Terry Sanford was a trim, petite, blonde, 41-year-old jockey, married to an Australian jockey named Young. Her story was as unusual as mine.

An unhappy home situation, combined with a love of horses, prompted her to leave her home in England and cross the Channel at age 17. She found a job at a Paris racetrack, becoming the first female jockey in Europe. She told us her grandmother was a mistress of Lord Cowley, and her mother took up with a charming drifter named Richard Clive Sanford who disappeared soon after Terry's birth, never to be seen again. She said RC Sanford was considerably older than her mother, and it occurred to us that he could have been the same Sanford who had run off to Europe with Nora Radenhurst. We have no proof, and may never have; in the meantime Terry and I continue our research.

My story of acquiring two sets of papers about Canada's last fatal duel, both involving the Radenhurst family, really got her attention. It seems more than co-incidental that I should find the only person named Sanford in Brussels, whose father might fit the profile of the man I was after, though Terry was clearly not Daphne, the daughter of Nora Radenhurst.

Returning to Canada, I was all fired up about this new angle to the case and tried to look up Marjorie Laidman, Nora Radenhurst's old friend who had stored the Radenhurst effects in her barn up until 1965. Alas, I was too late; Marjorie had been dead for five years. I interviewed her neighbours in north Toronto and one of them put me in touch with Ken Reese of Barrie, son of a family friend. The legwork paid off, as I was sent to see Margaret Stewart, a feisty 82-year-old woman who knew just about everything about old Barrie families, including the Radenhursts. I told her the whole story, which intrigued her, but she didn't think much of my angle on Sanford. She claimed to know who got Nora pregnant, and it was not a Sanford.

Gary French, a local lawyer and historian, got me a profile of Nora's father, George Radenhurst and his wife, who was also a Sanford. There are just too many co-incidences in this story to eliminate the Sanford angle. Something is not being told. All was not lost because Margaret Stewart, bless her, had Daphne Radenhurst's address in Bath, England. No wonder I hadn't found her in Brussels or Paris. I was eventually able to visit Daphne but she had nothing to contribute as all her family papers were in Nora's collection.

Acquiring more details about the Last Fatal Duel seemed possible when my old pal and fellow paperchaser Edward J Phelps, buying several heritage homes to restore, found Judge John Wilson's old office on Richmond Street in London, Ontario. When Ed realized that this Judge Wilson was the survivor of that famous duel, we both made a dash for the old building, hoping there might be some papers there, but alas, we drew a blank. Ed eventually sold Wilson's old office, as it proved to be much too expensive to restore.

At least four Canadian writers, including a judge, produced their own versions of this celebrated event in the 15 years after I procured the Inderwick papers and others relating to the duel, adding their own opinions to the documented material in the Ontario Archives.

> It was a ridiculous murder really ... young dandies preening and prancing like puffed-up game cocks [wrote *the Toronto Sunday Star's* Frank Jones], but in its way, the killing mirrored the pressures and antagonisms that four years later were to burst into the Papineau-Mackenzie Rebellion of 1837.

Maclean's Douglas Marshall ignored any connection to the future rebellion but pointed out that by the 1830s,

> Perth was already an anachronism, an 18th-century English county town blissfully isolated in the backwoods of Canada. Surveyed and laid out in arbitrary military squares in 1815, it was settled the next year by about one hundred half-pay army officers and their families. For two decades, Perth was a Colonel Blimp's paradise. Distinctions of class and precedence of rank were stringently observed.

The Reverend William Bell had said much the same in his journal covering Perth's early years, deploring "the haughtiness, pride, vanity and dissipation of the half-pay officers and their ladies. They minded nothing but dress, visiting and amusements."

In a special paper entitled *The Memorable Duel at Perth*, written in 1970 for the Perth Museum, Lanark County Court Judge Edward Shortt took another tack. Using public manifestos of two leading lawyers scant weeks prior to the duel, he showed how the legal fraternity itself undoubtedly contributed to the absurdly overheated, perilously touchy environment.

> Altho' I am fully persuaded that nothing I can utter will tend in the slightest degree to depreciate the character of James Boulton ... [screamed the broadside of lawyer Daniel McMartin in bold capital letters] [and] Altho' I am equally persuaded that nothing I can advance will heighten the infamy.... Yet having felt myself called upon to demand satisfaction at his hands and having met with a pusillanimous refusal, I am left with no alternative but to proclaim him ... a liar, a coward and a scoundrel....

Boulton's reply to McMartin's insults was more restrained, using nasty little digs and carefully chosen epithets, but no blaring black capital letters:

> I perfectly coincide in the statement of Mr McMartin, wherein he alleges that nothing he can utter will tend in the slightest degree to depreciate my character.... He seems by this admission to be perfectly aware of his own imbecility. If Duelling is any proof of courage (which I deny), I have proved that I am no coward by having given the satisfaction required by the laws of honour to a gentleman to whom I had given cause to call me out. But is there any reason because I choose to fight a duel with a gentleman, that I am to meet every low insignificant scoundrel that chooses to have his feelings wounded?

Maclean's essayed a tighter, terser wind-up:

> Everybody lived unhappily ever after, especially Wilson. He wrote impassioned letters to his beloved Joanna (which have recently come to light) but she refused to have anything to do with a man ... tainted with such a sordid affair. Wilson gave up in despair and moved to London, Ontario.

About two years later he returned and, as if to salvage some meaning from an utterly pointless victory, married his unclaimed spoils, the celebrated Miss Hughes. Although Wilson went on to become a Member of Parliament and a judge of the Ontario Supreme Court, his wife is said to have nagged him ceaselessly until the day he died in 1869. Mrs Wilson, her earlier becoming freedoms long forgotten, became a strict member of the Plymouth Brethren and died at the age of ninety-four.

Thus ends the story of Canada's last fatal duel.

CHAPTER ELEVEN
TAKING A COWAN AND OTHER METHODS

As a manuscript sleuth, I received leads to valuable collections for the Ontario Archives by any means that came to hand. In this profession, the adventure of seeking the material could be as interesting as the finding of it. Tips from friends provided the most frequent leads, followed by those from owners of papers I'd already acquired. Then might come combing of obituary columns, or running my own ads in local and international media. Then there was overhearing, or 'taking a Cowan.' This is a Masonic term of unknown origin and has various interpretations. One meaning is the finding of sources for research from what you overhear in another person's conversation, an information-gathering technique which has stood me in good stead many times.

In one memorable case, what I overheard involved the family of Sergeant John Hay, who helped defend Quebec against the Americans in 1775. I was in a Spark Street restaurant in Ottawa when I accidentally overheard one of Sergeant John Hay's kin, Dr Thomas Foran, a noted Catholic historian from the University of America in Washington, arguing about the disposal of his effects. Dr Foran was telling his friend, while I sat in the next booth, about a large collection of family papers his brother Phillip, who practiced law across the river in Hull, had asked him to work on. This work consisted of transcribing and translating hundreds of 19th-Century letters from French, Gaelic and Latin to English, a monumental task, for which Dr Foran, however, was well trained.

This incident occurred in 1960 while I was lunching with my brother Roy, who was *en route* to Germany as a 2nd Secretary in the Canadian embassy. I had already gleaned from the overheard conversation that the papers involved Foran's maternal ancestor Sgt John Hay, who emigrated from Scotland to Prince Edward Island, joined the 84th Royal Highland Emigrant Regiment, and at the end of the Revolutionary War settled in Glengarry County.

This was four years before I joined the Ontario Archives, but as I was president of the recently created Glengarry Historical Society, my antennæ for finding papers were already at work. Quickly introducing myself, I told them I lived in Glengarry and would be interested in these papers. Later, after I joined the Archives, this was one of the first of many major collections for which I made a bid. It was not to be ours for many years, until the task of transcribing was done. It was well worth the wait, because never again was I able to get a collection upon which so much tender loving care had been lavished.

I made many visits to the Seigneury Club at Montebello, Quebec where Dr Foran resided, also to the Foran mansion in Aylmer, Quebec where his brother Phillip lived.

Mary Hay Foran, mother of Thomas and Phillip Foran, had been trained in art by the Ursuline Sisters in Quebec City. The old Hay home on the Gleninore Road in Williamstown contains a permanent record of her artistic ability, but in a very strange place. Mary painted her mother with braided hair, in a low-cut gown, sitting at a table holding a hand of cards. The painting was done in oils on the inside of the back door.

Mary Hay Foran was part of a network of local historians who researched, wrote, and often met to compare notes, between 1900 and 1945. We owe them a great debt. Mary Hay Foran and Farquhar McLennan would gather with Carrie Holmes McGillivray, author of *The Shadow of Tradition*, Jack Greenfield McDonell, author of *Sketches of Glengarry in Canada*, and Archibald de Lery McDonald.

Also in this group was Msgr Ewan J Macdonald, my mentor, who had to be called in to assure the Forans they were doing the right thing in turning their papers over to the son of a Presbyterian cleric. At one point, Dr Foran was seriously considering giving the collection to his *alma mater* St Francis Xavier in Antigonish, Nova Scotia. It took the intervention of the Monsignor to squelch that idea.

The following quotations from two letters illustrate some of the more unusual problems facing a 19th century parish priest, in this case Father George Hay, son of Sgt. John Hay. The entire collection deserves publishing, but following are some examples.

Roderick McDougall writes to Father Hay from Lochiel, Glengarry on October 14th, 1839 with a strange problem.

> I am informed that Mr. Malcolm McKinnon of Eigg has been getting himself called [wedding banns being read] at St Andrews, with Christie McDonald daughter of Roderick. I have to request that you will stay all further proceedings in the matter as I have a claim on the young woman

having contracted to be married and have called twice at St Raphaels and St Andrews.

It is a wonder that Father Hay settled that request without incurring someone's wrath!

Father John McDonell writes Father George Hay from Belleville, Upper Canada on June 9th, 1831 with a much more unusual problem:

> George it is really too much! From the bottom of my heart I am injured innocence. But to the point at once, for this will be my last letter. I conjure you keep it secret! Well a lady of the first rank in Kingston, to whom I have never once spoke has blindly, deeply, irretrievably almost fallen in love with me. She wrote me on the 9th ultimo an anonymous letter couched in plain but illogical words. I thought it was a hoax, I laughed at it. Well, that day I got another inflammatory one, almost indelicate one. She told me all my difficulties, almost everything which happened and by everything sacred conjured me to forsake the gown and be united to her.

Some things just never change, and we are left hanging as there is no further reference to this potentially torrid romance. Could Dr Foran have done some judicious editing while translating?

Even after long years' experience, I was never able to judge beforehand how long it might take to have the written records of a subject's life in my possession. The seemingly simplest collection could run into one snag after another, or have conditions of release imposed that I could not accept. Again, following my most persuasive efforts, whole reams of important documents could suddenly be made available. In the case of RR McLennan, always called 'Big Rory,' it was a mixed bag. I knew where the papers were and who owned them, but it took close to 18 years to get them.

It started in 1964, when Dr Simon Fraser of Cornwall provided numerous well qualified leads. I was to see Randolph McLennan, a brusque Kingston entrepreneur with a passion for Glengarry history. His uncle Farquhar McLennan (no relation to RR) worked for Big Rory on railroad contracts from Florida to Lake Superior until the latter's death in 1907. Farquhar called in a carpenter, who made sixteen wooden cases in which to store all Big Rory's papers. They were stacked in the basement of the McLennan Block in Cornwall until I got at them in 1964.

Farquhar managed the McLennan estate until his death in 1948. He was a packrat collector, saving the most trivial scraps of paper, even all his receipts for haircuts. He was also a first class local historian who, over many years, had saved hundreds of historical documents. These were all meticulously filed, year by year with his diaries and business papers. Farquhar and Rory would be pleased to know that my persistence resulted in both collections being saved for future historians.

I have a most impressive picture showing the papers stacked four feet high, ready to be loaded into my station wagon. Many stories are told about Farquhar, including the observation that he was so tight he squeaked. He is reputed to have once phoned in an order to his butcher, including a half pound of liver for his cat, a few minutes later calling back to cancel the liver, as his cat had caught a mouse and he wouldn't need it.

I first heard of Big Rory (Col RR McLennan) when I was about 10. My father was telling me how Big Rory won the light heavyweight boxing crown at McGill when he was studying theology there. "My records," Father explained, "were nothing compared to those of Big Rory, who was the champion hammer thrower, not just in Glengarry but in the world. Why, many of his records are still unbeaten!"

Big Rory was born in 1842, son of a veteran of the Rebellion of 1837 and grand-nephew of the famous Finnan "Buffalo" McDonald, a huge Indian fighter and fur trader who in 1827 wrestled a wounded buffalo to the ground near the Saskatchewan River. Though fearfully gored and fainting from loss of blood, he survived to fight again. Big Rory himself was aptly nicknamed, being 6 foot 6 inches, strong, fast and agile on his feet.

Rory also had a good head for figures, a fine handwriting style, and a manner that instilled confidence in all who knew him. He planned to join the family trade, construction in all its forms, especially railroad-building, the mid-century's biggest and most bustling business.

Big Rory also ran and jumped, but early in his athletic career he won so many of these track events that he ran out of opponents. From then onward, he concentrated on tossing weights great distances, competing all over the world against the best in the field. At one point when doubts were raised about his legendary feats, the *Toronto Star* checked them out and issued an affidavit on Rory's records. These showed his victories, several against the great Scottish hammer-thrower, Donald Dinnie, to include the following:

May, 1865, Cornwall, 12 lb. hammer, handle inc, with a run 216 feet.
July 11, 1865, Buffalo, 10 lb. hammer, handle inc, with a run 285 feet.
Aug., 1865, Charlottetown, 16 lb. hammer, handle inc, with run 180 feet.
1872 Caledonia Games, Toronto, 21 lb. 5 oz. hammer, without handle, with run (swing) 130 feet 4 inches. with handle, 91 feet 7inches, from standing at a mark.
1872 Caledonia Games in Toronto, 50 lb. weight by ring, 37 feet.
1873 Buffalo, NY, 22 lb. ball, 36 feet 2 inches.

Big Rory invariably gave his opponents a hefty edge. When he won at Buffalo in 1865, for example, it was his 10-pound hammer against a man throwing only a 1¼ pound nail hammer. Considerable odds! At another advertised meet on Grand Island, near Buffalo, he threw a five pound hammer against all comers throwing a one-ounce stone, his only condition being that the one ouncer should not be flat. He beat them all.

Sadly, after the 1870s, Big Rory threw the hammer no more after a tragic accident at Cornwall, when a little girl dashed out of the crowd and was killed by his hammer. Ralph Connor worked the incident into one of his novels.

Rory was off building railroads in the USA when another Canadian, named Thomas Jeremy, who had just defeated Tait, Scotland's best hammer thrower, by a whopping 35 feet, challenged Rory to a world championship contest. There was a side bet of $1000. The mayor of Cornwall went looking for their native son, who came back, won the match, the money and the gold medal and then nonchalantly returned, by rail, to his other world-class vocation. There's no doubt that in this field Rory was Canada's greatest 19th-Century athlete.

Col RR McLennan's early railroad work was with Sir Sandford Fleming on the Intercolonial Railway from Montreal to Halifax, but he came into his own both career-wise and financially during the building of the CPR. Rory's method was to bid on a contract for a certain length of track to be finished by a certain date. He'd then hire experienced workmen from Glengarry, pay them well, with bonuses for their money-saving or time-saving ideas. Their confidence in him did the rest.

On a late-season 1883 CPR contract north of Lake Superior, Rory was having trouble obtaining supplies, which he solved in his typical fashion by buying the steamer *Enterprise*. Disaster struck when the ship sank in Lake Huron during a storm, with the loss of eight men. Within days he had a new ship, the *Argyle*, which finally delivered his supplies.

The north shore of Lake Superior was rugged, with the railway hugging the rocky shoreline. One of Rory's men came up with the idea of drilling the rock so the ensuing dynamite blast would hurl the shattered rock into the lake, eliminating the need to cart it away. He was rewarded with a Rory-sized bonus.

When lifelong bachelor Rory retired from the railway business after 1885, he had the money and the time to engage in many enterprises. One of these was a private bank, which lasted for nine years but was never a great success, partly because Rory was so accustomed to acting independently that as his partner delicately phrased it, "he often confused the bank's money with his own." Another venture was a newspaper, the *Cornwall Standard*. Five years later he was offering to sell it for $12,000 but found few interested buyers. Other endeavours proved happier. He had bought Glengarry Ranch in Alberta during railroad days and now used it to breed racehorses. One, called The Wandering Jew, won fame for itself and his ranch.

Made Colonel of the local militia, in 1890, Rory entered politics, was nominated by the Conservatives to run for Parliament, won election on his second try and held the post of MP for Glengarry until 1900, his personal contacts making him a popular figure around Parliament Hill. When he died in 1907, RR McLennan left an estate of nearly $400,000, including properties in Ontario, Manitoba and Saskatchewan.

Having no children of his own, Rory had always been generous with his siblings and their children, as well as local hospitals, charities and Queen's University. He'd taken in his brother Alex's Chilean wife and child after Alex deserted them, roundly chastising Alex for his "despicable" act. He was even more generous in his will, leaving sums of $10,000 to $25,000 to some of them and $275,000 and his papers to his nephew Alex.

This nephew was a big, taciturn man who lived in a double house with one side kept for guests and surrounded by fishponds. Acquiring these important manuscripts for the Archives required so many years of wheedling, coaxing and cajoling Alex that several times I despaired of ever succeeding. It was only in 1983, with the inducement of a $22,000 tax credit, that I obtained the 16 huge basswood cases, four tin boxes and other materials that chronicled Big Rory McLennan's astonishingly varied life and accomplishments on Planet Earth.

Another of my problems stemmed from a mistake made by the trust company when they delivered the papers to the National Archives instead of the Ontario Archives. It took me four months to plough through the necessary red tape to get them back where they belonged.

The Rebellion of 1837–38, pitting ordinary Canadians against the official oligarchy known as The Family Compact, had long interested me both privately and in my official capacity with the Ontario Archives. I had been weaned on tales of William Lyon Mackenzie, the fiery crusader who forsook reasoned journalistic arguments in favour of more direct armed confrontation. Anything to do with this hot-headed Scot who fled Upper Canada (Ontario) to escape hanging and set up a provisional government on an island in the Niagara River was for me the stuff of exciting historical drama.

This curiosity included his cohorts, particularly Anthony Van Egmond, William Lyon Mackenzie's military adviser during the 1837-38 Rebellion. Van Egmond escaped the gallows by succumbing to the cold damp conditions in the Toronto jail, dying before he was sentenced. This career soldier from the Netherlands left his mark on the history of Canada, especially in and around Egmondville, in southwestern Ontario. He left numerous descendents, one of whom was Matilda Fowler.

My curiosity was piqued by a picture of Miss Matilda Fowler, hoping this would lead to more papers connected with her great-grandfather, Anthony Van Egmond. Search as I might, I was unsuccessful in finding any important papers of Van Egmond's, but I did get a photograph of Ms Fowler in her youth, her beautiful hair cascading around her ankles. I was smitten with admiration. This lady, it turned out, had her own claim to fame.

Matilda had been a school teacher in the Seaforth area. She later studied art in Toronto, becoming known for her pencil sketches, particularly of horses, which she loved. She journeyed to Europe several times to study and to sketch, and died in the 1940s, at the age of 86.

I learned little else about her, except that the picture was probably taken shortly before her flowing tresses were shorn to more manageable proportions. I kept thinking I'd find further references to her in other Seaforth-area manuscripts. I never did, but one story persisted concerning Matilda's fine head of hair. The picture has her standing at a podium, and it was about this time she was reported to have won first prize at the Chicago World's Fair as the woman with the longest hair in the world.

Far more perilous in their implications were the papers dealing with the internationally sensational murder trial of a Canadian deputy sheriff named Alex McLeod, in Utica, NY, in October, 1841. I acquired these for the Archives from his great-grandson, Oscar McLeod of Niagara Falls, Ontario. Oscar's own career was as interesting as that of his ancestor. He was one of the first pilots with Pan American airways, and later piloted Sir Harry Oakes to and from the Bahamas.

As usual, Oscar McLeod was found by a circuitous route. I had first heard about a descendent of McLeod who was supposed to have family papers while I was literally digging papers from the plaster in the wall of an old house being demolished near Queenston, Ontario. These turned out to be a small, but valuable lot of letters belonging to Col John Claus of the Indian Department. I had been scouting around Niagara, and went to a local bar for a beer and information, as bartenders, like barbers, love to be consulted, and were often my best informants.

I was introduced to a local character, Norman Candler, who eked out a precarious living as a wrecker and diver for jumpers who commit suicide by throwing themselves over Niagara Falls. After a few beers with Norm Candler, the information was flowing freely, and I found that he was something of a collector. He took me home to see his collection of over two dozen ratty looking neckties, many of which were in shreds. When pressed for details, Norm said, "Well, you see when jumpers go over the Falls, their clothes are all torn off, but if they're wearing a tie, it is still on the body, and I keep 'em." This macabre collecting mania did not extend to female jumpers, because Norm just collected neckties.

Next day, we were off to rescue the Claus papers that Norm had spotted. Then he sent me to see Oscar McLeod, a balding, easygoing entrepreneur who ran a gift shop in downtown Niagara Falls. He was eventually able to provide me with what remained of Alexander McLeod's papers. He continued to be a prime contact in the Niagara area.

The murder trial of McLeod's illustrious ancestor related to William Lyon Mackenzie's 1837 flight to the USA and the government-in-exile he set up on Navy Island. There was an attack by British marines on the American vessel *Caroline*, which was allegedly supplying the Navy Island rebels. The vessel was cut loose and sent over Niagara Falls, killing one man in the process. Two years later, McLeod was overheard boasting in US and Canadian taverns that it was he who had set the *Caroline* adrift and killed a Yankee in the process. His arrest on his next stop at an American port enraged the British government, which arrogantly claimed it had a right to hot pursuit of its enemies even into US waters, and vowed dire consequences, perhaps even war, if government officer McLeod should be convicted.

There was no account of McLeod's trial in the McLeod papers I had acquired from his great-grandson Oscar, so on a hunch I went to Utica, New York, where the trial had been held. I interviewed a number of people, and eventually located a history buff, Judge Ryan, who had accumulated a vast assortment of information about the trial. From him I obtained a transcript and information about the trial proceedings.

Crack Utica lawyer Joshua Spencer was hired to defend McLeod. Anti-British vigilante groups calling themselves Hunter's Lodges (after their chief, a Vermonter named Hunter) swore to break McLeod out of jail and lynch him. A hundred militiamen were posted about the jail where Sheriff Moulton swore he would not let McLeod escape if convicted, nor be harmed in any way if acquitted. Before Judge Philo Gridley and a jury, the case proceeded smoothly.

According to the *Utica Evening Observer*:

> A reading of the testimony discloses that the prosecution had difficulty placing McLeod at the scene and the statement of his boastings came from persons obviously sympathetic to or members of Hunter's Lodges.... In addition, Spencer was able to produce witnesses who placed McLeod some miles from the scene of the attack. Judge Gridley's charge to the jury showed he understood only too well the gravity of the situation. "If you believe this man is guilty of murder, then, fearless of the consequences ... though they shall wrap your country in a flame of war ... look to the God of Justice and say whether the prisoner be guilty or not."
>
> [The story wound up:] In 28 minutes, the jury returned a verdict of not guilty.... The sheriff was happy to deliver his prisoner to Plattsburgh safely. McLeod received a hero's welcome in Montreal, Spencer received a fee of $10,000 from the British Government, and Judge Gridley was loudly praised by the London papers for his integrity and fairness.

The defence's strongest point, after making mincemeat of witnesses who claimed to have heard McLeod boasting of his misdeed, was to prove he was miles away at the home of Mrs Ellen Morrison the night the Caroline was scuttled. Mrs Morrison's father, a retired British officer, swore McLeod had dinner with them, then stayed overnight and all the next day with the family. Having no opportunity to question the accused, State's attorney Willis Hall concentrated on the ramrod-stiff British officer. His first question was a strange one:

"Was Morrison related in any manner to McLeod?"

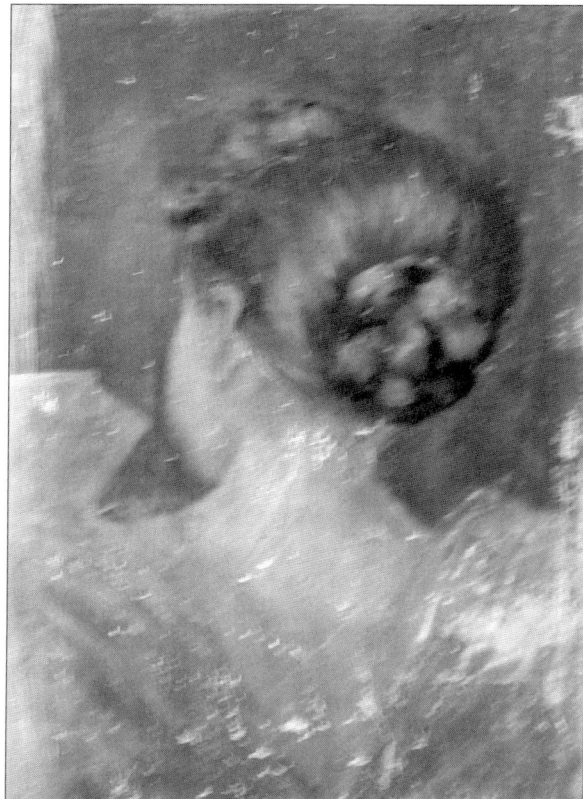

*"Kathleen Hay's work on the outer panel kitchen door at the former Hay house on the Gleninore Road in Williamstown."
... a woman holding a hand of cards, viewed from behind.*

When Morrison's voice, up to now ringing with sincerity, was a whispered "No," Hall called him a liar and asked Judge Gridley to dismiss all his testimony.

In the uproar that followed, Hall shouted, "Isn't it true that McLeod is married to your daughter, and that they lived together as man and wife in a house in Niagara until he was arrested?"

"Y-yes, it's true. But no, they are not married!"

"What?"

"Recollect I am on my oath," cried the crusty officer, in a strangled voice. "My daughter is married to a Southern gentleman named Taylor. McLeod persuaded her to leave him and come and live with him!"

"You ... you are a LIAR, sir!"

"Your Honour," shouted Spencer. "I object, most strongly!"

"Mr. Hall, do you have any proof that the witness is lying?"

State's Attorney Hall turned to face Judge Gridley.

"No sir. But the marriage records for 1840 in St. Mark's Anglican

Church, where they were married, are missing, although all other years back to 1796 are intact. Those records were removed to make this deception possible."

The judge remarked that this was merely supposition and that Hall must not question the witness any further on this point. Hall replied that in all humility, he had to question the wisdom of the court.

"Not another word about humility!" retorted the judge. "I'll permit no departure from the rules of propriety in this court."

Turning to the jury, he said, in a voice struggling for control, "Gentlemen, you will retire to consider your verdict!" The verdict of Not Guilty was greeted locally with skepticism and even the great jurist and orator Daniel Webster would say only "Smart Alex!" a term of derision that long outlived its creator.

Duncan McLeod of Westmount, PQ, brother of Oscar McLeod from whom I had acquired the McLeod papers, believes that his ancestor and Morrison were ordered to sacrifice their families' honour to prevent a war that neither country wanted. There are many clues pointing this way, Duncan McLeod declares, chief among them being the name "Mrs Alexander McLeod" on the list of communicant members of Lundy's Lane Presbyterian Church for the period. This wouldn't have been possible unless Ellen Morrison were legally married to McLeod. There's one final proof. In the graveyard of the church is a stone bearing the inscription "ELLEN MORRISON, WIFE OF ALEXANDER M^cLEOD."

From 19th-Century high drama to the inner workings of a 20th-Century labour union may seem an abrupt leap, but in my world they are both represented by the same highly useful basic material, paper. For a change, I didn't have to sweet-talk officers of the Mine, Mill and Smelter Workers Union into letting me handle their records. "We're proud of being the only local to have successfully resisted the raiding by the Steelworkers," Mine, Mill president Mike Solski told me when we met in Sudbury, Ontario, in August 1980. He asked only that I wait until he received his Canada Council grant and had his book a bit further along before he turned over the collection.

Earlier on, I had had great co-operation from Weir Reid, of Sudbury, who provided personal material on the union's struggles for recognition and suggested a dozen other sources from Ontario to BC to Pittsburgh, PA, where I might obtain more. Mr. Reid died shortly afterward, and his widow kept on supplying me with new material, new people to see, and new avenues of approach to other sources. I can't thank them enough. It turned out to be the only major collection of labour union records I ever acquired.

An interesting example of neo-conservative thinking occurred years later in Sudbury, partly as a result of the publicity engendered by my acquisition of those union records. In presenting honorary degrees at Laurentian University, Dr Henry Best, President of Laurentian University in Sudbury, looked for people whose careers had made some significant contribution. The career could be controversial, even bizarre, but they must have done something unique. Examples included Douglas Pollard, proprietor of the Highway Bookstore in Cobalt, Ontario, for helping bring culture to the north country, and Jackrabbit Johannsen on the occasion of his 105th birthday, for pioneering and promoting cross-country skiing. I received one myself for, as one wag put it, 20 years of amiably privateering papers from across Ontario. Bob Carlin was granted a degree for his outstanding contribution toward saving the Sudbury branch of the Mine, Mill and Smelter Workers Union. This degree cost the university several million dollars. INCO president Parker was no admirer of Carlin, so when he heard about the honorary degree, he forthwith withdrew his donation in a fit of rage.

One collection I found produced an unusual reaction. Sir William Mackenzie (1849–1923) with Sir Donald Mann (1853–1934) built the Canadian Northern Railway line, which would one day become the Canadian Northern Railway. Five trunks full of papers once belonging to Sir William's brother Alexander were in the basement of a house being sold by one of his granddaughters. In May of 1978, I discovered this through an alert Beaverton boy and his teacher, local historian Rae Fleming.

To my dismay, I found the five trunks of papers had been subject to floods in that basement for 60 years. When I tried to remove them, the trunks fell apart. The papers in the bottom half of each trunk were a sodden mass of pulp. It was late at night when I eventually got home with the papers I had salvaged from the mouldy, fungus-laden trunks.

Exhausted, I fell into bed. I awoke in the middle of the night to find my body covered in welts, accompanied by a high fever and aching bones. This was the start of major problems with allergies and bronchial asthma that I have suffered ever since. I should have been wearing a mask over my mouth and nose. Archivists today are instructed to do that when handling old and decaying material, but not at that time.

The Mackenzie papers proved what I had long known, that these two smalltown Ontario boys, Mackenzie from Kirkfield and Mann from Acton, grew up to be geniuses at selling themselves and their projects, however implausible.

Mackenzie and Mann built a totally redundant railroad based on virtually nothing but a magnificent gift of gab [said one review of their careers].

They acquired in the process the equivalent of a quarter billion dollars in public money. Their combined private fortune was estimated at $40,000,000.Yet they had the nerve to keep coming back, silk topper in hand, pleading broke and begging for more.

Photographs of the two show ex-school teacher Sir William Mackenzie looking more like a diplomat than a railroader, and ex-lumberjack Sir Donald Mann as just what he always had been, the tough construction boss in charge of pushing what turned out to be more than 16,000 kilometres of track across northern Canada. Described as "earnest, totally humourless Presbyterians" and berated by Prime Minister RB Bennett for their "shameless mendicancy," greed and falsifications, they were still revered by millions for opening up Canada's great northland to industry and settlement.

In a review for *Ontario History* of Dr Rae Fleming's award-winning biography, *The Railway King of Canada*, Mark Rosenfeld presents the following more balanced view of Mackenzie:

> One of the most interesting features of The Railway King of Canada is its attempt to understand the nature of Mackenzie's entrepreneurial mind. Here is Fleming at his most imaginative, drawing on art and literature to sketch his portrait. Mackenzie is presented as a visionary, an exemplar of creativity and optimism who could turn the era's infatuation with speed, efficiency, and consumerism into profitable ventures.... Like a film editor who creates an illusion of time and space, Mackenzie reshaped and edited the Canadian landscape with railways and hydroelectric plants.... He selectively edited his own past when recounting his personal biography.... Mackenzie was the grand illusionist, a conjurer who convinced others to believe in his dreams, a financial wizard who made those dreams happen. We also see a man sometimes plagued by self-doubts and prone to physical breakdown during periods of stress.

William Dunlop (1792–1848), an earlier Scot who also changed Ontario's landscape, died one year before Sir William Mackenzie was born. Journalist, politician, military doctor, world traveller, Dunlop served only brief, but hectic, periods in what is now Ontario. He was best known as "Tiger" Dunlop, for taking time out to fill the mandatory *pukka sahib* role of killing one of these great cats while he was editor of a Bombay newspaper. Dunlop was a devotee of snuff, and made good use of it in hunting tigers. He would ride in style on the back of an elephant with a small container of snuff lashed to a bamboo pole. As they approached a tiger the elephant jockey would lower the bait in front of the tiger, who would sniff at it and break into a fit of sneezing, at which point Dunlop would shoot the tiger.

A part of William Dunlop's work in Canada was with the Canada Company, a joint venture of the Province of Upper Canada and the British Colonial Office to allocate land around Lake Huron to former soldiers. His work for the Canada Company is now on record for all interested parties to see, but the following revealing items might be overlooked. Documents about his unusual career came into my possession, along with a 19th-Century transcript of his very illuminating will which I found in Goderich, Ontario.

Taken in conjunction with passages from R & K Lizars' book, *In the Days of the Canada Company*, it gives an amusing glimpse of the "Tiger" in his den.

First, he would bring out his military chest containing a dozen large bottles, which he called The Twelve Apostles. The brandy bottle was Paul, Peter held the whiskey, and the one containing water was called Judas. The Dunlop recipe for hot whiskey toddy was to put a spoon in the tumbler and fill up with boiling water; then pour out the water, fill with whiskey and drink quickly.

Years before his death, when the irreverent doctor was reading his proposed will aloud to his guests, his sister-in-law objected, but with no effect until he came to a description of herself as "outrageous and not to be borne." He finally agreed to expunge everything relating to her and leave all his property to his sisters, Helen and Elizabeth "the former, that no man of taste would have taken but was married to a minister whom (God help him) she henpecks, the latter because she is married to nobody, nor is she like to be for she is an old maid and not market ripe."

Among other bequests were:

> my silver tankard to the eldest son of old John. I would have left it to old John himself, but he would melt it down to make temperance medals ... and my books to my brother Andrew, because he has been so long a *jungley wallah* (bush man) that he may learn to read with them. One guest thought the will so *outré* that it might not be legal, but another opined that it was eccentric ... but not illegal ... reflecting indifference to what is called Fashion, even in testamentary matters.

Unlikely as it seems, Dr William "Tiger" Dunlop, the burly, brutally frank, bibulous globetrotter, wound up his Canadian capers as superintendent of the Lachine Canal.

While researching Captain Walter Sutherland, the British spy, I examined a letter Chief Justice William Osgoode had sent to his wife, mentioning a fatal duel involving Walter's brother David Sutherland. I suspected that another, unsigned, letter I had found, dated July 23, 1792, may also have originated with the Chief Justice, so I showed the two letters to an expert on handwriting. He declared them to be written by one and the same person. My hunch paid off and suddenly more exciting things developed, concerning my ancestor Walter and presenting an interesting question about William Osgoode.

The two-page letter, datelined Kingston, Upper Canada, July 23, 1792, written by Chief Justice Wm Osgoode to his wife in England, posed a puzzle for which I have never found an explanation. The letter describes Osgoode's voyage from England to Canada. As a person of some rank, he mentions that in Quebec he "had the honour of dining with Prince Edward, His Majesty's fourth son, who is in Garrison with his regiment there. He is a very fine figure, six feet high, very discreet in his Conduct and an avowed Enemy to Gaming and Drinking."

From Quebec, Justice Osgoode travelled by coach to Montreal, where he remained a fortnight.

> It is a much better built City than Quebec. The streets are regular and well paved, with much more appearance of Life, Activity and Business. The Elections for Members to represent them under their new Constitution were on ... and there for the first time I saw that Ladies were permitted to vote. The Returning Officer was an Englishman, which makes it most Extraordinary.

The puzzle is: under what circumstances could women have been voting in 1792 in Lower Canada, when it is a known fact they didn't officially get the vote in Canada until the early 20th Century? I have posed this question to many eminent historians, but none have come up with an answer. Could Osgoode's wife have been an early suffragette whom he was having some sport with? One more unsolved Canadian mystery, but my hunch may be right, in view of the fact that British author Mary Wollstonecraft had argued for the equality of the sexes in her book, *The Vindication of the Rights of Women*, which was published in that very year, 1792.

To examine some Canadian manuscripts for sale in Washington, DC, I took a trip to that city. After acquiring the collection, I came upon six documents written or signed by Walter Sutherland and a brother Joseph. Co-incidentally, I was called to Kingston to bid on more Sutherland manuscripts held by a trust company, after Marjorie Foxton, a reclusive and mildly eccentric Sutherland descendent, had died.

I was able to rescue some of her papers but not before the trust company's hired hands had taken 27 pickup truck loads to the dump. I never trust trust companies to act responsibly around old paper, even though this one said everything had been carefully looked over for anything of value, and only real garbage went to the dump.

Tom Foxton and his daughter Michelle (an archeology student at Queen's University) pleaded with trust company officials to be allowed to help them sort through the paper in the house. They were after any Foxton material, just as I was after Sutherland material. All their offers were rebuffed.

Tom was Reeve (a type of rural mayor) of the Town of Sydenham, where the Foxtons lived. The bulldozer driver at the dump alerted him to some china and papers that he had spotted. Tom retrieved some Royal Doulton plates that had come out from Ripon, Yorkshire, England with his ancestor. There were also some old letters that I have yet to see. So much for the trust company's careful sorting! Strange that they never throw out the art on the wall, the antiques, or the silver, but consider dirty old papers not worth saving. That these might have historical or monetary value rarely crosses the minds of trust officers, or auction people. They could call a local library, but typically don't.

Marjorie Foxton, a retired Latin teacher, had travelled widely with her husband Bernard, but they rarely invited visitors to their home, and always entertained out. I could understand why, when I was able to view the inside of their house. They lived in part of the living room, the kitchen, and one bedroom. One bathroom was used, the other didn't work. The rest of the house resembled a rabbit warren with furniture, china, glass, silver, art, and books piled from floor to ceiling in a jumble, a veritable heaven for an antique picker!

The bedroom where the police found Marjorie was a sad and depressing sight. Cobwebs, festooned with dead flies, hung a warning to us all; reclusiveness and eccentricity can be carried to extremes. I had phoned Marjorie at least once a year since the early 70s, but was only in the house twice, never further than the cluttered living room, and never shown the trunk of Sutherland papers. I now know why: the poor woman was too embarrassed. Assuming they wanted to save all the things they bought or inherited, it is ironic that a good part of what they kept was damaged or destroyed. Doubly ironic is the likelihood that many of the Sutherland papers she saved were in the end destroyed by her intransigence and that of the trust company.

On January 22, 1982, I placed the following advertisement in the "Information Please" column of the *London Times Literary Supplement*:

> Louis Drummond McRaye or McRae, born 1915, Battle of Britain pilot, graduate of Oxford, London School of Economics by 1952, son of Walter McRaye, died 1947, prominent Canadian lecturer. Wish to locate descendents and any papers extant, Hugh MacMillan, Archives of Ontario, Queen's Park, Toronto M7A 2R9, Canada.

A handwritten reply on flimsy notepaper bearing the heading "Roman Catholic Chaplain, University of Warwick, Gibbet Hill Road, Coventry," and dated a month later, carried this message:

> Dear Mr MacMillan:
>
> My attention was drawn to the notice in *The Times*. I am the son of Walter McRaye and a graduate of London (LSE) and Oxford universities, but not a Battle of Britain pilot. I served in the RAF from 1940–46 as a Medical Orderly. If you would let me know what information you would be interested in, I would do my best to supply it. I am his only son, a daughter who would have been my elder sister died very soon after birth. I look forward to hearing from you.
>
> Yours Sincerely,
> Louis McRaye.

The same day the *Times* ad appeared, I had sent off a letter to Mrs Betty Keller in Vancouver, asking about her new book on Pauline Johnson. "I have considerable information on Walter McRaye, who lived with her the last ten years of her life," my letter went on. "Am currently trying to track down a son in England. Should you have any letters or information, we would be grateful to receive copies." When Louis Drummond McRaye learned the sort of information I was requesting, he didn't reply. Mrs Keller's letter threw light on why he might have been so uncommunicative.

Betty Keller wrote:

> Copies of my book, Pauline: *The Life of Pauline Johnson,* will be in bookstores soon. Hopefully it will clear up many of the misconceptions that Canadians embrace about her, including the one that she lived with Walter McRaye. There are at least four other persons attempting books on Pauline at this time, as well.
>
> Louis Drummond McRaye was the son of J Walter McRaye and Lucy Betty Webling, whom McRaye married in 1909 in Vancouver. Louis was born in 1914. The following year McRaye went overseas with the medical corps and did not see his son again till 1919. Even then they had little contact, as McRaye went on the road again.
>
> In 1921, Lucy left McRaye and supported her son by writing and working in vaudeville. In 1924, she and her son went back to England. Louis never saw his father again, though he did receive birthday money from him for a few more years.
>
> Louis McRaye has flatly refused to discuss his father … out of dislike of him and loyalty to his mother, whom he believes was abused by McRaye … Louis holds no papers relating to his father, anything he did have being destroyed during the bombing of London.

So I was thwarted in my first attempts to obtain authentic manuscript material on two world-famed Ontario born theatrical artists, Walter McRaye, born at Merrickville in 1876 and Emily Pauline, daughter of Chief George Henry Martin Johnson, born on the Six Nations Oshweken reserve near Brantford in 1862. I would just have to look for other sources.

Their stories were well known, of course, though Pauline's was more familiar to Canadians in the 1980s than that of Walter McRaye, her younger compatriot.

Wearing the splendid Indian garments of the Mohawk princess she was in real life, adorned with intricate beadwork and other finery, often using the name Tekahionwake, she fascinated international audiences for two decades with readings of her own poetry. Tempestuous, flamboyant, and with the primitive beat of tribal drums in every word, according to one fascinated viewer, she rocked whole audiences back on their heels.

Walter McRaye was also a writer and lecturer, and like Pauline, possessed of a dramatic stage presence that thrilled and delighted his own international audiences. Unlike Pauline, however, he didn't promote his own writings but acted out the quaint character of the French-Canadian as portrayed in Dr William Henry Drummond's delightfully humorous poems.

The two Canadian stage luminaries finally met in late December, 1897, in Winnipeg. Pauline, 35, in the prime of her life and not yet married, had recently returned from another triumphal tour of Europe. While she was there, the first volume of her poetry, *The White Wampum*, was published to thunderous acclaim. McRaye, 14 years her junior, had just made his first professional appearance in Brockville and was on his first trans-Canada tour. They had Christmas dinner together, joined in several recitals, then went their separate ways.

They didn't meet again till two years later in Peterborough. This time, McRaye became Pauline's business agent and stage partner. Over the next 10 years, they covered Canada from end to end, even far up the Cariboo Trail to Barkerville during its gold rush. They then went off to London's fashionable drawing rooms and to an equally triumphant performance at Harvard University.

The partnership broke up in 1909, when Pauline became too ill to carry on, and Walter married London actress Lucy Webling. Broke and sick with cancer, with the help of fellow British Columbia writers, Pauline managed to produce some of her best work including, *Legends of Vancouver*. When Pauline Johnson died in hospital on March 7, 1913, Walter McRaye was at her bedside. Her last poem was to him. She was buried in Stanley Park, Vancouver, and her Ontario birthplace was preserved as a memorial to her genius. Walter's wife, Lucy Webling McRaye, who had the distinction of being the first to play the stage role of Little Lord Fauntleroy, toured Canada with Walter for four years, stopping only because of the outbreak of war in 1914. McRaye went off to war, and survived five of the biggest battles. Sustaining an eye injury from exposure to poison gas, he was then dragooned into service as an entertainer. At war's end, he joined the Chautauqua circuit, then bought a farm near Grimsby, where he lived on his memories till his death in 1947.

The McRayes' Chautauqua tours are well documented in scrap books of press clippings that I was able to acquire from Mrs. Tom Fuller of Merrickville.

Much of my knowledge of Pauline and Walter is from interviews with 94-year-old Mohawk Isaac Moses taped on the Six Nations Reserve at Oshweken. Moses had known both Pauline and Walter when he was young, but was sad when he confessed he'd never seen them perform. "She made my heart feel proud," he told me. "Nobody before had paid any attention to people like us."

The recent renewed interest in Pauline has been kept alive by Pauline Carey, who has portrayed her in a one-woman show. Sheila Ferguson of Port Dover, Ontario did a similar act. A real enthusiast, she took her show to Russia, and has been planning a new biography of Pauline. An excellent biography by Charlotte Gray, entitled *Flint and Feather, The Life and Times of E. Pauline Johnson,* was published by Harper Flamingo, Canada in 2002.

While the research proceeds and her story unfolds, as with so many of these engaging Canadians, the complete saga of Pauline Johnson is yet to be revealed. There are always more papers to find.

CHAPTER TWELVE
A GAEL FOR ALL SEASONS

In March 1974, I was on a field trip to Port Glasgow in Elgin County, Ontario, to obtain the papers of Finlay McDiarmid, first Minister of Highways for Ontario. Upon examination, I found included in the collection a copy of a letter dated January 6, 1899, by Duncan Fraser Macdonald to Aubrey White, Deputy Minister of Crown Lands in Toronto. Impressed by Macdonald's skill with words and especially with his use of invective in this political letter, I decided I must find out more about him. Perhaps there were more letters, or even diaries!

It took me over a year of wandering trails to discover Ray Smith, librarian for the Algonquin Regional Library System in Parry Sound. We had information to exchange and it soon became evident that Ray was considerably ahead of me in the chase. He had discovered a son of DF Macdonald, still living, who had his father's diaries along with other material. The son, Aubrey White Colquhoun Macdonald, had apparently known of my interest in manuscripts for the past five years. He had brought in a collection of pictures that his father had taken on the Wolseley expedition of 1870 for the Archives to copy and left word for me to come to see him as he had more material. I never received his message, but luck played a part when I met McDiarmid and later encountered Ray Smith.

The return of the Macdonald diaries to Parry Sound is an interesting tale in itself, with Ray Smith of the Algonquin Regional Library cast in the role of hero.

In the course of doing historical research, Ray came across a copy of a letter written in 1940 by CC Johnson, then Mayor of Parry Sound, to a clergyman named Macdonald in Thunder Bay. It referred to a diary kept by the clergyman's father while he was resident in Parry Sound. A colleague at a Thunder Bay library was only able to tell Ray that there were no Macdonalds of that ilk left in the area, but that a brother of the clergyman, AWC Macdonald might be surviving somewhere. Ray waded through telephone books until he found a WC Macdonald in Etobicoke. Yes, he was a son of Duncan Fraser Macdonald, and yes, he had some diaries. Ray and the local historian, Dave Thomas, went post haste to Etobicoke and brought back a couple of the diaries to read. Then Ray obtained the remaining 45 and devoted countless evenings to copying them in longhand for the Parry Sound Library. Later the Public Archives of Ontario microfilmed all the diaries.

Additions kept arriving for those microfilm reels as more material was located through descendents such as Mary O'Rourke in Thunder Bay, Hugh Macdonald in Edmonton, and Aubrey's son, D Ross Macdonald of Victoria, BC. Every one of them had valuable material for the collection. Later I located descendents of Aubrey White Colquhoun Macdonald and they have joined the search for more documents. The trick in such elusive paper chases, wherever possible, is to involve descendents in the chase, and make sure they get full credit for the roles they play in making the chase a success. The descendents tend to keep in touch with one another as they continue to exchange information, and often go on to work on a family history. In the process, many who had only been distant relatives end up becoming close friends.

John Macfie's book, *Now and Then*, is a collection of his columns on local history in the Parry Sound *North Star*. One of these is titled "A Year in the Life of Duncan Macdonald." Macfie's description of Macdonald is an accurate assessment of the man's many talents:

> Duncan Fraser Macdonald had a hand in just about everything that went on in Parry Sound for its first half century. When he wasn't at centre stage, he could often be found behind the scenes doing his best to manipulate the movers and shakers. Macdonald was a super Grit and political wheeler-dealer in a day when everyone wore his colours on his sleeve. He was also a bushranger, road builder, explorer, prospector, mapmaker, crown timber agent, linguist (Ojibwa, Gaelic, French), whitewater canoeist, gun nut, sportsman. And from time to time, as when an election went the wrong way, he was an unemployed gentleman. But most important of all, he was a keen observer and faithful chronicler of events, the closest Parry Sound has come to having a Samuel Pepys, the City of London [England]'s all-time greatest gossip. Macdonald kept a diary from 1872 until 1919 in small pocket journals which afforded regrettably little room for detail but which had the essential quality of being easily carried around. Macdonald was constantly on the go, usually where the going was hardest.

I would add to this description that Macdonald rarely lost an election and so was seldom unemployed. His most spectacular enterprise was as photographer with the expedition to Fort Garry, Winnipeg, to

*Duncan Fraser
MacDonald
1842-1922*

quell the insurrection of the Métis under their erratic leader, Louis Riel. Led by British General Garnet Wolseley, a small force of British regulars and Canadian militia left central Canada in May, 1870, and were in the capital of the newly created Province of Manitoba by mid-June. As would later be apparent from his diaries, details of Macdonald's *modus operandi* on this ambitious venture are conspicuous by their absence. Dry photographic plates were at least a decade away, so he would have had to prepare his wet plates at the site, expose them almost immediately and then develop them on the spot. Then too, cameras were huge and unwieldy, and stereoscopic slides, the most popular photographic form of amusement and education in middle-class Canadian homes, required two sets of images and a special viewer to give the illusion of depth. How the dauntless 28-year-old lensman journalist managed to keep up, much less be on the *qui vive* for photographic situations, boggles the mind.

Perhaps he didn't go all the way to the Red River with the expeditionary force, but turned back after they reached the Soo. This seems likely because on June 21st, two months before Riel gave up the unequal struggle and fled to the USA, an advertisement appeared in a Parry Sound Newspaper, *The Settler*, offering *Stereoscopic Views of Our Boys en Route for Red River*. Macdonald must have really hustled to be so on top of everything. The advertisement, included a list of slides available at 25 cents each or $2 a dozen. An editorial urged readers to support such a worthy local endeavour:

> We direct attention to the advertisement of our old friend Mr. Macdonald, late of Puslinch, who has been successful in taking a lot of splendid pictures illustrative of scenes and incidents connected with the Red River expedition. Mr. Macdonald is an accomplished photographer and we feel sure his photographs will be first class. Read his advertisement.

The advertisement listed the following:

SHADOWS FROM THE WARPATH
Stereoscopic views of our boys en route to Red River.

- Hudson's Bay Fort at Sault Ste Marie.
- Volunteers under canvas — Officers of No 3 Co, 1st Ont Rifles.
- Sentry on Duty.
- Red River Teamsters at Breakfast.
- Col. Bolton's Staff in group.
- Major Irwin's Tent and Officers of the Quebec Rifles.
- Pioneers Resting.
- Indian Wigwam.
- The Ontario Rifles Camp.
- The Quebec Rifles Camp.
- Some fine Winter Views.
- From the Wilds of Algoma — Voyageurs in Camp.
- Voyageurs on the tramp — Lumberman's Shanty on the Seguin River.

Also several more excellent pictures of Backwoods Scenes. Price 25¢ each, or $2 per dozen. Mailed free of postage to any part. Address DF Macdonald, June 21, 1870, Parry Sound, Ont.

At the same time, I also learned that Macdonald wrote a column for the Parry Sound newspaper, *The Settler*. The paper is not listed in the *Canadian Newspaper Index* and it is not known how long it survived. To illustrate Macdonald's talent as a writer, I quote from his column for August 15, 1873, which covers a trip he made by steamboat from Parry Sound to Collingwood on the Waubuno and from there to Killarney and Little Current, on Manitoulin Island, ending at the Spanish River Mills. The latter portion of the trip was on the famous blockade runner of the American Civil War, the *Chicora*, which ran cotton to England for the Confederate Army, bringing back military supplies in return. The *Chicora*, a fast stern-wheeler, was never caught, and was still sailing the Great Lakes into the early part of the 20th century. Macdonald wrote:

> Embarked on board the *Chicora* at 4 p.m. on Tuesday the 5th inst, having on board a large number of excursionists from various parts of the Dominion ... all going to "do" Lakes Huron and Superior. Let us stroll around and take a few notes of our fellow passengers, leaving our own motley crew out until the first night of camping. The first face we recognize in that health-and pleasure-seeking party is the martinet person of old Major B, well known to all the volunteer companies of the 30th Battalion. What a change has come over that once pompous form which has more than once caused a blush of vexatious shame to pass over the sun-tanned faces of that Battalion when his shrieking scream was heaping epithets more pointed than polite upon their patriotic heads; but that day has gone ... the scarlet uniform has given place to a seedy-looking coat, sash and sword belt to a greasy-looking haversack, the shining boots are replaced by a pair of coarse stogies ... and the once gallant Major is now going up to be something like an underboss on that public work of refuge, Dawson's Road. Close by him stands an editor from one of Queen City's leading journals. He is going to Nipigon and Red Rock to have a little trout fishing. The Pacific Scandal has used him up, and they say fish is good for the brain. I think he will require double rations!
>
> In two hours, the good steamer *Chicora* is moored up alongside of a rickety wharf at Little Current. Little Current of today is the same as it was ten years ago. If there is any change in its appearance it is more dilapidated; deserted houses and ragged citizens, one hotel, three groggeries, and two stores, three or four dwelling houses and a couple of lighthouses, a few scattered piles of cordwood, a half tumbled down Church, a number of bloated and dissipated looking "LOs" with a crowd of dirty and sickly children hanging around them, stared at the sight-seekers, who were busily engaged in viewing the wonders of Wabojeewang and its surroundings. A half dozen of sneaking, snickering, mock-modest squaws were busily plying a sale of some curiosities, and a score of

yelping, half-famished curs kept up a constant chorus of doggeral blasphemy … another blow from the Chicora's whistle and the lines are cast off and we are once more steaming up the channel.

Aubrey White Colquhoun Macdonald assembled helpful information over many years about his father's family background. An ancestor, Duncan "The Civil" Macdonald, of Invernessshire, Scotland, married Jessie Macdonald of Dornoch, Sutherlandshire. Her uncle, Captain Donald "Black" Macdonald, left the Black Watch to join the Fraser Highlanders. He was a rough, wild soldier of fortune who enlisted around 1756 to escape transportation to a penal colony. He spoke French fluently, and it is claimed that it was he who led Wolfe's troops up the cliffs to the Plains of Abraham, deceiving the French guard by his fluency in their language. He was killed in the sortie at Ste Foy in March, 1759, after the fall of Quebec. His frozen body was left buried in the snow until April when it was taken to Halifax for burial in the chapel at the Citadel cemetery, where he is recorded in the register.

Alexander Macdonald, born at Fort Augusta in 1815, was the son of Duncan the Civil and father of Duncan Fraser Macdonald. He married Mary MacPherson and they came to Canada in 1832. He was a big, powerful man with black curly hair, and a Liberal in politics. He took part in the Upper Canada rising with William Lyon Mackenzie in 1837, and was obliged to flee to the United States, where he remained for three years. When he returned, he settled at Bullocks Corners in West Flamboro Township, Wentworth County. He later moved to Puslinch township in Wellington County, where he died in 1871.

The Duncan Fraser Macdonald papers are permanently housed in the Ontario Archives. They consist of 52 diaries, dozens of letters, and several reports in his capacity as an Indian Agent, along with hundreds of photographs. Duncan Fraser Macdonald described himself as 5'6," 175 pounds, grey eyes, full-bearded. When Sir Wilfrid Laurier lost power, DF Macdonald stated that he would not shave his beard until the Liberals regained power. He had to await Mackenzie King's election in 1921, by which time he was living in Brandon, Manitoba with his family. According to the family, he kept his vow, going unrecognized on the streets of Brandon for some time!

John Macfie reports about Macdonald in the DF Macdonald diaries:

> He and a companion spent February of 1875 cruising timber in McMurrich Township, living in a tent in temperatures that froze whiskey, and snowshoeing all the day in 50 inches of snow. On February

25, he walked the 20 miles home from Rosseau to Parry Sound, then, the very next morning struck out on foot for Byng Inlet, nearly 50 miles to the north. He slept at Shasanaga and arrived at his destination at 4 pm the following day. Two hours later he was back on the trail to Parry Sound. When it got dark, he camped. But when the moon rose, he resumed walking and arrived back in Parry Sound before midnight. He concluded his walk without mitts, for part way along he had cut them up to make moccasins for his ever-present and now footsore dog. The only object of that three day hike, in the dead of winter to Byng Outlet and back, seems to have been to nail some sort of government notice on the doors of the Dodge Lumber Company's sawmill.

I may have implied that DF Macdonald was a gossip, which is not quite fair. Rather, he had the knack of bringing the people and times to life in the meagre space of his diaries with a garnish of insight and wry humour. For example, on March 7 Macdonald wrote: "Div A left this morning drunk as owls." Division B was to have its turn, for he added that AA Wright of Collingwood, who was in charge of the depot camp "gave a hogwash banquet at midnight, and the howl from the camp is a crazy drunken echo." Wright seems to have met an untimely end. In a list of crew members in the diary, Macdonald later penciled against Wright's name: "shot by an Indian, 1877."

Macdonald had a way of favourably impressing people, probably because he excelled at whatever he turned a hand to. One of the highly placed individuals who recognized and used his talent was Aubrey White, assistant commissioner of the Department of Crown Lands. Macdonald had helped White assess the standing drop of timber in Hagerman Township in 1874, and thereafter White frequently called upon him to handle bush-ranging assignments. The respect must have been mutual, because Macdonald named a son after White.

By November 23, 1874, the end of the survey was in sight and Isaiah Aisance was sent to Parry Sound with a message asking the steam tug *Mittie Grew* to pick up the party at Shawanaga Landing on the following Saturday. Nine days after that, on December 4, Duncan F Macdonald embarked on an adventure of a different kind by marrying Isabella George. Here is a description of the day in his own words:

> Bright, clear and beautiful, sunshiny and warm. I bummed around town busy all day. Mr Mosely drew out the documents and settled the boy for life. Present on the occasion Rev Mosely and wife and daughter, Mr and Mrs George, Judge McCurry and wife, McLean, Geo McLain Strain

and wife, Foley and Henley, W George, J George, Capt Skene, JC Miller, J McCurry, Belle George that was and DF Macdonald that is.

Jumping over 25 years to Macdonald's later career, we come to the 1899 election and the southern Ontario riding of West Elgin, where Grit candidate, McNish was running against Tory Finley McDiarmid. There was likely wrongdoing on both sides, but according to a report from the Toronto *Mail & Empire* on June 26, 1899: "West Elgin election voided and Liberals sign a sweeping confession of wrongdoing; Messrs DF Macdonald and WH Hoppins worked like beavers." In a booklet entitled *West Elgin Election 1899*, Macdonald is listed as a forest ranger in Nipissing who entertained deputy ministers of government departments with scurrilous remarks upon the electors whose support they were seeking. This is in reference to a letter he wrote January 6, 1899 intended for his longtime friend Aubrey White, deputy minister of Crown Lands. In that letter, Hoppins is listed as Macdonald's assistant saw filer in the summer and director of cabinet ministers campaigning in the winter. (It appears that the letter never reached Aubrey White personally but was published in a Toronto newspaper instead.)

A letter written to Macdonald on August 10, 1899 by a Post Office official in Ottawa reads in part:

> … you state that a letter you wrote to Mr Aubrey White did not reach him but was published in the columns of the *Mail & Empire*. You did not state whether you posted the letter and as to its receipt you do not mention whether Mr White has informed you as to whether or not he received the letter.

Aubrey WC Macdonald, son of DF, informed me "Father told me he suspected that some enterprising Tory in the Rodney post office steamed the letter open, did a transcript of it or sent the original letter to the newspaper." He further stated that his father sued the Post Office for tampering with his mail but that later on Sir Wilfrid Laurier persuaded him to call the suit off.

The west part of Elgin County was settled starting in 1818 by Highland Scots from the Western Isles of Scotland. Many of them had been driven from their homes during the Highland Clearances. A few years later, there was a large immigration of Germans. Macdonald refers to these two groups in his famous letter. His own people were from Invernessshire and he considers himself superior to those west coast island folk. His excellent choice of invective makes this clear. The excerpts from his diary before and after January 6 tell in his concise style some of the action that took place during the great election scandal. Macdonald was doing his best to manipulate the local movers and shakers.

Dec. 31, 1898 — Got up at 4:30 and got ready for the bus, but no bus. Hugh hitched up Billy, and Hoppins and I drove down to Rose Pt and caught the freight train and got out to Scotia 2 hours ahead of the North Bay train. We got to Toronto 4 hours later. I met Ted Taylor at the Walker House *en route* for West Elgin to help wee Donald McNish.

Jan 2, 1899 — Hoppins, Preston Carroll and Vance left for Woodstock on the CPR. We changed for St Thomas. Carroll went to West Lorne, Vance to Dutton, I to Rodney where I met McNish and put up at the Patterson House. I met JD Shaw, barrister.

Jan 3, 1899 — I met Angus McGugan at Shaw's office in the forenoon. We checked the voters' lists.

Jan 4, 1899 — Raining and cloudy, muddy roads — busy in Rodney all day, checking voter lists. At night we met in Shaw's office in committee. The landlord of the Patterson House showed his Tory sympathies by locking me out but we made him get up and let me in.

Jan 5, 1899 — Hoppins came up from St Thomas, nearly all the grits and Tories went down to Dutton to the nomination. Preston sent me $42.

Jan 6, 1899 — Hon. GW Ross and Mosscrip came in and held a meeting with Hoppins — came up and stayed all night. There was a big meeting at the hall.

Jan 7, 1899 — Haycock and I went over to Caras Corners held a rousing good meeting and came back to Rodney. Went to Shaw's office and saw a lot of the boys.

Jan 8, 1899 — Hoppins came up with me to Rodney. Penfold warmed young Morris' ears for him for listening at my bedroom door.

Jan 10, 1899 — Cold and raw weather. The Tories are mad, wild and at sea. I struck out to St Thomas and saw Preston and reported progress to him.

Jan 11, 1899 — Hoppins came up from St Thomas. The boys came in and reported progress. The Tories are wild. I wrote and wired Preston. We have a hot time in the Patterson house at midnight. McDiarmid and his gang went for Hoppins. We had a lively time McCarthy, Hoppins and I before the morning dawned.

Jan 12, 1899 — Went down on the train to St Thomas and had dinner. We left in the evening. I got off at Woodstock.

It is obvious that Macdonald and his crew were doing everything possible to influence this by-election in favour of the Grits, and the Tories would be doing the same. As usual, he understates the action, but it takes little imagination to realize that there was much more going on than he tells in his diary. When the letter appeared in the *Mail & Empire*, it was prefaced by this editorial comment:

A CONTEMPTIBLE LETTER

DF Macdonald is an official of the government who drew $1,421.61 of the people's money last year. Here is the blackguardly manner in which he slanders electors for the edification of his co-official, the Deputy Minister of Crown Lands in Toronto.

Rodney, January 6th, 1899

Dear Aubrey —
Here we are again, away from the rocks and charred pines of Nipissing and the nervous and excitable Frenchmen. Here's where there is hot work in store for us. Both candidates are popular and lots of good workers on both sides. Here's where you can meet the sons and grandsons of the men that Argyle drove from their homes, the islands of Mull, Islay, Tiree and Canna. As a class they are small in stature, dark and swarthy, with that greasy fish-fed look found among west coast fishermen. They are as tricky as pet foxes and as sly as a sailor's monkey and can lie as deftly as a Russian diplomat. They have pretensions of honour and pride from the teeth outwards. They are a slick, polished gang, no more to be

compared to the brawny and brainy men of old Glengarry than a mouth organ is to be compared to a Heintzman piano.

We have one ward here with 25 Pattersons on the voters list, 23 out of that are Tories, in the same ward or polling subdivision there are 29 Campbells, 14 of them are Tories. The McColls and McDiarmids without number are Tories, the McCallums and McPhersons are solid Tories, the Macdonalds, as usual, are divided. The McLartys, McVicars, McGregors, and McPhails are Tory through to the spinal nerve. The McKays are Gritty. The Purcells are Liberals to a man and the doubtful fish are the Swishers, Scheltzers, Schneckanburgers, Schmidts, Schills, Kranses, Kruppes, Keillers, Leibners and the Osterhaughts. When you get that German brood intermarried with the McPhees, McFaddens, McPhails and McAuleys they make a queer brood of Scottish Canadians from a doubtful ancestry!

They had a hot time at the nominations in Dutton. I was not there. They are going to have a hot time here in Rodney tonight. They have 500 torches ready for the flames to meet GW Ross at the station this evening. The brass band will be there. The McRaes, the McGugans, the McIvots, McRorys and McRitchies will be there. The Garchies, Dugalds, Duncans and Donalds, with Alberts, Conrads, Carlos, Gottliebs and Jacobs will be jumbled up in a British mixture, sauerkraut and porridge, limburger cheese and salt herring, bologna sausage and haggis, lager and hot Scotch, lambscouse and brose, and the riding is any man's today. I am going to St Thomas in the morning to meet Preston. We will win if we can. Keep our fellows fighting mad until Thursday night.

Hoping you are all well, I am, as ever,

Yours,
DF Macdonald.

A letter on February 27, 1899 from JR Stratton, a Grit official, brings out some of the problems faced by DF Macdonald:

> I don't think you require a recommendation from the opposition — a certificate of character from them would do you no good. Your friends know that you would not be guilty of any such acts as the opposition attributed to you in connection with the by-elections. I heard good reports about you in Lennox and east Wellington and for anyone to think

that you would go into a constituency for the purpose of bribing the electors is out of the question. A man has a perfect right in this country to exercise his own freedom on visiting his relatives in any part of the Province and if there happens to be an election on where he visits he has no way to stop it, if you could put in a good word for the government why should you not do so. I know that you are not employed by the Ontario government and that you don't know that you will ever be again.

On December 3, 1903, Macdonald was in his usual good writing form when he wrote JR Stratton, who at this time was Provincial Secretary in Toronto. Many of the problems deal with political patronage:

A Tory bartender Bradley is appointed gaoler where worthy liberals are ignored. The temperance element are making all the capital their busy tongues can raise. Moffat's son is acting as turnkey at the Parry Sound gaol for his father and he is not brawny or muscular, in fact he pays more attention to the brand of cigarettes he smokes than to the responsibilities of his work. Brainless bungling officials have done more damage to the popularity of the Ontario government than Whitney and his following ever could do in a lifetime. How many Liberal votes will we lose because a Tory whiskey mixer has been placed in a responsible and delicate position, among prisoners of all grades, male and female lunatics at times. On the eve of the Dominion election we will lose close to one hundred votes in this town alone. Votes and Victory is what I am looking for!

Although he signed most of his letters "Your obedient servant," it is unlikely that Duncan Fraser Macdonald was ever anyone's obedient servant. Brainless bunglers could count on his wrath. However, this man of many talents was not above taking on some mundane chores. His diary tells us that when the Earl of Dufferin came to town, Macdonald was out painting picket fences in Parry Sound.

Duncan Fraser Macdonald was a great outdoorsman, no outing being too arduous even when he was in his 70s. He exhibited a great regard for his family and in a letter to his son Allie written from Parry Sound on 2 March 1915, shows that he was still "on the tramp" as he puts it, often by canoe, or on foot, or in this case by snowshoe. He was 73 when he wrote:

I got home from a month's hard trip in the woods. The snowshoeing was very heavy, loose and dry. I waddled through and finished up. I had two Indian Packers. One was a good man and the other was dirty, hungry, sleepy and lazy. Jake and I decided to stuff his hungry protégé. I stayed in camp and boiled up 10 lbs of clear bacon, put it to freeze, boiled beans and baked them in sand, boiled rice in condensed cream. We had a bag of Naismith's special camp loaf bread. I had Armour's canned beef, canned apples, McLaren's cheese, creamy butter and a nice pot of beans. A dinner under canvas fit for a king, the Gods of Bush rangers. I filled that redskin so full that Sunday that he thought he never would be hungry no more. He left Monday morning so Jake and I finished the work shorthanded, but got through. The "Skeddler" sent his brother over the other day to enquire how much was coming to him. I told him to tell his brother to come here and I would settle with an Ironwood Missionary axe handle! ... I will write when I return from Toronto.

God bless,
Dad

Macdonald died in 1923 in Brandon, Manitoba, where he and his wife Isabella had moved to be with their family. Excerpts from several obituaries sum up Macdonald's impressive career:

> DF Macdonald was probably better known by more people than any other man in the Parry Sound district. He was a man of many parts, strong, virile, possessed of a rugged personality. He was the first photographer in Parry Sound, crown timber agent and Indian agent with an intimate knowledge of their language and customs. He was a great story teller in English, Gaelic, French or Ojibwa.

A terse comment from his diary for September 24, 1872 is typical: "Bothered last night by a hunting rattlesnake. Stomped him! Found a charred human skeleton on the portage."

A mistake I have made several times in my acquisition of private papers is to assume I have acquired all the papers. Suddenly some chance remark or event points up my error. This happened in the spring of 2001 when I called Mary O'Rourke, a granddaughter of Duncan Fraser Macdonald, in Thunder Bay, Ontario. I had last seen Mary over 20 years before when I was intent on assembling what I thought was all of Macdonald's superb collection of diaries, letters and photographs.

Mary remembered me after all these years, gave me the information I sought, then got my full attention by saying, "I have been trying to contact you to tell you that you missed some of Grandfather's papers."

I was startled, as I knew I had systematically contacted every living relative I could find in order to assemble the collection. I had acquired the bulk of it from his son, Aubrey White Macdonald, and recalled that he had shown me an old steamer trunk that contained his old uniforms from World War I. These were of little interest to me and I only gave them a quick glance.

When Aubrey died his cousin Mary O'Rourke and her niece Patricia Prokop of Orillia, Ontario, were clearing things from the house. They took the uniforms from the trunk and underneath was a cache of papers. Patricia shipped the papers to me for my assessment. They proved to be extremely valuable, and I paid her a significant amount for the collection.

The most important part was a bundle of over 200 letters, each three or four pages long. Most of the letters in this cache were written by Macdonald and addressed to the Millers, father and son.

John C Miller and his son JB Miller, successive presidents of the Parry Sound Lumber Company, maintained mansions in Parry Sound, Toronto, and California, and both were Liberal Members of the Provincial Parliament, the son being elected a few years after his father's death in 1884. It seems the Millers carefully kept Macdonald's letters and later returned them all to him. I had these letters scanned and sent copies to John McFie at Parry Sound. The letters, spanning 40 years from 1870 to 1910, along with the diaries, contain material invaluable for research on Ontario at the turn of the century. Aside from their great historical value, these letters to the Millers further demonstrate Macdonald's entertaining skill with words.

Describing a guide named Carufel, employed by timber cruisers working on the upper Spanish River in Northern Ontario, he wrote:

> This little fellow is a typical French-Canadian. A shantyman, prospector, trapper, guide and packer. Restless as a chained cub bear, as voluble as a chattering parrot, first in French then in Dr Drummond [Wm Henry Drummond was the author of a number of popular Québécois dialect poems, including "Leetle Bateese"] broken dialect with a smattering of Ojibway ... Carufel, constantly and continuously is very much disconnected. He generally has about half a dozen jobs on hand at one time, for instance patching his pants, washing dishes, trying to keep his pipe going while telling some yarn and whetting his axe, baking a bannock, trying to regulate the fire and watching a frying pan of spruce gum for his canoe. And when done, as he terms it, *'tout fini!,'* there is nothing completed to correctness and never will be.

Even the sparse words Duncan Fraser Macdonald squeezed into his tiny diary were colourful: "December 8, 1883: All's quiet except for a few drunken shantymen. McCullough and I marched Mr Peter Ramsay to the lock-up and we had a racket getting him away from the boys." That episode was described later at great length in one of his letters to the Millers. The collection is now in the Ontario Archives along with the Macdonald papers I had placed there years ago.

Duncan Fraser Macdonald played an important role in the organization of the Liberal Party throughout the Province. He participated in many a hard-fought campaign for successive Liberal premiers Mowat, Hardy and Ross. His timber-ranging extended from Ontario to Newfoundland, British Columbia and Arkansas. Most of all, he had an enviable and uncanny way with words.

A Gael for all seasons, a Canadian who should be remembered.

CHAPTER THIRTEEN
ADVENTURERS AND EXPLORERS

Most of us have minor eccentricities that help to shape us as unique human beings. Here are some great Canadian characters I've found whose eccentricities are more than minor. New information about many of these figures from the past keeps trickling in.

Robert, William and James Dickson come first to my mind. Shurley Dickson and several of her cousins have worked diligently at tracking their family antecedents. They are particularly interested in Robert, known to the Dakota Sioux as Mascotapah, the Red-Haired Man. He was an impressive and handsome figure, held in high respect by the Sioux. His country wife* was To-to-win, sister to Chief Red Thunder. Thanks to Robert Dickson's influence, the Sioux stayed on the side of the British during the 1812–14 war. Shurley has discovered the only known picture of Robert, among the Dickson papers in the City of Cambridge archives. She and a cousin went to South Dakota to meet descendents of Robert who live on the Sioux Reservation. While researching Niagara-on-the-Lake, they found evidence that Robert may have been married and produced a son before he went to Indian country. There has never been any proof that Robert sired James Dickson, "The Liberator," but this information may be a breakthrough.

William Dickson was a brother of Robert. He settled in Newark (now Niagara-on-the-Lake) in 1792, and was said to have walked away 14 years later from a duel which left a foulmouthed bully mortally wounded. William Dickson was so highly respected that he was permitted to practice law without full legal training and died an honoured citizen of Galt in 1846. His line of Dicksons became one of those families on which Ontario's early pride and prosperity were solidly based.

Somewhere along the way, however, even the most immaculate family trees may sprout a bad apple or two or, if not precisely bad, with a

---

* A genuine Canadianism: a native common-law wife.

deformity that compels them to worship strange idols, dream bizarre dreams, or tilt at impossible windmills.

Such a one was James Dickson, believed by many to have been a fairly close relative of the aforementioned William, and famous — or infamous — as "The Liberator of the Indian Nations."

I first became interested in James Dickson when Ontario Archivist Donald McOuat proudly announced that he had been out doing some fieldwork and had acquired a major collection of papers from Brigadier Crawford Grier, his old artillery battery commander. In one of the few cases where he got involved in fieldwork, McOuat had done a fine job of cutting a deal with the Brigadier. Sir Wiley Grier, the prominent portrait painter, and father of Brigadier Crawford Grier, had married a granddaughter of the Hon Wm Dickson. It was Sir Wiley who had gathered these papers over many years, and passed them on to his son, who in turn passed them on to McOuat.

Using a productive technique, I mined the papers for leads to more material. It was a long trail that wound from Galt (now Cambridge), Ontario, to Boston to Shreveport Louisiana. Ludwig Gindl, a German architect, had married Mary Dickson, sister of Shurley, great granddaughter of the Hon William, thereby acquiring *Cedarbrae*, one of the old Dickson homes, and along with it another major cache of Dickson papers which Ludwig had no intention of releasing, despite the fact that the papers were not his to give or keep. Mary acquiesced in Ludwig's every whim, and I was in a very poor bargaining position, made worse by the fact that Ludwig Gindl and I seemed to have formed an instant dislike of each other.

In the end, though, my persistence paid off. After Ludwig Gindl's death, I mounted a campaign to buy the papers for the Archives from Mary. After a series of devious moves, perhaps in a fit of pique directed at me, she sold the papers to the City of Cambridge archives for the sum of $120,000.

Mary had every right to do this, so I went after other Dickson papers in Boston and Shreveport. By this time, I had established a friendship with Mary's sister, Shurley, who had been at odds with the Gindl family for many years. Ludwig liked women to defer to his great man complex. It was obvious that Shurley was not about to defer to anyone, and especially not to Ludwig.

I met Shurley through her bibulous ex-sister-in-law who had been married to William's grandson, another Robert Dickson, and lived near Boston. When Robert walked away from this marriage he left many Dickson items with his ex-wife. She had been selling these off before I landed on her doorstep. Charming and evasive, she only wanted to sit and drink double gin and tonics. No documents were to be found but before finally giving up I took her teenage daughter, Robin, to one side and asked her to keep an eye out for any old papers. Robin, to her great credit, did watch for papers. When her mother died from alcohol abuse, Robin produced a valuable set of documents and maps pertaining to land that Wm Dickson had bought from Joseph Brant. More papers turned up through Robert in Shreveport and Shurley in Cambridge.

James Dickson, The Great Liberator, could well have been the model for Gilbert & Sullivan's Modern Major-General, for in 1835, when he began recruiting officers in New York and Washington for his alleged campaign to liberate North America's Indians, he called himself General Dickson. According to a story in Canada's *Beaver* magazine by Margaret MacLeod, a descendent of one of the officers,

> He had all the stage trappings: fine English tailoring executed with imagination, plenty of gold lace and gold braid, a handsome sabre-scarred face with beard and moustache. He wore small arms and a British general's inlaid sword. Dickson also had in his extensive military luggage a coat of mail for which he never found a use. He was well bred, a convincing talker and he had command of money. Officers and aides whom he recruited were lavishly equipped. Some carried with them extra beards and moustaches. The Major of artillery wore silver epaulettes, gold lace on his chest and silver lace down the side of his pantaloons.

By the spring of 1836, the Great Liberator's story varied with his audience. To US senators, he implied he was English and had lived for years in Mexico. There he had conceived the idea of liberating North American Indians from their bondage to chiefs whose sole aim it seemed to be to harass their white brethren. He would start by getting loyal Canadian tribes and Métis on his side and proceed from there. To other Americans, especially those still seething with hatred of the Mexicans for the very recent massacre of so many US heroes at the Alamo, he confided that his real target was not tribal chiefs but the political and military butchers now leading Mexico, whom he vowed, personally, to hang for their crimes against Uncle Sam.

From the USA, James Dickson and his new staff went to Montreal, where he hired other officers from among half-breed sons of Hudson's Bay Company officials. The explanation he gave about his past career was as colourful and vague as ever, but he disclosed the whole truth about future plans because, improbable and hare-brained though they were, their success depended on the Métis.

Even in far-off Mexico, it seemed, he had heard of their sagacious leader, Cuthbert Grant, to whom the Hudson's Bay Company had assigned the doubly vital mission of guarding the Red River Settlement against the Sioux and keeping it supplied with buffalo meat. Both of these being parts of Grant's own traditional activities, he had for the last dozen-odd years been the Mayor of Granttown, now St François-Xavier, a Métis community 18 miles west of Fort Garry, on the north bank of the Assiniboine River.

James Dickson hoped to persuade Grant and his band of superb guerrilla warriors to join him in a surprise attack on the US outpost of Santa Fé, some 1,200 miles south-west, where he had learned that a fortune in gold was kept for bribing hostile Indians to permit wagon trains to pass through. The plan was that after Dickson and his brave Métis allies looted Santa Fé of its treasures, they would continue on to California and set up their own wonderful empire, with themselves as lords of all they surveyed. To indemnify the Hudson's Bay Company for the loss of its Métis employees, Dickson was taking with him to Fort Garry drafts on well known Montreal financial institutions, representing enough funds to compensate for all who wished to join him in his enterprise.

Martin McLeod, 23, commissioned as a Major in James Dickson's army in Montreal, kept a journal, now in the Hudson's Bay Company archives in Winnipeg. He wrote:

> The party, consisting of some 60 people, left Buffalo, New York, on August 1, 1836, aboard the chartered schooner Wave. Her manifest said she was bound for Sault Ste Marie. There it would be necessary to change to smaller craft for the final thousand or so miles to Fort Garry. Before they reached the Soo, however, the party was shipwrecked.

An account in *The Beaver* continues:

> On arriving there, they were arrested on a trivial charge, the sailors had stolen a cow, so that American authorities could investigate. The Liberator had been talking freely of his plans.

Upon their release, a much smaller party of about 20 began following the south shore of Lake Superior in a Mackinaw Boat, passing the time studying Spanish for use in Santa Fé. Among the Spanish phrases given them to memorize were, "How many leagues to the next village?" and "Are there any soldiers there?" Others were "Are there many Indians?" "What say the people about us?" and "Where can we find horses?" They reached Fond du Lac, Wisconsin, about October 21 and with lakes and creeks fast freezing around them, had to move forward by dog team or any way they could.

The source of the mighty Mississippi was crossed on November 9 without even a written comment, and it was Christmas before they crawled into Fort Garry, destitute, in rags, with frozen limbs and starving, the sled dogs long since eaten. Of James Dickson the Liberator's force only the General and 11 others had survived.

Unknown to them, Governor Simpson had been busy, too. Travelling east in September, he had been startled by a Detroit newspaper story headed "Pirates on the Lakes," whose lurid prose informed him of the Dickson expedition. If he was alarmed at the thought of losing his Métis, he was horrified to learn that Dickson's Secretary of War was the son of the head of the American Fur Company, the Hudson's Bay Company's bitterest enemy. Cancelling all other appointments, Simpson concentrated on outwitting the menace to his colony. The visitors were well treated, fed, given new clothes, and their wounds looked after, but on Simpson's orders, Governor Alexander Christie simply declined to honour the bank drafts Dickson carried, thereby checkmating any plans he had to raise an army.

General James Dickson, the Great Liberator, couldn't even leave Red River without the Hudson's Bay Company's help, because all his provisions had been exhausted en route. "Also under Simpson's orders, the Hudson's Bay Company absorbed some of Dickson's halfbreed officers by offering them good positions," the *Beaver* story continues. "The others dispersed and Dickson, a defeated, deserted and deflated man, was stranded in Red River for the rest of the winter."

Most of this time was spent with Cuthbert Grant, whom he greatly admired. Cuthbert, honoured as The Warden of the Plains, must have held James Dickson in similar regard, for when spring came he outfitted him and provided guides to start him on his way to Santa Fé. Aware that this was his last hurrah, Dickson was equally gracious and gallant. "Guides, horses, drivers and carts were waiting beside the church at Granttown for him to begin his journey, and a crowd gathered to say good-bye," ran the eyewitness report. "He made a last laudatory speech of thanks to Cuthbert Grant. Then he removed his ornate military hat, bowed ceremoniously to him and ... said, 'You are the great soldier and leader; I am a failure. These belong to you, not to me.' In grandiose manner he removed his epaulettes, fastened them on Grant's shoulders, handed him his sword, mounted and rode away. Thus ended the great invasion."

As a footnote to this fascinating but frustrating episode in international relations, one which poses more questions than it answers, the Red River Colony's own bard, Pierre Falcon, composed a folksong simply titled *General Dickson*. After three verses describing why he came west, Falcon has General Dickson bid Grant farewell with these words:

> Mr Cuthbert Grant, Master of a Regiment
> My epaulettes of silver, I do to you present.
> Myself, General Dickson, I seek my own crown
> I seek my crown, where the Spanish may be found
> City of Mexico, very many generals
> Also many cannoniers, who wish to crown me too.

The story of James Dickson, The Liberator, has been around for years. Alfred Silver in his well written, well researched historical novel, *Where the Ghost Horse Runs*, brings Dickson into his story of Cuthbert Grant, the hero of that tale.

As often happens, my files tend to overlap. For years I have been trying to find out what became of Allan McMillan, the second oldest Métis son of James McMillan, first cousin to my great-grandfather, who was a partner in the North West Company. James mentioned him in his first will written at the mouth of the Columbia in 1813, giving as his place of residence the rather imprecise location "living somewhere on the Saskatchewan River." He next appears in 1823, when he is registered as having been baptized at St Andrews Church, Williamstown, Glengarry, Upper Canada. James came east that year when his father, Allan, died. James brought two of his Métis children the several thousand miles by canoe for baptism, disproving a common misconception that traders abandoned their Métis children.

Several years ago I was given an unpublished and unedited manuscript written by Henry Connoly, son of Wm. Connoly, a North West Company partner. The MS is now with the Robert Bell papers in the National Archives, Ottawa. Halfway through this rambling memoir, I was startled to find a reference to the missing Allan, and it had a direct connection to James Dickson, the Great Liberator. The following excerpt is from the Connoly manuscript:

> The Hudson's Bay Company's people had their eyes open and set to work to frustrate the General's scheme. When they heard of his plans

they sent dispatches to the officers in charge at Fort Garry. They sent a young man, Allan McMillan, a son of Mr. Chief Factor McMillan with the dispatches about the General's plans of getting the half-breeds and Indians. He was trying to stop them from joining. Although McMillan left Lachine pretty late in the fall, he managed to reach Lake Superior before the closing of navigation and had to make the remainder of the road on snowshoes. The distance may not have been quite so long as a certain gentleman is said to have made, without the use of the seven league boots. However, McMillan did his work well and got very little thanks for that. He was taken in the company's service but was looked down upon by some of the pale-faced fools in the service, so he left and went to St Paul. He was killed by some curs — poor Allan, he was a good fellow. His half brother, William MacMillan had settled at the Silver Heights on the Assiniboine River the next lot above the property of Donald Smith, Lord Strathcona. William died in the fall of 1904 at the age of 103 years, the eldest son of Chief Factor McMillan who was one of the Lords of the North. In the summer of 1837, General Dickson and his staff of officers reached the Red River but were coldly received by all hands, that is by the Hudson's Bay Company officials, so they had to disband and parted company. Some of these young men entered the company's service and that was the end of the scheme of the great Liberator of the Indian Nations.

Connoly wrote his manuscript about the turn of the century and died in 1910 *en route* to Labrador with the Hudson's Bay Company. He knew many of the people in this drama and makes other interesting comments about James Dickson. Later, in the Hudson's Bay Company archives in Winnipeg, I found that Allan may not have been killed by curs as he is shown having returned to Canada (the east) in 1841.

I found a special dispatch that Sir George Simpson sent Chief Factor Alexander Christie, Governor of Assiniboia in September 1836. This excerpt from the dispatch illustrates the clever way Simpson took to try to keep control of the situation.

> ... if they get to Red River they will give much trouble and occasion great excitement among the ignorant Canadian half-breed populace. It is highly desirable that the party should be broken up and to that end it will be well to let the people understand that the leaders are men of no character or standing in the civilized world, [that] they are self-credited Generals, Captains, Colonels and that the enterprise they have in hand is one of Madness and Desperation.

Let McLaughlin and McLeod be detached or separated from the party if possible, and engaged to the company on the footing I have already mentioned; I have engaged young McMillan who is the bearer of this as an apprentice clerk; he is a fine, spirited, powerful, active young man and being related to the Botash family he will have a good deal of influence among the Saskatchewan Half-Breeds who are the most troublesome people in the settlement. The influence of this young man I think may under existing circumstances be turned to good account; he will learn for you through his mother and uncles all that is going forward in the upper part of the settlement and if properly managed counteract all Dickson's plans; in short I think he may be a useful man in the event of the party being disposed to be troublesome.

These accounts illustrate Sir George Simpson's fine hand at intrigue and add a new dimension to the Great Liberator saga.

Michipicoten is one of the oldest names in Ontario. The island, a menace to navigation today, was recorded by Étienne Brulé in 1622 and noted on Champlain's map 10 years later. Michipicoten Bay, some 200 miles north of the Soo, was also the site of Ontario's first mining ventures. Some of them are still going strong today. *Michipicoten* is the Indian term for 'great bluffs,' quite appropriate because one of the great bluffs of Ontario's electoral history was staged in the area on October 17, 1903.

The Liberals had been in office steadily since 1872, but at the previous year's election in the newly created constituency of Sault Ste Marie, the Liberal candidate C. N. Smith, publisher of the Sault Express, had been defeated by Conservative candidate Andrew Miscampbell. Charges of irregularities resulted in Miscampbell being unseated and a by-election declared. The second battle between the same two men had one new element added, the Lake Superior Corporation, predecessor of today's huge Algoma Steel Company.

Backing Smith was the Lake Superior Corporation, the Soo's largest employer, owning the iron mines, the steel mill, the Algoma Central Railway, a hydro electric company, a pulp and paper mill and other enterprises. Lake Superior had been with Smith in 1902, but apparently believing he was a shoo-in, had done nothing unusual to help get him elected. This time they were taking no chances.

"On election day, the *Minnie M.,* a company steamship, crossed the St. Mary's River to Sault Ste Marie, Michigan, where it picked up some 20 Americans," declared a sworn statement in the *Sault Star* of

THE TRIP OF THE MINNIE M

Oh have you heard the stories,
Of the trip of the Minnie M,
How the Grits did fool the Tories,
And completely euchred them in.

'Twas in the bye election
They had up in the So,
The Grits made a selection
Of a drunken shameless crew.

On the twenty sixth day of October—
On the bye election day,
This crowd, not strictly sober,
Sailed up Batchawana Bay.

We had our instruction
To take them there and back,
To save Grits from descruction
By the festive Lumber Jack.

We went for them o'er the river,
And took on liquor at the docks,
The Jacks in the morn did shiver
As we pict them up at the locks.

But they soon got a reviver
From the stock we took on board,
And no longer gave a stiver
For the shame they did afford.

The Lumber Jacks were jolly,
'Twas a picnic unto them—
This trip of fraud and folly
On the steamer Minnie M.

The cost did not concern them—
That they'ed nothing to do with,
There was heelers there to learn them,
How to cast their votes for Smith.

They were each given a slip of paper
With the name they were to vote,
And the jacks, with wink and caper,
Did their willingness denote,

They said "if they should swear you,
You need not fear the law,
And let not the Bible scare you,
For the Bible's one of straw."

We stopped at Michipicoten
And a train stood on the line
To take all who were willing
Up to vote at Helen's Mine.

The whisky flowed both fast and free
And some were near undone,
But the votes for Smith were 23,
Miscampbell he got none.

The brought them back to Michipicoten
And said "here's where you vote."
Of course the thing was rotten
But they did not care a groat.

They went in, for Smith they voted,
Did this drunken, reckless crew,
And the ballot box denoted
They got forty against two.

The heelers came on board again,
Their work that day was through,
And we turned the steamer Minnie M,
With her head towards the Soo.

The Jacks were full and glorious,
Their mirth we could not stem,
And they carried on uproarious
On the deck of the Minnie M

They got all they demanded
And did all they had to do,
After midnight they were landed
Over at the American Soo,

I've made many trips up there & back
But this one was the gem,
What time we took the Lumber Jacks
Up on the Minnie M.

— G. C.

During a 1903 provincial by-election in Sault Ste. Marie, a steamship named the "Minnie M." crossed over to the U.S. Sault where it picked up 20 Americans hired to vote for the Liberal candidate. At both Helen Mines and Michipicoten Harbour, they voted in the name of dead or absent miners, were then paid for their services and returned to the American side.

November 24, 1904. "They were brought back to the Canadian side, where a special train of the Algoma Central Railway took them up to the Helen Mine. They voted there under the names of dead or absent miners, after which they were taken down to Michipicoten Harbour, where they repeated the exercise. They were then paid for their services and returned to the American side." Multiple-voting was not unknown. Indeed, it was practiced by both parties if there seemed a chance of it going undetected, but importing Americans to represent absent Canadian voters was a new twist. To complicate the caper, the Conservatives knew about their opponents' plans. They'd told Attorney General J. M. Gibson all about them days earlier, when he was in town to speak on Smith's behalf.

"Miscampbell appealed to Gibson to send special constables into the riding to supervise all the bush polls, but Gibson took no action," reported the Star. "As a result, the Conservatives chartered ... the tug Rooth to follow the *Minnie M.* with their own scrutineers aboard. But the Rooth was not licensed to carry passengers ... so was not permitted to sail." Using this and other underhanded tactics, Smith defeated Miscampbell by 247 votes, the first time the Soo had elected a Liberal to the provincial legislature. He didn't get much opportunity to warm his seat, however. The Conservatives, unable to persuade Liberal Premier George W. Ross to do anything about this blatant new brand of vote rigging, took them to court a year later.

Under oath *Minnie M.*'s purser, Nicholas Cole, was the hit of the show. Just before the election, the Sault Star reported, "Cole was ordered to load provisions for 100 passengers. At 2 a. m. (on voting day) the ship crossed to the Michigan Sault, where six or seven half-barrels of beer, a case of whiskey, a 10-gallon jug and cigars were loaded aboard. The ship traveled up through the American locks... picked up 20 lumberjacks and set sail.... They proceeded to drink as soon as we left the Michigan Sault." At Batchawana, organizers of this little excursion offered the returning officer a new suit if the men were allowed to vote. The unexpected arrival of the Conservative scrutineer put an end to the scheme. The little steamer arrived in Michipicoten ... where each of the pluggers was given a piece of paper with the name of a legal but absent voter.... They were warned not to make any mistakes and to vote for the right man. After they cast their ballot (at the Helen Mine), they were taken back to Michipicoten, where they were fed dinner, given more liquor and taken to the polling station there. All but three (one was too well known, one had too much mouth and another refused) voted again. The *Minnie M.* then returned to the Michigan Sault lumber camp, where the boisterous passengers were each given $2."

Partly owing to shenanigans like this, James Whitney's Conservatives dealt the Liberals a crushing defeat in the next election. The Soo's Liberal candidate, publisher Smith, cleared of complicity in the international vote swindle, was one of the few to survive the Tory sweep. The epic journey of the little steamer was immortalized in a poem, which is here reproduced.

This tale of political chicanery would not have come to light had I not found and acquired the papers of Captain Wm. Morgan Jones from Phillip Shakleton. Shakleton was the only dealer I was able to buy from consistently, year after year. Other dealers, including booksellers, seldom if ever came up with worthwhile lots of manuscripts or ephemera, but Phillip Shakleton had a great eye for papers.

William Morgan Jones was a steamboat captain in Lake Temiskaming. In 1884 he went with the Nile voyageurs to Egypt as a wheelsman at a salary of $150. per month. His experience as the captain of a stern wheeler stood him in good stead when he took a steamboat up the treacherous rapids of the Nile to help General Garnet Wolseley in his effort to relieve General Charles Gordon who had been trapped in Khartoum. Back in Canada Captain Morgan Jones came to Sault Ste Marie and became captain of the *Minnie M.*

In many cases I would go through collections I acquired to look for some unusual, humourous item I could copy for my collection of visual aids to use on the lecture circuit. Showing these to audiences would stimulate their imagination, so they might call out, "Why I have something like that in my attic." Guess who was the next person to visit their attic? In going through the collection I came on the picture of the *Minnie M.* What made it unusual, and drew my attention, was the verse printed down the side of the picture. This set me to building the story to go with the picture.

St. Joseph Island, a small chunk of fertile farmland in Lake Huron some 40 miles east of Sault Ste Marie, was for many years torn by the British-American strife which swirled around its shores. Fort St. Joseph, completed in 1800 to guard the navigation route to Lake Superior and maintain British influence for fur trade purposes, was demolished in 1814 by a naval force from Detroit and never rebuilt. My attention was first focused on St. Joseph's Island when I discovered that my great great grandfather, John Roy McMillan had been posted there in the 1790s when he was serving with his brother, Captain Alex McMillan, in the Royal Canadian Volunteer Regiment.

In 1968 I made my first trip to St. Joseph's Island, heard stories about Major Kingdom Rains and within a short time located some of the Major's descendents in the area. I teamed up with Marion Engel, author of Bear, the award winning book about Rains. Marion was working on a script for a CBC documentary about him as well. I acquired a diary kept by the Major, along with some letters and photographs and checked out many tips but, alas, could find no more papers of Major Rains.

In 1834, when St. Joseph's population was down to a few Indians and French-Canadians who lived by fishing and trapping, its fertility, beauty and particularly its off the beaten path serenity attracted the attention of upper-class Welsh immigrant, Major William Kingdom Rains. The Major, 45, had carved himself a distinguished career in the Peninsular Wars against Napoleon. Shortly after his release from the British Army in 1828, he emigrated to Upper Canada and settled on the south shore of Lake Simcoe. Like many others who sentimentally christened their Canadian abodes after those they left in the old country, Major Rains called his new dwelling Sutton Lodge. Today's thriving community of Sutton, Ontario, derives its name from the Rains estate.

One of Rains's Lake Simcoe neighbours was a retired British naval officer, Archibald Hamilton Scott. A friend of both of them was Toronto businessman Charles Thompson, who was having a steamboat built in Penetanguishene, the garrison town on Georgian Bay, planning to use it for moving goods and passengers around the burgeoning Upper Lakes. The trio also conceived the idea of establishing a farming colony on St. Joseph Island. They lost no time petitioning Lieutenant-Governor Sir John Colborne for a grant of land on the island, "to settle 100 families … and to form a steam communication through Lake Huron … and Lake Simcoe to the Bay of Quinte."

Though Montreal favoured the canal, Toronto didn't and this part of the trio's plan died, but by September, 1834, the steamer Penetanguishene was making daily runs to Coldwater, 15 miles from Orillia, from where road transport to Toronto was available. By 1835, they had their land and, using Thompson's money, they laid out a settlement on the eastern end of St. Joseph and put up a sawmill. Scott ran the mill, while Rains managed their company store.

Everything seemed to be going swimmingly, but it didn't last. Sales of lumber and supplies were meagre and bringing out settlers from England failed because Rains's London investment house made some bad guesses. The partners agreed to go their separate ways. By 1839, the island held only a few small houses, eight of them occupied by French-Canadians and half-breeds. Scott married a half-breed and took up farming on the other side of the island. Thompson no longer lived on St. Joseph, but the store he had financed sold tons of fish and maple sugar on the U. S. market. The navigation scheme had been abandoned.

A handsome, highly educated man who spoke several languages, Rains had married at an early age, but the union was not a happy one and though he had won a church separation, he couldn't arrange a civil one, which required an Act of Parliament. Making the best of the situation, he formed an extra-legal association with the well educated young English lady Frances Doubleday, whose mother had died some years before. In 1830 they had come to Canada, bringing with them their year old son and Lady Frances's sister, Eliza.

When the Major, his bride and son took up farming ten miles west of the original settlement at a spot called Rains Point, Eliza was installed in an identical house next door to them. There, though in reduced financial straits, the two households became one, with a harmony and happiness which lasted throughout their lives. "The sisters were devoted to each other, and both loved the same man, the eternal triangle," explained Mrs. Estelle Bayliss, of Cedar Rapids, Iowa, in 1938. This granddaughter of Frances Doubleday and Major Rains wrote: "There was no other man eligible, their equal in culture and birth. But the three, isolated in this lonely frontier, solved the problem harmoniously. The Major formed an alliance with both girls, providing a separate domicile for each.... The two families grew up side by side, with the deepest respect and affection for each other. The Major gave his name to his children and they were proud to bear it, respecting him and adoring their mother. The ladies seldom went anywhere, being content with their children and books.... They were keen, clever and witty women and endowed with more than ordinary beauty."

Today at least 50 families, most of them around Sault Ste Marie, but the rest in other parts of Canada and the United States, proudly claim descent from this unusual three way arrangement.

It is mildly ironic that Major Kingdom Rains, who had two wives at the same time, should have numerous descendents who are Mormons. A search is on to try and locate more papers relating to Major Rains and the Doubleday sisters.

The only recorded personal encounter between man and buffalo that I have come across was on the Canadian prairie on June 1, 1827. Scottish-born Finnan McDonald wrestled one of these huge beasts to a standstill and, though fearfully lacerated and nearly dead from loss of blood, survived in fame and honour as Finnan the Buffalo.

In a way, the two were almost even. Buffalo bulls are nearly six feet at the shoulder and weigh over a ton, with massive heads, ugly spiked horns and dispositions to match. At 45, Finnan was immensely strong, well over six feet tall, weighed at least 250 pounds, but was also noted for his sweet disposition. The huge weight difference was countered by Finnan's training. His normal method of capturing wild horses, according to one observer, was to "leap from his mount's back to theirs, grapple a nag to the ground by twisting its head down, then hold on till his companions could rope it."

Finnan Buffalo McDonald spoke English, Gaelic, French and several Indian dialects. Bright but not well educated, he had emigrated with his parents to Glengarry, Upper Canada, joined the fur trading North West Company and was sent to the Pacific coast to serve his apprenticeship under the famous map-maker David Thompson. An ally of the Flathead Indians against the Blackfoot, Finnan Buffalo McDonald was on a meat collecting expedition when he wounded a big buffalo. At this critical juncture, his horse stumbled stranding Finnan afoot on the open prairie. With the maddened beast thundering down upon him, he did the only thing possible, threw himself down and played dead. What happened next was described by several among the hunt party.

"This did not save him," wrote famous Scots botanist David Douglas. "He received the first stroke … a dreadful laceration laying open the whole back of his thigh to the bone." At this point, according to fur trader Edward Ermatinger, a dead shot, but afraid to fire because he might hit his friend, Finnan grabbed the buffalo by a horn and the nostril and just hung on despite five more such gorings. Someone did loose off a harmless shot, however, and the startled buffalo, "groaning and vomiting blood a great deal," gave a last sniff of the still-conscious human and staggered off. It was later deduced that a sealskin pouch "stuffed with gun waddings and pierced through and through" had saved Finnan's heart and his life.

Only a hardy Highlander could have survived such a ferocious hammering and subsequent crude medical treatment. Virtually unknown today but a legend in his time, Finnan Buffalo McDonald had founded the fur posts which became Spokane, Washington and Bonner's Ferry, Idaho. He had the good sense later that year to take his Indian wife and family back east, where he was highly respected. He died in 1851 and his body lies in a grave in the village of St. Raphael, Glengarry County, Ontario.

The story of Finnan Buffalo McDonald came to my attention soon after I moved to Glengarry County in 1952. My interest in the fur trade had commenced a few years earlier while I was living in British Columbia and discovered my relationship to James McMillan of the North West Co. who, along with Finnan, had served with David Thompson on the Columbia.

Soon after moving east I met Florence McDonell who had letters written by Finnan's brother John, a wintering partner with the North West Co. and later a Chief Factor with the Hudson's Bay Co. Because these four long letters reveal detailed information about the uncharitable treatment of Métis children of fur traders in Glengarry, they are probably the most historically valuable that I have ever acquired. They have been quoted many times.

John McDonald was writing to his brother Major James McDonald concerning the merit of sending Métis children to be brought up by relatives. He was much more in favour of placing them with strangers. The following excerpts from the letters express his concern. "I have only one more example and that is the case of our brother Finnan. Notwithstanding that I was sending down money with every exhortation to keep him in school as I was willing to be at the expense and wished him to have a liberal education, I was cruelly deceived by being told that he was constantly in school when it was quite the contrary, and he by his deception came to this country without education and what is the consequence? Why! that he cannot rise higher than the charge of a single post for the want of education, although he is possessed of every other quality requisite to entitle him to become a partner and want of education is the only cause that he has not become one before now."

John McDonald makes his point and a brief quote from a letter Finnan wrote in 1849 bears this out. It is well phrased, but phonetically spelt. Finnan had gone to Toronto to try to get his brother John's estate settled. John and his wife Magdeline Poitras had died suddenly of cholera in 1828 leaving a young family at Kempenfelt Bay on Lake Simcoe. Apparently, Finnan got in a row with the sheriff who threw him in the jail.

"Toronto Gale 11th May 1849,

Dear brother and son — I am sorey that I am not brought on as yeat I am badley of here without blankit nor bead.... I gote rashin of drie bread. Have no money to by aney thing. This day I met with young man McNab which is in gale for forgary. He call me aside and ask me if I was in the want of money I told him that I was he told me that he had hard of my situation he made me take one dollar.... I have no time to write long letter for I am to sent this to the postofis this evening."

The few letters of Finnan that survive show that he had no problem expressing himself. He must be one of the earliest school dropouts to be so well documented. A story is told in Glengarry about him and the country wife he brought from the west to Glengarry County.

The local folk had heard she was Indian but no one had yet seen her so the Glengarry women were after their menfolk to find out about her. Finnan was in Cornwall one day and stopped in a saloon enroute home. One of Finnan's neighbours kept trying to find some delicate way to discover if his wife was really an Indian. With the help of some whiskey he hit on a clever way to broach the subject in Gaelic. "By the way Finnan, of what racial origin is your wife from?" Finnan thought for a moment and replied, "Why she is a native of the western plains." The neighbour was quick to reply, "Oh. but 'tis glad we are to hear of that. We thought she was a squaw." The battle that ensued left the saloon and the neighbour worse for wear.

Finnan Buffalo McDonald's old home on the Gore road in Glengarry still stands, lovingly restored by Eric and Dorothy Winter.

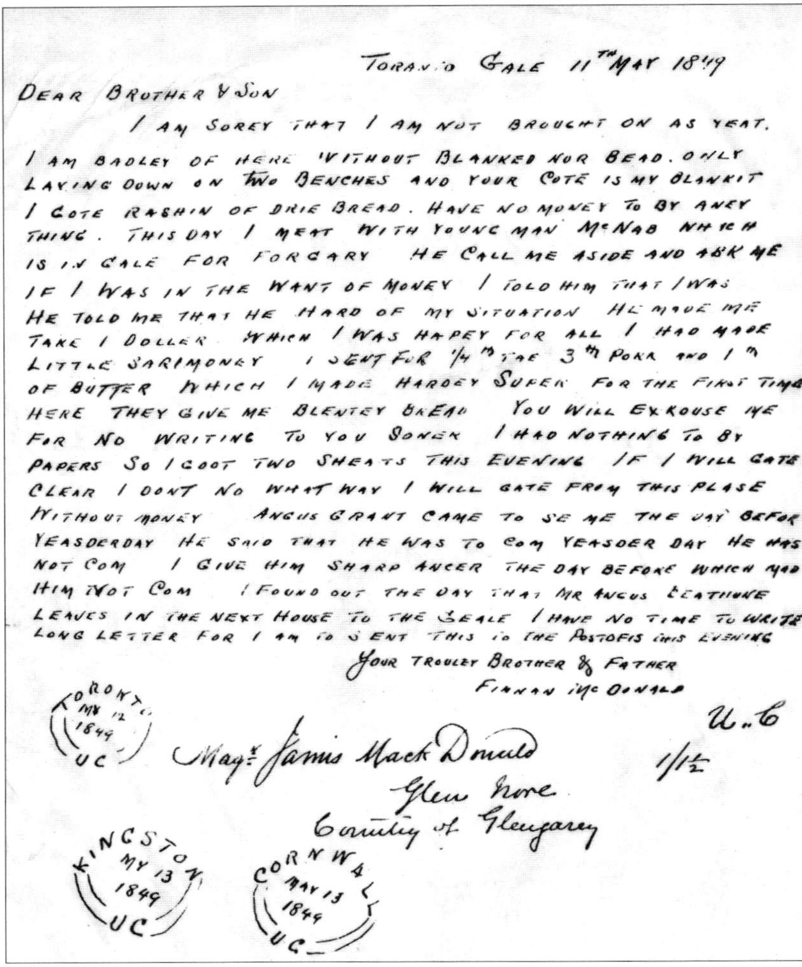

A letter from Finnan "Buffalo" McDonald, North West Company clerk, describing conditions in the Toronto Jail, 1849.

It was furs, for vanity, warmth and wealth, which brought Europeans to the northern portion of North America, and the reaping, treating and trading of the bountiful fur harvests which kept them there. North America's fur companies held sway over enormous areas, the wilderness equivalents of Spain's gold rich New World or the spices, rubber, tea and tin flowing from Holland's sprawling East Indies. The Hudson's Bay Company, whose initials, HBC, have been jokingly claimed to stand for "Here Before Christ," once held a monopoly over terrain which now includes most of western Canada and a large part of the western United States.

It took a formal ceremony at Fort Garry (Winnipeg) in 1869, and the handing over of some 300,000 English pounds to a representative of the then 200 year old firm, for Canada to win legal sovereignty over what an English king had carelessly bestowed as a gift on a court favourite. No treaty or cash was required to obtain a quit claim from the HBC's once fierce fur rival, the North West Company. This chiefly Scottish run coterie of aggressive free enterprisers, who ran rings around the poorly-paid, regulation-bound competition, included among its equal partners such luminaries as Peter Pond, Sir Alexander Mackenzie and explorer-mapmaker David Thompson. When fellow Scotsman, Lord Selkirk, won controlling interest in the Hudson's Bay Company he initiated an all out war against the Nor' Westers who were finally forced to give up the struggle. The take-over of the North West Company and many of its personnel by the HBC in 1821 resulted in the deliberate extinguishing of the North West Company's name, traditions and many accomplishments of its less than 40 year existence. During this brief existence of the North West Company, and the HBC's much lengthier one, some remarkable people made their marks on North America. I have always been deeply interested in every one of them and will go to any length to track down information on this subject.

Tips and leads come from many sources, not the least of which are the newspapers, including the obituary columns. I had colleagues in my network doing the same thing, and over the years this tactic produced excellent results. One day in my Toronto home, skimming through the Glengarry News my eye fell on a story about Mrs. Irons who came from Glengarry, lived in Toronto, and was celebrating her 100th birthday and was a great-granddaughter of Donald McIntosh, a North West Co partner. With me at the time was my 11 year old daughter, Jocelyne, who soon found herself, along with her dad, having afternoon tea with Mrs. Irons. This bright centenarian regaled us with stories and then told us her cousin in Montreal had a letter and paintings of their illustrious ancestor. Soon after that meeting I was in Montreal to strike a deal with Jessie McKercher, and pick up more tips. Unfortunately, none of these have translated into papers but the file is still open.

When six of his brothers were slain at the Battle of Culloden in 1746, John McIntosh left Scotland for America and settled near Albany,

New York. At the outbreak of the War of Independence, he again emigrated, this time to Glengarry County, Upper Canada. Donald, one of John's family of seven girls and two boys, entered the service of the North West Company and was with them until they amalgamated with the Hudson's Bay Company.

Donald McIntosh worked at various posts in the Canadian west until 1816, when he was put in charge of Fort Michipicoten, the North West Company's post on the north shore of Lake Superior, at the mouth of the Magpie River. The French had an outpost in this vicinity a century earlier. After the Conquest in 1759 it was operated, for a time, by two men: Quebecker Jean Baptiste Cadotte and American-born Alexander Henry, whose life Cadotte had saved during an Indian massacre. Henry is best known for his classic book, *Travels and Adventures in Canada and the Indian Territories between the Years 1760 and 1776.*

Alexander Henry's Nor'Wester son, Alexander, was also skilled at record keeping. The fascinating journal he kept for years at a prairie post, was published in three volumes much later. Five years before Donald McIntosh took over Fort Michipicoten, the Earl of Selkirk had won financial control of HBC and had used his new clout to start establishing colonies of dispossessed Scottish crofters in Canada's Red River Valley. Convinced that settlers could spell disaster for the fur trade, the Nor'Westers drove them from their new homes in 1815.

In June of the following year, while Donald McIntosh was still acquainting himself with his new post, a pitched battle took place at Seven Oaks, not far from Fort Garry, during which the HBC's governor Robert Semple and 19 of his men were killed. Selkirk was on his way to Red River with a troop of disbanded British soldiers when he heard the news. He immediately seized Fort William, the North West Company's headquarters and ordered all Nor'Wester chiefs to be arrested and sent back east to await trial.

Donald McIntosh, whose Fort Michipicoten faced a HBC trading post almost in sight of his own, was among those arrested. It doesn't appear to have bothered him unduly, however. Perhaps the suit brought against Selkirk by the North West Company for "having conspired to ruin its fur trade in the West," was enough to gain his early release. However it came about, no mention was made of imprisonment in Donald McIntosh's letter of August 17 that same summer to his sister Christy, back in Glengarry, Upper Canada. Much of the letter dealt with his children with his Indian wife.

I obtained the letter, along with a miniature painted of Donald on linen, from Ms L. McKercher, in Montreal, whose mother was a

McIntosh. Donald wrote: "I am glad to hear that John, my son, applies himself more diligently to his books. It is most time that he should be a scholar. For there are several that went down two years after him that are now apprentice clerks to the (North West) company and if I thought he was qualified to be a clerk I would have him at this place next summer and keep him a couple of years under my own eye. I therefore recommend to you to send him to a good school this ensuing winter, and to get him to learn the rules and principles of bookkeeping." A short time later in this same letter, he approves of one of his daughters under his sister's care being sent to a nunnery, if only "to learn how to sew and embroider, as well as receiving other education." He left this great news to the end. "I announce to you with satisfaction that I am admitted a partner of the N. West Company at long last. You'll say it is better late than never, but owing to the unfortunate contest between the N. West Co and H. Bay Co, prospects for returns are in no way flattering."

Unlike HBC employees, whose annual wages were fixed, Nor'Wester partners shared in the firm's profits, and in good times could become moderately rich quite quickly. McIntosh had waited twenty years for a partnership, only to see its value diminish by the bitter rivalry between the two fur giants. Not even the heady realization that he was now a master for his company of a vast area into which the whole of Scotland could be dropped unnoticed, was enough to assuage this disappointment. After alluding to the battle of Seven Oaks, with little sign of regret or remorse that 20 HBC men had died there, life in the great Canadian bush permitting little sentimentality, McIntosh mentioned that he'd received complaints from fellow Glengarrian Miles Macdonnell, Lord Selkirk's agent, who had been captured by the Nor'Westers.

Macdonnell's beef was "the North West Company was most severe upon him whilst he was their prisoner." McIntosh scornfully commented, "Not more so than he richly deserves. For had it been in his power, he would have got our throats cut, with all his heart." One could wish for many more examples of NWCo factor Donald McIntosh's writings, as much for what he leaves out as that which he includes, as well as his curious choice of words to vivify his descriptions. This one letter was all that I was able to acquire after much searching.

The fine miniature was located later with a portrait of Donald. I was able to persuade the owner, a descendent, to donate the two items to the Nor'Wester museum in Williamstown, Glengarry county where they are on view today. McIntosh closed the letter to his sister on a tender, personal note. "You requested the stature of my woman, she is about as tall as you are but very slender. I send you and my children a few pair of moccasins. I'm sorry I can send you no buffalo robes this year for they are very scarce at Fort William. You may depend on them for next year."

Donald McIntosh's career with the two firms had spanned nearly half a century when he retired in 1838 to St. Polycarpe, Lower Canada, just over the border from Glengarry. His father's old home and his own are still standing.

As a footnote to his own story, his grandson and namesake Donald, born at Jasper house on the Athabasca River, joined the U. S. Army, where he served as a supply clerk during the Civil War. At war's end, he was commissioned a second Lieutenant in a cavalry unit and, ironically since his mother was Indian, accompanied his regiment in the campaigns to bring the plains tribes under submission. On June 25th, 1876, his unit encountered a much superior force of Sioux and Cheyenne warriors and in a fierce 30 minute battle Lieutenant Donald McIntosh was slain, along with 14 other Canadians, and their commander, General George Armstrong Custer.

Evan Connell, in his book *Son of Morning Star,* does a fine job of documenting Custer and the Little Bighorn. He has an interesting anecdote about Donald McIntosh. A Lt. Wallace, who was not very handsome, rode up to Fort Rice to report to McIntosh. It was dusk so he went to McIntosh's house. Mrs. McIntosh opened the door and threw up her hands exclaiming, "My God, you are the first man I have ever seen who is uglier than my husband." It is not recorded what Wallace's rejoinder was to this comment. Donald McIntosh was not all that homely, but did have the angular features of his Scottish grandfather.

CHAPTER FOURTEEN
HOLY HERB

Herbert Emerson Wilson came to my attention while I was browsing through books in a thrift shop. I picked up a paperback titled *Canada's False Prophet* by H. Wilson. The back cover gave a fulsome account of Wilson's career: Boer War hero, friend of Sir Winston Churchill, and later a renowned Baptist preacher from Wyoming, Ontario. I bought the slim volume and was quickly caught up in the bizarre story of his brother Arthur, also known as Brother XII.

The preface claims that Herbert Wilson wrote the book to atone in some measure for his brother's sins. He tells a chilling tale about Arthur Wilson's religious cult, The Aquarian Foundation. Between 1928 and 1933, Arthur conned millions of dollars from gullible followers. Weird sexual rites, combined with torture and murder made for a gripping tale. I began searching for any extant papers of this Ontario preacher and his no-good brother. The chase led me to Herbert's publishers, Simon & Schuster, in New York. They gave me the name of a Vancouver lawyer, who informed me that Herb had died in 1968.

I flew to Vancouver early in 1970 and began searching at the office of the public trustee. This turned up an old address for Herbert's widow, Amelia, who had an unlisted phone. I managed to get the number but Amelia hung up on me, so I drove to her home. While we talked through the locked door, she kept threatening to call the police. When I assured her I would wait for their arrival, she let me in. We achieved a rapport, and she ended up talking for hours.

Amelia had burned most of Herbert's papers, but she did give me a few, along with his Boer War medal. I also learned that he had made an abrupt career change, from preaching the Gospel to blowing safes, a story spelled out in a lengthy story in *Collier's* magazine. In 1982, I was fortunate to meet West Coast poet Peter Trower and his companion, researcher Yvonne Klan, the present-day authorities on Holy Herb.

Herbert Emerson Wilson was born in 1881, in Wyoming, Ontario. His father was a soft-spoken, intelligent man, a carpenter by trade and an amateur chemist in his spare time. He died when Herb was 13. His father was a religious zealot, whose highest aspiration was that Herbert would become a man of the cloth. He grew up to be an utter scoundrel, a cheat, a liar and a con man, so smugly certain of his superiority over the rest of us, that search as I might, I could find only one redeeming act or feature to his credit, of which more later.

A story in the London, Ontario, *Free Press* of 15 November 1899 recounts how "The flimflamming, crooked career of Herbert Wilson, 19, has been checked for a time by ... three charges laid at the slippery chap's door by the local police." Herbert had tried to steal the purses of several working women. A tougher-than-average one had grabbed him and held on till the cops arrived. Within days, he drew a six-month term in Central Prison.

Herbert Wilson thirsted for publicity, but just after his book, *How I Stole $16 Million*, was published by Signet Books in 1956, he rained on his own parade. In his mid-70s, while living near Courtenay on Vancouver Island, and pestering the police to hire him to run an anti-crime campaign, he was caught and fined $100 for stealing $2 worth of groceries. He moved to mainland BC not long afterward.

Between these two sorry milestones in his life — stealing purses at 19 and groceries at 75 — Wilson carried on an amazing criminal career. It's true that at 21 he took part in the Boer War but it's not true that he met Winston Churchill, won a medal for bravery or had it pinned on him by Queen Victoria. It's gospel that he became a hellfire-and-damnation Baptist minister under the name of Holy Herb, but at age 35 forsook saving souls for the more lucrative trade of cracking safes.

He turned out to be a skilled practitioner of this line of work. Over a period of six years, beginning while World War I was raging in Europe, the Wilson gang demolished safes and vaults from one coast of the US to the other, baffling police departments and getting away with millions. But he was eventually caught, and spent 14 years in San Quentin and another six in Canadian federal prisons.

Herbert next surfaced in Vancouver in the early 1960s, operating the Arcade of Mysteries, a third-rate museum of crime, replete with wax figures, lurid paintings and crime memorabilia. About the same time, the poorly educated Wilson was setting up a vanity press to lure unwary would-be authors. His letterhead announced:

AUTHOR'S AGENCY AND PUBLISHERS
Professional Literary Consultants

Articles, Stories, Books, Poems, Songs, Movie, Stage
and Television Manuscripts Requested for Sales Consideration

During his prison terms, Herbert Wilson learned that another Wilson, Edward Arthur Wilson, *alias* The Great Guru, *alias* The Master, but best known as Brother XII, had far outclassed him in the flimflam department. Brother XII, a religious cult leader, spent no time in the slammer and got away with a bundle. Brother XII was not on the other side of the world and in another century, but just outside of Nanaimo, Vancouver Island, while he, Holy Herb, King of the Safecrackers, was getting his sunshine strained through San Quentin and Kingston Penitentiary's steel bars.

Early in 1967 came Herb's contribution to Canada's 100th birthday bash, a book titled *Canada's False Prophet: the Notorious Brother XII*. The illustration on the front cover showed a devilish man surrounded with money, beautiful nude women and a big number XII. Under a mug shot of a neatly dressed but steely-eyed Holy Herb, the back cover was equally eye-catching, not so much for the alleged author's photograph as for the brief accompanying biography:

> Born in Wyoming, Ontario, Herbert Emerson Wilson served as a soldier in the Boer War, where he befriended Winston Churchill, but was taken prisoner by the Boers. Upon release, he was decorated by Queen Victoria. Returning to London, Ontario, he was ordained a Baptist minister and preached for many years in Oregon and California. Mr. Wilson, through a sense of atonement, writes the true story of his brother and the religion he invented. It tells of degradation, murders, orgies, weird sexual rites, cruelty, greed, free love and black magic.

Obviously, if Holy Herb could summon Queen Victoria from her grave to pin a medal on his manly Canadian chest, arranging at age 86 to become a sibling of the notorious Brother XII through 'a sense of atonement' was mere child's play. Simon & Schuster of Canada accepted the lifelong con man's last and perhaps most successful deception, as did some well known commentators and personalities. Winston Churchill died while the book was being written, so he was unavailable for corroboration of his pal's nostalgic reminiscences about their alleged friendship.

You have to hand it to Holy Herb. Driven by his absolute abhorrence for honest labour in any form, he immediately saw the financial possibilities in a phony fraternal *mea culpa*. Even when Herb died the following year, 1968, leaving an estate of $33,000 but no will, most of the obituaries were more fiction than fact. To this day there are websites stating that Herbert E Wilson "worked as a newspaper columnist, artist, Museum of Crime curator, author and literary agent and that his brother was Edward Arthur Wilson, known as Brother Twelve, a religious cult leader" (University of British Columbia Library). Herb would have loved it, but died well before the Internet era.

From Lambton County, Ontario, records, I learned that Malcolm Wilson, Herb's chemist father, had nine children and was credited with inventing a method of hardening copper, the Wilson Sulky Plough, and a power-packed form of nitroglycerine, the 'soup' his errant eldest son would use to such criminal advantage. Herb bragged:

> I remember one night in Detroit when we blew nine safes in one building in less than three hours. When the ninth door popped with just a soft little whoosh, Big Harry Woods, one of my boys, laid his huge paw on my shoulder and blurted out, "Chief, I never seen nuthin' like this. Why dontcha proteck yourself and get a patent on this stuff?"

Herb's credo was laid out in the opening lines of *Collier's* 1949 five-part series. "I will never forget the last sermon I preached and the words I used: 'Thou shalt not steal.' I will never forget it because when I walked away from the First Baptist Church in East San Diego the next day, the church where I was pastor, I was on my way to a long career in crime. After 20 years in the pulpit, I became the most successful safeblower in American criminal history. I blasted 65 big safes and vaults from coast to coast and robbed the mails for a total take of some $15,000,000.... I studied burglary as a science, and mastered it. The burglar tools and techniques I invented set a standard in the underworld and are still being used today, though not with the same skill and nerve."

Holy Herb wasn't exaggerating. I learned from people in his hometown that he'd been building up to this master criminal role ever since he pilfered candy from village stores as a kid. He attributed his ambition to the fact that in his father's house, comic books were unknown and he was not allowed to read anything but the *Bible*.

The *Collier's* piece further reports Herb as saying that as his first officially recognized crime, he and another boy stole some things from a hotel, for which he spent only six months in Central Prison. The blatant lie about the nature of his crime was necessary because stealing from a hotel was a manly thing to do, but robbing poor working women didn't fit Herb's inflated image of himself.

Again in the false book about the False Prophet, he comes out with a statement that could well describe himself rather than Brother XII. "In retrospect I am ... struck by his total lack of any humanitarian feeling. Just as he was brilliant and observant enough to guess people's motivations ... he was brilliant enough to be aware of their reactions to his words, and thus must have maliciously enjoyed people's fear." The key to Herb's success as a safecracker was planning, sometimes for months, during which he and the gang would work out the smallest details of not one but perhaps a dozen possible heists. Then they might hit five or six major targets the same day, assuming odd identities like clergymen, cops or telephone repair people.

Holy Herb's favourite remark accompanying detailed explanations of his ingenious methods of operation, where any hit that yielded less that $100,000 worth of loot was written off as a failure, was, "We drove the Pinkertons crazy!"

A favourite strategy of Herb's was buddying up to night watchmen in buildings where, at certain times, the vaults were filled with cash. Many night watchmen lead lonely lives at home as well as at work. He or a member of his gang would take a room near the home of a particular watchman, strike up an acquaintance, buy him a meal or a few drinks, gradually gain his confidence and expertly pump him for information that would be of use in improving the gang's liquid assets. They also had their own fences, who could readily convert to cash "a million bucks worth of bonds or certificates, a priceless painting, a Ming vase or even an antique clock," Herb explained.

His first five-man crew consisted of his brother Lou, eight years his junior, a medical doctor named George Redding, whose main interest, Herb joked, was sick safes, Tony Masino, "a dead ringer for Rudolph Valentino" whose specialty was obtaining needed information from women, a chemist and nitro expert named David de la Pena, and Herb Cox. Before joining the gang, Cox had been a salesman for burglar alarms, time clocks, and safety wiring devices.

As time went on, Herb enlarged the gang, and found himself having to fire members who failed to produce or had drug or booze habits that made them dangerous to have around.

As the all-round master, he often brought in specialists for particular heists, to teach gang members new techniques or how to handle new equipment. He even included women among his regular operatives, all of them sworn to secrecy and paid generously enough to remain loyal. One of them, Helen Gillespie, a sloe-eyed brunette beauty with a college degree, was Herb's special assistant and sweetheart.

The gang's criterion for a worthwhile target was simple enough: it must contain lots of money. They robbed some of the USA's biggest department stores, as well as Sinclair Oil in Detroit, the National Biscuit Company in Pittsburgh, the Southern Railway in Cincinnati and even Harvard University, from which they lifted $100,000 the night after incoming students had paid their annual fees.

Holy Herb's gang never wore masks on the job. They used simple disguises tailor-made for each member; a bushy hairpiece for a bald man, all sorts of moustaches, glasses, hats, fake teeth, hair dye, phony tattoos. They also carried fake credentials, lodge cards, business cards, licences and stationery. They once bought out an entire private detective agency in order to obtain badges and gun licences. For a time they left out-of-town newspapers lying around the site of each heist to throw the cops off the track. They must have had very cool nerves indeed, because several times when it seemed that the jig was up, they ended up escaping scot-free.

While they were cracking the National Biscuit Company's safe, a guard they had tied up broke free and tripped an alarm. Shortly afterward the street filled with police. Stuffing the currency into flour sacks, Holy Herb's gang raced down the hall to a janitor's room where they had stored bakers' white coveralls, slipped them on, then grabbed hand trucks standing nearby and pushed them into a big room where a couple of hundred men were baking bread.

"Hey," Herb yelled. "I hear there's a gang of crooks trapped in the building. Let's beat it before the shooting starts!"

That did it. The bakers fell over each other getting to the exits, and pushed all of Herb's gang out with them. As the safeblowers pulled away in their cars, the police had floodlighted the office and were throwing a cordon around the plant. "It took me two hours to get over the shakes," Herb confessed.

One icy night in Detroit, after they had safely broken into a bank, a gang member named Big Harry slipped while carrying the acetylene and oxygen tanks into the building. The tanks went banging and clattering down the alley toward the busy street. The gang all froze in their tracks, but even when the cylinders slid noisily into the gutter, there was still no disturbance, no windows flew up. They finished the job without further trouble.

For one of their biggest jobs, they bought a millinery store across the street from a Chicago bank whose new vault was claimed to be burglarproof. They frosted the windows, put up "Closed for Alterations" signs, then settled down to study the habits of employees and customers.

Dr Dave de la Pena was lucky enough to get office space above the bank itself. He hung up a fake chiropractor's diploma and was in business — figuring out where to drill through his office floor, the bank's ceiling. "We spent about ten weeks on the preliminaries, tailing the night watchman, locating the juice that fed the alarm systems, establishing small accounts in the bank and mapping the invasion step by step," Herb explained.

"One dark Sunday night Jack Peer and Big Harry bracketed the watchman half a block from the bank. They flashed police badges and told the guard he was wanted at headquarters in connection with a gambling investigation. " 'Gambling!' he roared indignantly. 'Listen, do you know who I am? I'm the night watchman at the bank and I gotta get to work! Phone my boss, he'll tell you!' 'Okay,' said Jack. 'Let's phone him.' They walked into the bank with the sucker and two minutes later he was laid out on a long oak table, tied hand and foot. The rest of us were in Dave's room upstairs and we started tearing the wooden floor apart. It took an hour to drill a hole through the concrete floor under it. The loot ran close to half a million dollars and before morning we were counting it in our hotel rooms on Michigan Avenue."

Probably their most daring coup was substituting a cardboard mock-up of a safe that stood in Kroger Bros. department store window in downtown Detroit, while they emptied the real safe in behind it. One of Herb's men, dressed in the watchman's uniform, even gave the customary salute to the beat cop, sending him on his way suspecting nothing. Their biggest disappointment came after an all-night assault on a vault containing $14 million, when the oxygen tanks they had stolen from a public works depot ran dry. "Bloody crooked suppliers!" Herb raged.

Herbert Wilson claimed he was never suspected, never questioned, never stood in police line-ups. It's probably true, but with so large a gang it was inevitable that someone would eventually crack. It turned out to be Herb Cox, the former alarm-devices salesman. He got drunk one night, and bragged to a new acquaintance about the $200,000 he had stashed away.

Within a few days, he found the cops on his doorstep asking pointed questions for which he had no ready answers. "It was about a week before Christmas and Helen and I were as gay as a couple of kids on a spree," Herb recalled. "Cox had been on another train, heading home to his wife and kids in LA when he was arrested. Just after I got home, postal agents grabbed me for mail thefts, worked me over then turned me over to the local cops for questioning on the safecracking jobs. I swore I was innocent, claimed I was a retired minister. I didn't know they had Cox and that he'd been singing for two days."

In a breakout attempt, Cox was mowed down by police gunfire, but they hung the rap on Wilson and swore he would swing for it. He gave the District Attorney $50,000 and got off with only 14 years in San Quentin, later reduced to 12 (for a further payment, he claimed).

At the end of the stretch, he was deported to Canada, where he earned another six years in Kingston Pen for counterfeiting industrial bonds, a scam new to his native land. Most of the other members of the gang either committed suicide or were killed in shoot-outs. His sloe-eyed sweetheart Helen, he claimed, died of a broken heart.

Like others, I was fooled by Herb's claim to be Brother XII's brother, until that visit to the Vancouver area in 1978, when I contacted Herb's widow, Amelia, looking for any papers of interest she might have.

Then in 1982 I was given an informative article from the July issue of *Vancouver Magazine*. It was put together by the fine team of Peter Trower, writer, and Yvonne Klan, researcher, whom I had already met. It gave a *précis* of Herb's early career, then carried on with the following:

> "I was amazed one day in 1961 when I stumbled across the strange emporium called Wilson's Arcade of Mysteries and found it to be operated by the very same Holy Herb I'd read about years before. The place was eccentric to say the least, a minor league Black Museum containing such disquieting exhibits as a hangman's rope and the actual trunk where a body had once been secreted in a famous murder case. There were dummies of notorious underworld figures, including Al Capone.
>
> "Around the walls hung a series of lurid paintings ... ranging from Adam and Eve being tempted by the devil to appallingly graphic prison scenes of men being flogged or cut down from the gallows. They were, Wilson explained proudly, the products of his own brush, for while in San Quentin he had studied under a colleague of Diego Rivera, the Mexican muralist."

As a Vancouverite, Trower had, of course, known all about Brother XII long before Herb put out his phony book about his phony brother:

> The Brother Twelve legend is a classic piece of West coast folklore. Edward Arthur Wilson first surfaced in Victoria in 1905, where he was employed as a shipping clerk and spent his off-hours exploring the Gulf Islands by boat. Subsequently he left the coast and became a master mariner, wandering the world and delving into the occult.
>
> In Genoa, Italy, in 1924, he experienced, or purported to experience, a vision proclaiming him to be the twelfth brother of a group of meta-

physical entities who were instrumental in controlling Human Destiny. Following the revelation, he went to England where, promulgating a faith he called Aquarianism, he began to enlist disciples. Many of them were disillusioned Theosophists, former followers of the discredited Madame Blavatsky, and all invariably had money.

Claiming that he had seen it in a vision, the man who was already calling himself Brother Twelve elected to lead them to a Promised Land, where they would establish a colony. Thus, in 1927, Brother Twelve, accompanied by his wife Alma and a small flock of disciples, embarked to Canada and purchased property a few miles south of Nanaimo.

Once in residence on the island, Twelve blitzed the American esoteric papers with his propaganda and reaped an astonishing harvest of disciples: lawyers, successful writers, wealthy businessmen and even an ex-Secret Service agent.

Twelve converted their hefty donations into $20 gold pieces, which he stowed away in quart sealers and boxes. For the first year or so, as homes and administration buildings were being constructed and the forest cover cleared away, all was bustle, peace and harmony.

By 1928, one of the Aquarian Foundation directors had accused Twelve of misusing funds. Heard in Nanaimo, the case was more like a circus than a trial, with Twelve allegedly putting spells on witnesses and prosecutors, causing them to faint or forget what they were going to say. Twelve was acquitted, but from then on, the authorities paid much closer attention to the colony. From this point on things began to really slither down the pipe as Twelve's behaviour shifted inexorably towards the erratic and erotic.

On a train trip to Toronto ... he met a married woman named Myrtle Baumgartner and induced her to believe she was the reincarnation of the Egyptian goddess Isis, and he the god Osiris. Together they would create the new Messiah. When they returned to BC, Twelve's wife Alma left and the idealistic disciples were miffed, until he convinced them that this was all part of the Master Plan. But when the new Messiah was a baby girl who died at birth, 'Isis' went mad and Twelve's own sanity took another beating.

He took another mistress, Mabel Skottowe, soon called only Madame Zee. She introduced a regimen of harsh discipline, the colonists being worked from dawn to dusk and lashed for disobedience. Oddly, they suffered these new strictures with stoic forbearance.... After all, it was part of the Master Plan. When Twelve and Madame Zee left on a recruiting trip to Europe, the settlers enjoyed almost a year of peace.

But when they arrived home in a luxurious, newly purchased yacht, a new reign of terror ensued. The hard-pressed Aquarians finally revolted, trooping into Nanaimo and laying a batch of charges. Realizing the game was up, the pair ... wrecked the colony, scuttled two of the boats, boarded the third and vanished with the fortune in gold coins.

In 1939, a brief obituary in the Vancouver papers ... declared that Julian Skottowe, alias Edward Arthur Wilson, Brother XII, had died in Switzerland in 1934. No mention was made of Madame Zee.

I discovered, at about the same time as Peter Trower did, what we should have figured out much earlier, that Holy Herb was congenitally unable to tell the truth about anything if a plausible lie would serve him as well. His tongue might have been silver-plated, but his writing was juvenile. He couldn't have penned either the book boasting of his $16 million in thefts or the one about his supposed brother Edward, aka Brother Twelve.

Trower learned the truth about the two Wilsons when he and Yvonne Klan were setting out to write their own book detailing the amazing coincidence of two brothers being such controversial, flamboyant figures in totally different — though both criminal — fields.

From the veteran Toronto character actor Joe Austin, a regular in the TV series *The Beachcombers*, Trower got an eye-opening rundown on the slippery, mendacious Holy Herb. "He was a real old con artist," Joe told him. "I wouldn't trust him further than I could see him." When Peter suggested he must have had help with the Brother XII book, Joe laughed. "Help, hell! It was ghosted by a Toronto writer named Thomas P Kelley. He told me the whole story. Kelley got the money and Herb got the publicity." Joe also suggested that the book's ending (see below) was fiction. "They dreamed that business out of thin air and a few good belts of whiskey."

From others, Peter Trower learned that Holy Herb's widow, Amelia, was still alive. Herb had married her in 1951 in the euphoria of publicity after the mammoth Boston Brinks robbery, which the FBI thought he might have pulled off.

Trower tracked Amelia down too. He learned that she, not her husband or Diego Rivera's pupil, had created the grisly wall paintings in Herb's Arcade of Mysteries. She also confirmed that Tom Kelley had written the Brother Twelve book I had picked up in the thrift shop. I found and talked with Amelia four years before Peter did but she had never mentioned the Kelley connection to me.

Amelia swore that the last story in *False Prophet* was true. Herb had claimed that he was running a shop in Brisbane, Australia, in 1943, when Brother Twelve, broke and ill, dropped in. Amelia hadn't known Herb back then, but she thought that an encounter between Holy Herb and Brother XII had been mentioned.

It took one more witness, Vancouver writer John Oliphant, who had long been researching a book on Brother XII, to fill in the last pieces. He was able to redirect Peter and Yvonne's efforts from a book about the two Wilson boys to a book on one Wilson alone. "Oliphant was extremely knowledgeable about Brother XII and confirmed that he and Herbert Emerson Wilson were definitely not brothers," recalls Peter.... "And it was clear Yvonne and I had been scooped!"

I had worked through the same people, except for the actor Joe Austin and the writer John Oliphant, before getting to Peter Trower and Yvonne Klan in 1982, but I had stayed longer and gotten quite a lot of information from Amelia the second time around. With Herb's encouragement, she had been going to write a book on Brother XII and had gathered a pile of material. But while she was down in Hollywood doing some business for Herb (who was not allowed into the USA), he shipped all her material off to Tom Kelley, the ghostwriter.

Amelia told me she had married Herb not out of love but in the hope of discovering what he had done with all the money he had stolen. So far she had been regretfully unsuccessful. She regretted still more that she had thrown out boxes of papers after Herb's death, when I told her that I would probably have paid her a good buck for them!

Another woman involved indirectly with Holy Herb and very directly with Tom Kelley was Kelley's Toronto landlady, Mrs Teresa Winkler. She ran a high-class boarding house on Parliament Street where Tom and his wife Ethel took up residence around 1967. Mrs Winkler soon discovered that they were broke, but out of kindness she let them stay for several months, and looked after their estates following their deaths.

I knew Kelley mainly as the author of a book on the Black Donnellys of Lucan, Ontario. His father had been a famous medicine show operator. Tom had written a book about his career, which Holy

Herb hoped to sell to Hollywood or to the Canadian comedy team of Wayne & Shuster as soon as Stanley Kubrick filmed a blockbuster on his supposed brother, Brother XII.

It took me a long time to persuade Teresa Winkler to trust me. Only in late 1991 did she relent and provide me with a sheaf of documents, including letters Herb had written to Tom Kelley from the mid 1950s until Herb's death in 1968. Some of the topics discussed in them, such as a nude party Herb supposedly attended in Chicago with erratic Canadian evangelist Aimee Semple McPherson and an alleged effort by her to persuade Herb to join her in a suicide pact, are startling but not necessarily true. Three badly typed letters mailed from Vancouver to Kelley in late 1968, months after Herb's death, are mystifying. All of them have only typewritten signatures: "Yours as ever, Twelve."

The earliest document, dated November 10th, 1954, is an agreement with Wilson for Kelley to take facts supplied by Wilson and turn them into a book, presumably *How I Stole $16 Million*, the proceeds to be divided equally between them. A similar agreement was signed on July 1st, 1957, for another book, possibly *False Prophet*. There is a brief memo dated November 1964, on Herb's literary agency notepaper covering his $500 cheque for Tom's work writing the *False Prophet* manuscript. The following day Herb wrote again, part of the letter reading "Regarding Aimee McPherson: You will recall we have a book on her.... I never tried very hard to sell it. Should you want to do one, along the lines of *Ed and Me*, I could send the manuscript to you. Also how about a photo of me and my first wife, Alice, in clerical garb?"

The next two letters, in March and November of 1967, are from Kelley. They refer to other recent letters from Herb, presumably now lost. He first mentions the book he wrote about his father, which he was trying to sell, and *False Prophet*, which was due out any day. His postscript adds an odd note: "Herb, I did not write the Aimee manuscript for you. You wrote it some years ago and shot it on me to look at. Frankly I think it needs some changes and should be lengthened by at least 15,000 words before sending to a publisher. It could be a good follow-up for *False Prophet*."

Kelley's November letter mentions his pleasure at receiving Herb's, but he wonders if someone is intercepting his letters to Herb. Then he enthuses about a newsstand operator who told him how well *The False Prophet* was selling, and how the newsie enhances his own profits by "selling under the counter mags of naked dames at as much as six dollars a throw for some. Lesbians and queers in action and all that. Needless to say I made no mention of my connection with the book."

Many more letters must have been lost, because the next one on Herb's stationery is dated April 14th, 1968. It bears the inscription "Double Flash," Herb's code for haste.

> I have been thinking seriously about the best potential for money is that we concentrate on the darn good story of Aimee McPherson and me.
>
> First: After Prophet Joshua and his mob left Corvallis, Oregon State, a few miles from BC border, he organized another group of Holy Rollers in Chicago. It was a big success. For the fun of it Aimee and I attended their opening night, undressed with all the other males and females, rolled on the carpeted floor, singing and laughing while Joshua, naked, walked among us leading the singing and having as much fun as we were having. There were several naked musicians, men and women, who danced.
>
> Second: In the latter part of this story is about the time Mayor of New York Honest Bill O'Dwyer, was interested in the Holy Rollers.
>
> Third and most important when Aimee came to my home here in Vancouver crying and said, "Herbie, we have come to the end of our lives and I have with me enough sleeping tablets to end our lives, so Herbie here is your share, we can take them, go to bed here, and that will be the end of our interesting careers." I replied, "I cannot do that Aimee." She cried more. I telephoned for a taxi and instructed the driver to drive the lady to the railway station. The next day I read that she was found....

Herb penned another lengthy letter the next day, mentioning the previous one:

> ... relative to the McPherson article, posted before I received your encouraging letter, and your suggestions on Stanley Kubrick and Simon & Schuster. For the present, Tom, please do not be surprised when I inform Ethel and you that a few days ago I became ill. My advanced age cannot be changed, as much as I would like to. Fact is, folks, I felt I should make my will and have, with a carbon for you and Ethel.

He evidently survived the painful intimations of his own mortality, because he wrote again on May 25th, wondering when they were coming out to BC to see him. Another letter on the 27th praised contacts Tom had made with Ken "the General" Grant of Ottawa's CFRA radio station, Longmans Publishers and Toronto's notable Gordon Sinclair. A letter from Kelley a month later mentions their anxiety about him, especially as they couldn't join him because of critical negotiations in progress and the possibility of Tom doing circus midway king Paddy Conklin's life story.

Two short notes written by Herb the first week of July urge them again to head for Vancouver, where they can plot new ways of making "dough-ray-me." Another on July 8th is an offer to pay the Kelleys' way to the coast, a cool grand in cash for them on arrival and a trip to San Diego to see his last church, plus a brief visit to his old San Quentin friend, Dr Leo L Stanley. Herb's final letter congratulated Tom on the publicity for the *Fabulous Kelley* book and his meeting with Lawrence Productions for a possible movie deal.

Then in a "PS Flash Two" he made probably the last and possibly the only thoughtful gesture of his life:

> My original will, of which you have a copy, will be in my desk in the 'H' section. I am going to pay my rent here for three months, so if you come and I'm not here the caretaker will turn over to you and Ethel all my manuscripts, all my furnishings etc.... Live here as I have. Again, thanks to Ethel and you.

CHAPTER FIFTEEN
ARCHIVAL SECURITY

Collecting manuscripts, old letters, books and ephemera is on the rise as a hobby open to anyone. Not all collectors do it legally, and thereby hangs more than one interesting tale.

When institutions purchase manuscripts and ephemera, they are not always careful to check the provenance (origins) of the material. This worked to the advantage of a prominent cleric and scholar, now deceased, who emigrated from Scotland to Canada in the 1960s. For many years in Scotland, he was accustomed to doing research in archives housed in castles and stately homes. More often than not, the owners kept inadequate records of their holdings. This gentleman was in the habit of taking great piles of these ancient manuscripts home to continue his research. Over the years he would forget to take the material back, and in many cases may not have remembered which castle they had come from.

When he moved to Canada, the papers, maps and ephemera came with him, probably because he could not face having to sort the things out to return them to their owners. He was called to a rural Presbyterian Church in eastern Ontario, but ran into problems with his parishioners and had to move. Beset with financial problems, he began selling these papers to institutions in the USA and Canada.

After his death, I contacted his widow and his daughter in connection with some Scottish material that he had wanted to sell. On examining this material, I realized it belonged in Scotland, and should be returned there. I offered to take it back myself. David Galbraith, a friend in the Scottish Records office, took on the monumental task of figuring out which papers belonged where. I am still amazed at how successful he was in matching papers to owners.

I wish I could say this was an isolated case, but it is not. Unfortunately, important papers go missing, not always intentionally. For most of my working life, I have grappled with this problem. Genealogy and stamp collecting are two of the most popular hobbies in the world. They involve millions of people of all ages and billions of dollars, pounds, marks, francs, yen, and lira. Yet when thefts of precious manuscripts, stamps or stampless covers are perpetrated by knowledgeable individuals for huge profits, police and other authorities usually go after them with all the ardour and determination of a cop chasing a boy snatching an apple from a fruit stand.

Because many of the original manuscripts are tucked away in vaults as a general rule, only photocopies or microfilm are available for the public to study. This has not prevented some recent major thefts in Canada and the USA, perpetrated by *employees* of the institutions that owned the precious papers. Able to purloin the originals at leisure and sell them to fences or unsuspecting collectors, they know that the disappearances will only come to light, possibly years later, if some scholar insists on seeing the originals.

Archives and libraries tend to refrain from reporting thefts, fearing (rightly) that the publicity might discourage others from bequeathing their family papers to them. They would rather keep mum and swallow the loss than admit they might have been lax about security.

Some archival institutions will go through the motions of seeming alert to the ever present danger of major thefts only when the press or other media raise the question. Fortunately there are others that regularly invite outside experts to evaluate their security systems.

I invited an authority on security, Professor Philip P Mason of Wayne State University in Detroit, to Toronto in 1980 to encourage the staff of Ontario Archives to take greater precautions against thievery. At the conclusion of the lecture, Professor Mason asked if there were any questions and was met with silence until someone asked what the first precaution against thievery should be. "Change the locks on all your doors," replied Mason. "That's not necessary," the deputy archivist broke in. "All the keys are stamped 'Not to be duplicated.'"

Ignoring this retort, Mason told a story about a Canadian thief from Windsor who was apprehended with thousands of books stolen from Ontario and Michigan libraries. He was tried and later convicted of the theft of a valuable collection of Herman Hesse papers in 1969 from the Purdy Library of Wayne State University. "And do you know where this man is working now?" Mason asked. "He's with the Robarts Library, here at your own University of Toronto."

Shortly afterward, I was deeply involved in the case of Paul Carter, a photographer and fellow employee of the Ontario Archives, who in 1980 managed to make off with 756 items worth close to $500,000. Over the next 10 years, this individual would also be charged with bigamy, insurance fraud and threatening to bomb an Air Canada plane. Despite these serious crimes, Carter spent only a few weeks in jail, most of it waiting for someone to put up his bail.

Institutions, until recently, have been loath to admit that they have suffered from thefts, mostly out of a sense of embarrassment, which works to the advantage of thieves. Many thieves are keenly aware of the value of old letters written before the invention of postage stamps. Certain letters going across borders or across oceans can be worth hundreds, even thousands of dollars each. This point is illustrated in the story of how Paul Carter systematically looted the manuscript collections in the Ontario Archives.

Carter had limited knowledge of postal history values, so it can be assumed that someone coached him, because he took very few items valued under $100. With over 700 items missing, this adds up to a tidy sum. The Paul Carter case was well known to me, and for a short time hindered my acquisition of papers. It was easy for people to say, "But if I give you my papers, they might be stolen." When I encountered this objection, I had a press release to hand out that described our vastly improved security system.

Ontario Archives only discovered by chance that Carter was embezzling its treasures on a massive scale when Toronto dealer and collector Allan Steinhart asked archivist Leon Warmski to examine a valuable 1803 letter from John Strachan, which Steinhart had just bought in England. Delighted at the opportunity, Warmski checked the Strachan file and was dumbfounded to find it already contained a microfilm of the Strachan letter that Steinhart had bought. It had obviously been in the files of the Ontario Archives before it mysteriously found its way across the Atlantic. Several other originals, most of them microfilmed years earlier, were also missing. The Ontario Archives had concentrated on making its collections safe from outsiders, but overlooked a bigger threat from within.

Carter was arrested on 3 July 1980. He was charged with the theft of a camera and over a thousand documents. He resigned from the Ontario Archives on 21 July, pleaded guilty to the charges on 23 July and was sentenced on 9 September to two years in prison. The term was suspended, however, on condition that he help police recover the items he had sold and return them to their rightful owner.

One might have expected such an enormous loss would have William Ormsby, Archivist of Ontario, up in arms, bugging local police round the clock, alerting Interpol, offering rewards, *etc*, but not so. He seemed to be hoping the whole sorry *débâcle* would soon be forgotten, so that everyone — the police, the press, other dealers and especially myself, who made no bones about my displeasure — could go back to business as usual. Even when a hot tip showed us that a dealer in Newmarket, Ontario, had sold a number of the letters, it made no impression on Ormsby's attitude or actions.

The dealer claimed he hadn't known the letters and postal history items were stolen and had kept no records of the people to whom he'd sold them. This explanation was accepted. In 1984, when barely 5% of the missing papers had been recovered, no significant moves had been made by the Archives to put Carter behind bars or stir the police to any more action.

Of even sadder significance, Kitchener dealer Richard Lamb, a member of the Royal Philatelic Society, had sent Leon Warmski a sales sheet put out by a prominent British dealer, listing one of the Archives' missing items. "I gave the Sissons Catalogue with the document illustrated in it to management," Warmski wrote in a memo. "I heard no more on the subject."

Seeing Carter moving around with nobody watching him, free to peddle his ill-gotten wares to the highest bidder, the same kinds of wares I had worked diligently to acquire for an apparently uncaring boss, I became part of an anti-theft squad. Among its members were several Brits, including Dr Dorothy Sanderson, a Southampton collector who had been offered several of the missing Archives items, Richard Lamb of course, collector Michael Millar, Edward Phelps, Archivist and Librarian for the Regional Collection at the University of Western Ontario in London, Metro Toronto Police Inspector Keith Wilson, Sgt Joe Vertolli of the Ontario Provincial Police Criminal Investigation Branch, and Al Steinhart, postal history dealer.

My first attempt at recovering stolen goods was a dismal failure. A Scotland Yard inspector was sent out to assist in an investigation I had requested. I discovered that the Newmarket dealer divided his time between Canada and England, where he had a house. Hearing he had a stall at the August 14, 1985, Strand Stamp Fair in London, England, I called Scotland Yard and was put in touch with a Detective Inspector Clayton. When I told him what I wanted, and would be sending him a list of the missing items, he demanded that someone in authority, *ie*, the Toronto Police, call him and confirm the legitimacy of my request to have someone visit the fair incognito and see if the dealer was offering any of these items for sale. Some days later I got the news that Clayton himself had visited the Fair, identified himself and interviewed the dealer, who told him that of course he wouldn't think of offering stolen goods for sale.

The explanation of the fiasco came from a former Scotland Yard officer. He said the English police could not just go on a fishing expedition but had to already have a *prima facie* case against the suspect before they could act in the way I suggested. I realized that by asking Scotland Yard's help, I'd set myself back several years in the Carter case. Now the dealer was on his guard and would not offer any other items of ours unless he could see piles of cash and a *bona fide* ID beforehand.

Our inability to connect the dealer with anything illegal left Carter free to keep peddling his wares. Canadian law being in some ways as stiff as British law, we could not even get a search warrant now for Carter's home, unless we gave a judge some new evidence to support our claim. The devil was certainly looking after his own.

Five years later, Carter's luck was still holding. The headline in the *Toronto Star* read: "Fool avoids jail term for having three wives." As before, his new assault on Canada's laws was detected only by chance. First married at 23 in 1960, he had taken a second wife in Texas and later a third in Canada. In April 1989, his third wife was innocently checking the new Toronto phone book to make sure their address and telephone number were listed correctly. Noticing there were two Paul Carters, she phoned the other one and was amazed when her husband answered.

In court, Carter explained he was a geologist who had to travel a lot, so was able to spend six weeks at a time with each spouse. He begged the court's sympathy on the grounds that he could never make any close friends; he might run into them with one of his other wives, and also that he just couldn't face the agony of divorce. Even worse, he found it hard to save money. No mention was made of his conviction for stealing hundreds of thousands of dollars worth of Ontario Government property, and his lawyer skillfully made his client's bigamy sound like a harmless misdemeanor. "It started out as a captain's paradise that turned to Paradise Lost," he said, smiling. "It was more like a Walt Disney film than a sophisticated plan."

The court agreed with him. "This man is not a criminal, just a fool," decreed Mr. Justice Hugh Locke of the Ontario Court, General Division, on 18 December 1990.

Four months later, on 10 April 1991, Paul Carter broke a different section of the Canadian *Criminal Code*. This time the story read:

MAN HELD IN AIRCAN BOMB THREAT

A Mississauga man was arrested at a pay phone last night after an Air Canada jet carrying 161 people was diverted to Calgary by a bomb threat. The plane was *en route* from Toronto to Vancouver. A man was arrested at a Yonge Street [Toronto] pay phone while Air Canada officials were receiving a threatening phone call. The plane was parked away from the main terminal (while) bomb disposal experts searched the Boeing 767 jet and found no bomb. Each luggage item was also x-rayed. Paul Carter, 58, is charged with mischief and conveying a false message.

Absent at his first arraignment on 8 July, Carter was in hospital having tests for heart trouble which he claimed had come on suddenly a couple of days before. One of his ex-wives had warned the Mississauga police that her wily ex-spouse would probably pull some such stunt because he had done so previously in similar circumstances. No problem was found with his ticker then, either, but the alarm had served its purpose. The Toronto police did not mention her warning to court officials, who remanded Carter until mid-January, 1992.

Paul Carter made mincemeat out of the old dictum "Crime doesn't pay!" Anyone studying his record could be excused for believing that it's honesty that doesn't pay and the easiest, safest way to get rich is to steal valuable documents and sell them, especially when neither the owners nor the police care if they ever get them back!

After Carter's third wife learned of his criminal behaviour, not only theft but bigamy, she locked him out of their home. I located her and had several interviews. She was more than surprised when I showed her the list of nearly 800 stolen items, and told her of their value on the postal history market. I pointed out that many of the letters on the list were valued in excess of $1,000.

Paul Carter had carted around an old trunk full of such letters and had left them behind when he moved out. She notified the Metro Toronto police several times, but they made no effort to come and look at the material or to question Paul. I too contacted Metro police, but had no more luck. My timing in the matter was not good, since by the time I found out about the trunk, Paul had come and picked it up. More than likely the material was the balance of the letters, probably unsold only because they were too hot after the Archives' list was widely circulated.

Had it been art or antiques that were stolen, the police response might have been quicker. I told Peter Moon of the Toronto *Globe and Mail* about the Carter case, and was able to convince him that a detailed series of stories addressing the problem of the theft of papers and ephemera would be a service to the public, not to mention exciting reading. Unfortunately, his editor was of a different mind and the story never got past a rehash of the Carter case. A series would have helped inform the public.

Librarians, archivists, collectors and dealers are not the only ones who maintain files of historic documents. Fraternal societies, service clubs, churches, synagogues and many other organizations are interested in preserving records of their past. Like their lay counterparts, church archivists sometimes get careless about security, and discover someone has made off with their treasures. Too often (in my view, as someone who has treasured and tried to preserve historical documents for posterity) they are reluctant to track down and prosecute the transgressors.

Even when churches do ask police to help recover their treasures, they may still fall prey to official apathy or snafus and fail to regain their property.

This is just about what happened when the Committee on History for the Presbyterian Church in Canada, of which I was a member, offered summer employment in 1979 to a young divinity student from Hamilton, Ontario. His job was to help catalogue the Archives in the basement of Knox College, University of Toronto. What happened was similar to the Carter case, with equally dismaying results.

The Rev William Proudfoot was sent from Scotland to Upper Canada by the United Secession Church (now part of the Presbyterian Church) in 1830 as a missionary. Within a short time, he established a thriving witness in what is now Southwestern Ontario, with London as his base of operations. Much of the correspondence in the Proudfoot collection was from Mr Proudfoot's ministers in the field. It was of great importance to the history of the denomination.

I first heard of the theft of the Proudfoot papers from Leon Warmski, an alert member of the Ontario Archives staff. At about the same time, Kim Arnold, Archivist for the Presbyterian Church Archives, discovered there were items missing from the Proudfoot collection. As in the Carter case, a man had come into the reading room of the Ontario Archives with a few old letters for sale. Leon, ever vigilant, checked out the provenance of the letters. He soon discovered that they were from the Presbyterians' Proudfoot archives, and were likely stolen. The man with the letters said he had bought them for $7.00 each from the gift shop at Black Creek Pioneer Village, where they were being offered to the public along with the jams and jellies.

At this point, I began investigating how the letters came to be for sale at Black Creek. For Black Creek to be offering these letters to the public implied an unlikely (but in the event all too real) lack of responsibility. The letters would surely have a much higher value for postal historians. Where had they got them?

It took some digging to get the story from Black Creek officials, who by this time were beginning to realize that this was not one of their better sales ideas. Finally I found who had sold them the letters. It was a Toronto lawyer who dabbled in collecting, grew tired of the game, and sold his collection to Black Creek. He had bought them at an auction. When I was in touch with the auction house, they refused to give the consignor's name.

I didn't know that some members of the Presbyterian Church History Committee were well aware of the loss and were keeping the matter quiet. Shortly afterwards, the church history chairman confessed the whole story to his colleagues, and the pieces fell into place.

The student, though still in his early 20s, was already well versed in postal history, knew which stamped or unstamped letters were most valuable, with or without the written messages or the cancellation marks, and where he could most readily dispose of them for big bucks. The Proudfoot papers, most of them stampless letters, were his pot of gold.

He must have rubbed his hands in rapture when he saw them, hundreds of them, sitting neatly on the church's shelves. At this critical juncture, did divinity fly out the window and cupidity fly in? Or did he plan the whole caper beforehand, case the joint and its custodians, put the down payment on a Rolls Royce and promise the rest in the next (fully stamped) post?

The young student thief apparently wasted no time making off with selected letters from the collection, 246 stampless ones dating from 1832 to 1850, 10 entires from Scotland, and 25 cross-border covers, almost all of them addressed simply "Rev William Proudfoot, London, Upper Canada."

As early as August 1980, while still on the payroll of the Presbyterian Church, the daring divinity student was peddling his loot to dealers all around Toronto for as much as $500 to $1,000 per letter. Kim Arnold discovered the thefts shortly after she was appointed Deputy Archivist in September 1980. She drew them to the attention of the Archives Committee, but no action was taken. Like the Provincial Archives, the Presbyterian Church's governing body decided that making the thefts known would do their denomination more harm than good. This state of affairs continued, in spite of pleading from many sources, until 1984, when they found themselves confronted by highly critical forces they could not ignore; members of their own Historical Committee, some of whom were themselves knowledgeable postal historians, archivists, collectors and dealers.

"I am writing to you in connection with the removal and sale of certain items from the Rev William Proudfoot papers in the Presbyterian Church Archives," wrote Michael Millar to Dr Brian Fraser, Chairman of the Church's History Committee in Toronto. Millar was Chairman of the Anti-Theft Committee of the Royal Philatelic Society of Canada and a close associate of mine. I became involved in this matter when Kitchener stamp dealer Richard Lamb provided me with details in a letter to the Church office:

> I am a postal historian and a member of the Presbyterian Church in Canada (St Andrew's, Barrie, Ontario). The purpose of this letter is to urge you to take the necessary action to proceed with charges against this student.
>
> Much of the Proudfoot correspondence has now changed hands several times over. All postal societies, like my own, are publicizing the fact that there is no Proudfoot correspondence legitimately on the market, that all items currently in circulation have been stolen and should be returned.
>
> [But] with the apparent reluctance of the Church to proceed with a Criminal Action, it appears as if all our efforts are to come to nothing. If the Church will not proceed, the philatelic community will no longer feel an obligation to either return the material or to refrain from dealing in it, so the Church's refusal to prosecute is, in effect, going to legitimize this whole matter.
>
> That the committee did nothing in the autumn of 1980 is bad enough, but to sit back now when the Metropolitan Toronto Police and the philatelic community have spared no effort, time and money to assist with the resolution of this matter is far worse. The student has a Criminal Record as a result of his conviction for theft from the Library at McMaster University, and this alone should be reason enough to proceed with a prosecution.
> As a postal historian and a Presbyterian, may I urge you to light a fire under the Archive Committee and proceed with the prosecution.

A further note from Millar to Kim Arnold pointed out that Toronto stamp dealer Allan Steinhart was talking of instituting a civil action against the Church to recover monies he had expended in buying back

Proudfoot letters. So if action was not taken quickly, Millar declared, he himself would go before the Court of the Barrie Presbytery and lay a formal complaint, if only to save the Church from the unwelcome scandal Steinhart's action would involve.

One of my colleagues, Edward Phelps, Regional History Librarian at the University of Western Ontario in London, bought a dozen of the Proudfoot letters. When I told him they were authentic but stolen, he at once contacted Kim Arnold and arranged to return the letters.

Black Creek by this time had heard from me that they were inadvertently dealing in stolen letters. They finally reimbursed Ed Phelps for the $140 he had spent. Hopefully, they will stick to selling jams and jellies in the future.

An investigation was carried out by Sgts Douglas Cameron and William Mason of the Metro Toronto police, following which a warrant was issued for the student's arrest, but the warrant was not executed. The divinity student apparently divined that the fat was in the fire, and he did a disappearing act.

Twice the officers went to his last known Hamilton address and the church he was still reported to be attending, to serve their warrant, but without success. They discovered he was also wanted by Hamilton police. Frustrated, the police put the student's case on hold. I asked the two officers why they had not arrested the student when he was going into the Presbyterian Church he attended, since it was known he attended on a fairly regular basis. They replied "it's not very nice to arrest someone going to church."

On 8 June 1987, stamp dealer Allan Steinhart caught a glimpse of his elusive quarry at the International Stamp Exhibition in the Metro Toronto Convention Centre. He immediately alerted Toronto constable Wilkinson, on duty at the Exhibition, and had the student arrested.

Nothing more was heard of the case until October, when Church Archivist Rev Mel Bailey was contacted by another police constable and advised to appear in Courtroom 123 of Old City Hall, on 4 November at 10:00 am. "Should I bring any documents, anything of that sort?" asked Bailey.

"No," replied the constable. The rest of this sorry saga of woeful ineptitude is told in a complaint made by the Church's John A Johnston, DD. in this complaint dated 9 November to Ontario's Attorney General, the Hon Ian Scott, QC.

When Mr Bailey arrived at the Court, he was astounded to find that the two police officers, whose names I don't have, knew nothing about the facts of the case and had nothing prepared. This left the Crown Attorney with no alternative but to withdraw the charges.

Thefts of valuable records, stamps, books, paintings and other irreplaceable items are not, of course, limited to Canada. The disappearance of the Felix Frankfurter diaries and papers from the United States Library of Congress in 1974, was followed by thefts from the University of Virginia, North Carolina State Archives, Texas State Archives, Yale University, Franklin D Roosevelt Library, Indiana State Library, Ohio Historical Society, State Historic Society of Wisconsin and many others.

No single safety system fits all situations. In the early 1980s, it was seriously suggested that the Archives should be closed to the public. Citizens would then be allowed to examine manuscripts only in specified outside reading rooms or on videocassettes. This, of course, would not solve the problem of crooked employees who, like Ontario Archives photographer Paul Carter, would have the run of the premises.

"Today to see originals, anyone needs gilt-edged credentials," according to Dave Ross, of the New Brunswick Museum in Saint John. But Walter Neutel, head of a public archives security committee, counters this by noting that however well known and respected a visitor might be, he or she would still require watching. "A letter to your grandfather from a Prime Minister," he says by way of explanation, "may be too attractive to resist. Such an attachment can be just as motivating for even a distinguished visitor to lift a manuscript as a monetary gain to an ordinary thief."

A no-exception rule at the United Church of Canada Archives in the 1970s, requiring researchers to sign out documents they wish to use and sign them back in again, unexpectedly led to the recovery of archive material from all across Ontario. "In 1977, a researcher reported some historic pamphlets had been cut out of their bindings, [while] others in envelopes had been replaced with worthless paper," testified Glenn Lucas, United Church archivist-historian at the time. A peek at the sign-in list gave him a name. "I checked with a book dealer I knew and he showed me what he had bought from this fellow. The stitching on the pamphlets, which had been bound together, matched perfectly."

Police found the man at his home, busily bleaching identification stamps out of archive material. It required a station wagon and the trunk of another car to cart away all the material he had lifted. Included were rare books from Queen's University, Kingston, and the University of Toronto. "He'd had to climb a tall wire fence to get at the U of T's rare books," said Lucas. "I hope they use an iron fence to hold him."

Alarm-triggering micro-chips undoubtedly help foil thefts of books from libraries and archives, but suppose single pages in certain historic tomes are very valuable in the antique markets, do you attach micro-chips to every page? Sprays work well for some purposes too, but are not practical for manuscripts grouped together in file boxes. Curators are also loath to use stamps or sprays at all, for fear of marring the original condition. Even movement-sensitive cameras, ideal for some situations, have their drawbacks.

Equally complicated and baffling is what to do when thefts are uncovered months or years after the crime was committed. If the owner doesn't even know they are missing, he cannot alert the trade not to buy specimens offered for sale. Dealers, institutions and private collectors may have paid good money for them, featured them in exhibits, and resold them.

Even the most super-sophisticated, state-of-the-art precautions are of no use whatever against thieves like Frank Henry Robertson. Listed by Hugh A Taylor of the Public Archives of Nova Scotia as the perpetrator of "the most serious theft in the history of Canadian Archives," Robertson did not confine his talents to the Maritimes. Periodically he would sweep through the major centres of Southern Ontario or the USA with the speed of an express train, hitting dealers in their shops or homes and vanishing with their treasures before they could catch their breath, leaving consternation, havoc and panic in his wake.

Alerting police to Robertson's methods of operation did no good. If he thought they were forewarned and waiting, he'd postpone his raid till they relaxed. Then he might put it off altogether, or perhaps roar through using a different pattern, so they were always one step behind him, trying to guess where he'd strike next. Like many of the other thieves in my dossier, Robertson seemed to live a charmed life.

In the fall of 1984, Robertson, then 39, disappeared after a hectic summer making life miserable for archivists and dealers from Kingston to Ottawa to Toronto, some of them more than once.

But when he resurfaced the following spring, he did a surprising thing; he turned himself in to the authorities in Moncton, New Brunswick, stood trial in Kentville, Nova Scotia on 26 June and received a seven-year term in the penitentiary. The next time I was in Halifax, I contacted the Nova Scotia Archives and the Halifax police about Robertson. I assumed they would have a detailed file chronicling Robertson's raids on archives and dealers. With embarrassment, they showed me a file containing only a few press clippings, which gave no indication whether Robertson was in or out of jail.

I found much the same situation in the Carter case, where I had more complete files than the Ontario Archives did. Neither the police nor crown attorney had a copy of the trial evidence. Small wonder that paper thieves have it so easy! Though seven years may seem like a stiff sentence, it took into account only crimes Robertson had committed in Nova Scotia. If he ever visits Ontario, he can be charged all over again. The same applies to the United States, where the US Postal Service wants him for theft and sale of an imperforate pane of Project Mercury stamps from the Franklin Postal Museum in Philadelphia.

Robertson, described as a native of either Wolfville or Middle Sackville, NS, had been a criminal virtually all his adult life. The only break came between 1971 and 1977 when he was married, sired three children and worked as a furnace and oil burner technician. Caught with manuscripts stolen from the Public Archives of Nova Scotia (PANS) in 1977, he spent a year in the Halifax County Correction Centre.

The theft, referred to as the most serious of its genre in Canadian history, involved the disappearance of some 600 rare stampless covers. Robertson took these from PANS and also from the University of New Brunswick (UNB) and the New Brunswick Museum. In 1977 PANS archivist Hugh Taylor reckoned Robertson had purloined the stampless covers over a period of 10 years or more.

> The first indication that anything was seriously wrong [wrote Taylor] appeared when a philatelist who also knew of the PANS collection, asked for a check of some covers being offered to him. They were quickly identified as stolen property and an inventory of the collections revealed major losses. Other Maritime repositories were informed, and the full extent of the disaster was gradually revealed. Only the UNB had micro-filmed its collection ... and had a fully identifiable record.

The total value of the missing covers, only a handful of which were recovered, was estimated in the hundreds of thousands of dollars, perhaps as high as half a million.

Taylor drew up a list of 17 recommendations to help spare other archives "the terrible losses we have suffered," but made no comment on whether Robertson's seven-year stretch behind bars was enough to even the score.

Robertson's methods in his raids into Ontario were simple but effective. He used the loot slickly filched from one dealer to keep a dealer in the next city so enthralled with the high quality items being offered that he didn't notice Robertson pocketing the dealer's own treasures. A typical Ontario crime schedule, one of the last before he was put away for the long count in his native Nova Scotia, went like this:

4 June 1984: Ian Kimmerly, Ottawa stamp dealer and stamp columnist for *The Ottawa Citizen*, reports that a man shoplifted a horizontal pair of 3-penny Beaver stamps and a set of King Edward VII marginal imperf pairs from his shop.

6 June: Debbie Kosztandy of A Kosztandy Stamps of Toronto, says that copies of ½¢, $3 and $5 Jubilee stamps, valued at $1,000, were discovered missing from a stock book. She says she believes a man who looked at the material the previous day took them from the book. She said the man had shown her a pair of 3-penny Beaver stamps.

A belated report from another Toronto firm, George Wegg Ltd, revealed that on 5 June they had purchased a pair of 3-penny Beaver stamps from a man who entered their retail store.

- 9 June: Imperforate Edward VII stamps are offered to two dealers in the Kitchener, Ontario, area. One of the dealers, Harold Beaupré, later reported about $1,000 worth of Canadian plate blocks missing, including matched sets of the 50¢ and $1 stamps of the 1946 Peace series.
- 11–12 June: Officials at the University of Western Ontario in London believe "an individual using its archives" removed a quantity of stampless covers of the late 1700s and early 1800s.

Another late report from dealer Keith Greenham of London's Forest City Coins and Stamps states that on 9, 11 and 12 June, a man offered to trade Edward VII imperforates and historical material. "He was an interesting fellow, a very average kind of a guy," Greenham said, "easygoing, not demanding big discounts." Robertson and Greenham talked for seven hours, about everything under the sun. "Robertson returned several days later with War of 1812 documents, including military call-up posters and orders signed by Sir Isaac Brock. He'd bought them at a couple of flea markets, he said. He suggested lunch next day for some trading in various items."

The following day, on a hunch, Greenham called my colleague Ed Phelps, a member of the anti-theft organization, and discovered that the

1812 material had been lifted from the University of Western Ontario mere days before. Putting in an emergency call to the police, Greenham and Phelps headed for the train station, where an employee of Greenham's had spotted their man. When no police officer could be found in the large railway station, Greenham tracked Robertson, who ran off down the railway tracks, dropping a bag which proved to contain some $3,000 worth of rare stamps stolen from Ottawa dealer Ian Kimmerly a week or so before.

Robertson had been careless. Though he used various aliases, he'd shown dealers his driving licence on a couple of occasions. New tales of horror now flooded in. June 6th in Ottawa had not been the start of Robertson's odyssey, as they had thought. He'd hit Kingston, Ontario, stamp dealer Glenn McIntyre as early as 25 May, sold him a few coins and said he'd be back. Just about the same time, he'd relieved Queen's University of some 200 documents, among them stampless letters of great historic value.

Robertson did return to McIntyre's shop on 6 June just before heading for the capital, and left some stamps there, which were later discovered to have been stolen from Toronto dealer Andy Kosztandy. McIntyre's manager, John Meiboom, was congratulating himself on having miraculously escaped. But an inventory of items "which had last been shown to Robertson" revealed losses of at least $1,000. This was small potatoes compared to the losses of Toronto's JN Sissons. The slippery Maritimer spent two hours at Sissons' stamp auction on 15 June and walked off with $10,000 worth of rare Canadian stamps and printers' proofs of early stamps. "Our staff normally allows a customer to examine only one stock book of stamps at a time," mourned JN Sissons' Lex De Ment. "But with guys like that, as soon as your back is turned for another customer, you've lost an item."

Conservative estimates of Robertson's destructive spring swing through Ontario put his take at $50,000, which he may have used for a long, luxurious holiday in Florida or some other resort before heading back home a year later to face the music. Even though they knew his name and habits, the police couldn't stop him doing just about anything he wished, whether it was robbery, fraud or just a yen to travel.

It was thought that during the year Robertson was missing, he travelled to the US West Coast and committed dealer robberies in Northern California, Nevada, Washington and Oregon. It was later discovered that a man from Vancouver who matched Robertson's description and called himself "Louis Conti," was committing thefts using

Robertson's *modus operandi*. No arrest or recovery of stolen goods was made in this *doppelgänger's* series of thefts.

Checking recently with the National Archives in Ottawa and several provincial archives, I have found it evident that these institutions are now paying much more attention to security involving people using their reading rooms. The dilemma facing archives is to find a safe balance between security and public access.

Nevertheless, few of the historic artifacts stolen by Paul Carter and his ilk have been recovered. It is a great loss of public property — and of our historical heritage.

CHAPTER SIXTEEN
LOYALISTS AND OTHER TALES

Searching for Loyalist records and papers became almost an obsession for me, especially after I discovered I had three Loyalist ancestors. The United Empire Loyalists' Association of Canada has been active for many years, so very few Loyalist papers were still in private hands. Searching for papers that weren't in an archive was a challenge. Tracking down Loyalists brought me into contact with people I'll never forget, and occasioned some memorable incidents as well.

Lily Ross of Cornwall, Ontario had many Loyalist ties and was most generous in giving me leads to Loyalist descendents who had manuscripts. The first of these tips led me to Thunder Bay, Ontario, where I acquired the proceedings of a court martial involving the King's Royal Regiment of New York, a Loyalist military force organized by Sir John Johnson out of refugees from upper New York Province (as it was then) who had taken refuge at Chambly, Quebec in 1776. Miles McDonell, a young officer in the regiment who later became agent for Lord Selkirk at Red River, was part of the court that handed out a sentence of 50 lashes to a Private Newton for being disrespectful to a Captain Munro. Little wonder there were mutinies from time to time!

I last visited Lily Ross when she was 110 years of age, sharp-minded and as outspoken as ever. A staunch Tory, Lily remembered Sir John A Macdonald visiting her father's home. I asked her if she had ever considered getting married. Fixing me with her most penetrating look, she replied, "Hugh, I have known several men extremely well during my lifetime. There was only one that I wanted on a permanent basis, but Father did not approve. The others were loveable, but not full-time." When she died, she was 113. A most remarkable lady!

Through the efforts of Catherine Love, another helpful lady, some amazing letters came into my possession. Rev Samuel Rose, a Methodist circuit rider (horseback missionary) of the early 1830s, wrote them to his brother in eastern Ontario. Rose had a rare sense of humour, as evidenced by his description of York's (Toronto's) famous mud, noting that he was "sometimes under it and sometimes over it."

HUGH ON A ROLLS
I was chauffeured around Prince Edward County in 1986 in this very comfortable Rolls Royce by its owner, Bob Davis (centre) when I collected some papers from Larry Ackerman (right), secretary-treasurer of the Black Creek Cheese Factory. Good publicity for the work of the Archives.
(Photo by Dan Hinde, Picton Gazette)

His tolerance evaporated though, when, after driving his wagon onto a scow crossing the Grand River, he entered Mount Pleasant and learned of the invasion from the USA by those he called "Mormonites."

> They profess to have found part of the Scriptures. This they say was found by a man named Smyth, [Joseph Smith, founder of The Church of Jesus Christ of Latter-Day Saints] on gold leaf, and by him translated into English. No men can read it but those to whom it is revealed. Their converts profess to speak in unknown tongues. But what to you may appear most strange is that 14 persons … joined them and 3 of them were Methodist. I came to this place and found that those miserable imposters were at work here and that they were taking away some of our members. I told the people plainly that I believe them to be as great a set of imposters as ever was on earth.

(This quote from a letter by Rev Mr Rose is one of the earliest references to Mormons in Upper Canada.)

Catherine had that rare ability to make people feel good when they turned their papers over to her, or sometimes, as in this case, to me. Catherine Love was also instrumental in putting me in touch with the papers of a cheese company, which I picked up in my friend Bob Davis's Rolls Royce while promoting my work for the Archives in and around Milford. Many of the people who supplied milk for the Black River Cheese Company were descendents of Loyalists. I had *The Picton Gazette* cover the story, which got picked up by the wire services.

Hamnet Pinhey was first drawn to my attention by Phillip Shackleton, a great merchandiser of old paper, who offered me the papers of the Bytown & Nepean Road Co. This early toll road was one of Pinhey's many business interests. I followed my usual procedure: find more descendents, and the law of averages will see to you getting more papers. Turn up they did, in Northern Ontario, St Catharines, Toronto and Ottawa.

Hamnet Kirkes Pinhey was an English merchant. In 1819, he took up farming on the Ottawa River, a few miles upstream from the present site of Canada's capital. He had led a boisterous, exciting life before emigrating to Britain's North American colony. During the Napoleonic Wars, he persistently ran the French blockade bearing vital dispatches for Britain's ally, the King of Prussia. For these perilous patriotic endeavours he was publicly thanked and voted a sum of money.

Managing a 1000-acre farming enterprise was not enough for the energetic Pinhey. A leader in the community, he built the first grist mills and sawmills in March Township and erected the first stone church, mostly with his own money and labour. He also assumed the role of private banker for the area, served as warden of his district, and held various government posts. Hamnet Kirkes Pinhey's descendents have always been prominent in local and national affairs, with a range of interests from the law to the arts. Their progenitor, who died in 1857, is remembered for his pioneering agricultural, financial and social achievements, but more particularly among historians, for his superterse, neat records of everyday events.

Pinhey was a skilled writer. He used that skill to advantage in a column he wrote for Dr Christie's *Bytown Gazette*. I was able to meet Hamnet Pinhey Hill, a prominent Ottawa lawyer and grandson of Pinhey, through my mentor Verschoyle Blake. HP Hill had been directing papers to the Public Archives in Ottawa for years, but had become disenchanted with their slowness in pursuing his tips.

Pages for February/March 1833 from a diary kept by Hamnet Pinhey (d 1857) of South March, Upper Canada, near present-day Ottawa. A good example of concise diary writing. During the Napoleonic Wars, Pinhey regularly ran French naval blockades to carry dispatches for the King of Prussia.

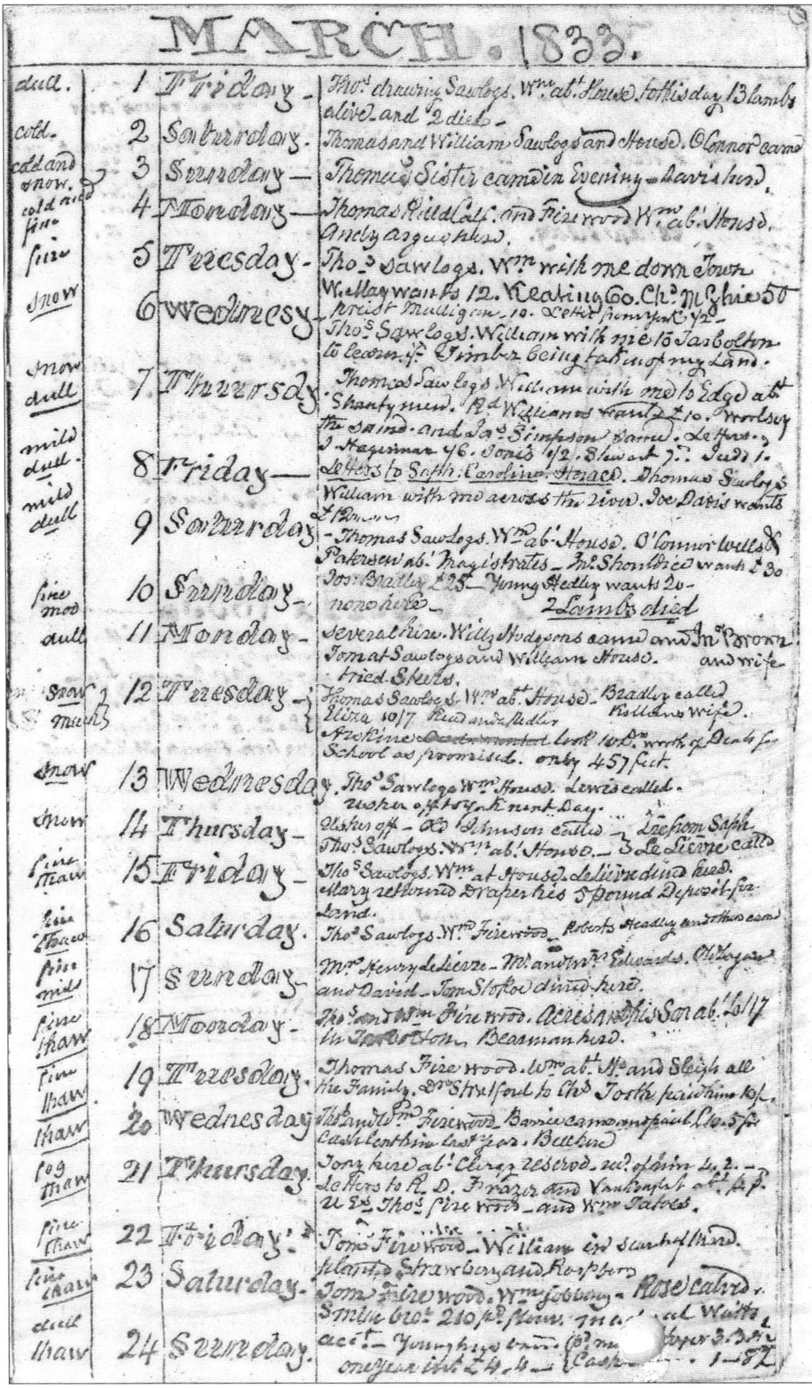

MARCH. 1833.

Weather	Date	Day	Entry
dull.	1	Friday –	Thos. drawing Sawlogs. Wm. abt. House. to this day 13 lambs alive – and 2 died –
cold.	2	Saturday.	Thomas and William Sawlogs and House. O'Connor came
cold and snow.	3	Sunday –	Thomas's Sister came in Evening – Davis here.
cold and fine	4	Monday –	Thomas Killd Calf. and Firewood Wm. ab. House. Andy Ayres here.
fine	5	Tuesday –	Thos. Sawlogs. Wm. with me down Town
snow	6	Wednesday –	W. May wants 12. Keating 60. Chs. McGhie 50 Priest Mulligan 10. Letter from York 4/2 – Thos. Sawlogs. William with me to Tarbolton to learn of Timber being taken of my Land.
snow dull	7	Thursday	Thomas Sawlogs William with me to Edge abt. Shanty men. Rd. Williams wants £10. Woolsey the same. and Jas. Simpson same. Letters J. Hagerman 46. Jones 4/2. Stewart 7. Judd 1.
mild dull.	8	Friday –	Letters to Saph. Caroline. Horace. Thomas Sawlogs William with me across the river. Joe Davis wants £[illegible]
mild dull	9	Saturday	– Thomas Sawlogs. Wm. ab. House. O'Connor Wells & Paterson ab. Magistrates – Mr. Shouldice wants £30 Jos. Bradley £25 – Young Hedley wants 20 – none here –
fine mod	10	Sunday –	2 Lambs died
dull	11	Monday –	several here. Willy Hodgsons came and Mr. Brown and wife Tom at Sawlogs and William House. tried Steers.
snow much	12	Tuesday –	Thomas Sawlogs. Wm. at. House – Bradley called Eliza 10/7 [illegible] Kellans wife. Erskine [illegible] took 10 Ds. worth of Deals for School as promised. only 457 feet.
snow	13	Wednesday.	Thos. Sawlogs Wm. House. Lewis called. [illegible] next Day.
snow	14	Thursday –	[illegible] – [illegible] Johnson called – Lre. from Saph. Thos. Sawlogs. Wm. ab. House – LeLievre called
fine thaw	15	Friday –	Thos. Sawlogs. Wm. at House. LeLievre dined here. Mary returned Draper his 5 pound Deposit for land.
fine thaw	16	Saturday.	Thos. Sawlogs. Wm. Firewood – Roberts Headley and [illegible] came
fine mild	17	Sunday –	Mrs. Henry LeLievre – Mr. and Mrs. Edwards. [illegible] and David – Tom Stokoe dined here.
fine thaw	18	Monday –	Thos. and Wm. Firewood. Acres with his Son ab. 16/17 in Tarbolton. Beaman here.
fine thaw	19	Tuesday.	Thomas Firewood. Wm. ab. [illegible] and Sleigh all the Family. Dr. Stratford to Chs. Forth paid him 10/
thaw	20	Wednesday	Thos. and Wm. Firewood. Barrie came and paid £10.5 for Cash lent him last year. Bell here
fog thaw	21	Thursday.	Tony here ab. Clergy reserve. [illegible] – Letters to R. D. Frazer and Vankoughnet ab. [illegible] Thos. Firewood – and Wm. Tables.
fine thaw	22	Friday.	Tom Firewood – William in search of [illegible]. planted Strawberry and Raspberry
fine thaw	23	Saturday.	Tom Firewood. Wm. jobbing – Rose called. Smith bro. 210 ld. flour. [illegible] Waite
dull thaw	24	Sunday.	acct. – Young [illegible] one year [illegible] £4.4 – { [illegible] 3.3 / Cash [illegible] 1–8 }

When I met Hamnet Hill, he complained to me that the Public Archives had failed to send someone to pick up the papers of Dr Christie, publisher of the *Bytown Gazette*. I immediately headed for Ottawa. The Public Archives were not overly amused when they discovered I had taken the Christie papers back to Toronto with me. Thanks to Hamnet Hill's son Charles Hill of the National Gallery, several more collections of Pinhey-Hill papers wound up with the Ontario Archives as well.

Charles Hill wrote to me later, commenting, "Your untiring patience and persistence in keeping after me to give you these papers finally convinced me." Convince him I did, and more leads followed. The papers are certainly unique. Hamnet Pinhey's daybooks were models of concision. He recorded an entire month's weather, crop and livestock data, trips and visits made, weddings, births, deaths, work performed on the farm or roads, in the mills or bushes, as well as any unusual happenings, on a single page. Pinhey's novel artistry makes intriguing reading.

Many other paper trails yielded far less than the Pinhey case, but another that proved to be extensive was the Bethune-MacKenzie saga which spans the continent and abroad. Both the Bethune and MacKenzie families produced many superachievers, including the famous Dr Norman Bethune of China and his great-great-grandfather, Rev John Bethune (1751–1815) chaplain to the Royal Highland Emigrant Regiment in the Revolutionary War. Rev John Bethune founded St Gabriel's Church, the first Church of Scotland congregation in Montreal, followed by the first Church of Scotland parish in Upper Canada at Williamstown, Glengarry. Rev John Strachan, the arch-Tory of York (Toronto), then lured two of Rev John Bethune's sons into the Anglican church, where they both became bishops.

In the pleasant Central Ontario community of Gravenhurst stands a house which for years has been a venerated shrine for officials and other visitors from the People's Republic of China.

When diplomatic relations between Canada and the People's Republic were established in the 1970s, delegations of Chinese began visiting Canada. It was a puzzle to find these groups didn't want to see the CN Tower or Niagara Falls first. Instead they wanted to go to the Gravenhurst, Ontario home of their great Canadian hero, Dr Henry Norman Bethune, who would blaze across the medical and political firmaments of several continents before succumbing to blood poisoning in North China in November 1939.

The Presbyterian manse in Gravenhurst was the birthplace, in March 1890, of Dr Bethune. Most Canadians, including the wife of the minister who lived in the house where Bethune was born, had no idea who Bethune was. One morning, she answered a knock at the door, and was startled to see a very large delegation of smiling Chinese tourists. With the help of an interpreter she was finally enlightened about why they wanted to look through her house.

A 1991 film about this icon of the history of the Chinese Communist revolution, entitled *Bethune*, starred Canadian actor Donald Sutherland. Eventually Prime Minister Pierre Trudeau had the house designated a National Historic Site, and the Canadian government bought it for Canada. It is now a major tourist attraction and the Gravenhurst Chamber of Commerce may bless the day Bethune was born in their town.

But I did not take a personal interest in rounding up Bethune family papers until I began researching another family, the McKenzies, who had been prominent in the North West Company. Nor'Wester documents are scarce, because after their merger in 1821 with the Hudson's Bay Company, many of the earlier records were lost. During the North West Company's short lifespan of less than 40 years, four brothers of the particular McKenzie family that I was probing were highly active. One of these, Donald, was the subject of *The King of the Northwest*, a book published in the 1930s by his grandson, Cecil McKenzie.

Huge as a bear, famous over half the continent as a dead shot, and with an Indian country wife, Donald McKenzie was rumoured to have turned down the offer of a knighthood from King George III because that obdurate English monarch refused to recognize Donald's wife as Lady McKenzie. "But if Your Majesty wouldn't mind," McKenzie is claimed to have retorted, "I'll take a pair of duelling pistols instead." The matched set of pistols became the proud possession of John McKenzie of Mayville, NY, a great-grandson.

Donald McKenzie left the North West Company and joined John Jacob Astor's fledgling American Fur Company in 1809. On July 4, 1810, Donald McKenzie was aboard the first American Fur Company Montreal canoe to leave Lachine for the gruelling run to Michilimackinac. He recruited a skilled crew of tough local voyageurs from among his personal friends.

A passenger on the trip was 27-year-old Washington Irving, the American writer, who later wrote disparagingly of the voyage: "Some [of the voyageurs] were able-bodied but expert; others were expert but lazy; a third class were expert and willing, but … broken down veterans, incapable of toil." Irving also claimed they "balked at their work, ever ready to come to a halt, land, make a fire, put on the great pot and smoke and gossip and sing by the hour." The heavily loaded craft reached Michilimackinac on July 17th, having completed the 900-mile upstream run in barely two weeks.

Donald McKenzie took part in the first overland journey to Astoria, Astor's headquarters on the Pacific Coast. When Astoria was captured by Nor'Westers during the War of 1812, he returned to his former employer as a partner. After the merger, he became a chief factor of the Hudson's Bay Company, and later Governor of Assiniboia.

Donald McKenzie's younger brother, Henry, duly serving his North West Company apprenticeship at Kaministiquia, later Fort William, became the McKenzie family's master of all trades. Back in Montreal in 1804, on the death of Simon McTavish, the first head of the North West Company, Henry McKenzie took over the management of McTavish's mills in nearby Terrebonne. Their famous kinsman, Sir Alexander Mackenzie, had been a North West Company explorer of overland routes to both the Arctic and Pacific oceans, at least ten years ahead of Lewis and Clark, thereby proving the long sought water passage from the Atlantic to the Indies did not exist. I acquired a miniature on ivory of Henry from a descendent, Mrs Audrey McCallum.

In 1808, when Sir Alexander Mackenzie left for Scotland, Henry, still only 28, also took over the handling of his North American affairs, including his extensive land holdings in Glengarry County, Upper Canada. During the acrimonious disputes between the Nor'Westers and Lord Selkirk, Henry McKenzie's pen became a mighty sword, regularly presenting the Nor'Westers' point of view in the influential Montreal newspapers.

McKenzie's public relations efforts undoubtedly helped turn public opinion against Selkirk's high-handed use of disbanded British troops to seize the Nor'Wester headquarters at Fort William, arrest several of its officers and send them back east for trial. Selkirk lost the civil action in 1818, was ordered to pay £2000 in damages and left for England, where he died two years later. Original letters to Donald McKenzie from Sir George Simpson of the Hudson's Bay Company have been lost, and the only place they are published is in Cecil McKenzie's book *King of the Northwest*, a rare copy of which I was able to acquire for the Ontario Archives.

In 1815, Henry McKenzie was elected a member of Montreal's Beaver Club, a men's social group. Each of its 120 members had to have spent at least one winter on a North West Company station, and was

Henry McKenzie (1781–1832) was employed by the North West Company Carried on a campaign in the Montreal newspapers against Lord Selkirk, who had seized the Nor'Wester headquarters at Fort William (now part of Thunder Bay). The company sued and won £2000. Selkirk returned to England and died two years later. Oil portrait on ivory. (Original in private collection)

required to wear a gold medal on a ribbon at all club dinners. Other amusing details of the club's elaborate ceremonial are preserved in minute books on file in the McGill University Library.

That same year, 1815, Henry McKenzie married Ann Bethune, the 17-year-old daughter of Rev John Bethune. This strengthened the McKenzie-Bethune connection. Bethune's eldest son and Ann's brother, Hudson's Bay Chief Factor Angus Bethune, had already married Louisa Mackenzie, the half-Indian daughter of Henry's older brother Roderick McKenzie. Louisa, whom Angus affectionately called Miss Green Blanket, bore him five sons and a daughter.

The second son of Angus and Louisa Bethune was Norman, born in 1822, who became a famous physician and surgeon. Norman's firstborn, Angus, tragically drowned in his late 20s in a ship collision off the coast of Florida. Second son Malcolm Nicholson Bethune became a minister in the Presbyterian faith. Their cousin, Anglican priest Charles Bethune, was an entomologist and the headmaster of Port Hope's Trinity College School for 30 years. The Rev Malcolm Bethune's marriage to Elizabeth Ann Goodwin produced a daughter, Janet, in 1888, and two years later a son, Henry Norman Bethune. Like his namesake grandfather, Norman Henry made his mark through medicine.

My search for the papers making the Mackenzie-Bethune connection began in 1966 and is still going on. A lead from the proprietor of the Downtown Gun Shop in Buffalo, NY proved fruitful, but another tip about a mass of valuable documents allegedly stolen from a house in Mayville, NY continues to tantalize me.

In the 1970s, while attending an architectural conference in Ottawa, I met Hazen Sise, who had been with Dr Norman Bethune in the Spanish Civil War. When I discovered Sise's connection to Bethune, I showed him the Bethune genealogy as it appeared in a small book called *Prelude to Norman*, written by another Bethune descendent, Mary Larrat Smith of Vancouver. Hazen Sise looked at the family chart and pointed out an error where it showed a Donald Bethune having no issue though he actually did have a family, one of his descendents being Robert Bethune, an architect in Buffalo.

I went to Buffalo and checked through the society of architects and found that Robert had a son, Charles, who became a dancer in New York. His only child, Zena, was an actress and led a dance troupe for disabled people in California.

Through Actors Equity, I found Zena and met her in Los Angeles. From Zena I was able to acquire for the Ontario Archives an unpublished history of the Bethune family written by her great-grandmother, Louise (Mrs Robert) Bethune.

I have had several interviews over the past 20 years with Zena Bethune, who had roles in the *Gunsmoke* and *Bonanza* TV series, among many others. Despite two artificial hips, she continued to be active in a special project helping disabled artists cope with their afflictions. Zena is made of the same tough stuff as the Nor'Westers themselves.

To my great embarrassment, I missed acquiring the library of Rev John Bethune. In 1965, I was in touch with the Smart family, who then owned the 1784 Bethune house. I made a search of the house and outbuildings, but obviously missed this rare collection of books.

Rev John Bethune lived in this house until his death in 1815, when it was sold to David Thompson, mapmaker of the North West Company. David Anderson, indefatigable researcher and curator of the Bethune-Thompson house, now owned by the Ontario Heritage Foundation, discovered my chain of errors because of his investigative nature.

Ontario Heritage held a sale when they acquired the property in 1977, but failed to examine the contents of a large, dirty wooden crate. It contained Bethune's library. The box was knocked down to Daniel Alguire as a junk lot for two dollars. When he got these books to his home in Cornwall, Mr Alguire discovered that they were all dated 1815 or earlier, and all signed by Rev John Bethune. Not being a collector himself, Alguire did the correct thing, albeit 10 years later, and took the books to the Rev Fred Rennie of St John's Presbyterian Church, Cornwall. Fred Rennie, who used to be on the Presbyterian Church History board with me, sent them to the Presbyterian Church Archives in Toronto.

The entire contents of this rare library should have been kept together but unfortunately this did not happen, and the collection was dispersed. As usual in the collecting game, we have to chronicle some mistakes along with the successes.

In a world-wide quest for manuscripts dealing with notable families and individuals with strong ties to Ontario, one of my most exciting finds were the papers of Reuben Sherwood (1775–1851). A New Englander whose family came to Canada after the Revolutionary War, Sherwood became such a thorn in the Americans' side during the War of 1812 that a hefty reward was posted for anyone who brought him in dead or alive.

Reuben Sherwood was a combination of Zorro, Robin Hood and the Scarlet Pimpernel, with a dash of Shakespeare's impish Puck thrown in. The Yankees never knew what he'd do next. The Sherwoods were genuine Canadian pioneers. Reuben's father, Thomas Sherwood, had helped recruit men for Jessup's Corps, a Loyalist military force operating near Albany, New York in 1776, the first brigade of boats carrying disbanded Loyalists up the St Lawrence. A surveyor by trade in peacetime, Reuben Sherwood pitched his tent on Lot #1, Concession I, Elizabethtown Township near today's Brockville, where he drew up the plans for the first settlement in Leeds County.

Surveyors in the 19th Century often took the time to record things in their notebooks that had nothing to do with surveying. We can thank these notetakers for valuable information that would otherwise have been lost. The Sherwood papers were my first major Loyalist collection. I have made contact with some of my historian son Ian's neighbours in Elizabethtown Township, home of the Sherwoods. Some of these neighbours are active genealogists, and hope to trace more papers.

From the papers I acquired from Bob Mucklestone, the Brockville surveyor, I discovered that Reuben Sherwood grew up on the heavily forested banks of the mighty St Lawrence River, which is the international boundary in those parts. Young Reuben enjoyed a bucolic world teeming with fish, bird and animal life. He benefited by a close acquaintance with all forms of water transport in both winter and summer, had the opportunity to see the first school built and the first court session held. He made friends with the aboriginal people and became familiar with their customs and languages.

Sherwood was a founding member of the region's first Masonic Lodge, the third oldest in Canada, which was established in Squire Sherwood's big, hospitable home and soon became the rallying point for disbanded Loyalist soldiers. Here eager youngsters listened enthralled to tales of their parents' wartime exploits, thrilled to their escapades, and soaked up the details of survival tactics for future use.

When the lodge moved to a new location in Brockville, valuable records were inadvertently abandoned. They were headed for the town dump when they were rescued by one of my network of pickers. He passed them on to his cousin Bob Phillips in Cambridge, who contacted me. Without this network, even fewer old papers would have survived. The records were deposited in the National Archives in Ottawa where Reuben Sherwood's name is prominent.

Returning to his birthplace in the Albany area of New York to upgrade his surveying skills in 1799, Reuben Sherwood became Deputy Surveyor, applying his newly acquired knowledge throughout Eastern Ontario. He laid out the original site of the now flourishing town of Perth. His brother Adiel Sherwood, who afterward became the area's sheriff, cut down the first tree in the town.

Though he could have settled down to a sedate, prosperous life in the surveyor's trade, Sherwood had his father's spirit of adventure. By 1803, the 28-year-old Sherwood was a lieutenant in the militia. One of the books in his collection is *Exercises for the Horse, Dragoons and Foot Forces*. He honed his military skills during the growing hostilities all along the border that eventually exploded in the savage War of 1812.

Sherwood's baptism by fire took place in September 1812, during an attack on Ogdensburg, NY from the Upper Canada settlement of Prescott, directly across the St Lawrence. Sherwood's contribution was to march 40 militiamen from Brockville to the staging site, where they joined the flank and rifle companies of the First Leeds Battalion in the amphibious assault on the American settlement. The attack proved disastrous for the Canadians, and they were forced to retreat. Reuben's own small detachment suffered one dead and eight wounded.

To improve communications between Canadian settlements and prevent raids by American guerilas on supply and munition transports, Sherwood was appointed to the unusual twin post of Captain-Superintendent of Guides and Assistant Quartermaster-General. The double duty was superbly tailored to his talents and desires. In the spring of 1813, Sherwood chose his own assignment, to infiltrate the huge US naval base at Sackett's Harbour on Lake Ontario. His journals describe the following adventure:

Taking with him one white friend and an Algonquin Indian known as Captain John, Reuben Sherwood canoed to within a mile of the base. Instructing his cohorts to hide for a few days, he walked into the town, declared he was a shipwright from Vermont and was immediately hired. Four days later, he'd seen all he wished to see and made drawings of all important installations. He begged permission to return to Vermont for his wife, and was reluctantly paid off.

As he left the pay office, he had the bad luck to be recognized by a man who had once been his neighbour but who, being a good egg, gave Sherwood an hour's grace before denouncing him to the American authorities. Sherwood used this time to good advantage, buying a bottle of whisky and some food before heading back to his hidden allies. Fearing pursuit by mounted men, he hid in a pile of saw-logs. Only minutes later, he heard the hue and cry. One of his pursuers even stood atop his woodpile to scan the countryside for the fugitive. Finally they gave up the chase, and Sherwood was able to join his comrades.

"We're not leaving yet," Sherwood told them. "We've got work to do." On their way to Sackett's Harbour he had noticed a solidly built blockhouse, obviously manned by troops charged with defending the approaches to the port. It was in a clearing, but with dense bush all around. From a chest he'd brought, Sherwood took a magnificent uniform fit for a Field Marshal, and an equally splendid sword. Leaving the whisky with Captain John, he ordered them to wait for a pistol shot, at the sound of which they should run through the forest uttering bloodthirsty Indian screams.

Reuben then entered the clearing, a flag of truce in one hand, the sword in the other, demanding to be taken to the commander. "It's useless to resist," he told the American major. "You must surrender the blockhouse and its garrison, or be responsible for their horrible deaths at the hands of my Indian allies. I have British regulars with me too, but they've never before been able to stop our allies from scalping everyone in sight."

When the white-faced, obviously shaken major still fumed and fussed, Sherwood strode to the door and fired his pistol. Instantly, the nearby woods resounded to the war-whoops of what sounded like hundreds of savages. Sherwood left the commandant's office and urged the terrified troops to lay down their arms. When they did so, the major had no choice but to capitulate. Sherwood released all the troops, took the apoplectic major prisoner, and torched the blockhouse. When he delivered his captive to Kingston and made his report, he was warned by the stiff British commandant not to act so rashly in future!

On another occasion, Reuben Sherwood disguised himself as an apple-woman and made his way into an army camp, where he sold his wares to the soldiers, making mental notes of the layout as he went. Once again he was recognized, this time by a distinctive ring on his finger, but he was so fleet of foot that he easily out-distanced them all and got away.

Reuben Sherwood is said to have been the only man to offer serious resistance when Forsyth's Raiders crossed the ice and attacked Brockville in 1813, carrying off munitions, releasing Yankee prisoners and taking 25 to 30 Brockville residents captive.

Not long after, Sherwood led his own assault on Ogdensburg, looting stores, burning the barracks and avenging the defeat of the year before. He was also in the thick of the action when General James Wilkinson's advance on Montreal was halted at Crysler's Farm and his army put to flight by a much smaller force of British regulars and Canadians.

Sherwood looked upon the War of 1812 as a way to harass rebels who had broken away from Britain, among them, regrettably, two of his father's brothers. His sheer zest for adventure was never more apparent than in a skirmish when American General Wilkinson had waylaid Canadian merchants heading west and appropriated all their goods. After the battle, it was agreed these articles would be returned to their owners, but Wilkinson broke his promise and was planning to auction them off for his own army's benefit. Learning of this on the night of February 6, 1814, the ever resourceful Sherwood brought a party of two officers, 20 marines and 10 militiamen across the ice in sleighs near Cornwall. They drove 10 miles into the interior of enemy country and took possession of the merchandise without the slightest opposition from the inhabitants. For this feat, Sherwood was thanked in general orders.

Sherwood lived a charmed life. For all his derring-do and seemingly reckless disregard for his own safety, he was never captured or even wounded, though there was a price on his head the last two years of the war. With the enemy barely a mile away across the St Lawrence along a 100-mile front, eternal vigilance was the order of the day. Luck, however, played its part. Apparently acting on a tip, American commandos made a lightning raid on the house of Adiel Sherwood, just west of Brockville, seeking Reuben. Adiel's wife was home alone, so the soldiers, in frustrated fury at having once more missed their elusive quarry, shredded the feather beds, smashed boxes and drawers and fired shot after futile shot into the walls as they departed.

After the war, warrior Sherwood returned to his trade as a surveyor, acquired fine farmlands and operated lumber mills along the Rideau Canal. British engineers were just then constructing this waterway, ironically to provide an inland transport route the Americans couldn't disrupt. Built between 1826 and 1832, the Rideau Canal was a bit late to save the St Lawrence River settlements from Uncle Sam's depredations. It was better late than never, though, for Reuben, who was among the first to send his timber rafts down the canal to Kingston.

Reuben Sherwood, who acted as if large-scale, international wars were invented solely for his personal amusement, died in Weston, a suburb of Toronto, in April 1851.

CHAPTER SEVENTEEN
THE SEMI-WILD WEST

My interest in the fur trade and the buffalo-hunting Métis of the western prairies became more focused when I discovered, to my surprise, that I had Métis relations of my own. My great-grandfather, Archie Roy McMillan's first cousin, James McMillan, became a wintering partner in the North West Company. Like most of his Highland contemporaries in the North West Company, he acquired several country wives at various times between 1806 and 1821. This accounted for descendents from three different mothers — that we know about.

William McMillan, who died in Winnipeg in 1903, was the best known. He had been in charge of the buffalo hunt at Fort Augusta (Edmonton), and later went to Red River (now Winnipeg), where he became a free trader.

Family anecdotes and tales came to light as I traced my Métis connections, one of the best ways to learn about history. It matters not whether your earliest ancestor in Canada is a first generation immigrant from Pakistan, or came here in 1792, we are all immigrants. Whether we ourselves or a distant ancestor chose Canada as a place to live, we should strive to acquire a basic knowledge of its history. This anonymous observation applies to us all:

> We stand to gain a new understanding about ourselves as we learn more about our ancestors and the lives that they lived. In today's mobile, often unstable society, it is important for people to have knowledge of their larger family connections, both here and abroad.

I am still searching for the rest of the story of Allan, the Métis son of James McMillan. The shabby and callous treatment that the Métis had received in 1839 was unchanged in 1870, as observed in the dramatic tale of Robert Cunningham, who by all accounts was a friend and admirer of the Métis. George Campbell's letters illustrate his bias towards the people he refers to as 'breeds.' There is a touch of irony in the fact that the Métis he despises have much more of a claim to be called Canadian than he does. Their antecedents trace back to the native people, intermarried with French-Canadian and Scots fur traders. By contrast, Campbell had arrived only a few years earlier from the island of Islay, off the west coast of Scotland to settle near the south shore of Lake Simcoe, Ontario.

This was a rare occasion when I was able to locate and acquire documents that describe both sides of a conflict, in this instance eyewitness accounts. We can only speculate that Cunningham's high regard for the Métis may have come from a liberal education in Edinburgh. As for Campbell, he would have imbibed a large dose of Orange Lodge bigotry from his friends and neighbours in Eldon Township. When he arrived in Winnipeg, he soon fell under the spell of another bigot, Frank Cornish, a former mayor of London, Ontario.

For 15 years after its 1870 entry into Confederation, the Province of Manitoba was in continuous turmoil. Most of it was caused by Irish Protestants from Ontario, who hated the French-speaking, Roman Catholic Métis and especially their spokesman, firebrand visionary Louis Riel. This mindless conflict did not end with the tragic execution of Riel in 1885. It broadened to become an English Canadian *vs* Québécois source of friction that has persisted, with intermittent ebbs and flows of rancour and bitterness, ever since.

Even during the years of turmoil, there were many English-speaking easterners who thought highly of the Métis. Once the acknowledged lords of the prairies, these tough, fun-loving human hybrids were still living lives white men envied but could not emulate. Among their admirers, journalist Robert Cunningham saw the Métis display their riding, shooting and fighting superiority when he accompanied the Wolseley Expedition to quell the first Red River Rebellion in the summer of 1870. Armed with an MA in history from the University of Edinburgh, Robert Cunningham had been in Toronto only a short time when he was hired by George Brown, a fellow Scot and publisher of the Toronto *Globe*, and sent to cover the uprising at the Red River.

A short time later, Cunningham left *The Globe* and started his own newspaper, *The Manitoban*, in Winnipeg. So enthusiastically did he support the natives and Métis in their quest for equality with the citizens of other provinces, that he was considered by one faction of prairie whites as a traitor on a par with Riel himself. His popularity with this group plummeted even further when he allowed his name to stand as a candidate for the House of Commons in the Manitoba riding of

Marquette. His manifesto, printed in English and French, had approximately the same effect as burning an effigy of King Billy or trampling the Union Jack underfoot. Here's an example of Cunningham's views:

> One of the most important measures for the people of Marquette and this province is that of the public lands. From the moment this act received the sanction of the Governor General, these 1,400,000 acres became the property of the Métis. If I am elected I will press the government to guarantee the rights of the Métis. Whether I'm elected or not I will always resist the least attempt that endangers these rights.
>
> As for the wooded lands, the best of which have been devastated by people who do not have a single right to these properties, I will do all I can to protect you against such vandalism. The question of the Indians is another issue. We have arrived at some understanding thanks to the treaty, but we have yet to settle with the large war tribes of the west. Any delay would be dangerous and any deception a folly. As for Education, it is in large part a question for the local legislatures. But as a member or simple citizen I shall do all I can to conserve intact Section I, Clause 93 of the BNA act, stating that no provincial law will prejudice the rights or privileges of any class of people who had legitimately, at the time of the union, separate schools and exclusive rights to administer religious doctrine.

There were a few other clauses among Cunningham's election pledges, such as insisting Manitoba's postal system be the equal of any other province and that the promised transcontinental railway must pass through Manitoba. All together, they were quite enough to incite a violent response. From a news viewpoint, the riot of Thursday, September 19, 1872, voting day in Winnipeg, was the scoop of the century because the main action took place in *The Manitoban*'s print shop, which was demolished, along with the printing presses.

A similar foray resulted in the razing of the Métis' own news-gathering office, and a serious attempt was made to set it ablaze. Shots were fired at French-Canadian candidates for office in nearby St Boniface. Though virtually at point-blank range, the bullets missed their marks, possibly because the rioters had psyched themselves up for the raid by quaffing copious quantities of prairie firewater.

Despite the savage, wanton sacking of *The Manitoban*'s office, the Saturday edition hit Portage and Main as an *Extra*, through the kind loan of a small hand-press belonging to Bishop Taché of Rupert's Land, and "a little type scraped together from the ruins," according to

Cunningham's lead editorial. The *Extra* edition, though no great shakes as prose, was a litany of outrage and defiance, in the finest tradition of journalism:

> The *Manitoban* office today is a wreck. The proprietors have laboured hard against difficulties which few can appreciate, to make the office one of the best appointed in Canada. They had succeeded, and everything was complete, but today the whole is a wreck, and the efforts of the proprietors have proved to be in vain. The presses are destroyed, the type is pie, the ink barrels were knocked in the head and overturned and even on the very lamps the dastards showed their malice and smashed them, and now we must crave the indulgence of our subscribers and customers and patrons for a week or two, until we can renew our plant … Anything more mean, more dastardly, more cowardly, was never perpetrated. The crowd that gathered round The *Manitoban* Office and sacked it on Thursday night, proved themselves by their conduct in every respect to be a scum fatal to the security, nay to the very existence of any community, and these men must be taught a lesson, and some of them may have learned it already, that there are institutions such as Penitentiaries, and that felons may run a fair chance of getting the benefits of these institutions."

The Hon Donald A Smith, rose from Hudson's Bay Company clerk through fur trader to financier, and was later honoured as the 1st Baron Strathcona. He is the white-bearded, silk-hatted dignitary driving home the CPR's last spike in the famous photograph of that 1885 event. The same Donald A Smith was running for federal office in nearby Selkirk riding. By 2:00 pm, according to *The Manitoban Extra*, "some 85 votes had been polled by the French Half-Breeds for Mr Smith, and only one vote for the other candidate, Mr Wilson."

It was at this hour that the crowd of rioters, armed with wagon wheel spokes and guns, marched on the police station to seize the poll books. Chief of Police Plainval stationed his men to prevent any rush and "though insulted, jostled and threatened, they behaved with the utmost forbearance and good nature," letting the rioters in one at a time even though none of them was on this particular voting list. The article continues:

> Thinking this was a good opportunity for clap-trap, Mr Frank Cornish mounted a waggon and made a most inflammatory harangue to the mob. The Lieutenant-Governor and the Hon Mr Smith were treated to

the most opprobrious epithets: the Sheriff was a perjured, base man, the Chief of Police a toad-eating Communist, the Military Commander knew nothing and would not be obeyed by his men, etc … but the polls were finally closed and the books having been safely got away, the military left.

Under a heading, "The Elections," editor-publisher Cunningham felt justified in congratulating three counties on the results:

> With Sir George Cartier for Provencher, Mr Donald Smith (Lord Strathcona) for Selkirk and Mr Robert Cunningham in Marquette, we conceive that Manitoba, in the matter of political experience and standing, business capacity and commercial position, as well as literary ability, has a position today in her representatives which any of the Provinces of the Dominion might well envy.
>
> As for Dr Schultz, the member elected for Lisgar, he is of no account whatever.

In the bottom right hand corner of the page were the final victory tallies: Mr Cunningham, in by the magnificent majority of 278.

In 1970, I was winter camping in Haliburton, Ontario while checking out some leads in the area. Once again a chance encounter gave me an opportunity to ask questions and tell stories. On our last day, camped out in 30° below weather, we ran short of grub. The next morning on the way home, we stopped for breakfast at the only café in Norland. I soon had the chatty owner telling all about his family background. He mentioned that a great uncle had been an active member of the Orange Lodge, and had gone west in 1871 to the new city of Winnipeg, formerly Red River. This led me to tell about how Robert Cunningham's newspaper office was wrecked in 1872.

Before I had a chance to add "… by a bunch of misguided Orangemen," the owner exclaimed, "I'll be damned! My old uncle, George Campbell, helped wreck that Papist-loving fellow's office, and I have a letter right here to prove it!"

Sure enough, he soon had the letters out for me to read. At this point I was grateful that I had not made my comment about "misguided Orangemen." Two hours later, I was headed south with the letters. It was a stroke of luck that we had run out of grub and stopped to get breakfast. In a letter dated 3 November 1872, George Campbell, one of the mob who trashed the office, tells the story from the other side, one of the few times I have acquired documents that describe a dramatic historic incident from both sides.

> I will now give you a few words about the row we had at the Election day [wrote Campbell]. That day I thought I would not work, I wanted to see some of the fun. I must tell you there was two polling places one in the town and one across the Red River. About 15 of us went and the head man told us he expected we would be imposed on by the half breeds and if we will, boys, look here I took a lot of wagon spokes with me to defend ourselfs and whenever the row starts you all make for the wagon. All went on quietly until about 2 in the afternoon when a quarrel arose between a half breed and a Canadian until it came to blows … so they made a rush on us. I think there must have been more than one hundred with sticks and everything they could get a hold of. The fight comenced hot and heavy. We drove them back but they got behind some old houses and we had no chance at all so we made a plan that we would run and they would think they scared us but we turned on them and fought like Divels … then a revolver was fired and the firing comenced, and we turned back, went in and took the poll book and burned it then we started to cross the river when we found the ferry rope cut so then we came over to the town to the polling so the row comenced with the police.
>
> The Captain got his head split, his revolver taken from him, and were all badley whipped. The military was called out by sheriff Armstrong and marched down within a hundred yards to shoot us down like dogs because we was fighting for our rights but the police was over powered and chased in to their station before the military arived so Lawyer Cornish, when he seen the military coming he took his stand on a wagon and spoke for an hour defending Canadians so when Major Irven heard Cornish explaining all about it he marched his soldiers in to Camp. So it was all over until dark when some boys went and smashed The *Manitoban* printing office and they were going for the land agents office but the military was called out and they kept guard all night. So the next [day] the news came that there were over 300 French half breeds armed across the river and that they was going to make a raid on the town that evening and kill every Canadian so all the arms the Canadians could procure they stowed in the Davis Hotel and when the evening came every man was armed with revolvers and rifles strapped around their shoulders but no half breeds made their appearance. This is not the half breeds alone we have to deal with but Hudson Bay and all those men

that is in power they are on the half breeds side but we have one smart man to stand up, Mr Cornish. I hope the day will soon come when we will have more of them. No more at present, but my love to you all.

I found Robert Cunningham's version of the story of mob violence and electoral vindication by tracking down his granddaughter, Mrs Helen Patterson, at Beamsville, Ontario in 1970. From her, I received the *Extra* quoted above, pictures, telegrams and letters. The *Extra* run off on Bishop Taché's little press, and the broadside published in French proved to be the only copies known to exist. This tip came to me from Bill Rannie, publisher of the *Beamsville Weekly* newspaper. He knew that Helen Patterson, a retired nurse, had a cache of priceless papers inherited from her journalist grandfather.

Bill Rannie became a bit of a legend in newspaper circles when he gradually took over much of the printing business for the French islands of St Pierre and Miquelon, off the south coast of Newfoundland's Burin Peninsula. This came about in the 1950s when Bill and his wife Kay, on impulse, flew to this outpost of the late French empire for a short holiday. Bill discovered by chance that all printing was shipped at great expense to the colony all the way from France. Also, there were no books about the islands for tourists to buy. Rannie soon began to bid on the islands' printing needs, and produced three books about their history.

Like most of the newspaper editors in Ontario, Bill Rannie regularly fed me tips. I seldom visited a town without a call to the local editor, and whenever I acquired a collection, I made sure the local editor got the story. This usually worked to our mutual benefit. One couldn't buy the publicity that accrued from this arrangement. A senior bureaucrat with the Archives thought I talked too much and received far too much publicity. He could have been right, but it sure beat being ignored.

Dr Donald Crawford was made known to one of my favourite tipsters, the irreverent Rev Orlo Miller of London, Ontario. Orlo had many careers, as a writer of books, including the well known *The Donnellys Must Die*, a playwright, an Anglican priest, and one of Canada's earliest professional genealogists. Sixty years ago, Orlo Miller was being paid 50 cents an hour to read tombstone inscriptions for American genealogists. He pocketed the train fare they gave him to get to various cemeteries and walked instead, keeping in practice for long distance walking competitions. He was an amazing man and a skilled storyteller, and he would feed me the odd tip in between recounting outrageous stories. It is unfortunate that his hometown university, Western, never awarded him a well deserved honorary doctorate.

Dr Crawford's papers added great detail to the Loyalist and Métis collections. Before World War II, he was a medical missionary in China, where he worked with Dr Norman Bethune. Crawford described Bethune as brilliant, but hell to work with. After I had several interesting discussions with him, he gave me his collection of family papers, including letters and diaries dating back as far as his Loyalist family's departure from Connecticut for New Brunswick.

Donald Crawford had long been intrigued by his uncle, Christopher Colin Crawford (1862–1891), known by his middle name, Colin. During his short life in western Canada, Colin developed a high regard for the skilled Métis buffalo hunters, which he expressed in his poetry. Colin, himself a superb horseman, probably joined them on one or more of their annual hunts.

Crawford's passionate admiration for the Métis was surprising, since his ancestors were Protestant Ulster Irish from County Tyrone. His great-grandparents emigrated to Stamford, Connecticut in 1733, but were living in New York Province when the revolutionary war broke out. After the war, most of the Crawfords trekked north, first to New Brunswick, and in the 1830s to prime farmland in Oxford County, Upper Canada, granted to them for war service.

During most of the 1880s, Crawford roamed the USA and Western Canada. He may have had journalistic training, but his literary works ran to poems and short prose essays. His odes included *The Battle of Queenston Heights, India's Golden Gate* and *Lines Written on the Death of late Mrs H Guppy*. He also wrote a pæan to the lords of the plains entitled simply *The Métis*:

West from Hudson's bleak and barren shore
To where the waters of the Rockies roar.
In this land lived many a loyal-hearted
British subject from his kindred parted.
[Suffering] raids on stock and cattle
For life was one incessant battle
To hold the warlike braves in check
Or make them flee before their beck.
Still no answer to their prayer,
Crushed are their souls with dark despair.
In this hour a voice doth rise

"Louis Riel, come help!" it cries.
"You're learned and for skills you're famed.
Our rights through you will be obtained."

On May 8, 1891, at the age of 29, Christopher Colin Crawford met his death in Montana Territory when his horse reared and fell over backward upon him

After many interesting visits with Napoleon Cantin, grandson of Narcisse Cantin, at his home in Royal Oak, Michigan, I acquired the Cantin papers. Napoleon, a businessman, appreciated my technique of constantly seeking qualified tips to more collections. The best of his tips concerned a neighbour who was related to Melvin Ormond Hammond, an enterprising magazine and literary editor at the Toronto *Globe*. More visits to this relative and others back in Toronto resulted in the acquisition of Hammond's collection of papers and photographs. The trail continued back in Toronto when the Hammond descendents sent me to meet the widow of Newton M^{C}Tavish, the legendary editor of the old *Canadian Magazine*. Here were more papers and the 1909 story of "The Last Great Round-up" that brought these two editors together in their wild adventure.

Several years later, I met George Coder of Cleveland, Ohio, who was doing a doctoral thesis on this last great buffalo round-up. The Ontario Archives was on his list of institutions to visit. He thought he had really hit the mother lode when he found Hammond's superb photographs and M^{C}Tavish's account of the round-up. One of the great satisfactions of these paper chases is matching up related papers, getting both sets, then making contact with someone like Coder who can make use of them. George was writing a book about the round-up that founded Canada's first captive buffalo herd. These two cases are examples of how one tip leads to another, turning common threads into the fabric of history.

> For weeks, ever since before the snows of a backward spring had melted from the lower hills and valleys along the Little Bitter Root, leaving the summits of the Mission Mountains white-capped and glistening in the sun, preparations had been making for The Last Great Round-Up.

So began the first of two articles in the October and November 1909 issues of the *Canadian Magazine*, under the byline of the Toronto publication's editor, Newton M^{C}Tavish.

This distinguished Canadian, a noted patron of the arts, director of the National Gallery, intimate of prime ministers and poets, had been fascinated to learn of the stirring event happening just over the US border from Calgary in mid-May, near places with names like Rattlesnake Cliffs, Pend d'Oreille River and Magpie Springs. When the notion of covering it himself struck him, he called close friend Melvin Ormond Hammond, magazine and literary editor of the Toronto *Globe*. "A buffalo round-up!" echoed Mel Hammond. "Count me in. When do we leave?"

It was no ordinary round-up for counting, culling or branding, but for shipping an entire herd by rail to Wainright, Alberta. Canada's herds of the huge, shaggy beasts, once numbered in the millions, were now almost as scarce as those of the USA. When Michael Pablo, a wealthy Flathead Indian-Mexican rancher in Montana, announced that he was willing to sell his private herd of over 600 buffalo, Howard Douglas, Canada's Commissioner of Parks, made the winning bid of $200 a head FOB. Sealing the deal was a triumph for Douglas, as it was for Pablo, since the herd represented the offspring of a small group he had bought for $2,000 from an American Indian named Walking Coyote 30 years before.

Not until Newton McTavish and Melvin Ormond Hammond, the two Toronto journalists, were actually in Montana studying the elaborate preparations for the round-up did it become plain that their light-hearted odyssey might be fraught with peril. They now discovered that the buffaloes to be loaded for transportation were the Pablo Outlaws, so called because they were the mean, unpredictable big bulls and mother cows, along with their recent male and female progeny now totalling some 350, which had escaped from among the tamer 400 shipped earlier.

The easterners' biggest worry was their own transportation at the site. Their only riding experience had been with the gentle beasts of Evans's Livery Stable in Toronto, where they'd started taking lessons on a snowy Good Friday, April 9, as soon as the trip west was confirmed. They doubted the mounts provided by Michael Pablo would be as docile. Starting on May 12, by rail to Calgary and then to Montana, and then in camp at the Flathead Reservation, Hammond was sending off local colour stories to his paper, along with reviews of the books he'd brought with him. McTavish was making plans for a fall series about the round-up. A third welcome member of the party was artist Charles Russell, Montana-born, Canada-loving cowboy painter, who would be doing his own paintings, and a fourth witness to the epochal event was Duncan Macdonald, son of the Angus Macdonald who came to Canada from Glencoe, Scotland, and was sent to the Hudson's Bay Company post in what is now Montana. Duncan held forth around the campfire with endless tales of Indians he had met.

The personal transportation problem was settled the moment they hit Ronan, Montana. Here everyone had to switch from iron horse to the four-footed variety and follow the well marked but rugged trail 25 miles to the round-up site. Hammond and McTavish took it in easy stages on the cayuses provided and were pleasantly surprised next morning not to be too sore wrote McTavish in his *Canadian Magazine* story.

> After the general cinching of saddles and donning of chaps and spurs, suddenly there is a sound of galloping and from the boss's camp comes a group of horsewomen who sit astride their saddles like their brothers and husbands. Their skirts are mostly of buff duck, divided, and they wear bright-coloured sweaters, gauntlets with bead trimmings and rakish-looking sombreros. The women do not follow the riders to the chase, but form a picturesque group on the side of the hill, or *butte* as they call it, and seated on the grass in the shade of their ponies, they await the results of the hunt.

The game plan for capturing and shipping the unruly giants of the plains was to steer them toward the mile-wide hilltop mouth of the fenced funnel Pablo's men had created, then drive them furiously down to the turbulent Pend d'Oreille (Ear Ring) River. Forced to swim across the swollen spring stream because there was no bridge for miles, and prevented by log booms from swerving either up river or down, they had no choice but to reach the other side and enter the mammoth corral built there. There was only one snag in this ingenious, carefully-crafted game plan however. The Pablo Outlaws had a counterplan of their own.

Hammond Diary, May 21: Start of hunt. Raining. MacT and I stationed ourselves on the far shore where we could photograph them coming. We had in reserve a tree each up which we could flee if the buffalo missed the corral and headed along the beach. 30 or more did escape going into the corral. Bad news.

McTavish's opening-day musings were quite different:

What a natural paradise for the buffaloes! It seems almost like vandalism to remove them from a spot to which they are so well fitted.... They

A bison being loaded onto a cattle car in Montana in 1909 for relocation to Wainright, Alberta, takes exception to the ride by bursting out the other side of the car. (K Ross Tooke Archives, University of Montana — Missoula, photo no 82 - 251)

start a slow gallop down toward Bitter Root Canyon and with that the riders rush after them with the speed of the wind. Even at this distance we hear the snorts of alarm and the wild yells of the cowboys and the thrill with expectation ... [but] the buffaloes have done what they might be least expected to do, swerving quickly into another draw on the right ... and all the King's horses and all the King's men would not stop them by daring to head them off ... it's a chase beside which fox hunting, wild boar killing or bull fighting would be as battledore or shuttlecock.

The next day was a lazy one for them, as the riders were off trying to recapture the runaways.

Hammond's Diary, May 22: Standing pat. Loafing. DF Macdonald regaled us with Indian stories. We had quite a discussion over the relative standards of morality of white and red men. He is well read and bright, though somewhat stolid as befits men with red men's blood.

Hammond's Diary, May 23: MacT and I had arranged to follow the riders in search of buffalo. So, tying our raincoats to the saddles and looking like war correspondents, we started up to the higher level. We were met with stray buffs being herded down, along with wild horses and their colts and all the excitement of a battlefield.

For this day, McTavish wrote:

The long fence-arms open wide to receive them and we fall into the impelling procession and for the first time experience the glorious impulse of the chase. For you, this is a lane that has no turning. You have passed from fear and trepidation into ecstasy and exhilaration. Ah, this is rare sport; it is sport for kings!

Hammond's Diary, May 24: We have learned this morning that the whole herd had escaped, even past DF Macdonald, but the riders got them back, all except five strays.

McTavish wrote:

Word goes out that Pablo is short of men, and it is evident that no progress can be made unless at least four riders can be stationed in the field, ready to drive them into the corral after they have crossed the river. Little Jimmy, a visitor, volunteers and Big Duncan, the Scotch half-breed who is in his 70s. Even plucky Charlie Russell, who came to paint and not to chase, is now chafing in his long boots and inquiring about a suitable cayuse. From this distance it looks as if he's certain he must take the bull by the horns. Then the bulls near the corral assume an angry attitude and horses and riders are being charged, but only to the spot where the horses stood. Suddenly you hear a shot and you see Charlie Russell's pony swinging about and young Pablo, smoking pistol in hand, leaning over a big bull that stands quivering, then falls. The camp will have a supply of fresh buffalo meat tonight.

Rounding up the buffalo, driving them across the river and trying to stop them escaping along the shore was a tough job. Equally hard was forcing them through the chutes into the special two-inch-thick plank crates to transport them to Ravalli, the railway shipment point 35 miles away. The first crates were smashed to flinders. Getting the buffalo into the railway's cattle cars was no cakewalk either.

Hammond's Diary, May 27: McT leaving for home. I rode with him to Ronan. Got two letters from wife. McT never seems to worry about letters from home. I couldn't sleep in the hotel, unused to the comforts of a bed.

June 2: Asked MP when he could begin the train ride for the buffs and he said not till they're all in, so I decided not to wait. Finished reading *The Bridge Builders*. Wrote a review of it.

June 6: Left Calgary for Edmonton where pics being developed. It was quite an experience to see the snaps of the loading and to be so near the caged animals.

June 11: Jumped aboard Supt Brown's private car and we were whisked off into the night with 343 buffaloes in the cars ahead of us.

June 13: At Wainwright ... saw unloading proceeding smoothly, then headed home.

After this very difficult, dangerous job reached its successful conclusion and the reports from two ace journalists who had gone to extraordinary lengths to be there were published.

CHAPTER EIGHTEEN
NIGEL DRAYTON: A REAL ECCENTRIC

I began hearing about Nigel Drayton in 1967 when I was working in the Rice Lake area near Cobourg, Ontario. William Van Buren, a bookseller and antique dealer in Bewdley on Rice Lake, had been trying for years to buy books and papers from him, but Nigel would never sell. Van Buren was a great source of documents, and I bought many collections from him for the Archives. He told me one time, "Hughie, you will never buy Nigel Drayton's papers, just wait till I get them." Had Nigel not outlived Van Buren, the latter's prophecy would likely have proved right.

Nigel and his wife Dorothy kept eluding me. They never seemed to be home when I phoned, or were just leaving for somewhere. I had several long conversations with Dorothy about our common interest in Scottish history. She told me she came from Scotland as a young woman to visit her brother and met Nigel. Once she figured out my line of work, she sometimes gave me tips. Sadly, we never met in person. On my last chat with her, she suggested I go to see Phyliss Arnoldi, whose father had been a friend of Nigel's. His grandfather was Col Arthur Williams, the hero of the battle of Batoche during the Riel Rebellion of 1885. He had been in charge of the Midland Battalion from Port Hope.

Phyliss Arnoldi was a striking woman in her 70s who lived by herself in Toronto. Her late husband had been a member of the Arnoldi silversmith family of Montreal. They were one of the better known makers of trade silver for the fur trade. Phyliss was one of the first half dozen officers to be commissioned in the Canadian Women's Army Corp during WW II. We soon became friends and, aside from the leads to some material relating to Col Arthur Williams, she sent me down another trail in search of Arnoldi descendents. That chase has yet to be resolved.

The book and antique seller Van Buren had found some of Col Williams's papers in an abandoned building at Port Hope. Much to Mrs Arnoldi's annoyance, Van Buren broke the collection up, but she bought much of it from him and eventually sold it to me. Thanks to her keenness in tracing more of the Williams papers, Dorothy Drayton put me in touch with Connie Fraser of Kingston. Connie's grandfather had been a partner of Col Williams in various Port Hope business deals, which is why the trunk full of Williams militia papers was shipped to his Port Hope office, then moved to Kingston when Connie's mother died.

Col Williams died of a rare fever aboard the steamer Northcotte on the Saskatchewan River *en route* east. Many of the papers in the trunk were related to his role in winning the Battle of Batoche. I owed Dorothy Drayton a debt of gratitude for assistance in finding these papers. Unfortunately, she died shortly before I was able to meet her in person.

I met Nigel Drayton through my longtime canoeing friend, Prof Kirk Wipper, founder of the Kanawa Canoe Museum at Dorset, Ontario (later moved to Peterborough and renamed the Canadian Canoe Museum). I was still searching for canoes that needed a home to add to Wipper's collection of over 600 watercraft. It was by far the largest canoe collection in the world. Kirk was a completely obsessed collector, although he didn't see himself in that light. He tried to enlist the support of almost everyone we met, even including my daughter Jocelyne. She and her friend Darlene Simpson had spent a summer working as kitchen wenches at Camp Kandalore, part of the Kanawa Canoe Museum complex, and Kirk informed the girls, as I had, that they must always watch out for more canoes.

Wipper discovered that Drayton had known many of the famous canoe builders on Rice Lake. He wanted a series of taped interviews and I wanted Drayton's papers. We got some of each but I wish I had met Drayton many more times. He was charismatic, and his wife Dorothy must have been the same. I will try to put his strange and bizarre tale into some order here.

As a rule, when I know something of a family's background, I have a pretty good idea what sort of family history they will be leaving for posterity. There will always be minor surprises, of course, an heiress daughter running off with the gardener, an adopted son involved in a messy financial scandal, that sort of thing. In terms of eye-bugging, jaw-dropping amazement over some twist of human eccentricity, I can recall only a handful of examples.

Heading the latter list would be Nigel Drayton, of Gore's Landing, a 175-year-old village on the south shore of Rice Lake. Drayton was regarded as a character, a term not conferred lightly in that part of Ontario. But the revelations about Nigel and his family went far beyond mere oddities of behaviour or speech.

Nigel Drayton, well into his 80s when I finally met him in 1974, came of the same British stock as the Traills, Parrs, Stricklands, Rubidges and other English gentry scattered throughout the Kawarthas. I heard that the first Draytons who came to Canada in the 1850s settled near Lake Erie and returned to England after the tragic drowning of their youngest child.

In 1871, another son, Reginald Charles Lumley Drayton, 21, returned from England to the Peterborough area and boarded with a Rice Lake farmer, Clinton Atwood, ancestor of Canadian author Margaret Atwood. Well educated, fluent in several languages, a fine singer, organist and painter, remittance man* Reginald Drayton enjoyed a carefree bachelor's life of sailing, hunting, trapping and nature study.

Around 1873, Drayton was selling Rice Lake furs in Germany, and he later held an art exhibit in Rochester, NY. He kept notes on everything from butterflies to rocks, and wrote fine poetry. His literary efforts included *Skunk Trapping in the Wilds of Canada*. In 1889, he married Agnes Rubidge, daughter of Peterborough farmer John Rubidge. They had one son, Nigel. Packed off to a good school, Nigel was soon bored and stayed for only one year. After that, Reginald took over his son's education. This resulted in Nigel growing to manhood almost a clone of his dad, but with special interests such as archæology and canoeing. He was an honoured shaman with Canadian Indian tribes.

Landscapes by both Reginald and Nigel Drayton are now among the holdings of the Ontario Archives. Nigel also unearthed a carved stone head near his home, Coldstream, and presented it to the Royal Ontario Museum. It is estimated to be about 3000 years old.

Reginald Drayton died in 1922, and his wife two years later. Nigel married Dorothy True, a recent Scottish immigrant, who was the daughter of an admiral in the British Royal Navy. Nigel and Dorothy had one son, Adrian.

The Draytons of Gore's Landing had never been affluent, but Nigel did a lot of travelling following World War I. In the late 1920s, he and Dorothy came into a fair amount of money from unknown sources. Suddenly Nigel was everywhere in his yellow and black Stutz Bearcat, while Dorothy sported a roadster of her own. They kept permanent hotel suites in Toronto and nearby Cobourg.

---

* 'Remittance men' were ne'er-do-wells from prosperous and respectable English families, shipped out to the colonies to avoid shame or scandal at home. They were given an incentive to stay in the colonies by regular remittances of money that were conditional on their staying out of England.

By 1939, they were broke. Nigel trapped, bootlegged a bit, gardened a lot, and shot or snared most of their food. He also guided hunting, fishing and archæological parties, rented out cabins he'd built and generally did anything that brought in a buck. Dorothy got a job in a Toronto war plant, then spent weekends concocting moonshine or hovering over a wood stove roasting ducks to feed cabin guests. The son, Adrian, attended local schools. After the war, Dorothy's factory job came to an end and the family continued to live off the land. I didn't seek them out until 1967, but gave up after many tries when I could never find Nigel at home.

In 1974, Kirk Wipper invited me, as one of the directors of the Kanawa Canoe Museum, to accompany him to meet a man who had known all the great Peterborough and Rice Lake canoe-builders of the past. The man we went to see turned out to be the elusive Nigel Drayton.

He certainly lived up to his advance billing. He was short and stocky, with a mare's nest of white hair, and dressed in tweeds and rubber boots. There were huge burn holes in his jacket and shirt, evidently from the oversized meerschaum pipe that was continually throwing off sparks. He reeked of dogs, fish and gasoline, but tobacco came off as the undisputed winner.

Nigel Drayton was vastly entertaining, encyclopædic about canoes and the men who built them, and had an unending supply of anecdotes, polished through long telling. He didn't mind me taping his reminiscences by the hour, though he was never ready to sell me his family papers, which were my primary interest.

It wasn't until Nigel died in 1976 that I acquired them from his son Adrian, an alcoholic then in his late 40s. Adrian made his living in the Arctic as a 'catskinner,' known in the south as a bulldozer driver.

Adrian usually came to Gore's Landing for a month or so each year to visit his parents. The visit would take place during the off season, and he usually brought his companion Irma with him. He claimed she was a slum landlord in Edmonton, and Irma never denied the claim. They made an odd couple in Gore's Landing, as they bore scars from many a night's hard drinking from Aklavik in the Northwest Territories to Edmonton to Gore's Landing.

After Nigel's death, Adrian and Irma combined fishing and drinking with selling the contents of the house. It was jam-packed with collectibles. Van Buren, the bookseller and antique dealer in Bewdley, thought he was in Paradise when he finally got Adrian into a selling mood, because Nigel would never sell to him.

I was Van Buren's one problem. I hung in for one last evening's tippling and bought the papers. As he put it, "that rascal Hughie from the Archives keeps buying in my territory." Van Buren figured that his territory extended for a 100-mile radius around Bewdley.

Adrian was not as well educated or as knowledgeable about Drayton family history as his dad or granddad, though he certainly appreciated the cash I offered for the documents, diaries, photographs and other Drayton relics.

Nigel had a side to his complex personality that completely surprised and startled me. The first intimation of what I took to be a wild imagination was when he and I were taking a shortcut up the hill that overlooks the village, on our way to his lakeside home. As we passed the old Anglican Church on the brow of the hill, Nigel pointed to the cemetery in its well kept grounds. "That's where the real Nigel Drayton is buried," he said solemnly. "You mean that's where you *will* be buried," I corrected, expecting him to laugh and agree that he'd used the wrong tense.

He didn't even crack a smile, but merely kept plodding on toward his home as if I hadn't spoken. I put it down as another example of his quixotic personality.

If I'd had the slightest inkling of the fantastic, labyrinthine byways through which this cryptic offhand remark of Nigel's would lead, I would surely have pressed for some answers on the spot. Unfortunately, however, I never saw Nigel Drayton again, and it was not until I was able to peruse the family papers that I began to suspect there was much more to Nigel than met the eye.

Missing pieces in the story of the Draytons of Gore's Landing pertain to matters about which the family didn't particularly want other upstanding residents of the lakeside community to know. For the Ontario Archives, I was not able to obtain anything in Reginald Drayton's own writing, or his son Nigel's, that would hint at skeletons in the family closet. It was some of the letters the Draytons had *received* that referred to alleged Drayton escapades over a 60-year period, and they paint an entirely different picture.

Alluded to and open to various interpretations are the possible switching of an infant male heir between *fin-de-siècle* Germany and Canada, criminal fraud, great inherited wealth, aristocrats galore, ancient castles on the Rhine, a famous German movie star, misbegotten royals in both Hollywood and Gore's Landing, a fatal pistol duel, a brutal beating, a desperate night ride, a foiled military uprising, and episode after episode of high drama in its *sturm und drang* form.

Father and son were a fascinating contrast: the father, Reginald, had popular authors like Conrad Bercovici and Sir H Ryder Haggard as friends, read Euripides in the original Greek, compiled an Ojibwa-English dictionary, and could play virtually any piano work requested; the son, Nigel, spoke Arabic and his interests transcended borders and distance. In mid-war 1915, when the Hun was the Allies' hated enemy, Nigel received a number of letters from Germany, sent *via* Tunisia. He was also embroiled in fistfights with Gore's Landing men, and his horse was mysteriously shot — a rare crime in that quiet community.

Were these just youthful grudge tussles or were the Draytons even then suspected of being too chummy with the Hun? Mere suspicion must have ripened to certainty in 1917, when a pretty young girl named Ottillia made her first visit to the Draytons of Gore's Landing. She seemed to have an already well developed crush on Nigel, who was 8 years her senior, and whom she called her cousin. Ottillia later became a film star and changed her name to Greta Nissen when she and Marlene Dietrich invaded Hollywood. By what mode of transport she reached Canada in wartime was not revealed. Nor is there any record of the effect of Ottillia's visit on the inhabitants of the Landing.

After World War I, Nigel did a lot of travelling, probably on funds derived from the family's estates in England. He was known to have visited Sweden, the Sudan and Algeria, where he studied at an Islamic seminary with an old pal, the future President of Tunisia, and an Afghani prince. Poring over the Koran was to become one of Nigel's lifelong pleasures. He also hunted big game further south in Africa. Letters from many unidentified people in Switzerland, England and other lands refer in sociable terms to these various pursuits.

Starting in 1928, the letters become much more compelling, urgent and puzzling. One, signed "Gertrude," calls him "beloved cousin Nigel." The writer was Baroness Gertrude Marie Drucilla von Lehenhöhe, of Castle Rustenburg, who once attended Girton Ladies College in London. She hoped that in spite of his English upbringing he still had "enough good German blood" in him to help a kinswoman in distress. Her 19-year-old daughter Resi, whom she once hoped Nigel might wed, has eloped with "a swine of an outlander" from Ireland, whom she met at art school. "Think of the disgrace," Gertrude rages. "The beautiful white body of a girl of our blood to be used by that animal for his pleasure!"

Gertrude promises that if Nigel will bring Dorothy to Germany, "we who are left of the great houses of Hesse, Darmstadt and

Papenheim would love her like a daughter, in spite of her hated race. If a son is born to you here, binding you anew to the Rhineland, everything we own will be yours."

Gertrude also mentions a recent visit to Schloss Rustenburg by Ottillia, her sister Hermione's illegitimate daughter by Prince Rupert of Bavaria. "The love [Ottillia] once had for you has turned to hate," Gertrude warned. "Be careful of her if she should come to Canada." Up to this point, Gertrude's alleged letter, translated into English in Nigel's handwriting, is fairly direct, if one can accept the bizarre possibility that an eccentric canoe expert who had lived most of his life in a small Ontario village might in reality be a Prussian aristocrat. As for Ottillia, there seemed little doubt that she, in the vibrant flesh, had visited him and called him cousin. Ottillia's aunt, a baroness, was claiming similar kinship.

Baroness Gertrude Marie Drucilla von Lehenhöhe, waxing nostalgic in her letter to Nigel, poses new puzzles. She recalled the old days at the great house when Regano (Reginald) was home from Heidelberg,

> … a handsome man, black-bearded and ever laughing, who sat at the piano and played Mozart, and Hilda sat beside him, her beautiful eyes on his face.

And then the Baron Leopold quickly rising swept your father's hands from the keyboard and slapped him across the mouth. Regano caught him as a man does an angry cat and hurled him through the great leaded window. I did not see the duel that followed, but this I know: that Leopold shot him when his back was turned (and) the signal had not been given. Leopold expected him to fall but, slowly, Regano turned and with blood spurting from his mouth, shot Leopold through the head, then fell. Well do I remember the fast galloping horses to cross the border before the hue and cry was up, and poor Hilda in tears. We are sending you a gift of money as a very late wedding present. I was too bitter at the time, but now I consider her a German. I still hate the English. God punish them! They killed my son.

The gift of money could have been what set the then newlyweds on Easy Street. But who was Leopold? Why did he hate Reginald? And when could Reginald have attended Heidelberg? Could it have been when he was taking furs to Germany? The only other recorded period that Reginald was in Germany was in the early 1890s, shortly after his marriage to Agnes Rubidge. Was Hilda Leopold's daughter, or his wife?

Did Reginald seduce her? As for Gertrude's son and heir, the only time he could have been killed by the English would have been in World War I. Was it this death that made them so anxious for Nigel to come on side?

A fanciful scenario was hinted at by Nigel himself when he said in the graveyard, "This is the real Nigel," and by the reported death of Reginald's first child and its possibly unauthorized burial, a precedent which had been set with the bodies of several cholera victims. Was Reginald being offered a substitute baby of Gertrude's family on certain conditions which he was later unable or unwilling to meet? Did the new Nigel discover his real identity in his teens?

Six months after the first letter, an even more heart-rending one arrived for Nigel, this time from Gertrude's husband, Heinrich, addressed on the inside to Baron von Hesse Darmstadt und Landgraf von Arn. He described how his pregnant daughter, Resi, had been beaten, robbed of jewelry and kicked out by her husband, but somehow made her way by night to the Rhine across from her father's castle. Summoning her last ounce of strength, she swam the river and fainted on the doorstep of the family swineherd. When Heinrich arrived later, Resi was near death. She was still shielding her stillborn baby when they were finally within Rustenburg Castle.

> As the great chimes of Oberhausen clanged the hour of noon [he wrote, tears staining the monogrammed notepaper], Resi Hildegarde von Papenheim, last child of the house, holding the hands of the Baron her father and the Baroness her mother, gave a great sigh and shudder, then passed away. Gertrude shed no tears, but from that day she lies in this little sanatorium at Valgarten, so weak she can't raise a hand.

The next message concerning the family in Germany is postmarked October 11, 1931. It came from Ottillia in Hollywood. Since her first visit 14 years before, she had seen Nigel at least three times, at Gore's Landing, in France and in Africa, the latter two visits probably taking place in 1926. The last occasion must have been a painful one, because her opening sentence recalls "the bitter hurt of the things you said to me that night." But after reminding him that she was now going under the name of Greta Nissen, she said bygones should be bygones, and began savaging the reputations of the movie capital's prominent citizens:

> As Hedy has told you, I am here in Hollywood but not a star and never can be. I am not rotten enough. I've had two big parts and many small ... I who thought to be a second Garbo, even to borrowing her

first name! That stupid Swede holds no attraction for me anymore. Miss Marlene Dietrich is rich and has a fine house in Catalina, due to being a mistress of Lasky, the great producer. But I don't really like her because she is one of the *hoi polloi*, the daughter of a Berlin riding master. She can't sing or dance or even walk, has legs like pipe stems and a bust prominent by its absence. The men here are so glutted with women that they become catamites, the women so glutted with men that they turn into … a collection of what you once called *me*, second rate harlots from all over the world.

Halfway through her long letter, she asked if she may drop in on Nigel and his lady at Christmas, *en route* to Europe, "for your house is the only home I have on this side of the Atlantic. Once again we two will meet, the last of the noble and once powerful House of Lehenhöhe, but no silver moonlight, no romance, no youth this last time, whatever will we do?"

Ottillia then alludes to the Draytons' baby son Adrian, who she assumes was named after her aunt Gertrude's grandfather. She also wonders who will inherit her aunt's money, the husband Heinrich having died of grief shortly after daughter Resi's own tragic demise. "First she left it all to me, then to the State and now it is all divided between you and the Church," Ottillia wound up. "I hope for your sake she dies tomorrow. Old friend, I hate her!"

Ottillia's hope was in vain, for some two years later, possibly half-crazed by the personal catastrophes which had befallen her, Gertrude was in a plot with Prussian General von Klooks to restore Kaiser Wilhelm II to power. She was betrayed by Johan Kauf, the long-time, supposedly loyal, *major domo* of Schloss Rustemburg, in the cellars of which police found tons of illegal military supplies.

Ottillia's letter of October 11, 1831, continues, confirming arrangements for her visit: "I want you to have about 8 dozen beers laid in, I will pay for it, and coffee, coffee! Black as night, hot as love and sweet as sin, not like this insipid US kind. And don't expect me to speak a goddam word of English!"

I tried to contact Marlene Dietrich to see what light she could throw on the whole still incredible saga, but to no avail. I then turned to New Yorker Charles Higham, Dietrich's biographer, hoping he could find out only two or three things. Knowing Ottillia, did Marlene also know Gertrude? Had she met Nigel, either under his Canadian name or the formal title by which Baron Heinrich Ludvic Wolf von Pappenheim addressed him, "Baron Wolf Konrad von Hesse und

Darmstadt?" I received a polite reply from Higham, but nothing in the way of information.

Some time later, I met a young woman, Susan Archibald, whose father, a Toronto lawyer, owned the lakeside house next door to Nigel's for many years. She herself had taped some of Nigel's reminiscences, with a vague idea of putting them into an article, or possibly a book. In hopes of obtaining more papers through her dealing with this intriguing family, I asked her to go through some of the material I'd bought from Adrian, but had never had time to read. Before doing so, however, I inquired, just as a formality, since she was a neighbor, if she had any information of her own about Nigel's connection with Germans of any stripe. I almost fell off my chair at her answer:

> As a matter of fact, I have, quite a lot. In 1975, I think it was, Nigel said, "Congratulate me, I now own two castles on the Rhine." As I was about to ask questions, he grinned and said, "All I have to do is pay the taxes owing for the last 40 years or so." A bit later, he said one of the castles the Baroness his Aunt Gertrude had left him was being used as a boys' school. The Third Reich had originally confiscated it when they were repatriating properties owned by foreigners. Gertrude must have already willed them to Nigel by that time, 1933 or '34, in a faint hope of saving them from the Nazis. But in fact it did just the opposite.

Though the evidence of Nigel's double life was mounting, I wasn't quite ready to go all the way with it. I still have more questions than answers. Among them, how did Reginald explain Nigel #2 to the neighbours and scrupulously refrain from the slightest mention of their quite important German connection? Was Nigel #2 a blood relation to the Draytons, perhaps Reginald's son from a sweet liaison in Heidelberg days with a maiden of Gertrude's family? Does that help explain Baron Leopold's rage?

Then again, how could Gertrude, surely in her 70s by 1928, have a 19-year-old daughter? My job at Archives was to get the important family papers, not question whether they were fiction or fact. I never had the time or opportunity for intensive study of family origins in European countries. Once my findings became public, I usually received communications from various sources about my subjects, and I trust that will be the case in this one.

I have to admit that the Draytons do fascinate me, far beyond my normal healthy curiosity, at least in part because it all seems so improbable. How did they keep their secrets for so long?

CHAPTER NINETEEN
BOLSHEVIKS, BUCCANEERS AND AMAZONS

Sitting on my desk is a Mason jar stuffed full of crumpled paper. A label reads "Finnish Record Management System." The tale behind this odd relic is about Johnnie Karjala, a Finnish prospector, woodcutter, and Communist party organizer. Karjala was reported to have a huge assortment of Communist *ephemera* in the form of pamphlets and flyers. One of my contacts in Thunder Bay, Steve Lukinuk, was the lawyer looking after Karjala's estate. On my arrival in Thunder Bay, he took me out to his farm, where the Karjala papers were stored. Lukinuk warned me that Karjala had an odd filing system. I had to agree when he took me to the storage shed, where I found a dozen 45-gallon drums. They contained hundreds of pickle jars, peanut butter jars and mason jars, each stuffed with crumpled up papers.

I braced myself for a lengthy session of opening jars to find the Communist Party material he was supposed to have saved. The only good thing you could say about his system was that the mice couldn't get at it. After hours of fruitless jar opening, Steve Lukinuk's daughter Monica, home for the summer from university, felt sorry for me and pitched in to help. By the second day, having worked our way through all the jars, we were hardly fit to talk to. All those jars proved to contain nothing but pulp wood sales bills, receipts and empty tobacco packages. Steve was apologetic and we decided Karjala was up there (or down below) somewhere laughing at how he had fooled this paper sleuth.

Our Finnish paper collector with the odd sense of humour had died before our case with him was concluded, as was the ardent seeker of a picture of one special steamboat.

The spectre of the windship *Helen S* with Bill Grimshaw at the helm still haunts me because from the time I met this driven man in 1977, he kept at me to get him a picture of the *Helen S* when she was a steam tug. By 1984 when I finally found the picture he wanted so badly, Bill was dead.

The Helen S converted to a brigantine (a 4-masted sailing ship) by her master, Bill Grimshaw, under sail in Hay Bay on Lake Ontario, near Picton, July 1980.

The Helen S was built in 1899 at Byng Inlet for the Collins Bay Lumber Co. She is seen here in her original conformation as a working tug boat. She was of wood construction. I was unable to locate this picture until after Bill Grimshaw, who converted her to a yacht, had died. (Ontario Archives photo no ACC-16649-8, reproduced with permission)

Grimshaw came to my attention through a full-page spread about him and his daughter Victoria in the *Toronto Sun* by a skilled writer, Ron Poulton, who had written about my searches for the Toronto *Telegram*. While bringing their sailboat to the dock in Picton, Ontario in 1973, they noticed a derelict wooden tugboat, the *Helen S*, resting on a sandbank in the harbour. Bill liked her lines, and being a man of impulse, decided he would try to buy her and convert her to a four-masted schooner. The ship, built in 1899, was over 100 feet long with a beam of 16 feet. She could carry several tons of cargo.

By the time I actually met Bill Grimshaw and the reclaimed *Helen S*, the conversion was over half done and the boat was tied to a dock in Deseronto, Ontario (near Belleville). Probably because of my own experience around boats, Bill saw me as a part-time helper. I got in the habit of scheduling my document-hunting trips so I'd end up staying overnight in Deseronto on the boat. Bill was a true artisan who could do anything in the line of mechanical or carpentry work. My skills in these directions were minimal, but I made my contacts available to him, finding people he could enlist to help with the refitting. I also did what I could to help in other ways.

Bill stripped the vessel down to the bare hull. He then rebuilt it with cabins below deck, the latest in mechanical gear, radar, sonar, auxiliary power, rigging and a suit of new sails. All this took hundreds of hours of work and much cash. Bill was a great scrounger and got many items secondhand. He was a genius at that, and was ably helped by his 20-year-old daughter, Victoria. Bill's wife did not buy into his dream, which she considered foolhardy and impractical. Their marriage ended over it.

But Bill never gave up and never slowed down. He was a skilled electrician, and in order to finance the venture, he worked long hours in Toronto. Every time he accumulated another few thousand dollars, he would come back to his first love, the *Helen S*, and his vision of her under full sail, performing humanitarian missions. After she was ready for sail, he carried a load of eyeglasses to the West Indies for *Médecins sans frontières* (Doctors Without Borders). Bill was a romantic visionary who put his dreams into practice.

In 1980, Bill married Sirppa, a Finnish woman who shared his vision. I went out with them on the *Helen S* every chance I got. Bill was able to make many trips, and had great plans for the vessel. He had assistance from a number of people, but it was his all-consuming drive that saw the venture to completion. He was always on the lookout for a picture of the *Helen S* as she had originally looked, and I kept trying to satisfy his obsession. But fate was not kind to Bill. The gruelling schedule he kept up, along with a bottle of rum a day, eventually killed him at the age of 50.

I nevertheless continued to put out feelers to find the Collins Bay Lumber Co's records. They had built the *Helen S* at Byng Inlet on the north shore of Lake Huron. A break finally came in 1984. When I was in Toronto two or three days a week, I would lunch at the Arts and Letters Club. One day I was introduced to a guest who had come to the club with another member. We were discussing the story of the *Helen S* and my long search for a picture of the ship and any papers of the Collins Bay company.

The guest listened intently to my tale, then hit me with a surprise. "Mr. MacMillan, my neighbour has the Collins Bay Lumber Company records and wants to find a home for them. If you will come with me, I will take you to his house." For at least half a minute I was speechless before I blurted out, "Let's go, your car or mine?"

Within two hours, I had the papers and an excellent picture of the *Helen S*. It was a bittersweet success, too late for Bill, but his 90-year-old mother was delighted to get a copy of the picture, as was his daughter, Vicky. Today the ship that he so magnificently restored still sails in the West Indies. The moral of this tale is that a paper sleuth should be on constant lookout for tips. I never had enough, because only a small number of them ever resulted in a find. My antennæ were always out, and I never stopped asking questions.

Whatever expertise I was able to develop in dealing effectively with a wide range of people came from working with Harry Dixon. From 1947 to 1951, when I was working on the tow boats out of Vancouver Harbour, I needed something to do when I was ashore between ships, sometimes for a month or more, so I answered Harry Dixon's ad seeking a person to sell 2-for-1 tickets to merchants in selected areas.

Harry was a tall spare man with a Hitler mustache, always well dressed. He was a superb storyteller with an unending stream of well told tales that extended back over 60 years. Harry ran away from home before 1900 to join Buffalo Bill's Wild West show in its last days. Later, he worked for Seal Bros circus and for various newspapers.

At another stage in his amazing life, he cranked out publicity for Porfirio Diaz, the Mexican revolutionary. Harry was married six times, his final marriage being the second time around with his second wife. He fluctuated from being wealthy to being broke, and often his fortunes were restored by one or other of his ex-wives, who seemed to keep a soft spot for him even after they split. The one I met owned a hotel in San Francisco.

Harry claimed to have invented the 2-for-1 ticket scheme. The deal was to sell large rolls of these tickets to one of each type of merchant in an area. They would give them to their customers with each purchase over a set amount. Each ticket would admit two people into a theatre, the circus, or some other attraction for the price of one. It was a great promotional idea for both the merchants and the entertainers, and while I was out and about selling the idea, and the tickets, I was also honing my skills as a salesman.

Before World War II, Harry had over 100 salesmen out in the Chicago area selling the 2-for-1 ticket deal. He was rolling in money, driving a Stutz Bearcat, and living the good life, until one day he had a visit from one of Al Capone's henchmen, who demanded a piece of the action. Harry closed the scheme down and went on to something else. In the 1950s, I apprenticed to Harry on tour across Montana with Seal Bros Circus. Later, on my own, I promoted the Great Orlando, an Australian hypnotist.

Harry Dixon once commented "Mac, you are a great salesman, but too damn interested in the past." He had that right, and I only wish I had asked him more about his own flamboyant career. He was largely responsible for any skill I developed in dealing with a wide assortment of people, the kind of confidence I needed and have been able to use all my life since meeting this valuable mentor.

One night in Madoc, a little town near Peterborough, Ontario, I was speaking to a women's group about the value of keeping papers. When I asked for leads or tips a woman stood up to say "Mr. MacMillan, if you would go to Windsor and see my friend, Danny Duck Pepper, you could be in luck. She has her grandfather's letters and diaries from the 1830s." Despite the unlikely name of the person to contact, I soon found this tip was for real, and within a week was away to Windsor. The lady with the improbable name of Danny Duck had married Howard Pepper, a former naval officer.

Danny was a charmer. A lively woman in her 70s, she had gone back to university as a mature student to do an MA in English. Her experience at the University of Windsor was enriched by the presence of writer in residence WO Mitchell, who became her mentor. She was already selling stories based on the diaries of her grandfather, who had travelled around Ontario with the Court of Quarter Session and commented on everything that caught his eye.

We soon made a deal for the Archives to buy her attic full of papers, a valuable collection. Danny became a good friend and another of my tipsters. WO Mitchell made use of these diaries in spinning some of his own tales. The most hilarious of them were acidic comments about the antics her grandfather had observed at the Legislature in York (later Toronto).

Two other women, younger but equally outstanding, were Viva Hilton and Barbara Bonnell. Viva was a free-spirited, handsome, gifted artist, who taught painting to hundreds of disabled and retarded people. Her mother was Lila Douglas (1876–1949), daughter of Judge William Douglas, descended from the Scottish Earl of Glenbarvie. Her father was LH Hilton, a professional gambler on the trans-Atlantic Cunard and White Star liners. Hilton claimed to be the son of Nellie Melba who went to Australia and became a famous opera star. After Viva's birth, her father, the abandoned son who became a gambler, himself disappeared, and Viva never saw him again. She was raised by her mother's Douglas family in Chatham, Ontario.

It was to that family's abandoned summer cottage on the northwest shore of Lake Erie that Viva invited me to pick up some very interesting documents. I did so, not without a bit of drama. I was walking towards the cellar door when rotting floor boards gave way and I found myself in the basement without benefit of stairs. Falling through a collapsed floor is not the conventional way to recover letters of a Prime Minister but this is exactly what I was after. I ruined a summer suit and had some bruises, but the basement of the old Douglas cottage yielded a fine array of political letters from Sir John A Macdonald to Viva's grandfather, Judge Wm Douglas of Chatham. Following that escapade, I kept in touch with Viva Hilton over the years until she died at 81, in 1991.

Viva's mother, Lila Douglas, lived in Montreal for many years and published Pets Gazette, a magazine about cats and dogs that carried advertising for pet food and related items. A regular writer of articles about pets was Eleanor "Happy" (Meyers) Bonnell, of Toronto. Happy had a daughter named Barbara. At 6 foot 4 inches, Barbara Bonnell was a statuesque lady of leisure with a private income from the estate of her grandfather, Dr DC Meyers of Toronto. Her father, Charles Bonnell, had been killed on New Year's Eve 1941 while trying to sink an Italian battleship from a midget submarine. He had been a lieutenant in the RCN Volunteer Reserve on loan to the Royal Navy.

Barbara Bonnell lived in a decrepit farmhouse near Lakefield, Ontario and hung out with people like Margaret Laurence and Rompin' Ronnie Hawkins. She was known locally as the Marijuana Queen of the Kawarthas, having been heavily fined at one time for baking and trafficking in marijuana cookies. I was taken by surprise one day when I bit into one of these, not knowing the ingredients. Barbara, by self-admission, was a slapdash housekeeper. She kept horses, and they seemed to live in the house, what with hay, straw, and horse droppings throughout, along with overflowing ashtrays (though to be fair, the horses were probably not responsible for the latter).

Barbara also fancied men. A story was told about several men being at her place repairing the roof when she took a liking to one young redhead in the work crew. Barbara drove off to Lakefield in her beat-up Land Rover and returned with a case of beer. She grabbed the young fellow under one arm, and with the case of beer in the other hand, marched him into the house. It is said they were not seen again for two days!

Barbara Bonnell and Viva Hilton, strong aggressive women, amazons by definition, saw each other several times a year. This may have been because of their mothers' involvement in the *Pets Gazette*, their own shared love of animals, or because of a shared interest in their family histories. Both families could boast of a variety of colourful and eccentric relatives. Barbara had a few Meyers family papers and led me to relatives who had more of them. Her mother, Happy Bonnell, had turned over the bulk of the family archives to her own sister Violet "Bay" Meyers, and their niece, Joan Eddis-Topolski. Barbara and Joan Eddis were first cousins. Their grandfather, Dr D Campbell Meyers, was another noteworthy Ontario medical pioneer.

A graduate of the University of Edinburgh, Dr Meyers established the first psychiatric hospital at Toronto in the latter part of the 19th Century. It was located at 72 Heath Street West near Yonge and St Clair Streets. At that time, it was on the very outskirts of town. The doctor and his family lived on the ground floor of the same cavernous mansion as housed his patients. The children were under orders never to enter the upper floors, where the patients lived. The family kept an assortment of livestock, including goats. One fine day, Margaret (later

Garth Dittrick

to be the mother of Joan Eddis) spotted a goat entering the house and bounded up the stairs to where the patients were. Against orders, Margaret chased the goat and found it perched on a bureau in a patient's room, gazing into the mirror, while the nurse stood on a chair shrieking. The patient, shell shocked in World War I, had been in a catatonic state and had never moved a muscle in the several years since he had been admitted. Suddenly seeing this tableau, he sat up in bed and burst into peals of laughter.

Margaret expected a tongue-lashing from her father for chasing the goat, but it never came. The incident propelled the patient to a rapid recovery.

I found a treasure trove of social history in Bay Meyers's house near Uxbridge, Ontario. Bay raised great black curly-haired Bouvier dogs. They had a free run into the living room from their compound outside through a dog-sized, double-hinged door at floor level. The living room had a royal blue deep-pile carpet covered with curly black dog hair. Scattered around the perimeter of this large room, almost devoid of furnishings, were hundreds of crumpled up empty Camel cigarette packages — a strange scene not easily forgotten.

In contrast to this untidy scene were several boxes of neatly arranged Meyers letters that revealed much about Toronto in the last decade of the 19th Century. Bay, a solidly built, unkempt woman, had been in the British Land Army during World War II. Her slapdash housekeeping was on a par with her niece Barbara's.

I was next sent off to see her other niece, Joan Eddis, in Chelsea, Quebec. A tall, elegant brunette who has written extensively on the Meyers family, Joan lived in a tidy cottage with her husband Alek Topolski. Here was the mother lode. Joan had two dozen detailed social diaries kept by her grandmother, Edith Burson, Mrs Campbell Myers. They were full of names and tidbits of gossip about the Toronto social scene around 1900. Joan's unpublished manuscript about her eccentric family would be a valuable contribution to Canadian historical literature.

CHAPTER TWENTY
TWO WILD RIDERS

On quite different military missions, Duncan Clark used a horse, while Angus Mowat, 130 years later, rode a motorcycle, each a Canadian hero in his way. Both were also writers who documented their work for posterity, and preserving their papers became part of my quest.

Duncan Clark was born in Scotland in 1785, came to Canada as an infant and eventually ran the Post Office and General Store in Edwardsburg, now Cardinal, Ontario. He is best known for shouting "To arms, to arms, the enemy is at hand!" as he rode through farms and villages on the night of November 4, 1813. Ten years before Clark was born, a similar lone rider gained fame through Henry Wadsworth Longfellow's famous poem, *The Midnight Ride of Paul Revere*. To our loss, no Canadian poet has immortalized Duncan Clark's midnight ride.

In his later years, Clark rose to the rank of lieutenant-colonel, but at age 28, he was a lieutenant in the 1st Flank Company of the Dundas Militia. He survived many battles of the 1812–1814 war. Assigned to scout out American General Wilkinson's troops assembling west of Brockville, Lt Clark needed to head east along the bank of the St Lawrence River to warn the British that the American general's armada of barges loaded with 10,000 troops was heading down river. He borrowed a farmer's horse and galloped the 15 miles to Prescott, changing horses in Brockville and shouting the warning to everyone along the way.

Clark's warning enabled Lt-Col Pearson and his troops at Prescott to ready themselves for the approaching Americans. The British, though heavily outnumbered, were able to win the Battle of Crysler's Farm the next day.

To the great benefit of future researchers, Duncan Clark's accounts of those earlier battles were published in the Prescott newspapers of the day. In 1818, he joined the North West Company as a clerk, but had already moved over to the Hudson's Bay Company when the Nor'Westers joined them in 1821. During his seven-year fur trading

Then Lieutenant Duncan Clark (b 1785, Scotland) rode a borrowed farm horse through towns and villages from Brockville to Prescott on the night of 4 November 1813, yelling "To arms! To arms! The enemy is at hand!" to warn of a sneak attack by 10,000 American soldiers under General Wilkinson. The British, though heavily outnumbered, defeated the Americans at the Battle of Crysler's Farm the next day. (Ontario Archives)

Angus Mowat and his travelling companion Elmer, on board Old Faithful, Kingston, 1942, as they tour military bases across Canada. Angus's report paints a dismal portrait of wartime military libraries. His son Farley wrote about Elmer in his popular book The Dog Who Wouldn't Be.

career he was stationed at Michipicotin and the Pic, and other posts on the north shore of Lake Superior. The money he saved during this period helped establish him in his mercantile career.

Clark's descriptive account of a Nor'Wester canoe brigade heading up the Ottawa River in 1818 attests that the canoes stopped at Alexander Grant's Daldraggen Hall, which is still standing today.

Clark also mentions Hamilton's Hawkesbury Mills down-river from L'Orignal. In the 1820s, my great-grandfather Archie Roy M^{C}Millan was able to earn enough money working at Hamilton's mill to buy a farm at Lochiel in Glengarry, part of which I farmed nearly a century and a half later.

Before Duncan Clark died in 1862 at the age of 77, he was able to make at least one trip back to Scotland seeking his roots. As well as a tireless recorder of events, he was one of Canada's early genealogists.

Clark came to my attention in 1965 when antiquarian book dealer Borden Clarke (no relation) of Morrisburg, Ontario, offered to sell me some of Clark's papers. I quickly discovered that Duncan Clark was a first-rate chronicler of events, with a wide range of interests, about which he made copious notes for later articles.

I was able to buy the Duncan Clark papers from Borden Clarke for the Archives of Ontario. Then I went across the river with Borden to meet Duncan's relatives, from whom he had purchased the papers.

The following is copied from Duncan Clark's writings about his military career. Some of it is derived from his own diaries, but much of which he wrote later is from memory.

A CANADIAN BATTLEFIELD, LUNDY'S LANE
from the Daily Globe, July 25, 1814

Whether we have a heroic age at present, or shall have it at some future time, we are not anxious to discuss, but that we have had a glimpse at least of what may very fitly be called by the name in past days, is beyond doubt to one who visits, as we did very lately, one of the few historical districts of the province. Close to Toronto, we are apt to overlook the interest the neighbourhood of Niagara Falls offers to anyone who takes the trouble to gather its traditions and memorials.

The village of Drummondville, within a few miles of the falls, was the scene of one of the sternest battles of the last war, that of Lundy's Lane. The village lies on the slope which rises behind, at a short distance, into a sandy ridge, on the crest of which now stands the Presbyterian Church. A tableland runs level and opens into the heart of the country. On the slope of the ridge and reaching the crest, stretches the churchyard, beautifully free to the sun in its southern exposure. The main road, known now forever as "Lundy's Lane," climbs the ascent about the middle of the houses, and reaches back to the interior in a straight line. Anxious to pick up … recollections or memorials of the struggle which has made the locality famous, we gathered what we could of them during a recent visit.

The agony of the battle was wrought out on the slope of the hill, where the dead lie now in the peaceful slumbers of God's Acre, as our ancestors called the graveyard. On the 25th of July, 1814, there was noise and tumult enough. The Americans had landed at Chippawa, and were pressing down to drive the British from the district. General Drummond, the head of the British forces, from whom the village took its name, had his headquarters at Beaver Dams, about 7 miles back, and hearing of the invasion, at once marched to meet and repel it. From behind the hill, our people stretched along its height to drive back the Americans, who were determined to get possession of it. The battle began at dusk … and raged fiercely until midnight, when the Americans retreated with great precipitation to their camp beyond Chippawa.

On the following day, they abandoned this camp, threw the greater part of baggage, camp equipage, and provisions into the rapids, and having set fire to Street's Mills and destroyed the bridge at Chippawa, continued their retreat in great disorder, toward Lake Erie.

The recollections of the inhabitants of Drummondville who then lived in the neighbourhood are very interesting, and throw light on many details of the struggle.

One elderly man pointed to us a spot where 80 of the Glengarry militia had been killed in mistake by our own side; the poor fellows having passed quickly from Queenston, and coming up the hill in the dark night earlier than the British had expected, and being taken for Americans endeavouring to turn our flank. Our informant was then a boy and told us how he had sat down close to a working party wondering what they were doing digging a cellar in a field, and watched them without his wondering lessening till he saw them begin to put the 80 bodies in the one unshapely grave. The ground has long since been plowed over and every year now crops of wheat or corn grow over the mouldering bones of the brave.

Where is there not the dust of the British soldier? It was very warm weather at the time of the battle, and there was no time to bury the dead — who were very numerous, one force having to bury for both sides. Large piles of branches and cordwood were therefore made at various points, and the bodies were heaped on them and burned. Many a fine fellow had this strange end. The conflict must have been terrific at some points, if we may judge by the number of ball holes in a wooden house, the only one still surviving the battle. We counted not less than 50 bullet holes in the one building — some of musket balls, some larger sizes, and one a clean round hole cut by a cannon ball. What is now the churchyard was the scene of the fiercest strife. Close to the upper fence and just where the British battery was fixed, there is a headstone with these words:

"Here lies the body of Abraham T Hull, captain in the 9th Reg US Infantry, who fell near this spot in the Battle of Bridgewater (Lundy's Lane) July 25, 1814, aged 28 years."

There is close by an older memorial, a wooden slab, somewhat differently worded:

"This was erected to mark the spot where Captain Hull, US Army, fell in the memorable action of Lundy's Lane, 25th July, 1814, gallantly leading his men to the charge." This is the only American gravestone in the churchyard.

A massive flat monument in the middle of the ground tells a sad story. It bears the following inscription — "Sacred to the memory of Honorable Cecil Bishopp, 1st Foot Guards and Inspecting Field Officer in Upper Canada, eldest and only surviving son of Sir Cecil Bishopp, Baronet, Baron de la Zouche in England. After having served with distinction in the British Army in Holland, Spain and Portugal, he died on the 16th of July, 1813, aged 30 years, in consequence of wounds received in action with the enemy in Black Rock, on the 13th of same month, to the great grief of his family and friends, and is buried here. This tomb erected at the time by his brother officers, becoming much dilapidated, is now (1846) renewed by his affectionate sisters, Baroness de la Zouche and the Hon Mrs Pechell, in memorial of an excellent man and beloved brother." On one side of the tomb are some lines:

Stranger, whose steps ere now have stood
Beneath Niagara's stupendous flood,
Pause o'er this shrine where sleeps the young and brave,
And shed one generous tear o'er Cecil's grave;
Whilst pitying angels point through deepest gloom,
To everlasting happiness beyond the tomb,
Thro' Christ who died to give eternal life."
Thus ends the English baronetcy! Clay cold but glorious,
Poor Cecil saw his native land no more!

Near at hand a broken board attracted our attention, and turning it up, the inscription, nearly effaced, ran thus:

"Sacred to the memory of Lieut Thomas Andrew, 6th Reg, who died in consequence of a wound he received when gallantly leading on his company before Fort Erie, Sept 17, 1814, aged 26 yr."

Poor Andrew is hidden somewhere near Colonel Bishopp, but who could now tell where? A half rotted fragment of a wooden head mark, blown by the wind, is all that tells us he ever lived. Oh life! life! life! What a dream art thou! It is well to keep a memorial of all who have their names left as having been laid here red from the battle. Two marble slabs side by side, over two friends, who gave up their lives for us in that struggle, are inscribed thus:

"Sacred to the memory of Lieut Wm Hempshill, of the Royals, who fell at the battle of Lundy's Lane, on the 25th of July, 1814. This stone was placed by his son, Lieut-Colonel Hemphill, of the 26th Camerons, 17 July 1854."

The other is thus: "To the memory of Lieut Gordon and Captain Torrens of the Royals, killed at Fort Erie during the campaign of 1814. Erected by Major Barry Fox, late of said regiment, their friends and companions, June 20, 1851. Captain Torrens was very likely a relative of General Torrens who died from the effects of the Crimean hardships. Here he sleeps, sweetly we trust, as he died nobly."

These are all the tombstones in the churchyard. Only one out of many [of the dead] is here and there recorded — the multitude are forgotten forever. Yet surely they live in the gratitude of every Canadian. With their lives, they defended this country and saved it to us as our heritage.

All that we are and have as a British people, we owe to them and their fellow warriors. Light lie the sod on their breasts!

Thus ends Duncan Clark's description of the battle and the cemetery. Not only is there much war history to learn from Clark's notes and articles, but he also bequeathed information about his few years with the Nor'West Company. His original fur trade papers were sold by Borden Clarke, the book dealer, in 1964 to Jerome Peltier of Spokane, Washington. I acquired copies of these for the Ontario Archives, but was never able to lay hands on the originals. Here is an entry in his diary from Spruce Grove, Edwardsburg, written on June 25, 1859:

> Leaving the NW Brigade of canoes 16 May, 1818, at the foot of the Long Sault Rapids, Ottawa, Mr McTavish and Mr McDonald went to Mr Hamilton's Hawkesbury Mills and Messrs Fraser, Scott, Chisholm, Nelson and myself crossed the river at Barron's Point and walked to Mr Grant's and on the arrival of the canoes the following day, May 17th, left Point l'Orignal with a merry song and reached Fort William, Lake Superior, on the morning of the 24th June, performing the voyage from Lachine in 44 days.
>
> On the 22nd of July, Mr Chisholm and young Mittleburger left in a light canoe for the Pic and I left on the 26th by the vessel for Sault Saint Marie, where I was stationed about 2 years with the exception of one winter at Michipicoton. I returned to Fort William again on the 9th of July, 1820 and on the 22nd left for Michipicoten department with Mr McIntosh, Mr McTavish and young McKay, the two latter for the Pic, where we arrived on the 28th at 8 in the morning, and passed the day and the night with our friend Roderick Chisholm, who was most happy to meet with his fellow voyageurs, Mr McTavish and myself. Mr McIntosh and myself got to Michipicoten on the 30th and on the 8th of August I left for my wintering station at Brunswick Lake. A Montreal Light canoe passed down the bay on the 7th, supposed to be Messrs McGillivray, McKenzie and Hughes, and Mr Chisholm might have been on board.

Duncan Clark never married, but there are descendents of relatives in Fort Frances, Ontario, who may have more of his records. I have reason to believe that one of them may have his red uniform from the war of 1812. The search continues.

Soon after I started searching out papers connected with the history of Ontario, I was chasing after those of Sir Oliver Mowat (1820–1903), a highly regarded and astute politician. Donald McOuat impressed on me that though we had Mowat's political papers, none of his personal papers had been found. Using reverse genealogy I located descendents, mostly in Ontario, and searched old Mowat homes and the family cottage on Sturgeon Lake. The search yielded papers of John Ross Robertson, a Toronto newspaper tycoon, but nothing on Oliver Mowat.

My first break came when I located Angus Mowat (1893–1977), father of the well known author Farley Mowat. Angus was a librarian, and as unique a character as his son Farley, whom I knew. In fact, Farley and I looked so much alike that I was often taken for him on the street, at public functions, and even at a book signing, where one customer would not believe me and insisted that I sign the Farley Mowat book she had just bought. I signed my own name, of course, and this must have baffled her when she got around to reading the inscription.

Farley helped me locate his father, Angus Mowat, who was living with his second wife, Barbara Hutchison, at Pinch-Penny, Ontario. As instructed, I drove to an isolated point north of Kingston, where I was met by a kilted Angus Mowat chauffeuring a Volkswagen Beetle. He was rebuilding a derelict Lake Ontario fishing boat, which he later named *Bonnie Prince*, and the National Film Board was in the midst of filming a documentary, *The Old Man and His Boat*, about the restoration. Our meeting was auspicious. We became friends and I acquired many of the Oliver Mowat papers I sought.

Proud of his Scottish heritage and that of his grandfather, Sgt John Mowat, who had come from Caithness in northern Scotland to Canada as a career soldier, Angus nevertheless detested pomposity and self-important bureaucrats. His 40-year career as a librarian started in Trenton, Ontario. Before it ended in 1960, Angus had been head of library services for Saskatchewan, where he was able to come to work each day in his canoe. His last posting was as head of library services for Ontario.

Angus Mowat had a great affinity for native people. He once went on snowshoes into a remote native settlement in Ontario, pulling a tobogganload of books. It was no wonder that native people loved him. The first library at Moose Factory Island on James Bay was named the Angus Mowat Library.

For the 1954 annual meeting of the Canadian Library Association in Halifax, other delegates arrived by car, train, and by air, but not Angus

Mowat. With his son Farley, he sailed his 34 foot ketch, *Scotch Bonnet*, from Oakville, down the St Lawrence and around the coast to Halifax, arriving two days late. When the weathered, salt-stained Angus came to the podium, his speech, as always, was laced with ribald tales.

Though he had suffered an injury to his arm in World War I, Angus Mowat enlisted for overseas duty during World War II. The Army discovered he was much older than he had claimed, and shipped him home in 1943. They had to find something for him to do, and a perfect solution came up when rumbles of discontent were heard about the quality of books available for servicemen in Canada. The Department of Defence sent Angus Mowat across the country to report on the state of armed forces libraries. Not content to travel only by train, he went part way by motorcycle. On these journeys, he was accompanied by his dog Elmer. Bundled against the weather, this wild Scots sailor must have been a colourful sight, tearing across country on his Indian motor bike with Elmer riding pillion. Mowat's assigned task, as he recorded it in his diary, was:

> to go across the country and bring together and get working together all the various organizations that are working for camp and command and division libraries, and organize them into groups by provinces, and set up regional committees to govern them ... imagine any committee, regional or otherwise, governing in one bed the IODE, General Motors and the Canadian Jewish Women's Association!

Although he called it a "preposterous job," he produced an excellent report, which elicited great praise from Lorne Pierce, Editor of Ryerson Press, who deemed it "an ideal scheme if it could be put through, but it will take a revolution to stir the Government to appoint an Inspector of War Library Services." Angus Mowat's report and recommendation for Libraries for the Services in Canada, dated December 29, 1943, is there in the Ontario Archives for anyone to study and act upon.

Mowat's typed 1943 report on Service Libraries was thorough, irreverent and colourful. The following snippets are copied from a deteriorating document:

[KINGSTON]
Norman Rogers Air Station (RAF)
Library is in the padre's office which is crowded and in any case any library that gets into the hands of the padre is almost certain to sink.

Fair selection of poorish fiction in good condition. Nobody could tell me how many were used in a month or why, so I got my wet ass on the motorcycle again and hurtled back to Kingston.

HAMILTON
Army Trades School
Now here's something different again. The Sally Ann has 2000 books. They stoutly intend to keep them. Let them. Nobody else wants them, least of all the men in the camp. But the unit has built a damn fine recreation and education hut, with a damn fine library. And they have a personable young trained librarian in charge.... IODE will contribute 1000, but only 250 at a time. I suggested that in the meantime they get after the Legion for a selection from their general reading new books. This library is worth watching. It is starting out with a good librarian, decent quarters and NO bloody deadwood to kill it at the start. Misjudged my time and failed to get to Mount Hope RCAF. But I got an idea about their books and take a dim view of what I might have seen anyhow.

LONDON
Wolseley Barracks
500 books, half of them useful, in glass locked cages in men's recreation room and in charge of a corporal who is category on account of his peculiar head. Try and get a book while he stands behind you jingling his keys and hurrying you so that he can lock the case again. They don't lose any books. Have an antiquated system.... I fear they don't know what they're talking about. A bum outfit.

Westminster Hospital
One more library in charge of a mental case. He carves little things and piles the book cards in piles in fantastic patterns on a table kept for the purpose. ALL the books will have to be junked. Also the room in which they are kept. The padre is responsible and seemed rather confused about the whole thing.

WINNIPEG
No 3 Wireless Trng School, RCAF Winnipeg
This library could go places if it had a few more useful books. The quarters are good. In an excellent recreation room, such as only the RCAF knows anything about. A WD is in charge. She isn't a trained librarian but appears to have a very good personality and is interested.

A marked contrast to the bum army libraries I have seen in W'peg and elsewhere. The Legion, IODE and purchase account for the books. But as usual there is a lot of trash that ought to be hove overboard.

No 8 ARD Winnipeg
This is a padre's job, and looks it. There is a WD sitting at the desk but the poor thing hasn't been taught anything and doesn't know what the hell's bells this is. There are 1000 books. I'd throw out half of them.… What the God damned hell is the use of me spending this citizen's money running round the country looking at crap such as I have been seeing.

HMOS Chippewa Winnipeg
If you want to buy a stamp or borrow a book, go to the wicket and ask the WREN in charge. But you can't handle the stamps and you can't handle the books and I don't suppose you can handle the WREN either.… The boss of this library is Lt Langton. He bullies the WREN and knows EXACTLY how everything should be run. Balls again.… I am told that the Navy is so popular that they don't have to draw on anybody for books. The public bring them and leave them on the doorstep. Wonder if they leave their illegitimate babies there too. Be funny to see them in the library, but they'd be as much use as most of the books — that can't be touched.

REGINA
RCNVR Regina
Two long shelves in the school room … so high that you'd have to get on a table to reach the books if you wanted to. But you wouldn't want to. And in any case you couldn't take them out of the classroom. However, I had a good beer in the Ward Room.

CALGARY
No 13 District Depot
This is the Old Curiosity Shoppe under the famous Sgt Low who'd talk a steer into a miscarriage. It's all damn nonsense as far as library is concerned but the ferns are growing well.

VANCOUVER
Command Depot Little Mountain (Army)
SFA here. Major Anderson, 2i/c assured me that the unit could not take responsibility for books. Is it any damn wonder the whole army is voting CCF?

Georgia Dugout Hostess Hut
A collection of volumes. Nobody'd want to read them. Nobody....

No 3 RD Vancouver
Quite a decent little room next door to the recreation room and well filled with books, most of which should be thrown into Burrard Inlet or whatever happens to be the nearest large body of water. Also thousands of pulp magazines, very old and carefully piled on top of shelves where nobody could reach them. The Educ officer, Helmer, knows it's all bad. Circ 200 for pop of 1400. A WD temporarily i/c but she's awaiting posting and doesn't know what it's all about.

NAVY
Got in touch with the appropriate Navy bloke who told me they hadn't anything and suggested that everything is in Victoria.

VICTORIA
Well, the first night in Vic I had an all-night blather with Miss Clay the public librarian, Mr Morrison the provincial librarian, Miss Holmes who runs the book depot and two other ladies whose names I forget. I tried a couple of times to get hold of the chairman of the Coord Committee, but no luck and everybody says he is a nitwit anyhow so I'm too busy to keep on trying. All books, IODE, collections, donations come to Miss Holmes in the Metropolitan bldg, who puts in cards, sorts and sends out. And these are absolutely the God damndest of all the God damned rotten rubbish I've seen anywhere since Camp Borden in 1941. What in hell do our damn citizens think soldiers and sailors' minds are made of anyway! This is the last bloody limit! I'd go and get drunk if I could get a bottle. But you can't in this country. I don't see that there's much use going on late into the night writing notes about this kind of nonsense. However, this is what I saw in Victoria.

ARMY
Work Point Barracks, Victoria
The books are behind chicken wire. A damn good place for them. Bloody bloody bloody.

EDMONTON
Main Library
Books are behind glass but the cases aren't locked. There'd be no need to lock them. Nobody would steal much from that collection of

mildewed punk. There are 1500 to 2000 derelicts, eked out (Now who and the hell for example, would think of purloining the *Memoirs of Baron de Marbat,* vol II only?) ... Various people come out from town at various times to act as voluntary librarians.

Major Mowat's final thought in his report on Canada's Service Libraries in 1943 was for the Manning Pools, of which he wrote, "None of these manning pools have libraries. Each has a collection of junk."

On this bright note, our copy of Angus Mowat's report of Canada's military libraries in 1943 comes to an abrupt end.

It is clear that Angus didn't enjoy the cross-Canada library tour but it is also obvious that he enjoyed writing his daily accounts of what he saw. I've only skimmed the high- (or low-) lights. His complete document is in the Archives, great background material for researchers today, and for years to come.

Available to the public at the Ontario Archives is more information about the illustrious Angus Mowat, nephew of Sir Oliver and father of Farley, whose own role in the story of our country has considerable significance.

My search for original papers of Sir Oliver continues.

CHAPTER TWENTY-ONE
NOR'WESTER TALES

My job title of Ontario's official liaison officer was abolished in 1989, but my paper sleuthing didn't stop; in fact it just continued. As is obvious from all the foregoing chapters, treasure hunting for manuscripts, relics and *ephemera* is a vocation, avocation, occupation, preoccupation and a game I will continue to enjoy as long as I live. From the moment I retired until today, I have continued this lifelong interest as a part-time dealer in antiquities.

Not simply a matter of having in my possession items of historical interest, the obsession also includes trying to solve historical mysteries, locating art treasures, and finding the best destinations for certain valuable historic items.

Shortly after my retirement party, when I related some of my misadventures to friends and relatives gathered at the Arts and Letters Club in Toronto, Muriel and I set to work on our own business called Nor' Wester Partners.

With Muriel as editor, we have published four catalogues so far, listing items ranging in value from $25 to $85,000, and the chase continues on into the 21st Century.

We chose the name Nor'Wester Partners because though we have branched out considerably, we originally intended to specialize in finding and selling reproduction trade silver, and publishing journals about the North West Company. We operated fur trade canoe brigades for pleasure, provided costumes for heritage movie footage, organized tours to historical pageants and fur trade canoe races, and presented slide shows and lectures on the history of the fur trade. We also conducted tours to Scotland, following our interest in Glengarry antecedents.

Through all these related activities, we built a network of history buffs and developed useful leads to manuscript collections. Similar to the original North West Company, our Nor'Wester Partners company is a commercial venture. The original Nor'Westers explored much of Canada as they conducted the fur trade; we explore the same territory while conducting our trade in papers and objects of historical value.

Aviation pioneer Hyacinthe Lambart (1904–1988) with her de Havilland Gypsy Moth after landing on the Plains of Abraham, Quebec City, en route to an aviation conference in Holland, 1932. Hyacinthe corresponded with Amelia Earhart. (Author's collection)

Some museums, archives and other public institutions miss important collections because of poor rapport with intermediaries. I discovered early on that establishing good relations with dealers in antiquities benefits the public archives and all those who use them for research.

Every item that has appeared in our Nor'Wester Partners catalogues is a story in itself, from the very start up to yesterday's acquisition. Our first major coup was acquiring the Lambart Papers.

Hyacinthe Lambart (1904–1988), a woman to be reckoned with, had a regal bearing and spoke her mind freely. In 1973, she took offense at something I said, didn't speak to me for 10 years, then suddenly phoned to apologize and offered to sell me some manuscripts.

These were letter books from the old Hamilton Brothers Mill at Hawkesbury across the Ottawa River from where she lived in Cushing, Quebec. They had considerable historic value so I bought them for the Ontario Archives.

In 1990, two years after Hyacinthe Lambart died, her executors got in touch with me to offer Miss Lambart's family, business and personal papers. They revealed much detail of this illustrious family, a real coup for our new antiquarian company.

Hyacinthe's great-grandfather, the Earl of Cavan, had brought his son Octavius Lambart to Canada in 1874. Hyacinthe's father Frederick, son of Octavius, became a surveyor in Canada and built Vine Lynne at 7 Rideau Gate, across from the Governor General's residence in Ottawa, which is now used as a residence for visiting VIPs.

The letters in this collection define Hyacinthe Lambart as a fascinating Canadian. At McGill University, she studied under Hugh McLennan and Stephen Leacock. One of Canada's first female pilots, she corresponded with Amelia Earhart.

In 1932, Hyacinthe Lambart flew her Gipsy Moth aircraft to Quebec City, landing it on the Plains of Abraham. A striking photograph shows her wearing a stylish tweed suit, standing beside the plane *en route* to Holland to attend an international aviation conference. A photograph in the same collection shows her as the only female, still wearing her tweed suit amidst a group of sober-looking male aviators.

During World War II, she was secretary to the Association of Canadian Flying Clubs based in Montreal. Hyacinthe went on to historical research and writing. We eventually placed her family papers, some 2000 items spanning four generations, with the National Archives in Ottawa, where they can be read by interested researchers.

Included in the collection were papers of her two brothers, Arthur and Edward Lambart. Arthur left the RCMP for special duties with the RAF and was killed early in WW II. Edward was with the Royal Canadian Horse Artillery in Italy when he was killed by a German sniper.

An unusual item in the Lambart collection was a fine sleeping robe made of lynx paws. Her father had brought it back from the North, where he took part in the Yukon/Alaska boundary survey. This item is now with the National Museum of Civilization in Gatineau.

Serendipity was at work a while later when we were able to place the James Finlayson Taylor Papers with the Heritage Committee in Aylmer, Quebec.

We acquired this collection from Philip Shackleton, an Ottawa dealer who had moved to Western Canada. His late wife, Marjorie Taylor, was descended from James Finlayson Taylor (1800–1877).

The papers included militia, business and municipal records, as well as family letters. An amusing item was a wedding announcement in the

January 19, 1843 issue of the *Bytown Gazette* for a wedding performed on the ice at the Chaudière Rapids. The item read: "Taking it Coolly — James F Taylor, Esq, of Hull married Miss Betsy Eady of Hull. The ceremony was performed on the ice."

In 1992, I met Patrick Evans, chronicler of Philemon Wright, the Vermont Yankee who founded Hull in 1800. Evans solved the mystery of the wedding on the ice by observing the couple were from Lower Canada (Quebec) whereas the Methodist preacher was from Bytown, Upper Canada. He had no authority in Lower Canada and solved the problem by drawing a line in the ice. He stood on the Upper side while the bride and bridegroom remained in the Lower.

Neither the National Archives nor the Quebec Archives would buy the Taylor papers, but co-incidence struck when Quebec journalist Bob Phillips suggested I contact the Aylmer Heritage Committee. Suddenly, I was in luck. When I told the Heritage chairperson why I was calling, there was a long pause, then she exclaimed, "Serendipity is at work. Please come for lunch and bring the papers, which I will buy. I live in James Finlayson Taylor's old house!"

Another exciting object we acquired from Philip Shackleton when he moved away from Ontario was the Swan Inn Guest Register for 1890–1910. The Swan is a 600-year-old public house near Guilford, in County Sussex, south of London, England. The 8x10 leather-bound register contained 160 pages with guests' names and pen-and-ink renderings of the English countryside contributed by many of the visitors. Notable guests included Rudyard Kipling and Bertrand Russell. Both had artistic talent and penned fine sketches in the register.

Philip Shackleton's father, himself a competent artist, acquired this guest register at auction in Toronto in the 1930s. Who had brought it from England to Canada, and when, remains a mystery.

Placing such an unusual item is always a challenge. In this case I asked Toronto art historian Robert Stacey, grandson of the great illustrator CW Jeffreys, to see if he could find the Swan Inn for me on a trip he was making to England. This he did, and on our next trip to the UK, Muriel and I stayed at that very place. The current owner was anxious to recover this missing register, so we were wined and dined. He happily paid us £1000 for it. Getting it back where it belonged proved a very satisfying effort in every way.

Major Kinzie Bates (1839–84) was a free-spirited letter-writing veteran of the American Civil War, later serving in the Indian Wars in what became the State of Montana. I found his letters in Cambridge, Ontario, and bought them from Shurley Dickson, a descendent of Major Bates's Canadian wife. An American collector in Maine laid out $7,000 for this rare collection of letters.

An example of Bates's prose is the following description of New Orleans during the Civil War period: "The people here are as disloyal as they were in 1861. The place is populated by gamblers, ruffians and devil née [sic] care women. It is the Paris of America in its debauchery and crime. Duelling is as common as can be."

Bates spent much of his time unsuccessfully trying to capture Sitting Bull, the great Sioux chief, after the Battle of the Little Big Horn. It was at this time he first met up with the Canadian Métis. He remarked on their famed Red River carts. Because they were all wood and had no grease on the axles, the screeching noise they made crossing the prairies could be heard for miles.

A prolific letter writer, Sir Charles GD Roberts (1860–1943), carried on correspondence with numerous ladies. One was Montreal writer Eleanor Williams Moore, who eked out a precarious living from the 1930s to the 1960s. She met Roberts at the Canadian Authors' Association, of which she was a founding member.

I bought their letters from Jean Morrison, a writer and historian friend, who had salvaged them at an auction. Queen's University bought the Roberts-Moore collection.

The papers reflect the difficult times those were for a writer, especially a woman. Roberts's letters reveal that he pursued Eleanor with great ardour for about a year, and apparently the affair was kept secret. One letter tells of Roberts hiding Eleanor in his clothes closet. She had come from Montreal by train, and had to do a fast disappearing act while he held a meeting of the Canadian Authors' Association in his apartment on Wellesley Avenue in Toronto.

A lock of hair from a hero becomes valuable in the hands of some collectors. We had one of these in our catalogue, a swatch of General Sir Isaac Brock's hair sewn onto a 2 by 2 inch square of rag paper, centred in a crimson matte in a gold frame, surrounded by pictures of Brock,

A lock of General Sir Isaac Brock's hair taken after his death at the Battle of Queenston Heights. Also in the frame are a portrait of Brock, a photo of his bullet-riddled scarlet tunic, and a photo of the stone cottage at Queenston to which his body was carried. (The lock of hair is now in the possession of Brock University) (Author's photo)

his bullet-riddled scarlet jacket, and the stone cottage at Queenston to which his body was carried.

This relic was kept by the Jarvis family, descendents of Brock's friend, Ensign Samuel Peter Jarvis, who was also at the Battle of Queenston Heights. It was exhibited at the 1899 Canadian Historical Exhibition by Amelius Jarvis, along with a letter to the wife of Ensign Jarvis from her brother, describing the battle in vivid detail.

Jon Jouppien, a knowledgeable collector, bought the gold-framed hair of General Brock display, then sold it to another collector, who donated it to Brock University, where it now graces the President's office.

Items like this are usually better put into the safekeeping of a known collector or institution. In the hands of descendents, they are always in danger of being lost or destroyed.

It could have been a wild goose chase when, in 1998, I travelled across the continent to California to buy six buttons, but the journey paid off when I sold them to a Montreal collector for a significant sum. There are six more of these buttons, probably in California, and one day I expect to find them.

Canadian mining magnate Merrill Denison acquired them from a woman in New Jersey and I tracked them to California, where they were in use on the vest of Denison's stepson. When I piled enough hundred dollar bills on his coffee table, he snipped them off and handed them over.

The significance of those little one-inch buttons was not simply that they were sterling silver, but that they were authentic Michilimackinac Hunt Buttons, crafted in 1802 by London silversmith E Morley. Each was engraved with a different animal or hunting figure with the words "Michilimackinac Hunt" separated by a tomahawk on either side. The figures on the set I found represent wolf, beaver, porcupine, hunter, canoe and snowshoe.

I was informed that the other six are in the possession of "a woman in California." Who is she, and where is she? Someone will come up with the information and we'll get the whole dozen back together.

Tips come when least expected, from all parts of the globe, and sometimes from close to home. Right here in Ottawa, cartographer Ed Dahl, retired from the National Archives of Canada, put me in touch with a map dealer buddy of his in England. Within days of my arrival on my next overseas jaunt, I had acquired most of the existing papers of Sir David William Smith (1764–1837), Surveyor General for Upper Canada. This was my very first collection of a true antiquarian.

Though Sir David spent only a few short years in America, his collection included a great number of individual items, meticulously catalogued right up to the year of his death.

I was able to sell 20 volumes of his military history manuscripts to a Montreal collector, while five of his watercolour drawings went for an average of $2500 each to other collectors and institutions. They depicted the fortifications of old Montreal, Fort George at Niagara, and the officers' quarters in Detroit, where his father had been in charge

I was foiled in getting Mabel Stevens's Baptist Church records. They went to McMaster University, but I did get the bear story. Mabel's parents had a farm during the depression of the 1930s. They found a stray bear cub and kept it in a cage near the road to attract tourists. People would stop to see the bear and buy their farm produce. Mabel's brother made his own beer and it was a sight to see him drive his Model T into Athens with the bear sitting beside him sipping beer. The locals were used to it but it did startle the tourists!

before the American takeover from the British in the latter part of the 18th century. One of those paintings of tremendous interest showed the disposition of the British and French troops at the 1759 Battle of the Plains of Abraham as recreated for visiting royalty 28 years later, in 1787.

It is always a thrill to bring such antiquarian treasures back to Canada.

Another thrill of the chase is in trying to solve mysteries like the curious photographs of Russian gold piled on the deck of *HMCS Rainbow*. Two photos of the bullion were in an album of 112 pictures including sharp, clear, neatly captioned naval photos by E Froggatt, dated Christmas 1916.

I acquired this album of pictures along with a slightly battered but still playable brass bugle, engraved "Presented by Surgeon EW Boak to

HMCS Rainbow," from a dealer in Victoria, BC. These treasures, passed up by several west coast maritime museums, should have stayed on the West Coast, but the Maritime Museum in Halifax bought them.

The first vessel in the history of the Royal Canadian Navy, *HMCS Rainbow* had served the Royal Navy in Britain from 1893 before she was sold to Canada in 1910. On active duty until 1920, she was used for training, ceremonial visits and fishery patrols until the First World War, when she defended the West Coast as far south as Panama. The *Rainbow* also visited Mexico, Nicaragua, Cocos Island and various ports on the Pacific coast, as evidenced by photos in Mr. Froggatt's albums.

In 1917, the *Rainbow* transported millions of dollars worth of Russian bullion from Esquimalt to Vancouver, where it was taken by train to Montreal, then to New York, probably destined for Britain and Sweden, in payment for arms and munitions. It had been delivered to Esquimalt by the Japanese navy, piled on the deck of the *Rainbow*, and provided an intriguing photo opportunity for Mr Froggatt. As well as a talented amateur photographer, he was probably a member of the crew, but he had no idea where that Russian gold was going, or why.

Along with mysteries, we also encounter hoaxes, and here is a grisly one. It's a little jeweller's box containing a faded note and a piece of tanned hide that purports to be the human skin from a Sioux chief hanged at Mankato, Minnesota in 1862.

In fact, after testing at the University of Chicago Medical Centre, it was determined not to be human skin at all. It is probably from a dog or other small animal, but the accompanying note is signed by an Indian Agent in the US who wants us to believe he collected this, and many other such samples, after the massacre and subsequent hangings during the Sioux uprising of 1862. Apparently there are numerous such little boxes containing questionable bits of skin of questionable origin. Owning one should be one more than enough, but for some strange reason, they are still considered to be collectibles, as a conversation piece if nothing else.

Of far greater interest are such genuine articles as the 8 foot long, linen-backed, colour-coded chart showing the descent of Queen Victoria from William the Conqueror and Robert the Bruce. Mounted on pine rollers, this treasure was compiled by George Sim and produced by Johnson and Hunter of Edinburgh in 1851.

People buy antiquities like this for various reasons. In this case, the lady who acquired it was particularly delighted because she believed that in a previous life she had been one of Queen Victoria's maids. A close friend of hers had also made a particularly happy find, a leather-bound biography of Mary Queen of Scots written in French by a Russian Count. The volume had been taken apart and rebound at a later date with many plates relating to the Royal Stuart family added. This practice, known as grangerizing after its 18th-Century originator, added several thousand dollars to the worth of the book. The proud new owner believes that in a previous life, she was Mary Queen of Scots, another interesting reason to buy the book.

The most expensive collection we ever sold was that of Viola MacMillan, known as the "Queen Bee" in Canadian mining circles. Her husband was my third cousin, George, of the Glenpean line of MacMillans. He and Viola were a formidable pair in the mining world for many years, and she was awarded the Order of Canada.

Viola MacMillan presented $1.25 million to Ottawa's Museum of Nature for their unequalled exhibit of sparkling gems and for the Viola MacMillan Mineral Gallery and Activity Centre. Her papers fill more than 60 transfer cases. The collection includes 1000 slides and photographs, 25 cans of film about mining, travel and records of mining claims.

This valuable collection eluded me for many years. It was only after her death at age 90 in 1993 that her estate executors entrusted to us the daunting task of sorting through 120 cases of papers. We reduced it to about half by discarding duplicates, and eventually placed it with the Museum of Nature in Ottawa.

In contrast with such expensive properties, we also dealt with small items, such as a letter about financial matters, on a single worn and slightly torn page, listed at $50. It was written on March 6, 1771, in French, by François Dambourges, a soldier and merchant, from St Thomas, West Indies, and was addressed to a M Beaubien at Quebec City. A militia colonel and member of the Legislative Assembly, Col Dambourges was a leader in the defence of Quebec against the Americans in 1776. Coincidentally, Dambourges had been in the only company of French Canadians in the 84th Highland Regiment, which fought the rebels in the American War of Independence.

It is always a delight to be able to place an item with exactly the right person. Such was the case with this letter, listed as no 84 in our catalogue. At a Scottish conference in Guelph, my friend Gavin Watt, Colonel of the recreated King's Royal Regiment of New York, introduced me to a Captain Ross from Detroit, a mercenary soldier in real life who was also a captain in the recreated 84th Highland Regiment.

I handed one of my catalogues to Watt. When Ross looked it over, he became very excited, asking if I still had item 84. When I told him I did, he insisted we rush home so he could get it right away.

"It's a good omen," he explained. "It's item 84, a document signed by Dambourges, whose role I play, and I am number 84 in our recreated 84th Highland Regiment." We had a very happy customer.

Some of our major finds require patience and persistence over long periods before we finally get our hands on them. We were on the trail of one valuable collection for almost 30 years.

In 1963, I met Katherine Ferguson, whose husband, Col Malcolm Ferguson, was curator of Fort Frontenac at Kingston. She knew I was about to become the liaison officer for the Ontario Archives and urged me to contact her friend, Dr Marion Bonnycastle.

Then a professor at Princeton University, Marion was a Bonnycastle by marriage but was by birth a McLaurin with Glengarry connections. A trunk full of the papers of her great-grandfather, Rev John McLaurin, was being kept for her by an aunt, Mrs Whitehead, at their family cottage in Muskoka.

In August 1965, I met Marion Bonnycastle in Muskoka, where her aunt allowed me to examine the papers but said they were not leaving the cottage. In the collection were letters from Duncan Cameron, a Glengarry North West Company Partner, and vast material from Marion's great-grandfather, the Rev John MacLaurin, the Church of Scotland minister of Martintown, Glengarry. This was a veritable goldmine of letters, notes and sermons, many of them in Gaelic. I never abandoned the effort to acquire these for the Archives, and I continued to be frustrated for my entire tenure as their employee.

Mrs. Whitehead died in 1969. I was then dealing directly with Marion Bonnycastle, who had transferred from Princeton to the medical faculty at Yale. We had great difficulty trying to arrange a time to meet at the Muskoka cottage, and in 1986, before this could take place, Marion also died.

The next person to come into possession of this trunk full of valuable papers was Marion's daughter, Sarah, a classical scholar who seemed to commute between the University of Michigan in the US and Oxford University in England. Sarah proved to be as elusive as her mother, and in 1991, she also met an untimely death. A few months before she died, Sarah had married Brian Rigley, who agreed to meet me at the cottage the following year. Though reluctant to sell the papers, he finally accepted my offer. This important collection is now lodged with the Glengarry Historical Archives in Williamstown.

Some collections came my way by sheer chance. That was the case with the HP ("Horse Power") Davis (1878–1962) collection of several thousand photographs and pieces of *ephemera* connected with the founding of Cobalt, Ontario.

The photos define the era, including the first major shipment of silver ingots, the first Salvation Army band, the first three hookers in town, streetscapes and events, mining and logging camps, aircraft and fires. When Davis, an American from Nevada City, California, went to Cobalt in 1903, he noted and kept track of every piece of paper or picture he came across, saving it all for posterity.

Davis was investing in claims and selling mining stock on Wall Street, but he must also have spent considerable time in Cobalt to organize this comprehensive collection. In 1960, he gave the entire collection to Bill Galloway, who had come to interview him for a National Film Board movie about mining in northern Ontario. Four years later, HP Davis died in Nevada City.

I met Galloway in 1974, when he was pioneering the search for Canadian film footage for the Public Archives of Canada. Galloway still hadn't found a permanent home for the Davis collection, but when he died a few years on, I acquired the Davis collection from his estate, had some conservation work done on it, and prepared a detailed inventory.

In April 1999, we were able to purchase from James Read, a dealer in Victoria, British Columbia, 200 photographs of early mining in northern Ontario, the work of another American, Paul C Leddicum.

These photos were a perfect enhancement to the Davis collection. The combined collection then found an appropriate home in the Porcupine-Timmins Museum. It was only by a fortunate series of happenstances that these collections were saved and made available for the use of the people most concerned with their contents.

Quite often when we're off on the trail of something we deem to be important, another far more significant item suddenly comes our way.

One of my early assignments at the Ontario Archives was to locate more private papers of Edward Blake, the second Premier of Ontario. I was helped in my search by his grandson, VB (Verschoyle) Blake.

Vers was a historian with our department. He shunned the sort of publicity which I had come to realize was necessary in order to succeed in this unusual line of work. Despite our differences on this point, we went on many joint expeditions. On one of these searches for Blake material, we met Phillip MacKenzie, a Montreal architect who gave me 40 letters written to his uncle William Hume Blake, author of the classic *Brown Waters and Other Sketches*.

The letters had been written by an Irishman, Gerald Fitzgibbon, and as they were of no interest to the Ontario Archives, they remained in my library for years.

Soon after setting up as a private dealer I decided to have them appraised for historical content by Jack Richardson, an Ottawa historian whose description of the Fitzgibbon letters highlights their significance.

Gerald Fitzgibbon of Dublin was a Member and Deputy Speaker in the Irish Parliament. He at one time claimed to be "as thick as thieves" with President de Valera. The letters covered the worst years of the Irish Troubles, beginning with the Easter Rising of 1916 and continuing until 1923. Every letter contained a significant and often very extensive firsthand account of events with comments and analysis of the developments and motives of the participants. Trinity College in Dublin was happy to pay for the collection.

Some searches become complicated, with too many parties involved who are difficult to track down. Among these convoluted exercises were my efforts to obtain the "Spanish John" manuscripts.

I was particularly interested in 37 letters written by "Spanish John" Macdonell's three children, Miles Macdonell, agent for Lord Selkirk in Red River, John Macdonell, a North West Company partner, and Penelope (Macdonell) Beike, whose husband was a clerk in the legislature of Upper Canada at York. These letters were written to their brother, William Johnson Macdonell, between 1792 and 1837.

One of my best tipsters at the Ontario Archives spotted copies of these letters in a 1930s issue of the Unitarian Church publication, *The Onlooker*. Seeking the owner of the letters, I learned they had been given to a Mrs Lumbers in Toronto by Barbara Heyden, but I wasn't able to locate either of these women. I put my search for the originals on a back burner.

Suddenly, years later, I received a call from freelance CBC producer Carol Warren, who had heard that I was looking for the letters. She said they were in the possession of her father, Donald Warren, a Mississauga lawyer, and Carol was acting as his agent to find the right home for them.

We were then able to answer some questions that had plagued me so many years before. The mysterious Mrs Lumbers was Donald Warren's aunt, and Barbara Heyden was the sister of a book collector, Lawrence Heydon, Jr, who had been in contact with one of Macdonell's illustrious grandsons, known as Chevalier WJ Macdonell. The Chevalier was also an antiquarian book collector. He had emigrated to Toronto, where he was influential in the founding of the St Vincent de Paul Society. Lawrence Heydon acquired the entire Macdonell collection, which passed to his sister Barbara, and then to her friend Mrs Lumbers, thence to that lady's nephew Donald Warren, and finally into the hands of his widow, the mother of Carol Warren, CBC freelance producer.

Knowing the route those letters had taken solved half my problem. Getting them was another matter. After the death of Donald Warren, his widow began selling items from his estate. An art dealer friend of mine, Bill Roberts, happened to be visiting her to buy some works of art. When he found she also had some papers that she thought would be of interest to me, Bill bought a box of unsorted manuscripts on my account.

The contents were from the 18th and 19th Centuries, letters, photographs, ledgers and diaries. All had been part of Lawrence Heyden, Jr's collection. Also among these papers was an 1804 diary of a Shetland Island town. This, too, was a mystery, because we didn't know who had written it. We sent some photocopied pages to the archives of the Shetlands and discovered it had been written by Charles Fothergill (1782–1840), a Yorkshire Quaker, naturalist, politician, author, printer and publisher who emigrated to Canada in 1816. The diary was one of a series and the search continues for the other three.

Another name on the Heyden family tree was Robert Baldwin. His leatherbound pocket ledger for 1848–1856 was included in that trunk full of papers. The collection hence became known as the Heyden/ McDonell/Fothergill/Baldwin collection.

Some of the papers that I chase after are exceedingly elusive. Thanks to his history-conscious descendents, the papers of William Lyon Mackenzie have been very hard to obtain. His grandson, the Right

Honourable William Lyon Mackenzie King, saw to it that nearly all those documents were safely ensconced in the Ontario Archives long before I began my field work there in 1964.

In 1998, I discovered some of the Mackenzie papers were still out there, and possibly available. Barry Penhale, who published my book, *The Lochaber Emigrants to Glengarry*, called me to suggest I get in touch with Rev Chris Raible, a semi-retired Unitarian Church minister, a great admirer of Wm Lyon Mackenzie and a former curator of Mackenzie's old home on Bond Street in Toronto.

Raible said someone in Calgary had two volumes of scrapbooks for sale, which Mackenzie had kept during 1832 and 1833 while he was in England taking his grievances to the British Parliament. Raible wouldn't say who the Calgary owner of this treasure was, but he did mention that the scrapbooks were bought in 1979 from a Toronto dealer, Jerry Sherlock, who had bought them from a dealer in England. The mysterious man in Calgary wanted them, I was told, to research a reformer called Marshall Spring Bidwell, but was now prepared to sell them for $3,500.

My informant said he couldn't afford to buy the scrapbooks, but wanted to see them if I were to buy them. At this point, I asked the semi-retired minister if the man in Calgary might be a lawyer by the name of Edward Bredin. Raible was so startled he actually dropped the phone.

No, I wasn't clairvoyant. It just happened that I knew Edward Bredin's brother James — who was one of my best tipsters. I often stayed at his house in Cornwall, where he would regale me with stories of his adventures piloting Lancasters in World War II, being shot down, taken prisoner by the Germans, and planning the Great Escape. He also told me about his brother's interest in Marshall Spring Bidwell (1799–1872), a Methodist member of the Legislative Assembly, from Lennox and Addington County (near Kingston), who was forced into exile by the lieutenant-governor for his criticism of the Anglican "Family Compact."

Ed Bredin was willing to part with the scrapbooks, which I sold to the Scottish Studies Foundation Inc, which I had helped to found 10 years earlier. Allan McKenzie (no relation to Wm Lyon Mackenzie) then bought the scrapbooks for the University of Guelph, which has a huge collection of books and manuscripts about Scotland, second only to the collection in Edinburgh. The Guelph collection was instituted by Dr Stanford Reid, first head of Scottish Studies there. He was assisted by Lauchlan Farquhar MacRae, head librarian of the university. They were delighted and surprised to receive this gift.

As for Chris Raible, he was able to pursue his interest in Mackenzie at his leisure. In 1999, he published a book about the "Firebrand," *A Colonial Advocate: the Launching of his Newspaper and the Queenston Career of William Lyon Mackenzie.*

My final little story is about love letters between two great Canadian poets and their special friends, perhaps the most endearing documents I've been able to track down and place in public archives for all to enjoy.

The poems of Pauline Johnson, frequently billed as a Canadian Indian Princess, and John McCrae's poem of remembrance "In Flanders Fields" are well known Canadian classics. Now we can access the love letters they wrote (though not to each other). Surprisingly, the correspondence I discovered was unknown to their many biographers.

Though neither Pauline Johnson (1861–1913) nor John McCrae (1872–1918) ever married, their letters reveal that both had special loving friends, and as my research into each continued, I discovered that these friends happened to be brother and sister.

John McCrae (1872–1918), author of In Flanders Fields. *This studio portrait was probably taken in the 1890s, either in Guelph, where he was with the Number 2 Artillery Battery or at the University of Toronto, where he was with the Queen's Own Rifles of Canada. (This picture and his letters to Laura Kains, are now in the McCrae House Museum in Guelph, Ontario.)*

A Canadian Bank of Commerce branch in a tent, Cobalt, Ontario, 1905. This is part of the collection of HP ("Horse Power") Davis (1878–1962) of Nevada City, California, who collected thousands of pictures and other ephemera connected with the founding of Cobalt. (Now in the Porcupine-Timmins Museum)

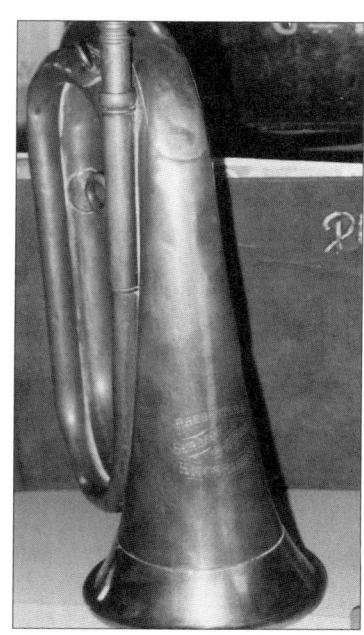

A battered but playable bugle from HMCS Rainbow, the Royal Canadian Navy's first warship. The inscription reads, "Presented by Surgeon E.W. Boak to HMCS Rainbow." (Now in the Halifax Maritime Museum)

Pauline's lifelong friend, was Archibald (Archie) Kains (1865–1944), a Canadian-born banker who escorted Pauline around New York and introduced her to the art of painting, among other things. Though he eventually married another woman, Archie helped Pauline Johnson financially when she became ill. She died of cancer at the age of 51.

In 1991, I went to Little Silver, New Jersey to meet Joan Ritchie, the daughter of Frank Ritchie, who had inherited the Kains and MacMillan papers from his uncle Archie, a wealthy banker in the US. When he retired to Ottawa in 1925 and lived at 9 Rideau Gate in Rockcliffe, Archie Kains spent many years researching his Kains and McMillan family history. His nephew, Frank, who fell heir to the collection, unfortunately handed out many of his uncle's papers and relics, leaving very little track of who got what.

I am still searching for any relics that Archie Kains's grandfather Captain Thomas Kains may have saved from *HMS Victory*, aboard which he was purser during the Crimean War. At that time, the *Victory* was a hospital ship in Portsmouth Harbour.

I acquired part of the Kains-MacMillan collection in 1991, though not nearly all of it. In 2000, I asked Dr Susan Kains to go to New Jersey

Laura Kains (1873–1949), the sister of Archie C Kains. Laura was the friend of John McCrae early in his career, and Archie romanced the Mohawk poet E Pauline Johnson. Laura lived for a time at 9 Rideau Gate in Ottawa, next door to the Governor General. The siblings were descendents of Captain Thomas Kains.

Garth Dittrick

This tale was related to me by a half-brother of William Dummer Powell Jarvis. In 1940 he was off to war with the R.A.F. He had just inherited two million dollars and established his wife in a mansion at the east end of Cobourg. But dear, she exclaimed, "there is no bus service and we have no car." He solved that problem by ordering ten pink Cadillacs from nearby Oshawa. In due course they were delivered in crates to the Cobourg station. Each year for the next ten years a crate was opened and a new Caddy hit the pavement.

and meet Joan Ritchie, who very generously handed over the balance of the papers to Susan for return to Canada. The lot included the Johnson-McCrae letters.

At about the same time as the Kains-Johnson friendship was flourishing, Archie's sister Laura was having a romance with Royal Canadian Army physician John McCrae, whom she had met in Guelph. Laura had grown up on a farm near London where her family had moved from Cushing, Quebec. In Ottawa, she lived with her brother Archie at his elegant home across the street from the Governor General's residence. She held various government jobs and never married.

I was able to place her letters from McCrae with the McCrae House Museum in Guelph where he was born, and the Johnson letters to Archie Kains are now in the National Archives in Ottawa.

That they are available to the public illustrates the importance of the research and field work done by archivists and collectors. Had I not happened to be tracking down descendents of the Kains-McMillan families and received help from many of their descendents, these letters might not have survived.

As I close this collection of stories illustrating my never-ending search for historical papers, I must reiterate my 'mission statement':

> We must remain vigilant in seeing to the preservation of written and pictorial records. Make sure that those letters of your aunt, mother or other relatives are saved. Let an archives or museum decide if those memorabilia are worth preserving. It is unnecessary — indeed impossible — to save every scrap of old paper; just make certain that the worthwhile material is not discarded.

Paper sleuthing has been called an addiction, even a disease. Whichever it is, I, for one, will never be cured.

APPENDIX 1
THE MACMILLAN METHOD FOR SAVING CANADIAN HISTORY

In the employee lunchroom of Canada's National Archives there is a figured mug for sale. The face on the cup is that of Sir Arthur Doughty, the second Dominion Archivist and a legend among Canadian archivists. Sir Arthur made his name by the aggressive and ingenious methods he used to acquire historically important papers for Canada, whose collections were then in a state of infancy.[1] Hugh P MacMillan, the first field officer in the history of the Archives of Ontario, has created a method of archival acquisition which is broadly based on what he calls "reverse genealogy." It is a recipe for saving history, and stands in the best tradition of Sir Arthur and those of his table, so to speak.

If we "reverse engineer" the material that Hugh P serves forth in this, his present book, we can savour the recipe as well. First, take a generous large-hearted interest in other people and their stories. Pay no heed to race, religion or gender, but do use them to enhance the flavour of the results — this from a man whose personal library has a long shelf labelled "social justice." Listen carefully and sincerely for clues that may connect the person back to a thread or a character in history. Knead relentlessly on said connection until it starts to leaven.

The seeking (and finding) of good subjects involves a preparation time: become richly read in history and biography; contrive to sketch out a family tree and walk, write or telephone your way down the disparate branches thereof. At all times follow the trail of the family story and find who got the papers, portraits or artifacts. Never give up. Once on to the scent, take van (or Caravan) and show up on doorstep. Engage subject in purposeful conversation, even through the crack in the door if the situation calls for it.

Brush aside protestations that "the attic is a mess," or that they "need time to go through the boxes." Give receipts, tax credits, or *in extremis,* money, and get the material in its rough state back home to the professional archivists, the sedentary guard, if you will (to use a fine old term from the War of 1812.)

Before leaving, break bread with the new friend, and continue to be such a natural good companion that the proffered spare bed of the host is impossible to refuse. Never forget a name or a genealogy. Return when next in the neighbourhood and bring forth more and more connections to add to the intricate living web of characters, friends, papers and history. Through it all, keep a wife of abiding good sense (Muriel) and a family of international extent.

There are no secret ingredients in the MacMillan Method, but few have mastered it or served it up as well as our good friend, Hugh P.

David G Anderson
Williamstown, Glengarry County, 2004

---

[1] Doughty is the only archivist to have a statue on Parliament Hill.

APPENDIX 2
A NOTE ON THE SPELLING OF NAMES

Scots Gaelic surnames not being in the English language to start with, tend to vary in their transcription, even within a single family. Thus you will find *MacDhòmhnuill* englished as McDonald, MacDonald, and Macdonald (not to mention MacDonell and McDaniel and *their* variants). I have used the spelling the individual himself preferred or the one most commonly used in records (or history books) about him. Where several members of a family are referred to and they do not share an opinion on the spelling, I have taken the position that my opinion is as good as anyone's, and spell the name however I damn well want.

As a general rule, though, the abbreviation M^c (with a superscript c to indicate it was an abbreviation of Gaelic *mac*, meaning 'son,' or sometimes an apostrophe or open single quote if the printer's typecase didn't run to superscript letters) was usual until about the end of the 19th Century. After that, some people, especially social climbers and recent emigrants from Scotland, adopted the full Mac ('son of _____') spelling.

They may have been trying to differentiate themselves from the then less prestigious and more conservative Irish immigrants who had begun coming to Canada in very large numbers since the 1830s. Historically, the abbreviated spelling did not distinguish between Irishmen and Scots, and just as many people in Glengarry will argue that M^c was used by Protestants as will claim it is distinctively Irish. I suspect that a literate and socially secure generation of Scots families, many of whom were Protestants, saw no reason to change the spelling that they had been using for generations, especially to accommodate the conceits of recent immigrants, who could change their *own* names if they were so inclined.

APPENDIX 3

The following four letters are unsolicited comments regarding the need for an aggressive field work policy to locate and acquire historical papers.

When historians publish their research, they alter what others believe about the subject in question. They also alter what other researchers will choose to study. And so it goes on. It is irreversible; it is creativity. And this, too, is what Hugh MacMillan has done over many years in his tireless search for manuscripts for the Ontario Archives. What he has recovered in the way of manuscripts will influence our future researchers and dictate the form their work will take.

As for the man himself, read this work. It is important, because Hugh has been important. It is interesting, because Hugh is interesting. He is a fine private scholar, and this is a book for scholars. Over the past forty years, Hugh's work has constituted a new segment in the intellectual and social history of English Canada. I have long admired him heartily. Let us be glad that we now have this fine, eloquent, first-hand record in print.

Royce MacGillivray

Formerly Professor
University of Waterloo
Waterloo, Ontario
February 2004

It was with great interest that I read Frank Rasky's article on your work at the Ontario Archives and the sad news that you are soon to retire. I thought the article a well-deserved tribute to your work.

Over the many years you have been there you have brought in a rich harvest of material. I must confess I am not well informed about it all because I seldom get to Toronto, and more seldom than that, to the Archives. But I do know from past experience something of what you have done work that no one else seems to have been inclined to do. At times it must have been arduous and often thankless.

When you retire, I hope that you will find the time to write up some of your experiences as an archival sleuth; I know it would be absorbing and worthy of record. Do consider it.

Have you salvaged any material on Ontario Indians? Anything in the way of original manuscripts, letters or illustrations, etc? I am always on the look-out for such things.

All the best for the future, Hugh, and my own personal thanks for what you have done for all of us.

Sincerely,
Kenneth E. Kidd

Professor Emeritus
Trent University
Peterborough, Ontario
7 December 1988

I would like to say that I admire the way you work. It is just such an aggressive (in the most positive way) outreach that ensures the acquisition and preservation of archival material. Certainly your visits and contacts were enjoyable for me even though it took me a few years to make up my mind what I wanted to do with the papers, always hoping to be able to work with them myself.

I know from my own line of work as Curator of Canadian Art at the National Gallery that there are many people who just don't know the importance or value of what they have or don't know what to do with papers, photographs, portraits, etc. It is just such unsolicited contacts as you made with me that can give people some direction, and hopefully result in important acquisitions.

It's refreshing to see so much real commitment to content in a world of systems planners and managers.

Charles C. Hill

Canadian Art
National Gallery of Canada
Ottawa, Ontario
17 December 1985

I was wondering why you did not show up at Katie Gil's sale. It is one I will remember for a long time to come! The weekend before the sale I helped the auctioneer move furniture from the upstairs of the drive shed down to the fur-

"Adventures of a Paper Sleuth"

p. 129 – indenture agreement extract

p. 137 – pistols from S. Jarvis – Ridout duel in July 1817 stolen in 1970s
– S.P. Jarvis collected hair sample from Brock's body at Queenston Heights

p. 122-3: Wm Sawyer & Schram connection

p. 160: Gary French mentioned

p. 190: Robt Dickson (only photo in City of Cambridge archives).

p. 341 Diary Robt Clouston (1838-56)
p. 343 Clouston family history

niture from the upstairs of the drive shed down to the ground floor, and also to sort through the incredible amount of Katie's estate.

In several of the trunks in the drive shed we found hundreds of old letters and documents. Many of these were McLennan documents, although many were also from the Woods family. To our horror, the housekeeper insisted on destroying all of the old letters. She said they were Katie Gil's personal letters and should not be sold. The earliest date that I noticed on some of the ones that we looked at was 1809! At least one dealt with someone's nephew leaving school and going into the northwest in the fur trade.

Unfortunately, we could not talk the housekeeper out of ripping up the letters. I do think that a few went to the Museum. There were also quite a few old (1880-1920) photos which were also destroyed. I even tried to explain that as a distant cousin of Katie Gil, I could use the letters and photos as genealogical research material — but to no useful end.

Bruce Kennedy

A Glengarry Resident
15 February 1984

APPENDIX 4
LIST OF ACQUISITIONS 1964-1986

A representative list of manuscripts and pictorial material acquired for the Ontario Archives by Hugh P. MacMillan
  To obtain more information about any of these collections, contact the Ontario Archives, and ask to see the comprehensive list of all Hugh MacMillan's Acquisitions from 1964 to 1989

1964
3783 McGillis family letters (NWCo.) 1812–42
3782 Muster roll Glengarry Highlanders (6th C0.)
3785 Pamphlet, Gaelic and English, 1877
3817 Papers, letters, diaries of Farquhar D. Mclennan 1806-1916
4797 Hamilton Bros. letterbooks, 1st lumber operation on lower Ottawa River
3809 3 letters of John "LeBarge" MacDonald 1819-25
3819 H. Pinhey Journal, 1829-40; Bytown Road Co. Records 1851-1922
3822 Crib raft lumbering ledger and journal, 1860-63
3820 Diary of J.H. Purvis, British Army, Quebec, 1838
3810 Bishop Alex McDonell papers, 1792-1838
3923 Joanna and Robert Lees letters re: Perth duel, 1838
3924 Photograph album of early C.P.R. railway construction
?   Photo: Sir George Simpson family

1965
3928 Journal of settler, S. Cole, Point Fortune, 1787-1823
3932 60 glass negatives, 1860-93
3970 D. McTavish–Sir George Simpson letters, 1864
4006 "Prescott Journal" and other newspapers, 1837-1900
4246 2,000 letters of Simon Dawson, surveyor of Dawson Road from Lakehead to Red River, 1858-60
4098 Rev. John McLaurin letters
4099 196 letters of Thos. Radenhurst, Perth, Ontario, 1822-50
4123 Rev. S. Rose letters, Methodist circuit rider, 1835-41
4245 NWCo. Journal, 1818-19; NWCo. letters, 1796-99

1966
4523 Father John MacDonald letter, book and letters, 1802-46
4683? Photos: HBCo. post and steamer
4684 Carpenter letterbook of Dawson Trail, 1874-1909; railroad photos
4678 Scrapbook of Senator D. MacMillan. 1878-1911
4257 Papers, clippings, court files, newspapers, maps, 1887-1940 (major collection)

LIST OF ACQUISITIONS 337

4561 "Brockville Antidote" 1833; "Quebec Gazette" 1764
4513 812-page letterbook 1767-1891, Catholic mission to St. Regis Mohawks
4824 Journal of Serg. Cox, 24th regiment of Foot, 1820-37
4596 Capt. McMartin's 1839 order book
4292 Maj. Duncan Clark military papers, 1812-14
4294 29 boxes Quarter Session records, Leeds and Grenville, 1798-1873
4381 Wm. Douglas letters, 1854-90
? Sepia print of Ellen Grant, family of John "LeBorgne" MacDonald, NWCo.
4391 HBCo. account book, Ft. William, P.Q., 1849-1853
4523 5 cartons letters and diaries of Father J. MacDonald, 1782-1896. "Spanish John" Macdonell papers, 1802-40

1967
4714 Letters, Wm. McGillivray, (NWCo. and Voyageurs Corp.)
4786 Letters, "Spanish John" Macdonell, 1773-1847
4815 Transcript of diary, 1801, of M. McDonell, Fort George
4821 Original McNiff map, 1786
4819 Miniature of Henry McKenzie, NWCo.
4911 Autobiographical notes, John McDonald of Garth, NWCo.
4851 Photos: Wm. McMillan and wife, Margaret Dease, HBCo., Red River
6035 Jarvis papers, 14 boxes
4852 6 photos: HBCo. "Flying Post"
4889 Duncan Clark letters, 1788-1836
4903 King's Royal Reg. N.Y., discharge, 1783; Dingwall family letters
4927 Photo, D. Clark, NWCo. notes and bibliography; data to add to Clark Paper
? Wm. Douglas family papers, photos and diaries
4996 Letters to and from John Cameron, 1797-1807
4980 Sir S. Fleming letters, diaries, maps, 1832-76
4979 Alex McMartin papers, land documents, sundries, 1813-1980

1968
? MS Rev. John Bethune letter to parish, 1815
6178 Ermatinger fur trade papers, 1808-54, 300 letters, memos, journals
6045 Photos: Marg Fraser, granddaughter of Simon Fraser
6131 Portrait: Peter Pangman, XY and NWCo's
6199 Sudbury Mine, Mill and Smelter Workers union papers, 1917-65
6259 Paris Militia papers of N.H. Baird, 1862-74
6319 Sir Sanford Fleming papers: letters, maps, business records
6310 Jas. Edgar papers, 1881-1940

1969
6355 Papers of M.O. Hammond, editor of Globe; photos
6377 C.P. Treadwell, letters and journals
6378 Hamilton Bros. letterbooks, 1845-1911: early lumbering, Hawkesbury

6376 HBCo. papers, Temiscamingue District, 1842-75
6329 Papers and photos: Donald MacKenzie, fur trader
6343 Copies of MS letters of Angus Roy (The Mast) McDonell, 1771-1858
6337 26 MS letters, W. Osgoode, 1st chief justice, U.C.
6327 236 letters: Hon. John Hillyard Cameron, c. 1850-70
6375 Letters: D. MacKenzie, American Fur Co., 1783-1851
6430 2 vols. MS letters Canadian artists and writers to Newton McTavish, publisher, "Canadian," 1908-61
6492 "Pickled Rod," 1878
6484 Photo: Nancy Campbell
6610 Map: 1831, Col. Bye; MS re Rideau Narrows
6605 Unfinished MS of Judge Chas. Oakes Ermatinger family history; 2 fur trade pictures
6387 MS by Donald MacKenzie re fur trade

1970
6670 Photo of Kilkotah (Marguerite) c. 1808-73, blanket wife of James McMillan
6678 Cameron papers, NWCo., Temiskaming; 9 North West Co. journal (MS) ledgers; 1 North West Co. agreement for 1795 (copy); 4 vols. journals and letterbooks; letters to Aneas and Angus Cameron from various NWCo. partners
6704 183 letters of the Hon. Hillyard Cameron to his wife (comments on the political scene in Ottawa)
6715 1 box letters, maps, briefs from estate of Wm. Douglas, attorney, Blenheim
6722 2 vols. letterbooks Stephen Tucker Sr. and Jr.; 1 diary kept by Stephen Tucker Jr.
6732 1 map (copy) 1837; 1 transport report on the landowners of St. Joseph's Island, 1876; 1 historical data given Mrs. J.E. Bayliss in 1926 by Mr. Owen Rains, grandfather of donor
7563 1 vol. "Spanish John" by Col. John McDonell of Scottos
6678 128 letters from Sir Geo. Simpson to Angus Cameron of Temiskamingue, 1826-60; 142 letters of Angus Cameron to his uncle Angus Cameron, 1844-64
6907 Silver Islet material: pictures; 1 pkg. 4 large plates; photo album, Silver Islet area; album—ships; box of 11 small plates, Brown photo album. Envelope of Silver Islet and Mine pictures; Private Manuscripts: Mine Reports a) 1873 b) Nov. '73-Dec. '74 c) '72-'73 d) '75-'76. Smelting correspondence; Journal; Silver Island time book 1884; cheques, Report etc. 1875; Diary; J.W. Cross; Director's report. 1879-84; Bureau of Mines, 1896
6646 MS letterbooks 1893-95, '95-'97, 1900-02, 1897-99, 1893-1904, 1904-05, 1905-07, 1907-12, 1910-12, 1912-13; 3 vols. census returns 1899-1901; 1 vol. cash books 1857-82; 2 vols. Indian Land Sales books, 1854-95; 1 vol. scrap book re: agency

LIST OF ACQUISITIONS 339

6884   Papers of Robert Cunningham, M.P. for Marquette, Winnipeg, publisher of "Manitoban," former reporter with the Toronto "Globe," went with the Woolsey Expedition; letters, pictures—1 newspaper (extra); telegrams; Indian treaty (copy) MS 1837-74
?   Typed transcripts of Gen. Sir Geo. Airey (1761-1833) letters and Richard Airey (1803-81) letters relating in part to Col. Thomas Talbot's colonization; photo of Sir Richard Airey
6906   Collection of approx. 4,000-5,000 glass negatives taken by Duncan Donovan photographer in Alexandria, Glengarry Co. c. 1895-1924
6938   MS material: Commissions, reports, letters to do with Col. James Fitzgibbon

1971
9229   Papers of Richard Hardisty, HBCo. Chief Factor (father-in-law, Lord Strathcona), letters, genealogical data, estate papers
8504   1 report (printed) of 1870 expedition by Gen. Woolsey—signed by himself—incomplete, 3-4 pages missing (rare); 1 map (paper) of Simon Dawson's survey
9203   Papers of Col. S. Barnett, Niagara Falls, Ont.—1,500 misc. letters, posters, agreements, engraving 1865-81 re: Niagara Falls Museum, 44th Reg. Militia, plus personal letters of his family while in South America, business correspondence
9111   Typed genealogy of family of Catherine Christy McKay, Glengarry Co. Ont. by L. W. McLennan
9208   14 boxes of business, political, and military correspondence of Col. R.R. McLennan (uncle of donor), M.P.P. for Glengarry and C.P.R. railway contractor c. 1870-93
?   Scrapbook, Jan. 1950; Pinhey legal papers, letters, land grants; Christie letters, 1870-80; box of Christie letters, St. Louis; Christie letters and material, 1854-60; photos (Christie) and misc. papers; Christie letters, 1863-70; historical file folders—2 boxes 13 vols. Christie letters, 1816-1906
6977   Crawford family papers, letters, diaries, poetry, genealogical data; photostat of New Brunswick newspapers
?   Private MS papers of Narcisse M. Cantin of St. Joseph's, Ont. Letters, journals, maps, pictures, newspapers and clippings, etc. c. 1892-1950; 20 cartons papers
?   14 boxes of letters from Sir J.A. MacDonald, Abbot, Mowat, Thompson and other political figures, also letterbooks of Sir J.R. Gowan, 13 reels microfilm
9378   Journals, correspondence, diaries, reports of Geo. Duck Jr. (lawyer), Geo. Ridley Duck (his son who went to the northwest) and his father Geo. Duck Sr.; also letters of Mary Arin Duck (wife of Geo. Duck Sr.) c. 1836-87. 1) Portrait of parliament (report) and transcript; 2) Narrative of the rebellion, 1837-38; 3) reports on newspapers (undated); 4) 6 vols. reports of inspection of clergy reserve for the western district by Geo.

Duck Jr.; 5) journal of Geo. R. Duck during Riel Rebellion, also collection of his letters from the west; 6) journals of Geo. Duck Jr. including his reports (including letters of Egerton Ryerson) re: inspection of schools by Geo. Duck Jr.; 7) folders of correspondence; 8) map—plan of Morpeth

1972
9351   1 folio—letters to Nicol H. Baird
9397   1 photo, Col. James MacDonald; 1 photo, daughter of Finan MacDonald; 1 photo, grandchildren of Finan MacDonald
9436   1) List of officers Royal Canadian Volunteer Regiment (1797-1802); 2) Framed clipping re: capitulation of Detroit; 3) Signed proclamation to Electors of Glengarry by John MacDonell, 1812; 4) 3 photos of Sir John A. MacDonald; 5) copy: Capitulation order for Fort Detroit; 6) Photo of Father Campbell, priest at St. Raphaels 1919-48; 7) Photo of Bishop Wm. MacDonald, 2nd Bishop of Alexandria 1905-21; 8) Group photo (names added) opening of Alexandria; 9) Cairn at Lancaster Post Office, 1905
?   1 newspaper "Life at the Springs"; letters written by Wm. C. O'Brian to his father Peter O'Brian, barrister, L'Orignal; 1 letter re Fenians, Cornwall, 1866; 1 letter re: school, L'Orignal, 1969; 1 letter re: elections, D'Arcy McGee, 1863; 8 letters re: life at McGill, 1870-74 by William to his father at L'Orignal; 5 letters re: Wm. O'Brian in Cornwall; 1 letter 1929 by Carrie Twiss Burgess re: history of Twiss clocks; 1 copy MS "County & the River" by Lewis O'Brian
?   Business papers, maps, phone directories, voters lists c. 1901-11 of A.N. Morgan (deceased W.W.1), grandfather of David Marshall, who was a shareholder (founding) in and solicitor for the Temiscaming Telephone Co. of New Liskeard
?   1 transcript of letter written by great-grandfather of Robert B. Douglas (Andrew Bell) in Sept. 1825, to his father in Scotland
9586   3-hour taped interview with Thomas Eddy, only remaining grandchild of Donald Mackenzie, Nor'Wester, partner of John Jacob Astor and later Governor of Assiniboia for the Hudson Bay Company
?   3 volumes journals from HBCo. Post at Mattagami 1828-35 and 1879-84; 1 letter by Donald Grant from Flying Post 1848; 7 canoe bills of lading 1883-84

1973
?   Moravian Mission Reports 1819-80
9770   Genealogical data, Sutherland, Campbell, Schram, Sawyer
9916   Hon Archie McLean letter to Sir A. McNab re: memoirs 1812 war, Blake diary, Indian Agent
9842   1802-29 letterbook (1 vol.) Archie Murlaggan MacMillan
9841   1802 MacMillan ship contract and photo (copy) Allan Glenpean MacMillan
9913   Edgar family papers 1860-1960

1974

10117 Papers of Wm. Urquhart, U.E.L. lot 18-19 south side river Raisin, Glengarry Co.—who came from Mohawk Valley with his son Alexander, and other members of the family 1746-1831

10596 23 letters and papers of Hon. Finlay G. MacDiarmid, Minister of Highways 1914-19, 2 political broadsides, 11 telegrams re: church union

10219 1858 Diary of Robert Clouston (brother James Clouston, HBCo.) 1838-56, from his arrival in Canada until shortly before his death in Honolulu

10232 Collection of glass slides, approx. 3,000, of Bartle Bros. travelling photographers, c. 1895-1905; 7 newspapers (Cornwall)

10354 1 broadside, Perth 1857; 1 envelope; 33 letters to Col. Alex Fraser; 2 political broadsides; 5 bundles legal papers and letters; 5 vols. family genealogy (De Bereford)

10441 Copies of biographical and historical data re: John MacDonald of Garth and family

10489 Biographical data collection of private papers from estate of the Hon. T.B. McQueston

10467 5 letters Glengarry area, 1811-38

10498 Photo album once belonging to Jack "Greenfield" McDonell, various notable people, mostly from Glengarry

10587 Unpublished book manuscript of Bethune family, compiled by Louisa Blanchard Bethune, from secondary sources, family letters, and local history

1975

10595 Unpublished MS telling the story of John McGillivray, NWCo. Partner and his descendents who owned "Dalcrombie" at McGillivray's Bridge, Glengarry Co.

10577 Autobiography of Reginald Charles Leemley Drayton, 1830-1922, who came from England to Gore's Landing in 1870

10599 7 vols. reports, pictures re: Trent Canal

10607 Taped interview with Angus Mowat, former head of library services for Ontario

10973 Business papers of Col. A.T.H. Williams and family, 1850-95; 1 trunk of land records, letters, etc.

10977 Genealogical data to add to the Farquhar McLennan papers

10978 Papers of Col. Asa Danforth re: Danforth Rd., Dundas St.; also of Walter Pleuthner, and his collection of the papers of Timothy Green (1753-1813)

11075 Papers and letters, Father Geo. A. Hay, 1807-76, son of John Hay, 1749-1824

11042 St Gabriel Church registers of births, marriages and deaths, 1796-1869. Minutes of Presbyter. Of Quebec, 1831-35, 1835-42

11073 Personal and business correspondence of Sir Roderick Cameron and family, c. 1840-1918, approx. 2,000 items, incoming and outgoing

11070 Memos, notes, newspaper accounts, letters to and from Capt. Alex. McLeod, 1837 Rebellion

1976
11174 Glass slides (coloured and glass negatives of Northern Ontario and Quebec) Indian canoes, fishing, HBCo.—taken by Frank Schoonover 1903-11; also black and white prints, etc.
11315 1 loose-leaf binder of biographical information on Maj. W. Kingdom Rains of St. Joseph's Island, Ont.
11532 McQueston papers, 702 items (1830s)

1977
11561 Map (McNiff), Van Kougnett, Cline papers; will of John Sand; pictures
11616 Duncan Fraser MacDonald papers, Parry Sound
11912 Proudfoot MSS Presbyterian clergy
11887 John Graves Simcoe and Stamfort family history; 51 letters, J. Ross Robertson family papers
11940 Papers of John MacDonald of Garth and his family, NWCo. Partner 1793-1836, approx. 1,100 items
11943 Newspaper clippings 1921-31 of Walter McRaye, lecturer on Canada, 1921-31 literature

1978
12905 Captain Jones papers and pictures (Nile voyageur)

1979
12825 5 albums rail construction 1879-1942 by A.J. Isbister
12889 1923-36 letters H.R. Morgan, editor of Brockville Recorder from Curzon Lamb
1289? Papers of Dr Ebeneezer Hunt and Henry Hunt, 1788-1907; diaries, letters, journal
12904 Diary Rev. Wm. Bell, Perth; 19th-century Ontario newspapers
13096 6 letterbooks 1894-1918 by Farquhar McLennan, railroad building

1980
13703 Business records of Old Author's Farm, 1920s-60s, one of Canada's oldest antiquarian book dealers
13509 Chewett family papers, letters, diaries, posters
13545 24 vols. diaries by P.S. Van Wagner 1853-1905; political, agricultural
13558 W.R. Gregg letters 1872-1918
13793 Col. R.R. McLennan Papers (additions)
13931 Dr C. Meyers Papers
13930 Dr C. Meyers Papers

1981
14469 66 boxes Murray Watts business records, surveys, maps, pictures, corres. 1928-75

14310 21 cans film, 7 daguerreotypes, 1 box letters, paper re: Norman Bell

1982
14815 Papers of Doug. S. Robertson, re: John Ross R. and Toronto Telegram; family history by Lilian Westgarth Grant
14876 1 Geo. Washington letter; 9 letters of Thos. Ridout and part of journal; 3 letters of Bishop Strachan; bundle of Masonic material; Indian Dictionary 5 comm.; History of St. Andrew's Lodge; History of Ridout Family; T. Ridout obit. in Loyalist newspaper 1829; 2 profiles Mrs. T. Gibbs Ridout and daughter; invitation to meet Prince of Wales 1847; letter to T. Gibb Ridout; Thos. Ridout letter to brother in England; 1822 Journal York, Upper Canada
15067 1921 pictures Cornwall Motor Sales; Blanchard & Nissouri Cheese & Butter Co. 4 vols. minutes 1881-1974; daybook 1899-1912; cash book 1887-1912

1983
15597 Diaries E.A. Birson Meyers re: Myers Institute, 1901-50
15839 Biographical sketch of Sally Ainse 1728-1823 and Nicholas Montour
15966 Box of papers of Sir Geo. Perley from grandson
16112 Genealog. and bio. data re: Hon Wm. Dickson

1984
16554 Haultain family papers and pictures c. 1880-1930; letters and pictures RMC; letters and pamphlets W.W.1; canoeing pictures, glass negatives RCNWM Police; files Pict. Denistoun fam.

1985
16660 Rossin House records; minute book #2 1938-47; Rossin House Hotel share book, minute book, reports; photos, journals, ledgers
16654 14 file cases Gillies Bros.; timber licences, corres.; maps re limits

1986
16789 Map 1809 by Jeremiah McCarthy of Indian Lands
16811 12 boxes manuscripts. society correspondence re: Women's Canadian Historical Society; Durie papers, maps
? Clouston Family History
? Papers, pictures, ledgers of Capt. A. Steckler, steamboat owner, Lancaster, Upper Canada
? Papers Dodge Lumber Co. 1868-1941, Georgian Bay Lumber Company
? Medical Journals of Dr Donald J. McIntosh; newspapers—Life at the Springs

ARCHIVES
OF
CANADIAN ARTS
CULTURE & HERITAGE

PENUMBRA PRESS
www.penumbrapress.com